Feminism and Socialism in China

Feminism
and Socialism
in China

Elisabeth J. Croll

Routledge & Kegan Paul
London, Henley and Boston

First published in 1978
by Routledge & Kegan Paul Ltd
39 Store Street,
London WC1E 7DD,
Broadway House,
Henley-on-Thames,
Oxon RG9 1EN and
9 Park Street,
Boston, Mass. 02108, USA
Photoset in 10 on 12 Times by
Kelly and Wright, Bradford-on-Avon, Wiltshire
and printed in Great Britain by
Page Bros. Ltd, Norwich
© Elisabeth Croll 1978

British Library Cataloguing in Publication Data

Croll, Elisabeth Joan

Feminism and socialism in China.
1. Feminism—China
I. Title
301.41'2'0951   HQ1767   78–40293

ISBN 0 7100 8816 7

'The thoroughgoing liberation for women is not something ready-made. . . .'

Woman Correspondent, *Renmin Ribao*, 8 March 1973

Contents

Acknowledgments

This study was begun in 1972 at the School of Oriental and African Studies of the University of London, and I would like to thank Stephan Feuchtwang and Charles Curwen for their help during that year. That the study has been completed in its greatly expanded form is to no small degree due to the stimulus and encouragement provided by the women's movement in Europe and North America. In particular I am grateful for the impetus provided by the North Kensington women's study group, the women in anthropology group and the local and national women's conferences. I would like to thank my parents and friends who have been unfailing in their personal support and particularly Felicity Edholm and Hermione Harris who read the manuscript and made valuable suggestions. Luxing-she Travel Staff in Peking and the Society of Anglo-Chinese Understanding in London both made it possible for me to travel in China and talk with local and provincial leaders of the women's movement in 1973. I would also like to take the opportunity to thank Jim Croll who more than anyone else has shared in this project and in the care of Nicolas. Above all, though, the research for this book has been a part of my own consciousness-raising and in this I am indebted to the experience and analysis of Chinese women themselves who throughout the twentieth century have fought long and hard to redefine their position in society.

Elisabeth Croll

Note on romanisation

In this study I have mainly used the Hanyu Pinyin system of romanisation. The exceptions are composed of well-known place names such as Peking, Tientsin and Canton and persons such as Chiang Kai-shek. Where Chinese authors and titles have been written in, or translated into English, they remain as they are presented in the available texts. Where the source material refers to persons in an unusual spelling, and it has not been possible to check for the original spelling, I have used the form given in the source consulted.

Abbreviations

ACDWF	All-China Democratic Women's Federation later became the National Women's Federation (NWF)
CCP	Chinese Communist Party
CQ	*China Quarterly* (London)
CR	*China Reconstructs* (Peking)
CWR	*China Weekly Review* (Canton)
FLP	Foreign Language Press, Peking
NCH	*North China Herald* (Shanghai)
NCNA	New China News Agency also *Xinhua she*
PC	*People's China* (Peking)
PR	*Peking Review* (Peking)
RMRB	*Renmin Ribao* (*People's Daily*) Peking
ZF	*Zhongguo Funu* (*Women of China*) Peking
ZQ	*Zhongguo Qingnian* (*Youth of China*) Peking

Introduction: The Women's Movement in China

They too were fired with a fanatical desire to fight to the death for the revolutionary cause. This very remarkable phenomenon of women taking an active part in the Chinese Revolution was observed in Shanghai as well as in the south.

(F. Farjenel, 1911)[1]

One of the most striking manifestations of social change and awakening which has accompanied the Revolution in China has been the emergence of a vigorous and active Woman's Movement.

(Irene Dean, 1927)[2]

The revolt of women has shaken China to its very depths. . . . In the women of China, the Communists possessed, almost ready made, one of the greatest masses of disinherited human beings the world has ever seen. And because they found the keys to the heart of these women, they also found one of the keys to victory over Chiang Kai-shek.

(J. Belden, 1946)[3]

Travelling through China we saw old women with feet painfully crippled from foot-binding, younger women working in the fields and operating machinery in factories, and middle-school girls shooting rifles in a militia drill. These contrasts convinced us that the changes in the lives of women since liberation may be one of the greatest miracles of the Chinese Revolution.

(Group of American Students of China, 1971)[4]

At every stage of the continuing revolution in twentieth-century China, one feature which has immediately impressed observers has been the active participation of women in the revolution, and the parallel changes in their public and domestic roles. What had been described as a 'remarkable phenomenon' in 1911, a 'striking manifestation of social change and awakening' in 1927 was said by 1946 to have 'shaken China to its very depths'. In the 1970s an impressive array of *prima facie* evidence has caused many observers, like the group of American Students of China, to contrast the occupations and confidence of women in China today with the reports of bound-footed, hobbling and secluded women that reached Europe and America in the nineteenth century. Even at the turn of the present century women could still describe themselves as leading the existence of a 'frog in a well'[5] and Peking was observed to be 'a city of men'.[6] In the twentieth century women emerged as a new social category of public economic and political consequence. No longer did they think of themselves 'as different from men as earth was from heaven', but as half of China holding up or constituting the other 'half of heaven'. Despite the impressions of contemporary observers at each stage of the revolution and the changing self-image of Chinese women, the details of this national and conscious attempt to collectively redefine the position of women in society has until recently remained largely undocumented in Western literature.[7] There has been considerable research and debate on the role of peasant and labour movements, their history and contributions to the victory of the Communist Party, but these same scholars have largely ignored the fact that women, too, formed a significant group in Chinese society which in attempting to improve their own position could potentially furnish a separate and organised basis of support for the revolution. Only recently have students of Chinese society begun to document their life-patterns, the history of their separate movement and its relationship to the revolution.[8]

Throughout this century two forces, the wider revolutionary movement and the separate and organised women's movement, have worked to redefine the role and status of women in China. The term 'wider revolutionary movement' is used to refer to the continuous attempt to redefine economic, political and social institutions in the twentieth century. It began with the reform and republican movements which culminated in the 1911 Revolution during which the Manchu dynasty was toppled, and it continued with the development of a nationalist revolutionary movement, led initially by Sun Yat-sen and later by the Communist Party, to unify China and establish a socialist society based on the principles of Marx and Lenin but adapted to the special social and economic conditions of agrarian China. The establishment of the Communist Party as the government in 1949, the period of social reconstruction, the Great Leap Forward (1958–60), the Cultural Revolution and the recent movements to criticise Confucius and Lin Biao (Lin Piao) all constitute stages in this continuing revolutionary process.

The organisation of women to achieve new rights of equality marked the emergence of a new social movement. The women's movement in China as elsewhere is distinguished from other social movements by the sex of its members and its specific interests and pursuits. The redefinition of the role and status of women in public and domestic spheres required not only the ending of legal, social, political and economic discrimination against women, but also an analysis and consciousness of their position in society, together with a total change in their beliefs, self-image, obligations and expectations. That is, all those activities contained under the general rubric of the 'emancipation of women', the 'liberation of women' or 'woman work',* which have deliberately been left as open-ended concepts by Chinese women to allow for constant redefinition. Feminism is not an easy term to define. In China its meaning has been constantly reinterpreted. For the first two decades it was used to denote the exclusive advocacy of women's rights, later it referred to the women's movement which worked to forward the interests of its members within the context of the wider revolutionary movement to alter the basic structures of society. In the last two decades the term feminism has become much more a term of abuse referring to those who exclusively pursue women's interests without regard for the forms which political and economic systems take. It refers to those who survey or describe women's oppression but stop short of an explanation which requires a class analysis and class struggle.

In China the integration of feminism with socialism has demanded that in addition to improving the status of women, the women's movement also arouses an awareness of class interests and responds to all forms of oppression. While in theory the women's movement was to be a separate but not autonomous part of the socialist revolution and the achievements of the goals of each were seen to be mutually interdependent, in practice the uneasy alliance between the wider revolutionary and women's movements have sometimes brought competing claims on the identity of women. The balance of these dual demands has directly affected the history of the women's movement. At various stages certain conditions have favoured a strong group identity among women which has led to its criticism for following an independent feminist policy and disregarding the wider goals of the socialist revolution. While at

* Woman work is a popular term describing the education and organisation of women for struggle within their own and the wider revolutionary movement. Hereafter woman work refers to this type of activity in order to differentiate it from women's work, the more usual translation of *funu gongzuo*. Women's work is reserved for reference to work or occupations to which women are traditionally confined.

other times women have displayed a weak group identity in the face of these competing claims with the result that their interests have been neglected. The history of the women's movement shows that it has been marked by certain ambiguities which have surrounded its position as an independent power-base in a society in which class struggle is viewed as the motivating force generating social change. The special oppression of women did call for the separation of women into their own solidarity groups, but women did not form a class however the term was defined. This book examines the historical and fundamental relationship between feminism and socialism in China.

The attempt to redefine the role and status of women in China has recently attracted the attention of members of the women's movement the world over. Like many other contemporary analyses of the position of women in China, the present study arose out of a joint training and interest in the study of Chinese social institutions and an involvement in the women's movement in London in the late 1960s and early 1970s. One of the main issues that has concerned the women's movement in Europe and North America has been the relevance of radical societal change, revolution and socialism, to the emancipation or liberation of women. Some have concluded that socialism alone promises to change the social order enough to enable women to acquire new rights or to exercise in practice those rights increasingly accorded in principle. But it is this question which has divided the women's movement in Europe and North America from the turn of the century to the present day. The apparent successes and the evident failures of the movement to redefine the position of women in China have equally been used by both sides to support their points of view.

I began this study fairly committed to the view that only the broader economic, social and political transformations that have occurred in China have made the unquestionable changes in the lives of women in China possible. And while not deflected from this view, the present study has raised a number of important questions. For example, how has the women's movement, whose programme essentially suggested a struggle between the sexes, been integrated into the broader class struggle of the wider revolutionary movement? How have the problems of women been defined in relation to the definitions of class struggle in theory and in practice? Has the revolutionary movement as the government satisfied the expectations of women aroused in the early years of struggle when it required their support? Has the implementation of socialist policies and institutions brought with it a concomitant rise in the status of women? The way these questions have been defined and handled in China reveals that in practice the alliance between the women's movement and a political party committed to radical social change is inherently uneasy, complex and, at certain junctures, antagonistic. Indeed in China it has been these same issues which have divided the women's movement itself around the question: which should come first, political or class struggle and the establishment of socialism, or the struggle between the sexes or feminism? Tension between the two sets of priorities has marked the history of the women's movement in China. But to grasp the full complexities of this alliance requires a detailed examination of the changing social, economic and political background of China.

The history of the wider revolutionary movement can be divided into a number of distinct phases each of which had particular implications for the ideological and structural development of the women's movement in China, and raised pertinent questions for women's movements elsewhere. First, this book identifies and summarises the ideological, physical and economic factors responsible for the oppression of women at the turn of the century (chapter 2). It examines the degree of suppression experienced by women at each stage of their life-cycle and for each social class, the forms of protection afforded to women and the attempts made prior to the twentieth century to challenge their subordination. The first two decades of this century were marked by the questioning and confrontation of the old and traditional ways and the search for new social and political institutions. The source of inspiration for the reform movement of 1898, the Republican Revolution of 1911 and the new Thought and Cultural Renaissance of 1916 which were all attempts to redefine social and political institutions in China, was the Western powers of North America and Europe which seemed to hold the secrets of wealth, power and stability. The period which saw the height of Western influence in China in political, social and economic thought and institutions was also marked by incidents of foreign aggression and penetration at the hands of scrambling foreign powers and capital. It was the age of the *Punch* cartoon in which China was shown as the enticing melon or cake ready to be portioned by the foreign powers at the Party table. The increasing incapacity of China's governments of the day to respond to this challenge fed the reform, republican and patriotic movements of the first two decades. Along with other radical movements, the women's movement developed in response to this foreign encroachment, to the growing urbanisation, and to the influence of Western principles of individualism, freedom and self-fulfilment. The women's movement that emerged was primarily confined to, and its platforms reflected, the dominance of the privileged defined in terms of wealth and education. Its members were labelled and harassed as aberrant individuals engaged in quixotic combat with a predestined and established social order. It is the history of the early patriotic, romantic, revolutionary and feminist struggles of the women's movement in this period (chapters 3 and 4), which raises a number of questions to do with the construction and development of similar movements elsewhere. What are the social conditions and the specific condition of women that may produce a revolt? What are the effects of a new imported ideology and/or new economic relations on the size, class-nature and activities of its participants? Where in society should the women's movement identify the agents and institutions of power?

The second phase in the 1920s was marked by further penetration of foreign capital and the steady decline of the power of the central government in the face of competition from a number of regional warlords. The establishment of new economic relations in the cities contributed to the growth of urban areas and new social classes and the decline of the rural economy. In response to the deteriorating economic, social and political conditions of China there emerged a single new revolutionary movement made up of the Communist and Guomindang (Kuomintang) Party members under the leadership of Sun Yat-sen. It was dedicated to the unity of China and the reform of political and economic social institutions, but the latter were subordinated to the immediate military goals of defeating regional commanders and establishing a new and strong central government in China. The structural integration of the women's movement into the nationalist revolutionary movement (1922–7), whereby feminism became linked to a social alternative, marked the turning point in the history of the women's movement in China (chapter 5), and it also raises a number of fundamental questions concerning the integration of feminism and political movements. How did the expanded women's movement go about soliciting the support of peasant and working women and attempt to establish a mass base to the women's movement? What is the relationship between feminist struggle and the struggles of the oppressed? What conditions make for co-operation or conflict between the women's movement and the wider revolutionary movements? What are the revolutionary theories or strategies that accords a distinct place to women's oppression and their movement?

Following the split between the Communist Party and Guomindang Party in 1927 and the suppression of the Communist wing of the nationalist revolution, the Guomindang Party as the government turned to the traditional ideology of Confucianism and nurtured the traditional economic relations based on land rents, and the new economic relations of capitalism in the urban areas. They solicited and increasingly came to rely on foreign aid to restore national unity, mend the social fabric and defeat the Japanese invaders. However, the government was challenged by the growing revolutionary movement led by the Communist Party, which introduced a new ideology and new economic relations based on the writings of Marx, Lenin and later Mao Zedong (Mao Tse-tung) and the experiences of the Soviet Union. The 1930s and 1940s were punctuated by periods of co-operation, mutual tolerance and deadly rivalry or civil war between the two. The division of China into two areas, one governed by Chiang Kai-shek and the Guomindang Party and the other by Mao Zedong and the Communist Party, provides a unique opportunity to follow the development and fate of the women's movement within a decaying semi-feudal society with capitalist trappings (chapter 6) and a burgeoning socialist society (chapter 7). Its study raises the questions which are of great relevance to the reform versus revolution debate within the women's movement. What are the differing political and social interests affected by the demands of women and how far can they be accommodated within certain political and economic systems? How can government policies affect the composition and platforms of the women's movement? Is a change in the socio-economic structure of society necessary to the redefinition of the position of women? Must women wait till after the revolution to achieve their aims? What are the effects of economic development and modernisation on the status of women in rural and urban areas?

The proclamation of the People's Republic of China in 1949 marked the beginning of a nationwide attempt to introduce new political, social and economic institutions in China. A number of major reforms were initiated in the early and middle 1950s: land reform, involving the redistribution of land and the organisation of peasants; the publicisation of the new Marriage Law; the founding of modern industry and the gradual displacement of individualised peasant production by collectivised agriculture. The period of the Great Leap Forward which followed from 1958 to 1960 is perhaps best known for the formation of the new forms of rural social organisation (the people's communes), its utopian flavour, and the subsequent expansion of production. From the 1960s and culminating in the Cultural Revolution, the emphasis has been on the further consolidation of new forms of social organisation, socialist education to raise the political awareness of the people and the struggle against bureaucratic, routinised, capitalist and feudal forms of thought and behaviour. Within the context of these general programmes designed to change the economic base and create new social institutions and values, the women's movement has worked to introduce the new policies and support the interests of women.

The history of the women's movement since 1949 provides an opportunity to study its strategy, its theoretical basis and implementation in practice, in a developing socialist society (chapters 8–11). The relationship between the role of women in the economy and their status in society, the conflicting demands of production, reproduction and the accommodation of domestic labour, the structure of the household or kinship organisation in defining the position of women, and the nature of the labour process, are all current and formidable research problems facing the social scientist and members of the women's movement. The direct and neat correlation between participation in social production and the degree of participation in political activities which gives women access to and control over the strategic resources of society has been questioned. Recent analyses have suggested that although female productive labour is a necessary condition for female status, it is not a sufficient condition, for other factors, often not identified, may interfere with and discourage access to political power. What might these factors be? What are the ideological and structural constraints which continue to inhibit the redefinition of the position of women in Chinese society? How far does socialism bring improvements in the position of women in its wake? What are the role of female solidarity groups and how far can they constitute an independent power base in a socialist society? Is the tyranny of a tight organisation comparable to the tyranny of structurelessness? In sum can the struggle between the sexes and between the classes be combined in the one strategy? I cannot, of course, pretend to be able to discuss all these questions in depth or even that I fully understand the complex nature of the many questions themselves.* But a consideration of how the government and women's movement in China have assessed, analysed and attempted to resolve some of these problems cannot but be of interest and relevance to those concerned with developing analyses and strategies to redefine the role and status of women in society.

In any study of women it is difficult to maintain a balance between presenting an outline of the socio-economic structure in which they are located and the details which directly affect the role and status of women. This problem is magnified in the case of China, where the cultural and political frameworks may be unfamiliar to many readers and where individuals and groups of women should be allowed to relate as much as possible their own observations of and participation in the struggles to redefine the position of women. The documentary sources upon which the book is based fall into two main categories. The first category is composed of official documents of both the government and the women's movement, including authoritative theoretical discussions in the media and educational materials of all forms. These documents include descriptions of role models or public reference groups, commonly used to define the goals of the respective movements and promote the strategies devised to achieve these goals. The reactions to these goals of women in and out of the movement and their perceptions of the events in which they participated or observed has required the use of a second category of materials such as diaries, autobiographies, letters, magazine articles and interviews conducted by anthropologists and journalists. This study exemplifies the problems of documenting the history of a social category hitherto hidden from history by their omission from any of the established and recognised sources for historical analyses, and it has often been necessary to rely on the less formal historical sources and in particular on eye-witness accounts of those who alone at the time thought the movement important enough to attend some of their meetings and interview leaders and members. To maintain balance these accounts are based on a wide variety of political persuasions. At each historical stage the majority of the English-language sources are contemporary to the period in

---

* There is one important set of questions missing from this list and this is the difficult one of sexuality. This topic is probably subject more than any other to the dangers of simplification and ethnocentrism. I have preferred to leave its consideration to future studies.

question. For the Chinese-language sources the historical chapters are based on a study of the general histories of women and the women's problem published in China in the 1930s,[9] while the chapters devoted to the People's Republic of China are based on an extensive reading of contemporaneous Chinese magazines and periodicals and my own interviews in 1973. Without the advantage of broad surveys and statistics allowing for the compilation of tables and membership maps it has been necessary to rely on individual group or community case studies to reveal the intricacies of general large-scale structural changes. These have been chosen to illustrate general patterns and trends of development, less to demonstrate the degree of social change than to delineate the problems involved in combining the goals of feminism and socialism in a single strategy.

The history of the women's movement in China is the history of a long and many-layered complex struggle. It was summed up recently by Jin Zhifang, a peasant woman living on a commune in Jiangsu (Kiangsu) province.[10] In 1973 she described the changes within her lifetime. In the past, like their sisters in other parts of the country, the women of her commune suffered multiple oppression—they were inferior to men, had very little say in the family and were dependent on their husbands economically. Indeed there was an old saying that 'women were always busy, either beside the kitchen stove or at the far-off riverside'. This, she said, aptly described how the labouring women of her village were tied down from morning to night with household chores such as cooking, fetching water and washing. Besides heavy housework they had also to row boats, fish and collect firewood and some even worked as maids in the big houses of the neighbourhood in order to earn some money for their families. 'Some women', she said, 'were so poor that they had to leave six-month-old babies at home and become wet nurses.' Now their position had changed. Both men and women took part in the political, social and economic life of the community. For example, nearly 500 women held leading posts in the commune and popular organisations, women composed 46 per cent of the commune's labour force and now were receiving equal pay where they did equal work. To help women assume a public role, the commune had established a number of neighbourhood organisations such as creches and permanent and seasonal canteens. In describing the present position of women in her commune today, Jin Zhifang constantly referred to their continual battle against old and persistent conventions and ideas.

'Old institutions were rigid, old moral concepts and old customs lingered.' She concluded with real feeling that their new position had only been 'hard won after many, many struggles'. This book is an attempt to analyse the many many struggles of women like Jin Zhifang to win 'half of heaven'.

2 'A Frog in a Well': Mechanisms of Subordination

The past in China was a pit,
Grim, bottomless, accursed,
Where common folk were trodden down,
And women fared the worst.

(Old Folk Song)[1]

Over the centuries the position of women in traditional China gradually deteriorated until the degree of subordination and control of women, whether in the family or in society, has become proverbial. The most apparent means for ensuring the acquiescence of women in their own subordination was the dominant use of ideological mechanisms. The cosmological foundations for this elaborate code of subordination were to be found in ancient Chinese beliefs dating from the first millennium BC. These held that the universe was composed of two interacting elements, 'yin' the female and 'yang' the male. The 'yin' elements displayed dark, weak and passive attributes in contrast to the 'yang' elements which were characterised by all that was bright, strong and active. The rhythms of day and night or the sun and the moon and summer and winter fitted the balancing roles of male and female. While man was endowed with the 'firm nature of heaven', woman partook of 'the yielding nature of the Earth'.[2] Originally conceived as interacting and complementary, these elements were soon arranged in a hierarchical relationship juxtaposing superiority to inferiority and goodness to evil. In time, 'yin' elements came to stand for all that was negative and inferior in the universe. The revised cosmological belief was incorporated into the teachings of Confucius and his disciples which became the established and ruling ideology from the second century BC. Confucius himself had been mainly concerned with the form and content of ideal social relationships between prince and ruler, father and son, husband and wife, brother and brother and friend and friend. In the Confucian classics are to be found the rules of conduct appropriate to each type of social relationship. Confucius is believed to have said of women that they are as different from men as earth is from heaven. 'Women indeed are human beings, but they are of a lower state than men and can never attain to full equality with them.'³ The *Book of Changes* noted that 'Great Righteousness is shown in that man and woman occupy their correct places; the relative positions of Heaven and Earth'.⁴ According to the *Book of Rites*, compiled in the second century AD and later to become one of the venerated Confucian Classics containing rules of correct conduct, 'to be a woman meant to submit'. Women were to take no part in public affairs: 'A man does not talk about affairs inside [the household] and a woman does not talk about affairs outside [the household].'⁵ From these principles establishing a position of submission and the division of labour, practical rules were derived governing women's correct behaviour be they daughters, wives or mothers. These latter were elaborated in a particular set of books expressly written in the first few centuries AD for a feminine audience.

The aim of female education was to develop perfect submission and compliance rather than to cultivate the mind.⁶ Among the books of instruction for girls were the *Nü Jie* or *Precepts for Women* and the *Nü er Jing* or the *Classic for Girls*. The *Nü Jie* was written by the famous woman scholar, Ban Zhao (Pan Chao), in the first century AD. She was educated, and fulfilled the functions of court historian following the deaths of her scholared father and brother. In the *Nü Jie* she wrote 'The Yin and the Yang, like the male and the female, are very different principles. The virtue of the Yang is firmness, the virtue of the Yin—flexibility.' She exhorted women to be obedient, unassuming, yielding, timid, respectful, reticent and unselfish in character. 'First others then herself.' A woman should endure reproach, treasure reproof and revere her husband for 'A husband, he is Heaven' and 'Heaven is unalterable, it cannot be set aside'. 'If the wife does not serve her husband, the rule of propriety will be destroyed.'⁷ The *Nü er Jing* similarly catalogued the ideal qualities of women. It outlined in more detail what were known as 'The Three Obediences' and 'The Four Virtues'. Throughout her life-cycle a woman was subject to the three authorities of her father and elder brothers when young, of her husband when married and of her sons when widowed. The four virtues comprised, first, a 'general virtue' meaning that a woman should know her place in the universe and behave in every way in compliance with the time-honoured ethical codes; second, she should be reticent in words taking care not to chatter too much and bore others; third, she must be clean of person and habits and adorn herself with a view to pleasing the opposite sex; and fourth, she should not shirk her household duties.⁸ The *Lie Nü Zhuan* or

Series of Women's Biographies was first arranged by Liu Xiang in the first century AD. The general preface to these biographies reads: 'The wife leans on the man. Gentle, yielding, she early listens to the words of others. She has the nature and emotions of those who serve others and controls her person in the way of chastity.' The biographies themselves include filial daughters, chaste maidens who would sooner meet death than dishonour, and ideal sisters-in-law, wives, mothers and widows whose chastity and devotion to duty is above reproach and worthy of emulation.[9] One breakdown of the *Lie Nü Zhuan* includes 19 examples of women who were far-sighted and benevolent; 19 who were celebrated because of chastity; 18 who refused to marry after widowed whether by death of husband or betrothed; 18 who were celebrated for far-sightedness and widowhood; 18 who should be considered as warnings for girls; 16 who were great mothers; and 16 who were celebrated for their docility and constancy.[10]

As Confucianism was gradually institutionalised, the Classics and these Books were increasingly adopted as the authorities on feminine conduct. They set the ideal standards and were used as textbooks in the education of girls throughout succeeding generations. From the first centuries AD onwards an endless succession of Confucian writers extended these texts and perpetuated the belief that women were as different and inferior to men as earth was to heaven. In particular, the Neo-Confucian philosophers of the Sung dynasty (960–1279) further elaborated the code of feminine ethics by re-emphasising the practices of segregation and seclusion, and introducing the practice of bound feet. In theory the division of labour in society was complete. Most could not read the Classics for themselves. For the illiterate, quotations from the Classics were repeated to them by village gentry and bits of homely philosophy were handed down by word of mouth from generation to generation. Male superiority, embodied in proverbs and folklore, became an attitude prevalent in popular thought. The persuasion of an ideology became the forces of fate, inescapable. But the lives of women in traditional China were not influenced by the ideological mechanisms alone. In examining the position of women their socio-economic or class position in the social structure was as important a factor in defining their field of activities. Normally traditional Chinese society was divided into four social classes—those of the scholar-gentry, the peasants, artisans and merchants. Outside this classification lay those without a recognised place in Chinese society—the 'mean' people or the boat people, actors, storytellers, prostitutes and other like social categories. Each of the four official 'classes' was associated with a distinctive occupation and life-style which affected the lives of their women by modifying the division of labour, the amount of seclusion and their particular positions in the household. It was the interaction of economic with ideological and physical mechanisms of subordination which finally determined the degree of subjugation and control experienced by women in society and in the household.

In the social, political and the economic affairs of the country, the most important distinction common to all classes was the sexual division of labour between household or domestic affairs and non-household or public spheres of activity. If ideally women did one and abstained from the other, in reality it was the prerogative of the richer classes to live up to these norms. Among the poor, economic factors interceded to a greater or lesser degree to modify these standards in practice. But from earliest times all women were taught that they should not concern themselves with public affairs. The *Book of Rites* clearly stated that women should have no public influence or knowledge of affairs outside the home. 'A wife's words should not travel beyond her apartments' and 'a woman does not discuss affairs outside the home'.[11] The classical writing and literature go so far as to suggest that there is something inherently vicious in the female nature that brought men possessed by women to an evil end. The compilers of one of the Classics thought the contemporary lack of harmony and disorder in the state was caused by the interference of women in public affairs:

A woman with a long tongue
Is [like] a stepping stone to disorder.
[Disorder] does not come down from heaven;
It is produced by the women.[12]

In literature it is often women who divide brother against brother and bring men to ruin with their 'sexual aggression and dangerous cunning'. In the popular novel, *The Water Margin*, the heroes sacrifice the company of women so that the heroic code among sworn brothers may endure.[13] Women were denied participation in any of the government or local community institutions. They had no access to the system of examinations which furnished the major path to political office in traditional China. All the significant Confucian ceremonial roles in society could only be fulfilled by men. In the provinces of southwest China for instance, women were not even permitted to witness the rituals and rites which were held annually to pray for a prosperous year with good crops.[14] Even in the wider kinship units whose boundaries often coincided with those of the village or local community, the leadership and ceremonial roles were reserved for men. Only they could perform the ancestral rites of central importance in the clan or lineage. Women in general tended to turn to Buddhism and especially to the Goddess Guanyin, the female protectress, for help and solace in their troubles. Theirs was a private and individual religion usually confined to the domestic sphere. Within the household they kept images, recited beads and sometimes they visited temples and shrines to pray and plead for a son, good health and good fortune. Likewise they were responsible for placating the Kitchen God with offerings in order that prosperity visit the household in the coming year.

The confinement of women to the domestic sphere was further reinforced by the concern for, or almost obsession with, the preservation of the virtue, honour and chastity of women. Perhaps the most striking feature of social life was the segregation of the sexes. It was deemed desirable that men should have no public social relations with women, and even within the home boys and girls seven years or older were not supposed to sit or eat together.[15] The cult of feminine chastity and ideal of segregation led to the increasing isolation of girls from all save the women of their own family and the seclusion of women in the richer and poorer households. The very word for woman became '*nèirén*' which literally meant 'inside person'. In the upper classes a woman tended to live within the confines of the women's apartments occupying herself with her toilet, embroidery, the management of household affairs and parlour amusements. The contrast with the life of her brother was self-evident. In the words of the poet Fu Xuan:

> Boys standing leaning at the door
> Like gods fallen out of Heaven,
> Their hearts have the Four Oceans,
> The wind and dust of a thousand miles. . . .
>
> When she grows up she hides in her room,
> Afraid to look men in the face.[16]

If men entertained at home, rather than at the customary teahouse, women were seldom in evidence. At such times women were not supposed to even peep outside the doors of their apartments; advice to husbands was:

> Let not your guests behold your wife,
> And secretly lock the postern gate.
> Restrict her to courtyard and garden,
> So misfortune and intrigue will pass you by.[17]

In the eleventh century, a time when the value of seclusion was being forcefully reiterated by the neo-Confucianists, the poetess Li Jingzhao expressed her thoughts and longings as:

> Silence, solitude, deep in women's enclosure,
> A single inch of soft intestine holds a thousand
> threads of grief. . . .[18]

In the novel *The Family* Ba Jin (Pa Chin) describes the New Year custom which persisted into the twentieth century allowing women into the streets:

> The women of the family . . . walked smilingly through the main gate and out on to the street. This was the women's annual comedy of 'going abroad'. It was only during this brief interval each year that they were permitted to travel freely in public other than in a closed sedan chair. The women feasted their curious eyes on the sleepy little street. Then fearful of meeting any strange man, they hurried back into the compound.[19]

In peasant households women customarily had more freedom of movement. Their living quarters afforded them less seclusion than the rambling courtyards characteristic of gentry dwellings. The very size of the peasant dwelling allowed less segregation and where the light inside was poor, peasant women frequently sat and worked on their doorsteps. In the village, peasant women sometimes gathered water from the well, did their washing at the river, and had no servants to shop and market for them. They had more contact with local shopkeepers and pedlars and in some areas of China such as the southern provinces women traditionally worked in the fields alongside their menfolk during the busy seasons. Women of the non-Han ethnic minorities, boat-women, water-carriers, servants, fuel gatherers and scavengers tended to come and go freely. But despite the influence of their living standards and type of work on the ideals of segregation, the movements of most village women were still restricted. They were often not permitted to leave their courtyards for the first three years of marriage,[20] and one traveller in nineteenth-century China found that tens of thousands of women had never been more than two miles from their villages and this was often only on the occasion of their marriage.[21] They were generally said to live the existence of a 'frog in a well' and one lady told the Englishman, A. H. Smith, that in her next life she hoped to be born a dog for then she might come and go where she chose.[22] The common sayings 'A man travels everywhere while a woman is confined to the kitchen' and 'An incompetent man can get about in nine counties but a competent woman can only get around her cooking stove' arose because appearances of women outside their household yards were rare.[23] One working woman recalled how she and her elder sister were not allowed on the city streets after they were thirteen years of age and if a stranger came to the door they had to disappear into an inner room. Women were not always welcome as visitors in the district in which she lived. They could not visit on the first or thirteenth day of any month and could not, when visiting, lean against the frame of the door. They should not stand or sit on the doorstep or even touch it in crossing, for to do any of these things might give them power over the family they were visiting and so ruin it. 'Women', she said, 'were not considered clean.' She also recalled that when a family wanting to know more about a girl who had been suggested as a prospective daughter-in-law, asked neighbours for an opinion, the highest praise and compliment in response was 'We do not know, we have never seen her.'[24] Symbolic of the status of women in one village in northeastern China was the reply given to male visitors when the men of the house chanced to be out. The customary answer to the question 'Is anybody at home?' was 'No, there's nobody in'—given by the housewife herself![25]

The physical mobility of most women in China was devastatingly affected by the practice of footbinding which itself has become a symbol of their role circumscription. The practice is said to date from the fashion of small bowed feet current among the court dancing girls in the tenth century. The custom was first practised among the upper classes, but because bound feet were then associated with wealth and status they eventually became an essential prerequisite to an advantageous marriage and any form of social mobility. The degree of binding did vary with each social class. Matchmakers were asked not 'Is she beautiful?', but 'How small are her feet?' A plain face was said to be given by heaven, but poorly bound feet were a sign of laziness and poor breeding.[26]

Many an aspiring mother subjected her daughter to this painful process and soon girls of all but the poorest families had lost their freedom and agility. The painful memories of women contrast starkly with the poetic appreciation of men[27] though there were a number of specific groups in Chinese society among whom the practice of footbinding was not common. For example: Manchu women, Hakka women, the so-called 'hill tribes' of China and the boat population of Canton.

Where it was practised girls of seven and eight years of age had their feet tightly wrapped and bent until the arch was broken and the toes permanently bent under. The memories of those first years of agony remained forever etched in one woman's mind:

> I was inflicted with the pain of footbinding when I was seven years old. I was an active child who liked to jump about, but from then on my free and optimistic nature vanished. . . . My feet felt on fire and I couldn't sleep; Mother struck me for crying . . . I tried to hide but was forced to walk on my feet. . . . Though I wanted to sit passively by the *kang*, Mother forced me to move around.[28]

Another recalled that her 'feet hurt so much for two years that I was forced to crawl on my hands and knees'.[29] The intense pain and suffering were summed up in an old saying: 'For every pair of bound feet a bucket full of tears.' Women were condemned to the life of a cripple while men praised their aesthetic and erotic qualities. The small feet, measured steps and the gentle swaying gait were thought to be reminiscent of the willow or poplar in the wind. The body shimmered all over and looked ready to fall at the slightest touch. Lin Yutang, the writer, thought that looking at a woman with bound feet walking was like looking at a rope-dancer, 'tantalising to the highest degree'. He considered the bound foot the highest sophistication of the Chinese sensual imagination.[30] The cult of the 'golden lotus' or 'golden lily' occupied an important place in sensual poetry and song. Su Dongbo (1036–1101) wrote one of the earliest verses in praise of footbinding.

> Anointed with fragrance, she takes lotus steps;
> Though often sad, she steps with swift lightness.
> She dances like the wind, leaving no physical trace . . .
> Look at them in the palm of your hand,
> So wondrously small that they defy description.[31]

The practical implications of the bound feet were not lost on men or women. They restricted the physical mobility of women thus preventing them from moving about freely and unchaperoned. A verse in the *Classic for Girls* asks of women:

Have you ever learned the reason
For the binding of your feet?
'Tis from fear that 'twill be easy to go out upon the street.
It is not that they are handsome when thus like a crooked bow,
That ten thousand wraps and bindings are enswathed around
them so.[32]

A similar attitude was expressed in a Yuan dynasty rhyme 'Why must the foot be bound? To prevent barbarous running around'[33] or in a folk ditty from Hebei province: 'Bound feet, bound feet, past the gate can't retreat.'[34]
Although the prevailing social ethos reinforced by physical constraints were instrumental in confining women to the domestic sphere, as important a factor was the absence of any available independent economic role in society and their total dependence on the family unit. There were few public occupations open to women. They were excluded from the civil service which was the main source of income of the ruling class. Women scholars, artists and writers were rare and practically never derived any income from these activities. They were prevented by the laws of inheritance from owning property in their own right, and as the anthropologist, Fei Hsiao-tung, pointed out, in a community where land is the main foundation of the economic structure, the dominance of the landowning sex is to be expected.[35] The unilateral principle of inheritance excluded women from any matter concerned with land. Only her jewellery represented convertible savings. Leisure was the hallmark of the lives of women of the upper classes and among the poor the few occupations that were open to women were mainly associated with magic or procreation. They could become midwives, marriage-brokers, prostitutes, courtesans, procuresses or spirit diviners. Peasant women and wives of artisans were far from idle, but their productive roles were largely confined to the household. The family unit was to a large degree self-sufficient and was the chief organisational unit of production and consumption. Within the family there was a sharp distinction drawn between the processes of production and transformation or those performed immediately prior to consumption. In the main production was carried out by the men of the family and the bulk of its preparation

for family use fell to the feminine side of the family. Although women's share of the total labour time expended on transformation activities (grinding corn, pounding rice, etc.), child care, cooking, making clothes and sometimes livestock rearing and cultivation might be equal or greater than that of men, the production of the latter was held in higher esteem. Denying importance to women's work helped to maintain women's subordinate position.

In the southern provinces some peasant women laboured in the fields during busy seasons, but they never played a large part in the agricultural cycle. J. L. Buck who did a survey in the early years of the twentieth century found that women supplied only 16.4 per cent of all farming labour.[36] Peasant women, especially in the north of China, might participate in domestic and handicraft industry such as spinning and weaving, but because these were performed within the confines of the family unit and hardly distinguishable from household work, they were supervised by the men of the family and afforded the women no independent source of income. Except in a few areas given over to the silk industry, any non-household jobs were rarely of sufficient duration or quantity to provide the women with a viable source of economic support alternative to that afforded by the family unit. As a result the men of the family had an extremely strong economic basis for power; women ordinarily could not produce or consume without male sanction. The tradition of economic dependence, even in hard times, is evident in the following extract from an autobiography of a working-class woman.

> Day after day I sat at home. Hunger gnawed. What could I do? My mother was dead. My brother had gone away. When my husband brought home food I ate it and my children ate with me. A woman could not go out of the court[yard]. If a woman went out to service the neighbourhood all laughed . . . I did not know enough even to beg. So I sat at home and starved. . . . How could I know what to do? We women knew nothing but to comb our hair and bind our feet and wait at home for our men. When my mother had been hungry she had sat at home and waited for my father to bring her food, so when I was hungry I waited at home for my husband to bring me food.[37]

In effect the individual woman held no publicly recognised position in the public sphere and her confinement to the activities of the household ensured minimal co-operative links with other women which might have mitigated the effects of male dominance. Ideological and economic factors interacted to deprive women of the opportunities of independence or association which might have arisen from participation in public, social, economic or political activities.

Women's activities were mainly confined to the domestic sphere. The family, the primary unit of the social system, was from the time of Confucius and his disciples consciously cultivated as the ideal foundation of an orderly state. It occupied a central position in society assuming a multiplicity of economic, educational, religious and even political functions, with few additional organisations and associations being available to serve the individual's social needs. Ideally several generations were to live harmoniously under one roof. Large extended families were usually confined to the richer classes who had the economic resources to maintain such a household. The peasants rarely achieved more than three generations under one roof—the grandparents, parents and their children. The structure of the Chinese family was based on a hierarchy of the generations and the sexes with well-defined patterns of authority. The locus of power and responsibility was overwhelmingly in the hands of the male members of the household. Within the patrilocal, patrilineal and patriarchal family institution women played a subservient role until they became the sole representative of the senior generation. Women's life-cycles were dominated by two states: first they were 'temporary' and then they were 'outsiders' or 'strangers'. In their early years they were temporary members of their natal family destined to leave the family on marriage. On their marriage they entered their husband's family as outsiders or strangers. The stability and ideal harmony of the family organisation was not maintained without considerable stresses and strains, and these were particularly apparent in the lives of women. Since the subordination of women formed what was one of the most potentially disruptive lines of tension within the household, a number of ideological and economic factors combined to reinforce their position of dependence within the domestic sphere.

It was not always true, especially in the richer classes, that in the words of the poet Fu Xuan, 'No one is glad when a girl is born and by her the family sets no store',[38] but certainly a girl was welcomed into the family with fewer expectations and less ceremony than a boy. *The Book of Poetry*, one of the richest and most authentic

source materials depicting social life in ancient China, recorded the
unequal treatment of the sexes from birth:

> When a son is born
> Let him sleep on the bed,
> Clothe him with fine clothes,
> And give him jade to play with.
> How lordly his cry is!
> May he grow up to wear crimson
> And be the lord of the clan and the tribe.
>
> When a daughter is born,
> Let her sleep on the ground,
> Wrap her in common wrappings,
> And give her broken tiles for playthings.
> May she have no faults, no merits of her own
> May she well attend to food and wine,
> And bring no discredit to her parents.[39]

There were reasons why a daughter was generally less welcome than
a son. Daughters cannot offer ancestral sacrifice, cannot glorify the
family through official appointment or perpetuate the family
name. Sons were of overwhelming importance to the family
because of their potential role as providers of the family income
through office-holding, commerce, landownership or labour and
handicraft skills. Even after death it was the sons, as sole
performers of the religious rites, who were responsible for the
welfare of their departed parents in the spirit world. 'Men rear
sons', says a proverb, 'to provide for old age, just as they plant
trees because they want shade.'[40] Daughters consumed rice, needed
clothes and their weddings were usually a drain on the family
resources. The expression a 'commodity on which money has been
lost' was a paraphrase sometimes used for a girl.[41] After her
marriage she became the exclusive property of her husband's
family and was thereby as beyond the control of her own parents as
'water which has burst its banks'. An old saying that 'a boy is born
facing in and a girl is born facing out'[42] reflected the transient
nature of her life with her parents and the loss to her natal family
on marriage. Indeed the relative advantages of sons and daughters
were emphatically indicated in the meanings of the names
sometimes given to girls after a succession of daughters, such as
'Better luck next time' and 'Wish you were a boy', and the maxim
'Eight lohan [model] daughters are not equal to a boy with a

limp'.[43] In extreme cases girls were reckoned of so little account that a father would leave them out of his calculations when asked the number of children in his family. In these circumstances it was not difficult to understand the preferential treatment often accorded to sons in times of economic hardship and, for the majority of the peasants who constantly struggled for a living, the lower economic value of a daughter accounted for much of the general discrimination against the female infant.

Girls were the main, if not exclusive, victims of infanticide and tended to have a higher infant mortality rate in times of poverty and famine. In a nineteenth-century survey conducted in several different provincial villages, the 160 women over fifty years of age who were interviewed, and who between them had borne a total of 631 sons and 538 daughters, admitted to destroying 158 of their daughters; none had destroyed a boy. As only four of the women had reared more than three girls, the field workers felt that the number of infanticides confessed to was considerably below the truth. The greatest number of infanticides owned to by any one woman was eleven. Sixty per cent of their sons had lived for more than ten years as opposed to 38 per cent of their daughters.[44] In other areas there was no sign of female infanticide. On the contrary there was much evidence of parental care and affection. In remote and poor northern Shanxi where girls were more scarce they were a precious commodity and did not suffer any obvious childhood discrimination. In conversation with Jan Myrdal an old resident of Liuling village in northern Shanxi elaborated on this point. He said that there was a shortage of girls in all northern Shanxi, he didn't know why this was so. 'It was just a fact that far more boys had been born here than girls.' He quoted the figures for his own family, of 9 grandchildren 3 were girls, and for his village where 36 out of 58 children were boys.[45]

Apart from infanticide it was also a fairly common practice among the poorer peasants and townspeople to free themselves of the expenses of rearing a daughter by either selling them into domestic service and prostitution or offering them as child-brides to be brought up as adopted daughters-in-law in their future husband's family. For the husband's family this arrangement spared them the later expenses of a wedding ceremony, secured an additional household worker and ensured that the young girl was conditioned early in the habits of their household. One anthropologist described the fate of the daughters of the poor in the villages in south China:

Poor families need money and have too many daughters. The daughters consume rice and need clothes; when they are grown up they leave the home and furnish additional service to the productivity of the economic family of the group into which the girl is married. The parents in poor families consider it better therefore to get rid of the girl at the first opportunity and thus free themselves of her expenses and at the same time get some cash.[46]

In contrast, in social classes where girls were less of an economic burden, they grew up and occupied an affectionate place in their families. Many scholars lamented the death of or marriage of a much-beloved daughter in the verses of their poetry. In all social classes however it was recognised that girls were destined to become a daughter-in-law and wife in another family. As the *Nü er Jing* stated 'You should study as a daughter all the duties of a wife'.[47]

Generally these duties did not include the advantages of literacy. The richer Chinese families were stimulated to educate their sons by the ambition to have them hold a government position, but the daughters had no such argument to advance. Only the privileged daughters of the scholar-gentry class sometimes shared their brother's tutor and enjoyed an opportunity to develop their minds and cultivate their talents. One Chinese professor estimated that only a very few girls 'learned something of books' and the main works taught to them were the four classics especially written for girls.[48] The line of demarcation between the ideal boys' and girls' education was drawn in the following poem:

When he grows to years of boyhood,
Then a teacher call at once,
Who will books and manners teach him, that he may not be a dunce.
Lazy habits in his study will good people all annoy,
And his indolence the prospects of his future life destroy.

For your daughter in her girlhood,
To learn fancy-work is best,
Ne'er allow her to be idle,—lolling to the east or west.
If in youth you do not teach her, when full grown 'twill be too late.
When she marries it will bring her only shame, disgrace and hate.[49]

Generally, knowledge was widely believed to be a bad investment for an 'outward-facing' girl, and was considered unnecessary or even harmful. For 'a woman without talents is virtuous'[50] while 'a woman too well educated is apt to create trouble'.[51] Girls were almost exclusively trained for their duties in the domestic sphere. The chief aim in a girl's education was the inculcation of ancient stereotypes of female conduct. All the older members of the family assisted in informing what she may, or may not do, in all sorts of situations, particularly in relation to her brothers, father, mother, uncles, and her future husband and his parents. The possession of propriety, the right attitudes and correct conduct, were some of her greatest assets for a desirable marriage contract, and for the successful adjustment in her new home after marriage. For the practical achievements of this vocational aim, daughters in peasant households were early initiated into the household chores by their mothers. Household chores in a peasant subsistence economy were numerous. Girls learned to sew, spin, cook, wash, clean and care for younger children, poultry and pigs. In the southern provinces the girls sometimes learned the skills required in the fields during busy seasons. In the richer households girls destined for a more leisured existence learned household arts rather than chores of a more utilitarian nature. By the time the marriage took place girls of all classes had received much of the domestic knowledge which their mothers possessed.

Early marriage was well-nigh universal. Marriages were arranged between families of different surnames and usually of a similar social standing by 'matching a bamboo door with a bamboo door and a wooden door with a wooden door' to procure the services of a woman's reproductive powers and domestic labour. Negotiations regarding the choice of the marriage partner, the bride-price and dowry were conducted by a go-between or broker and the young people were strangers to one another upon marriage. Romantic courtship played no part. Any overt intimacy or affection would be bound to strengthen the conjugal tie and threaten the dominance of parental affection, loyalty and authority. The new bride entered her husband's household as an outsider and embarked on the most difficult and personally humiliating period of her life. The most important role she assumed on marriage was that of daughter-in-law, and many institutional devices were brought to bear to subjugate and integrate the daughter-in-law so as to prevent a division or break-up of the Chinese extended family. The obligations of the new daughter-in-law towards her husband's parents were numerous. According to the *Book of Rites*, she was 'to revere and respect them', 'never to disobey them day or night', and 'serve them as she served her own parents'.[52] The *Classic for Girls* established her priorities:

As a wife to husband's parents,
You should filial be and good,
Nor should suffer imperfection in their clothing or their food,
Be submissive to their orders, all their wants anticipate,
That, because his wife is idle, they your husband may not hate.

Be submissive to your husband,
Nor his wishes e'er neglect
First of all in this submission is his parents to respect.[53]

In the *Twenty-Four Patterns of Filial Piety*, the only girl held up for emulation nourished her old and toothless mother-in-law with milk from her breast by which means she was able to keep her alive. She walked several miles every day to get river water for her mother-in-law because she preferred it to that from their well. She made similar efforts to provide the old lady with minced fish to gratify her desires.[54] A Tang-dynasty poem ruled that as far as the new daughter-in-law was concerned 'The husband's mother ruled the roost'.[55] In the daily household routine the daughter-in-law was under the constant surveillance and discipline of her mother-in-law. It was said that when a mother-in-law wanted to find fault with her daughter-in-law she was as thorough as a donkey going round and round the rolling millstone: she did not miss a step.[56]

It was as if, having been trapped all their lives, women turned around and with the authority of the mother-in-law expressed their new security and compensated for their own former suffering and impotence as an outsider by repeating the very process of domination that they themselves had suffered. Indeed, in peasant households the abuse of a young daughter-in-law was so common a circumstance, especially in situations where the family had incurred heavy debts to procure a daughter-in-law, that unless it was especially flagrant it attracted little attention. The new wife in a richer household was spared the rigours of constantly supervised domestic labour but the mother-in-law normally acted to maintain her influence with her son. In cases of conflict a wife could not necessarily count on her husband's support. Sometimes he sided with his wife, but more often with his mother. The husband, who was himself in a subordinate position in his parent's home and was a stranger to his new wife, was discouraged from showing any public or strong favour or affection towards her or from taking her side during any conflict with his parents. He was often torn between his loyalties to his mother and new wife, and in extreme cases a mother-in-law might use her son to enforce authority. Her husband's family had the institutional right to send her back to her parents' home on many traditional grounds and the story of the obstinate mother-in-law who threw the wife of her son out of the house and drove the daughter-in-law or both of the young couple, if she was beloved, to suicide, is a recurrent theme in classical literature.

Young women were taught to exercise forbearance and self-sacrifice and accept their fate. Such sayings as 'Obey heaven and follow fate' and 'When you marry a chicken, stick with a chicken; when you marry a dog, stick with a dog', were constantly used to remind her that her 'rice was cooked'. The term for divorce, which literally meant 'oust wife',[57] closely reflected the unilateral nature of divorce. Tradition allowed a husband, under certain circumstances, to return his wife to her own family. Grounds for this action included failure to obey and serve his parents, failure to produce a son, lasciviousness, jealousy, contraction of a malignant disease, garrulousness and thieving. This right was overruled if his wife had no family to return to, she had passed through three years' mourning for his parents, or she had married him when he was poor and he now had become rich. A woman had no such reciprocal rights. Not even the death of a husband released a woman from her vows. If a woman had the misfortune to be widowed while she was young she was ideally to remain eternally true and chaste and many a monumental arch lined the Chinese roads to honour the virtues of the faithful and life-long widow. As long as the husband's family could support her, the death of the husband did not affect the nature of the marriage bond to his family or alter the wife's status and obligations as a daughter-in-law. Among peasants and the urban poor, widows did often remarry on account of economic pressure. In these classes, the husband's family usually exacted a price for her and she was permitted to take neither her sons nor her husband's property, for these belonged not to her but to her first husband's family.[58] Lu Xun (Lu Hsun) has described a poor widow's fate in his famous short story entitled 'The New Year's Sacrifice',[59] in which a widow, whom everybody called Xiang Lin's wife ('They did not ask her her name'), was sold by her dead husband's relatives to a family in the nearby mountains. The arrangement was said to be a good bargain for no one was willing to marry someone deep in the mountains and the cash price was high. Xiang Lin's wife struggled and fought all the way. Widowed again, some years later, she entered a rich man's household as a servant where she was taunted by the other servants. As a woman twice married, they said, the King of Hell would have no choice but to cut her in two when she died, one half for each of her husbands. These threats affected her mind and she later died in penury on the streets. As this story shows a second marriage was usually one of downward social mobility for there was a certain amount of social discrimination against the remarriage of a widow—it was like 'taking a second-hand article'.[60]

A woman's prestige in the family increased immeasurably once she had presented them with a son and heir. This was a family event of the utmost importance. As the famous injunction by Mencius suggested 'there are three unfilial acts and of these the lack of posterity is the greatest'. In her son or sons the new young wife found new protection and security. Margery Wolf, the anthropologist, undertook field work among Hokkien-speaking women resident in two villages in the Taipei basin of Taiwan in the 1960s. She found that women did not share the same definition of the 'family' as the men. The latter were conscious of the obligations to their ancestors and future descendants and viewed the family as a line of descent encompassing all the members of a household: past, present and future. She has suggested that women tended to define the family in terms of the temporary and contemporary social unit consisting of the mother and her children. Margery Wolf argues that this uterine family was no less real because it had no ideology, formal structure or public existence.[61] It was by forming and cultivating their own small circles of security that women found a source of power in a social structure dominated by men. Consciously and unconsciously a woman tended to weave ties with her sons that were personal and exclusive. Any threat to this relationship struck deep. Hence her response to the threat later posed by the entrance of the new daughter-in-law into the family. The mother of a son became more and more an integral part of the family, while on the other hand her failure to bear a son made her lot worse. Small girls were sometimes adopted in the belief that this practice would stimulate the birth of a son, but failing this expedient poor families might adopt a son, or a son-in-law and thus reverse the normal patrilocal practice, and in richer households a childless wife might be forced to accept the presence of another woman brought into the household to bear the heir, although this practice does seem to have been confined to the gentry and richer merchant households. In a survey of rural Dingxian (Tinghsien) for example there were concubines in less than 1 per cent of the families.[62]

Although custom and law allowed only one principal wife, husbands could take secondary wives or concubines ostensibly for the purpose of providing them with sons. In practice, and limited only by their wishes and financial ability, men were free to gratify their personal desires by this means within the context of an arranged marriage. Concubines were often attractive girls purchased from poorer families or were courtesans who had attracted the husband on one of his visits to teahouses. The latter were often skilled in music, dancing, conversation and poetry composition, and merchants and scholar-gentry frequented the houses of courtesans for such feminine companionship. They often supplied the need for courtship and romance which many men had missed in their youth and many later became concubines. Some wives co-operated with their husbands in such ventures. The wife of Xi Men in the sixteenth-century novel *The Golden Vase Plum* amiably received and co-operated with new concubines often mediating between them and her husband.[63] Others felt very threatened by the presence of a concubine or concubines, and like Phenix in another novel, *The Dream of the Red Chamber*, reacted to competition with venom.[64] Phenix was ultimately responsible for the death of her husband's concubine. The presence of several women competing for the favours of one man often caused intrigue, rivalry and jealousy in larger households or in court circles. The character for the word 'peace' denotes 'one woman under one roof' and there was a common saying in this situation: 'Do you ever see two spoons in the same bowl that do not knock against each other?'[65] The concubine herself was placed in a precarious position and families were often more reluctant to dispose of their daughters in this way. Not only was she often the focus of aggression and jealousy, but she was completely dependent on her male sponsor. No formal marriage ceremony marked her entrance into the household and just as a 'hall was not a room' she was never accorded full membership status in the family unit.

With old age, a woman enjoyed certain advantages arising from the subordination of the young to the old. The old mother and grandmother were greatly respected and the old matriarchal figure at the head of the household is a familiar enough person in Chinese literature. By the time they reached the venerable position of the eldest surviving member of the senior generation after a lifetime of resorting to struggle, manipulation and duplicity, some women made the most of their new vantage point in order to dominate the affairs of their family. Formally, however, a woman remained subordinate to her husband while he was alive. Even as widows women only had a powerful position so long as there were no male adult relatives to act as family heads and manage the children's property. A widow might benefit from the patterns of filial piety, but in the last resort the real power of the sons was written into the codes of law. Widows were never officially recognised as the heads of the family for just as 'a mare is not fit to go into battle, a woman cannot take a man's place'. In peasant households a lower life expectancy and insufficient economic resources to maintain large households meant that wives, though they might be spared the domination of the older generation while young, were also less likely to live to an old age where they might enjoy a certain measure of leisure and respect.

The fate of a woman generally depended on her luck in bearing a son, on the position of the man to whom she was attached in the hierarchical family structure and the class or position of her own and her husband's family. In the larger gentry and merchant households, women were not subject to economic pressures and lived a more secluded, leisured and aesthetic existence in their separate apartments. Ordinarily they had servants at their disposal to spare them from arduous physical labour in the household. Indeed, the ennui of women in the wealthier houses contrasted with the fatigue of women in humbler conditions. The behavioural patterns which characterised the life of the richer classes approximated the ideal, but the vast majority of the population followed the life-style of the peasantry. Among the peasants economic factors frequently countered ideological factors. Their direct contribution to the subsistent economy of the household could affect and did often improve their position within the family. It is difficult to generalise about domestic life in traditional China for it was often said that customs 'varied every ten li' and in all classes the inferior position of individual women might be mitigated by personality factors, family affection, their personal assumption of power roles or a man's fear of conflict and avoidance of disruption. But the widespread notion of a nation of henpecked husbands and Chinese dowagers wielding enormous power does not stand up to analysis. Individual cases of female domination cannot invalidate the general argument that any status accorded to women was informal, delegated and dependent in nature. As the sociologist E. A. Ross observed in China at the end of the nineteenth century, an individual woman might slip from under the thumb of an individual man, but never could women free themselves from the domination of the male sex.[66] Men had all the artillery at hand—time-hallowed teachings and economic power. Within the domestic sphere, men were the institutionalised source of all authority and women had no public, social, political or economic position or role with which to negotiate and improve their position within the family.

If women had little choice but to submit to the male dominant family institution what were their rights of protection against ill-treatment? How true was the proverb 'A wife married is like a pony bought; I'll ride her and whip her as I like'? The law itself afforded women little protection. The rights of a husband to discipline his wife, if necessary by means of force, were recognised by the law. A husband could kill his adulterous wife with immunity. There were no such reciprocal rights. Except in cases where death resulted, magistrates were reluctant to interfere in family affairs for 'Even an upright magistrate can hardly decide family disputes'.[67] This was the responsibility of the patriarchal figure. Just when discipline became abuse it is difficult to ascertain, but it is evident that a certain amount of ill-treatment such as beating was tolerated. It was usually considered the natural right of a husband to beat his wife. The Chinese themselves are reported as estimating that six or seven out of ten husbands regularly beat their wives.[68] Without legal protection a woman was forced to rely on informal means—her value to the household, the family's concern for its reputation, the intervention of her natal family and threatened suicide—all of which might or might not be effective.

The expenses associated with the marriage ceremony and the acquisition of a wife meant that those in the poorer classes were reluctant to take action which would ultimately mean embarking on the process a second time. The number of unmarried men or 'baresticks' present in every village served as a reminder to poor peasants and townspeople that wives were not always easy to come by. The young wife was valued for her reproductive functions and in poorer households her labour was essential to the subsistence and well-being of the home. In gentry families, economic factors were less important, but the reputation or 'face' of the family was of major concern to all.

The amount of gossip and village opinion was a powerful force for justice. Daughters-in-law were often actively discouraged from talking with outsiders for fear they would betray the secrets of the household and in particular would gossip about the faults of their mothers-in-law. Indeed it was often the women's community of the village which, by initiating gossip around the common well, brought pressure to bear against the mothers-in-law or the men of a particular family. Margery Wolf made enquiries as to just what 'having face' amounted to. She found that when no one was talking about a family, you could say that it had 'face'.[69] When a man behaved in a way villagers considered wrong the gossip and talk was enough to inform him that he was bringing shame to the family and his ancestors and descendants. In the last analysis fair treatment of women was guaranteed by village opinion and gossip to the extent that continuous ill-treatment would jeopardise the possibility of securing advantageous marriages in the future. The inhabitants of one family or village might decide not to marry their daughter into another because of their reputation for mistreating new young wives and daughters-in-law.[70]

Active intervention of a more direct nature by a girl's natal family was less usual. The potential protective role of her natal family was minimised for, except on ceremonial occasions, visits by the wife to her own parents' home were discouraged. The ritual closing of the door after the bride had left her home symbolised a lasting break and she was rarely reinstated in her old home. Should she return there was usually no provision for her support. Enough land was normally set apart for the maintenance of the parents and the remainder was divided among the brothers, with no lot or portion allocated to any sister. After marriage, sustained contacts between daughters and their parents were only common among gentry families who could better bear the expenses of travel and board, and spare the domestic services of their daughter-in-law. If word of unusual mistreatment reached her family, the wife's clan might intercede and the issue could become a point of contention between the two families. Extreme cases might involve the threat or use of force and in one such example cited by a foreign observer in the nineteenth century, a large clan force went to the house of the mother-in-law and destroyed the furniture before severely beating up the members of that household.[71] Where early death occurred, the father or brother of the girl would sometimes insist on the right to see the body to ascertain that her death was not from unnatural causes. But constant protection for daughters was more the exception than the rule, and for 'adopted-in' daughters-in-law almost non-existent. Families were inclined not to interfere unless the abuse was flagrant. Even in these cases they could not be counted on to act and the outcome of any intervention was largely dependent on the strength and influence of the wife's family. According to one anthropologist, the unusual proportion of unsuccessful suicide attempts gave reason to believe that attempted suicide was also used as a last resort for the redress of wrongs.[72] The occurrence of an attempted suicide suggested that all was not well in the household and caused 'loss of face'. But set against the effect of this form of blackmail was the possibility of miscalculation and permanent physical injury and death. A woman was not completely devoid of protection, but within a wide range of abuse, she had little real hope of ameliorating her position or redressing wrongs for the only means at her disposal were informal, unreliable and extreme.

Without more than minimal means of protection and with no effective rights of divorce or independent economic means of support, avenues of escape from the strains of family life were severely limited. Romantic literature in the form of novels, dramas and short stories, read or told aloud, provided a form of release from the realities and pent-up emotions of everyday life. There were a number of myths, legends, fairy tales and popular stories which portrayed patriotic and romantic heroines serving their country or meeting their beloved ones in clandestine meetings at Buddhist monasteries or inns. One love story, told in many variations and dramatised under the title of *The Westchamber*, enjoyed great popularity. Other fictional characters were rebellious wives and women who stepped outside the traditionally circumscribed role. One of the perennial favourites was the story of the courageous warrior, Mulan, set in the sixth century AD. She was the daughter of an old and ailing general who was suddenly called up to lead the Imperial troops into battle. To save her father she donned the dress of a boy, left home and for twelve years fought in the army. She was a leader of men, performed great feats of courage and was rewarded for her heroic service to the Emperor. None suspected her sex, her chastity was preserved and it was not until she returned home and exchanged her linked-iron tunic for a skirt that her true identity was discovered. In her autobiography, one young girl described how when she was about seven she sat on her mother's knee 'round-eyed and still, and listened enchanted to the old legends of the past'. Of all of them, the story of Mulan was her favourite and she never grew tired of hearing about her and begged for the story over and over again. She described what the story of Mulan meant to her mother who was herself the daughter of a general and had led an unhappy life. As a young girl she had dreamed of freedom and happiness, all of which dreams had been frustrated. Physically timid and without education, she had suffered as a junior member of a large stifling household. The girl thought that since her mother was a victim of this and other facets of the system, 'the story of Mulan is actually a projection of the dreams she held originally for herself and later gave to me'.[73] In the novel, *The Dream of the Red Chamber*, the women of the large household surreptitiously read romances and openly arranged for dramatic performances to celebrate festive occasions. For the poorer women old ballads passed down from mother to daughter, and old tales spun and embellished by the roaming storytellers sufficed to serve the same function. In one market town in Siquan (Szechwan) a resident anthropologist noted that women loved to hear the stories, especially the love stories,[74] and in Phenix village in Guangdong (Kwangtung), an observer found that popular ballads exercised a powerful control over the imaginations of women and girls who often identified themselves with the heroines of the simple stories which were told in a rhythmic and popular language. The village men went as far as to say that cases of moral delinquency and much of the suicidal tendency on the part of women came from listening to those stories. Such was their influence that the men had had many of the stories rewritten in an attempt to impose upon women male-dominated norms of behaviour.[75]

Few places existed to which a woman could flee and from which she could not be returned upon discovery. Buddhist convents offered one possible refuge for girls who were generally from the richer classes. Some girls, like two of the young heroines of the classical family novel, *The Dream of the Red Chamber*, shunned the realities of a conventional marriage and preferred to put on the grey robes of a Buddhist nun. The convents were sometimes endowed with small pieces of land which supplied in part the living of the sisterhood. Most depended on the charity of the lay worshippers who received instruction and solace from them. Not only did young women take the vows of Buddhist nuns, but many widows, when they could arrange their family affairs so as to permit it, found a refuge in the cloister for the remainder of their lives. Women were sometimes to be found in the Taoist religious sects and secret societies which were the traditional poor man's protective brotherhood. The Taoist philosophy had long recognised the importance of women and as far back as the second century AD there is evidence that the membership and leadership ranks in these societies were sometimes accessible to both men and women. In mixed sects and societies women were able to meet with men and fulfil roles denied to them by Confucian principles and customs. Married women could join the 'Water Lily Society', for instance, and were under oath not to reveal their membership to anyone, not even their husbands. If both husband and wife belonged whoever had joined first took precedence in the society.[76] Père Leboucq observed of the secret societies in the north of China that although women were not admitted to the high positions or jobs, they were given assignments and positions of responsibility to make up for their official obscurity. 'This seemed to console them', he noted.[77] In the south of China where women had a less disadvantaged position in society, women played a large part in the secret societies and those who became leaders were known as 'female polished sticks'. Many were sworn members, and mothers and wives were often the able assistants of male members. They spied out the land, hid the booty and screened the guilty.[78] Women often split off to form autonomous all-female associations as at the time of the White Lotus Rebellion in the 1790s. During times of unrest and peasant rebellion many of these bands took to roaming and looting to support themselves. The Green, Blue and Red Lanterns, associated with the Boxer Rebellion in the closing years of the nineteenth century, were made up of young girls and widows from poor peasant backgrounds. The Red Lanterns, for example, were composed of young girls between the ages of twelve and eighteen years who carried red handkerchiefs and red lanterns in their hands. New recruits had to undergo a period of training ranging from 48 days to 5 months. They were taught an incantation and when possessed by spells practised walking on the surface of rivers and ponds with a view to eventually taking to the air. The leaders of these groups were purported to be able to loosen the screws of the enemies' cannons from a distance of some miles. It was said, when their magical powers failed to match up to the claims, that the impurities associated with 'yin' had interfered with the spirits and rendered the spells ineffectual.[79] But despite these isolated instances, it was not easy for women to free themselves from their traditional ideological and economic shackles.

It seemed to many women of all classes that virtually the only means of escape, when their situation became excessively unbearable, was suicide. Chinese literature contains endless stories of women who threw themselves down the household well and ended their lives in ways which were numerous, and as ritualised as the marriage ceremony itself. Suicide statistics collected during the first two decades of this century indicated a high number of successful suicides among women in their early twenties—the most difficult period of adjustment. Revenge would be lasting for all cases of suicide were supposed to be investigated by the district magistrates and it was widely believed that the spirits of those who committed suicide returned permanently to haunt the household they inhabited. Many a foreign resident in nineteenth-century China commented on the frequency of suicide among young wives and described such incidents.[80] One traveller described a scene he stumbled upon in the course of his journeys.

> A village is startled by the report that a woman has thrown
> herself into a well. Someone happening to pass by at the
> moment observed the poor creature with flushed face and
> flaming eyes throw herself headlong into it. At once everyone is
> mad with excitement. The women run shouting and screaming to
> each other, expressing their loud commiseration; the men move
> along with sphinx-like faces to see if help can be rendered, and
> the dogs tear about yelping. . . . The unfortunate woman is
> hauled out of the well. . . . She is quite dead.[81]

Apparently she had had words with her husband, blows followed and the woman had responded by avenging herself most thoroughly on the man who had injured her 'in the only way she knew possible'. It was said that in some regions scarcely a group of villages could be found where similar events had not recently taken place. Without full statistics it is difficult to know how exaggerated or not these claims were, but there is no doubt that the act of suicide constituted the individual woman's protest *par excellence* against the traditional forces of 'fate' and provided the final route of escape. It symbolised what she felt to be her hopeless subordinate position, and from what would appear to be its widespread use, it reflected the absence of an institutional formula for the readjustment of a woman's position in the family.

The lack of any real form of escape from the family institution, or any chance of improvement in the status of women in society did not mean that their subordinate position passed unnoticed or unchallenged. The poetess Li Jingzhao, among others, had bemoaned the solitude and isolation characteristic of the women's apartments. But few women had the educational skill or opportunity to express their discontent publicly in writing or by their actions. A number of men intellectuals raised voices decrying the inferior position of women in Confucian society. To cite but a few: there was many a poetic line contrasting the fate of men and women as in the poetry of Fu Xuan. Even in the third century BC, he had exclaimed 'How sad it was to be a woman! Nothing on earth is held so cheap.'[82] In the twelfth century Yuan Cai mourned women's inequality and their enforced dependence on husbands and sons. One scholar in the sixteenth century deplored the injustice of the traditional divorce procedures and two centuries later, another, Yuan Mei, included pleas for a system of education for women and mutual sexual licence in his anarchist revolt against the entirety of the Confucian system. Contemporaneously, Yu Zhangxian in four essays on chastity denounced the double standard of morality and castigated the custom of binding feet. Perhaps the best known of protesters was Li Ruzhen who attacked the very ideological foundations of inequality. 'I believe,' he said, 'that the essence of heaven and earth is never endowed exclusively in any one sex in particular.'[83] He wrote a whimsical novel in 1825 which was called *Flowers in the Mirror*. In it the roles of men and women in society were reversed. The fantasy Kingdom of Women was inhabited by men dressed in voluminous petticoats and subjected to the tortures of footbinding. Domestically and publicly they were ruled by women who, with the exclusive advantage of education, entered the state examination system to take up positions in the government bureaucracy. Li Ruzhen used the novel to question the inequality of women in society and the double standard of morality. He emphasised the injustice done to women and later in the twentieth century his novel was heralded as the first 'Chinese Declaration of the Rights of Women'.[84] The inequality of women was thus not without its critics, but ranged against them was the whole weight of the Confucian ideological tradition.

At periodic intervals in Chinese history, peasant women expressed their discontent and, however inadvertently, protested against their class and sexual position in Chinese society. Traditionally women of the poorer classes had in times of peasant rebellion aligned themselves with their menfolk, who with no voice or power in the existing political structure, rose to challenge the rule of the Emperor and his officials. There is some evidence that in the second century AD during the 'Yellow Turban Uprising' and during the eighteenth-century 'White Lotus Rebellion' there was a certain assertion of women's rights.[85] This bid to improve women's position reached its fullest expression in the extensive and widespread Taiping peasant rebellion of the mid-nineteenth century. This is one of the features which distinguished the history of the Taipings and has been partly responsible for its interest as a forerunner of the twentieth-century revolutions. Their attempted reforms, if implemented, would have amounted to a revolution in the position of women. This rebellion, which first arose in the southern provinces of China out of agrarian distress, unemployment and inflation and was influenced by an admixture of indigenous religious and Christian influences, acquired great momentum as it spread northwards to establish a capital in Nanking. The Taiping platforms which included revolutionary programmes for the redistribution of land, the establishment of communal property and the equality of the sexes were influenced by the more mobile and less subordinated Hakka women, one of a number of non-Han ethnic groups who were founder members. Edicts were issued which banned footbinding and women were permitted to sit Taiping examinations and take up official positions ranging from women chiefs-of-staff and chancellors in the Heavenly King's court. Women were at first confined to segregated women's quarters where they were taught handicrafts and organised into service corps which could be called upon to dig ditches and carry salt and other useful physical labour. Within these quarters the women were chaperoned to protect them from the advances of men and even those of their husbands. These segregated corps were dissolved in 1855.[86] An Englishman, A. F. Lindley, who fought with the Taipings, noticed then the open presence, the 'free intercourse and elevated position of the women' in Taiping-occupied Nanking, an occurrence that was said to be in marked contrast to the rest of the country.[87]

Women substantially contributed to the fighting capacity of the Taipings. They were organised into their own separate army corps under the overall leadership of Hong Xuanjiao, a sister of the Heavenly King. According to contemporary chronicles she was a sight to behold, 'a beauty so charmingly clad galloping as if she were flying'. She led the big-footed and strong Guangxi (Kwangsi) women clad in gorgeous clothes who were good at using firearms and were dead shots.[88] Their very presence was said to have broken the morale of the imperial armies set against them. A Taiping folk chant which has persisted into the twentieth century commemorates her formidable exploits:

Women able to follow Hong Xuanjiao
able to use fire arms, do sword play;
At Niu Bai Ling, Hong Xuanjiao prepared
her defences, throwing the enemy
with broken backs down the hillside.[89]

By the time the capital was established in Nanking there numbered
forty women's armies each with 2,500 soldiers.[90] The number of
early women followers, mainly from the minority nationalities of
the southern provinces, had been augmented by numerous village
women. Sometimes whole families joined the Taiping forces. A
folk poem from a village in Jiangsu (Kiangsu), recorded in the
1950s, still celebrates the skills of one of their past inhabitants—an
unknown Widow Pai.

Widow Pai is young, one who
ran away from her village
to become a Taiping leader; first
in the barracks a common soldier
using sword and rifle so well
and praised by Prince Tsun
himself, was raised in rank
becoming a Taiping woman commander;
famous for her eyesight, seeing
clearly for three li, and whenever
enemy troops came lurking
within rifle shot, why Widow Pai
Widow Pai brings one down dead
each time she fires.[91]

The Taipings were defeated in civil war but not before the women,
like the male members of the Taipings, had been betrayed by their
leaders. Like many of the Taiping programmes, projected reforms
were to remain little more than paper proposals and they did not
always rest on well-developed principles at that. The attitudes of
the leaders towards women were riddled with inconsistencies at
best, and at worst were downright repressive. Though women were
assigned certain privileges denied them elsewhere, many of them
were officials in name only and were actually the concubines of the
men leaders whom they served.[92] Women were used as rewards for
courageous fighting. The number of women a man received was
determined by his rank; the highest ranking men in the armies
received more than ten women and the number decreased as the

rank lowered.[93] The leaders, the Kings of the Taipings, had unlimited licence and had early set about collecting concubines. A poem composed by the Heavenly King himself clearly defined their role.

Women in the rear palaces should not try to leave;
If they should try to leave it would be like hens trying to crow.
The duty of the palace women is to attend to the needs of their husbands;
And it is arranged by Heaven that they are not to learn of the affairs outside.[94]

Moreover the writings of the Taiping leaders still extolled the three forms of obedience, and the Confucian principle that the way of a woman was to 'cherish chastity' and 'never approach a man' was constantly reiterated. Only if she maintained her proper position within the family 'would all happiness be hers'.[95] The old Confucian ideology persisted. But in spite of the contradictions and inconsistencies of the Taipings in practice, the utopian ideals and military exploits of the women members passed into the folklore of the villages and the experience of the Taipings clearly indicated that women formed one of a number of oppressed groups in the social structure which could potentially contribute to a movement to improve both their sexual and class position.

A new challenge to traditional ideology and customs appeared in China in the nineteenth century following the first Opium War in 1840 when certain ports were opened to foreign residents. The Christian missionaries in particular were horrified by the low esteem in which women were held. They reported to their home countries the effects of the practice of footbinding, seclusion and arranged marriages on the position of women and their enforced ignorance of the written word and public affairs. Many wives of missionaries and single women missionaries set about to remedy the situation by taking the unprecedented step of opening small schools for girls.[96] Miss Aldersley, a member of the Church of England, opened the first school for Chinese girls at Ningpo in 1844. In 1847 the Presbyterian mission in the same city started another girls' school with two pupils. Their example was followed in other treaty ports and schools were opened in Shanghai in 1849, in Fuzhou (Foochow) in 1851 and in Canton in 1853. By the Treaty of Tientsin in 1858 missionaries gained the right to establish mission centres in any part of the country. In 1864, 7 girls in Tientsin and 5 girls in Peking entered the first mission schools established in north China.

In 1872, 13 girls entered the Presbyterian mission at Chefoo. The first school in central China is supposed to have been founded in Kiukiang by the Methodist mission in 1873.

Through the schools the women hoped to put an end to the binding of feet, introduce the idea that women were capable of learning and establish a regular audience for Christian teachings. At first their schools were scarcely popular and they opened and closed at a considerable rate much to the discouragement of the missionaries. They came up against all the traditional prejudices. An education was wasted upon girls who were anyway scarcely capable of bookwork. There were practical difficulties of overcoming the bounds of seclusion and in most families there had to be good reasons to convince them that they could spare the domestic services of a young daughter or daughter-in-law. Above all, the close proximity of foreigners was feared and their influence resented. When one school opened in Peking the little girls ran as fast as their bound feet would carry them at the sight of the strange-looking foreign ladies.[97] Rumours persisted and fed suspicions that parents would never see their daughters again for they would either be whisked away in a big ship or furnish medicines or opium for foreigners. Despite considerable missionary efforts these fears and traditional prejudices and customs were responsible for the very small number of pupils.[98]

The slow growth in the numbers in mission schools in China can be seen from the following figures estimated for Protestant schools:

1849	3 schools (probably fewer than 50 pupils)
1860	12 schools (approx. 196 pupils)
1869	31 schools (approx. 556 pupils)
1877	38 schools (approx. 524 pupils)[99]

Many of the pupils were, in fact, slave-girls, foundlings and beggar girls picked up off the streets. Only the very poorest families pressed by the bribes of the missionaries in the form of a cash payment and the promise of food and lodgings responded to mission approaches and risked sending their daughters to the schools. The missionaries were thankful for any response and were well aware that it was usually the promise of rice and lodgings which brought them pupils.[100] Sometimes girls only stayed long enough to receive a new warm suit of clothes.

Even when the parents responded some of the young girls themselves rebelled and refused to allow the missionaries to influence their lives. Three times the Christian father of one little pupil tried to have her feet unbound and each time she refused as soon as his back was turned. Her unbound feet were the source of constant comment and ridicule far more galling to her than the pain of the tight bandages. Neighbouring women used to say, 'Rather a nice girl, but those feet!' or 'Rather a bright girl, but those feet', and the phrase 'those feet', 'those feet', was all she heard, until she was ashamed to be seen and rebandaged her feet at the first available opportunity.[101] The resentment at missionary interference was recognised by the Chinese government which officially condemned the activities of women missionaries in 1877. It attempted to put an end to their work among women. In order to preserve the strict propriety of Chinese women it was ordered that 'no Chinese female should enter the chapels nor foreign woman propagate the doctrines'.[102] Public feeling frequently ran high and lady missionaries were forced to keep out of sight as much as possible at certain times. The missionaries in their bid to challenge existing social norms and improve the position of women had few followers in the early and middle nineteenth century.

It was only in some parts of the southern provinces of China where women traditionally raised silkworms and wound silken thread that there was any evidence of women forming exclusive associations specifically designed to challenge their traditional fate of marriage. Chinese newspapers in the nineteenth century frequently made references to those organised societies called 'anti-marriage associations' or associations of 'Girls who do not go to the family'. They were made up of young girls who solemnly vowed never to wed and swore to protect each other from such a 'miserable and unholy' fate. Usually ten or so girls lived together and developed a sisterhood cult with the avowed intent to collectively drown themselves if opposed or if one of their number was threatened. Irate parents solicited the aid of officials who from time to time tried to check the formation of such sisterhoods, but the threat of collective suicide usually rendered their efforts ineffective. Others, who had been forced to go through a marriage ceremony by their parents or by the fear that a woman must be married in order to guarantee a home for her spirit after death, reimbursed the expenses incurred by their husband's family from their incomes and left their husbands after three days.[103] One case was reported in the Chinese newspaper, *Shi Bao*. A band of young maidens ended their existence by drowning themselves in a river because one of them was forced by her parents to be married. It was reported that she had been engaged in her childhood before she had joined the sisterhood. When her parents made all the necessary arrangements for her marriage, she reported the affair to the other members of her sisterhood who at once agreed to die for her cause, if she remained constant to her sworn vows to be single and virtuous. As there were many persons set to watch her movements it was almost impossible for her to escape, but by bribing the female servants she was taken one night to her sisters under the cover of darkness. The sisters at once joined with her in terminating their lives by jumping into the Dragon River with its swift currents, which rapidly carried them off.[104] This movement was apparently quite widespread among the silk workers of Guangdong province, but in addition some female labourers and domestic servants made similar arrangements. The rebellious spirit and alternative life-style of these primitive feminist associations constituted a consciously deviant form of behaviour. But while opportunities for an independent economic life were limited and there was no new ideology, the challenge was more potential than real in the nineteenth century. The anti-marriage associations were an expression of opposition to the traditional forces of 'fate' but they remained at the level of rejection and furnished a form of escapism rather than a significant force for change.

The traditional position of women therefore did not pass unchallenged, especially in the nineteenth century, but their subordination constituted and remained an integral part of the institutional framework of society. The interaction of ideological factors upon economic dependence continued to reinforce the physical constraints that held women in their place. Isolation and lack of identity made it difficult for them to actively articulate their own oppression and relate to other oppressed groups; any unified expression of protest or concerted group action was well-nigh impossible. It was not until the twentieth century that each of these three embryonic forms of challenge or forces for change, the intellectual questioning of the traditional social institutions, the formation of feminist associations and the linking of the fortunes of women to those of other oppressed groups, combined to give rise to a women's movement in which women began to widely and collectively protest against the traditional role and status assigned to them in the family and in society.

New Expectations: Patriotism and the Vote 3

Men and women are born equal
Why should we let the men hold sway?
We will rise and save ourselves,
Ridding the nation of all her shame.

(Jiu Jin, 1907)[1]

The women's movement had its origins in the crisis of confidence in the traditional social, political and economic institutions and the consequent search for the sources of wealth and power seen to characterise the foreign powers. Towards the close of the nineteenth century the reforming intellectuals came to the conclusion from their study of Western philosophical works and their observations of European and American societies that the source of their enormous productivity and strength and power lay not in the mere acquisition of material hardware, but was more a question of developing man's innate capacities and potentialities. They became convinced that the energy which accounted for the development of the Western powers resided within the individual and only needed to be released and fostered in all its forms— intellectual, moral and physical. In attempting to create an environment which would liberate the individual energies of men, the reformers turned their attention to cultivating one of the greatest of the country's 'undeveloped resources'—the women of China. Their conviction grew that China could never become strong while in each generation boyhood years were predominantly spent in the company of ignorant and crippled womenfolk.

During the 1890s, footbinding came to be viewed by radical intellectuals as an outmoded vestige of the past which crippled half the population and caused loss of 'international face'. Indeed the custom had prevented China from taking its rightful place in the modern world. The leader of the reform movement, Kang Yuwei, noted that in the eyes of foreigners nothing so much as footbinding made China appear so culturally backward:

> There is nothing which makes us objects of ridicule as much as footbinding. . . . With prosperity so weakened, how can we engage in battle? I look at the Europeans and Americans, so strong and vigorous because their mothers do not bind feet and

therefore have strong offspring. Now that we must compete with other nations, to transmit weak offspring is perilous.[2]

One reason for the weakness of China was seen to lie in the physical weakness of the progeny of the bound-footed women; another lay in women's enforced illiteracy and ignorance of the affairs of the world. One reformer, who toured Western Europe in 1890–1, attributed the prosperity and strength of the European nations to their systems of contemporary education for boys *and* girls.[3] Yuan Shikai, the reforming governor of Zhili (Chihli) province, observed that: 'the Sciences of the East and West which lead to the strengthening of a country all give due importance to the practice of educating women and making the women the equal of men.'[4] The education of women, like the movement against footbinding, had an ulterior and utilitarian purpose. Since the 'natural' function of women was considered to be the bearing and raising of children, their education became a form of insurance to guard against the further decline of China or more particularly of China's sons. No scheme of reform was thought to be permanently effective unless it included measures for the improvement of women as 'mothers' and it was on this basis and largely due to the work of a number of radical intellectuals and foreign women that a movement was launched for the abolition of footbinding and the establishment of schools for girls.

Theoretical attacks were launched on footbinding with increasing frequency during the last decade of the nineteenth century. Two of the chief proponents were Kang Yuwei and Liang Qichao. Kang Yuwei's most eloquent writing on the subject was probably the memorial which he submitted to the throne in 1898. In it he described the abnormal and inhuman treatment of the young and innocent child whose limbs were so impaired that she had to 'get up by holding on to the bed and cling to the wall for support when walking'. Surely this meant that the poor were seriously inconvenienced in the performance of their many tasks, while the rich transmitted weak offspring as a direct result of their being physically harmed. He proposed that prohibition orders should be circulated and reinforced by a system of penalties; remiss officials should be deprived of their privileges and householders should be fined for every pair of bound feet in the family.[5] Liang Qichao wrote a number of persuasive appeals to his fellow gentry in the Chinese press. In one, he likened the binding of feet to the most cruel and despicable punishment of cutting off the lower legs. He described in detail the effect of footbinding on the health of women and its contribution to the lowly position of women in society. He suggested that the custom originated in either the mind of 'a corrupt prince, an immoral ruler, a robber of the people or a despicable husband'.[6] In contrast to the past praise of the 'golden lotus', the bound foot came under increasing poetic attack. One of Liang Qichao's contemporaries, Lin Jinnan wrote a number of poems each entitled the 'Tiny-footed Lady'. The first and last few lines of one read:

Tiny-foot lady, whose daughter are you?
Three-inch bound shoes beneath her skirt.
She trembles in the blowing wind,
As if she's gone ten thousand miles. . . .

How inconceivable, that in reducing the foot,
Her flesh and bones are so distressed
That she loses her appetite for food.
So much of her fragrant youth
Spent weeping by the fallen flowers;
She hears the chirping of the birds,
But her bowed foot is like a tiny grave.[7]

A number of tracts, essays and poems which challenged this centuries-old practice were written and circulated by the reformers. At first they were less than effective. Although in individual gentry families there might be talk of change, in practice few were prepared to take the first steps and alone face the inevitable prejudice. Zhu De (Chu Teh), one of the leaders of the Red Army in the 1920s, remembered that in many families there was talk of the end of footbinding but nothing was done for 'what man would want to marry a girl with big feet'.[8] Even the wives of some reformers made ready stockings and shoes, but put off unbinding until they could find other ladies who would join them. Anti-footbinding societies were formed by both reformers and foreign ladies to provide the necessary mutual support.

Kang Yuwei had organised the first 'Unbound-Feet' Society in Canton in 1892 and after the Sino-Japanese War this society opened an office in one of the principal streets in Shanghai. It was eventually to have more than 10,000 members and following on from this example 'Natural Foot Societies' began to spring up in the main cities and nearby rural areas. The *North China Herald*, a Shanghai newspaper, reported attempts by prominent intellectuals to form new societies. One report from Sichuan described the founding of a new society in Yangjing county in 1903. Edicts against footbinding were first published and for three days gongs were beaten up and down the streets calling the people together to hear the street preacher's exhortations against footbinding. A meeting was then held at the Cantonese Temple at which fifty or sixty men held consultations and decided on the establishment of an anti-footbinding society. They arranged a feast in the town to which all women would be invited, but only those who would agree to join the society and unbind their feet would be allowed to sit down at the tables and enjoy their food. The others were allowed to look around and were then relegated to the status of onlookers standing at the door. The correspondent writes that all those who sat down to the feast were the wives of the chief men of the villages and towns of the county. It was hoped that they too would hold similar feasts in their localities and establish mutual support societies. Apparently the whole proceedings were viewed by the inmates of a nearby teahouse and ridiculed to such an extent that it had to be summarily closed down for the occasion and the impertinent men given a beating![9] One society which was instrumental in organising opposition among important officials and received a lot of attention in the Western press was the 'Natural Foot Society' which was founded in 1895 by a number of foreign women resident in Shanghai. This Society, led by an English-woman, Mrs Archibald Little, published upwards of thirty pieces of literature, edicts, proclamations, placards, poems and folders of photographs.

These anti-footbinding societies enlisted the support of influen-tial persons, imported neat patterns of Western ladies' shoes, held meetings and circulated articles and simple poems and songs to popularise their cause. Members would vow not to bind the feet of their children and every effort was made to influence the parents of daughters against this profitless and injurious custom by graph-ically highlighting the physical defects and emphasising the worth of a daughter who could 'move with speed to aid parents and parents-in-law'. Poems, often set to music, on the sorrows of footbinding were designed to move women to reflect on their lifelong pain and suffering. Slogans such as:

Once feet are bound so small
Such effort to do any work at all.

Once feet to a sharp point are bound
The women's cries to Heaven resound.[10]

were designed for quick and popular appeal. An argument that was
often resorted to was the helplessness of bound-footed women in
times of flood, fire or armed attack. One of the most popular
ballads tells a typical tale of woe:

The mounted enemy comes,
The mounted enemy comes,
Bandits bearing down upon us
Amidst dust and confusion
Making the most of chaotic times. . . .
Eight out of every ten villagers have fled,
For there is butchery from door to door.
My neighbour a healthy wife,
With feet bare and unbound,
Escapes to the valley, babe in arms,
Another wraps her turban like a man,
Rice in bag, pot on shoulder,
Lucky she can hide her femininity from bandit eyes.
A delicate lady nearby, lovely as jade,
Finding it so hard to travel on tiny feet,
Holds her head and weeps afraid.
Bandits swoop down before the weeping ends. . . .
Because her steps were so tiny, so hard to take.
Her husband's children share the bitter fate![11]

Parents of sons were encouraged to vow not to allow their sons to
marry girls other than those with natural feet. This move,
tantamount to a masculine boycott, hit directly at the basic social
tenet that bound feet were a necessary prerequisite to a good
marriage. According to the *North China Herald* the custom only
received its deathblow when a growing number of Chinese men
joined the societies and took the oath that neither they nor their
sons would marry a small-footed woman.[12]

These societies and those organised by the foreign women
resident in China petitioned officials of the government and
encouraged them to take a public stance in support of their
campaign. They received the backing of the Court in 1902 when a
decree by the Empress Dowager exhorted the 'gentry and notables
to influence their families to abstain from the evil practice and by
this means abolish the custom forever'.[13] It was proposed that the

custom, as it had been initiated, should be abolished by gentry and official example. As a result of this decree regulations were drawn up and a system of rewards and punishments instituted. The Viceroy of Nanking issued copies of the following regulations to check footbinding.

> According to the regulations anti-footbinding proclamations and literature will be distributed when the local officials take a census of the people. The officials will instruct them in the disadvantages of footbinding and the necessity of unbinding the feet of the women and girls within the space of one year. Fines will be inflicted or rewards given according to violation or observance of the prohibition against footbinding. From the first year of Xuan Tong, girls under ten years of age are not allowed to have their feet bound, and fines for violation, or rewards of observance of the rule, will be given out accordingly. Anti-footbinding societies should be extensively established, throughout Liang Kiang, and where success has been achieved memorial tablets will be awarded to parties concerned, for their services in discouraging the practice of footbinding.[14]

It is the feature of these early footbinding societies that they were instigated by the reformers, foreign ladies and government officials. Chinese women were rarely the moving force and of those involved many were the wives and relatives of the patrons. In 1908 when one society founded by foreign ladies was handed over to a committee of Chinese women it seems to have ceased to function within a very short time.[15] It was the impression of most observers that in these early years these reforms had not penetrated far beyond the cities and were limited to official and gentry families. Even among this category the abolition of footbinding could be interpreted as an unnecessary alien idea originating in the West. The new idea aroused much opposition. As the following extract shows, one member of the gentry, at least, was aware of the likely repercussions of the reform on his position.

> Footbinding is the condition of life bringing dignity to man, and contentment to women. Let me make this clear. I am a Chinese fairly typical of my class. I pored too much over classic texts in my youth and dimmed my eyes, narrowed my chest, crooked my back. My memory is not strong and in an old civilisation there is a vast deal to learn before you can know anything. Accordingly

among scholars I cut a poor figure. I am timid, and my voice plays me false in gatherings of men. But to my footbound wife, confined for life to her house, except when I bear her in my arms to her palanquin, my stride is heroic, my voice is that of a roaring lion, my wisdom is of the sages. To her I am the world; I am life itself.[16]

Leaders of the societies to unbind feet were ridiculed by their fellow gentry. The leader of the Shanghai society was reputed to be in constant fear of his bound-footed wife at home and forced to lick her feet in punishment. He was nicknamed 'the supervisor who licks feet' which was a play on the words 'natural foot supervisor'.[17] Beyond the cities progress was slow and some idea of the initial impact of the abolition movement in rural areas can be obtained from a number of surveys undertaken in the 1920s and 1930s. The figures for Dingxian (Tinghsien), a rural area 125 miles south of Peking, show that between the years 1900 and 1909 there was a significant breaking down of the custom. The proportion of girls with normal feet rose from 18.5 per cent in 1900 to 40.3 per cent in 1905–9.[18] These figures contrast with those assembled by a Japanese sociologist for the interior province of Shanxi (Shansi) which was found two decades later to have been much more conservative.[19] But if women were less the moving force they were the direct recipients of the reform and the movement for physical mobility received impetus from a contemporary movement to educate Chinese girls. Most of the schools be they mission, gentry or government sponsored did not admit girls with bound feet.

The new century was marked by increasing popularity among certain classes for the education of daughters. Mission schools for girls began to expand and multiply in number. After a long struggle to establish their schools, the missionaries no longer had to bribe and pay pupils to attend, and to a certain group of Western-oriented Chinese, the mission schools, with their high teaching standards and foreign equipment, seemed to provide the most advanced courses for their daughters. Others of the gentry class, unwilling that the education of their daughters be left entirely in foreign hands, began themselves to sponsor the establishment of girls' schools. The first Chinese schools for girls were established under the patronage of reformers and officials. In 1897 a number of wealthy merchants and officials in Shanghai, led by the Manager of the Chinese Telegraph Company, formed a society for the purposes of establishing schools for the women of their families.

The provisional prospectus opened with the following words:

> In opening schools for girls we are reverting to the illustrious custom of the three dynasties. In order to open up the intelligence of the people, we must certainly make women free and afterwards customs can be changed.[20]

According to this same prospectus the raising of funds and the administration of the school were to be left to the control of their wives and daughters. There were to be provisions for 4 Chinese teachers and 40 pupils between the ages of 8 and 14 who had to be able to read a certain amount on entrance and have dispensed with footbinding. Funds were to be made available for the payment of fees on behalf of the poor, but it is clear that the major entrance requirement to the school was a respectable family background:

> It is the intention of this school to make no distinctions of rank, but since in the future, pupils from the school will be leaders and teachers in other schools, only respectable families will be admitted.[21]

No pupils were to be given as concubines to avoid 'tarnishing the purity' or 'disgracing' the high standing of the school. The school was modelled on the Methodist Mission School for 'high-class' girls, the McTyeire School of Shanghai. Among the subjects taught were English, reading, spelling, Chinese, arithmetic, geography, drawing and handicrafts such as spinning, weaving, knitting and crocheting which were considered skills of great importance and befitting to a woman's role. The promoters of the school, constantly seeking sources of funds, published a monthly paper known as the *Chinese Girls' Progress* and organised a society for the 'Diffusion of Knowledge among Chinese Women' to promote girls' education and establish further schools. It was a great blow to their hopes and plans when in obedience to the orders of the Empress Dowager the school was forced to close in 1899 less than two years after its opening. In common with many other reform movements it was swept away in the reaction which followed a 100 days of reforms in 1898. The period of reaction was short, and after the turn of the century a number of schools were founded by educational associations of radical intellectuals and officials to educate the women of their families.

The cities of Shanghai and Peking led the way. With the Boxer Uprising over, the Empress Dowager reversed her policy and issued an edict permitting the opening of girls' schools. At her order, a large Lama convent in Peking was transformed into a school for girls and the Manchu Princesses were quick to follow her example. The Princess Imperial opened a school for girls at court and soon there were several schools in Peking founded and managed by the Princesses and others to teach girls of 'good' families arithmetic, needlework, Japanese, music, drawing, Chinese language and history.[22]

In Shanghai, the centre of reform and radical activity, the new schools were mainly sponsored by a number of associations of radical intellectuals. For instance, the Shanghai Patriotic Girls' School, founded by the 'Educational Association', whose members included the foremost revolutionary activists, became the nucleus of a new group of girls' schools founded there. These and similar privately established and financed schools were commonly called 'gentry schools' and although they were to be found in many cities in China it was not until 1907 that similar schools were to be formally provided for by the government.

Girls' schools had been excluded from the new official system of education as it was first outlined in 1902, but a year later certain government provisions had been revised to permit girls to enter the lowest primary grades. When an Imperial Commission of 1906 was sent abroad, it was charged to study women's education in other countries and its findings led to the Board of Education's decision to establish a national system of women's education in China.[23] The new code issued in 1907 stated that 'the good education of the citizens of the empire depends upon the good education of its women.[24] Provisions were therefore made for establishing government schools for girls. According to the *Peking Gazette* in 1907, girls' schools, normal and primary, were to be founded first in the provincial capitals, afterwards in prefectural cities and later in the county districts; primary schools were to be established wherever possible.[25] Thereafter a number of gentry and government schools for girls were established. In Peking, schools which numbered 5 in 1906 rose to 26 in 1908;[26] in Tientsin 20 were established between 1905 and 1908;[27] in Nanking the first school was founded in 1906 to be followed by 11 others (2 gentry and 9 government) with a total of 752 pupils in the next three years;[28] in Nanchang (capital of Jiangxi province) there were 13 girls' government schools,[29] Shanghai had 12 girls' schools with a total of 800 pupils[30] and in Canton 23 government and gentry schools had been established by 1908.[31] These schools were predominantly, but not exclusively, confined to city locations, but in Zhili province there were 121

C

government schools outside Peking with 2,523 students.[32] Even in far Sichuan province there were 49 government and gentry schools for girls with a total of 1,897 students in addition to the 297 elementary schools which enrolled boys and girls as pupils.[33]

A certain prestige soon accrued to acquiring an education. One woman of wealth and position in Peking described how she had bought a beautiful new silk gown to attend an 'entertainment', but found herself quite eclipsed by the presence of a quietly dressed little lady who was educated and could talk about a great world which she herself had 'never seen and knew only of dimly'. No one paid any attention to her rich gown or showed any envy, and as for herself, she started to despise it and longed to 'know what the quietly dressed lady knew and talk as she talked'.[34] The quest for an 'education' was not just confined to the young and single. Many married women sought entrance to the schools and put their hair up in a braid as was the custom with schoolgirls. Daughters and wives persuaded fathers and husbands to subscribe to the new institutions and one story was cited by a Professor at Peking University as a warning to the men of the land. A certain teacher in Hangzhou lacked funds for the school she had established, cut a gash in her arm and then sat in the temple court during the day of the local fair with a board beside her on which was inscribed the explanation of her unusual conduct. After the first year she wrote letters to the officials of her province, in which she asked for subscriptions and urged the importance of female education, to which cause she said she was willing to give her life. When the officials paid no heed she committed suicide. Her letters were subsequently published in local and general newspapers, and at memorial services, which were held in various parts of the Empire, funds were gathered for schools to encourage the new learning among girls and women.[35]

The new learning was largely confined to city locations in the treaty ports and provincial capitals, and their pupils were drawn from certain classes for whom expense was no problem and a daughter or daughter-in-law's labour dispensable. One report on the establishment of mission schools in China noted that now whenever girls' schools opened 'they are supported by the upper classes who readily send their girls and loyally support the school both financially and morally.'[36] Another observer wrote of the government schools:

The Chinese now have under consideration schemes for establishing schools for girls under government control and a system of land-tax is to be instituted to support them. These schools will be for the benefit of girls of the wealthy class, for the board and tuition will be free as in the government schools for young men, yet there are so many other expenses connected with the school that none but the well-to-do can take advantage of them.[37]

Among these classes the new education was viewed as a means towards a very desirable end; the strengthening of half of the population of the country. Women's rights might become a common phrase among the radical and intellectual in gentry and official circles, but the phrase referred solely to reforms in education and anti-footbinding, and these had an ulterior purpose. An educated Chinese official who published the *Girls' Reader* explained in its preface:

A good girl makes a good wife, a good wife makes a good mother; a good mother makes a good son. If the mothers have not been trained from childhood where are we to find the strong men of our nation. If then we say as China has said for so long: Let the men be educated, let the women remain in ignorance, half at least of the nation cannot be as useful as it should. It is as if one half of a man's body were paralysed; these members not only being helpless but proving a weight, a hindrance to those not affected.[38]

The government official Zuan Fu, who was mainly responsible for influencing the Empress and introducing the reforms, thought that the government would ultimately benefit.

With a constantly growing number of educated women, children will have in the near future the valuable privilege of a mother's teaching at home, the real school for patriots. None, he says are greater patriots and more loyal to the government than women.[39]

Although the new education of women might be officially circumscribed and there was to be no intended change in their role and status, the new reforms inadvertently led to the development of a recognisable women's movement.

The establishment of the new schools be they mission, gentry or government sponsored, provided for the first time an institutional basis and a communications network for the development of a collective identity among women. Their environment served to insulate girls from the exclusive influence of their families and traditions. As one sociologist travelling in China noted, even in the mission schools, which primarily taught girls the qualities of restraint and obedience, every lady principal was at heart a sworn enemy of the subjection of women in China. He said that this

> Is not her role of course—she will fence with you at first, but
> finally if you seem trustworthy, she will own up. She
> does not egg the girls on to assert this or that right, but strives to
> build up in them a personality which will not accept the old
> status.[40]

There are numerous letters and accounts left by missionaries of their encouragement of girls not to accept the terms of a traditional betrothal or marriage at a young age. They were encouraged to train as teachers, doctors, Bible women or at least to be a 'help-mate' to a pastor husband. Under their auspices girls were sent abroad to train, a practice which was later taken up by government agencies. For a number of women of scholar-gentry background who had had the benefit of an education, the need for women teachers, especially in the gentry and government schools, provided opportunities to escape from an intolerable family situation and acquire a position of economic independence through the new opportunities for such employment. The sudden expansion of schools created a demand for teachers which could not be met by the supply of mission-school graduates. Clause 17 of the rules of a new government school for girls in Tientsin is indicative of the shortage of trained women teachers. It stated that 'if any educated ladies care to offer their services as teachers they will be accepted'.[41] A remarkable feature of many of the biographies of the women who were later to lead in the women's movement was the early influence of their defiant mothers who had often courageously broken away from their families to become schoolteachers of independent means. Many of the early activists were themselves women schoolteachers of gentry background who in their early 20s or 30s had typically had the benefit of a classical education at home before voyaging to Japan or Shanghai for a modern education.

These new opportunities for education in schools not only took women teachers and students out of the confines of their homes, but also introduced them to current revolutionary ideals, Western literature and institutions and the new concept of 'feminism'— current among English and American suffragettes. Political tracts such as 'A Warning' and 'Wake Up' by Chen Tianhua exposing the sinister rule of the Manchu government and calling upon the people to rise and make revolution were circulated in the schools. In 'The Revolutionary Army', the young intellectual Zhou Rong called on the 400 millions of the great Han race, his fellow countrymen, 'whether men or women' to carry out this revolution against the Manchu rulers.[42] In these schools, girls first came into contact with the Three People's Principles of nationalism, democracy and improving the people's livelihood which were the platform of the Revolutionary League led by Sun Yat-sen to overthrow the government. The unprecedented congregations of literate and articulate girl students in the new schools provided a natural unity from which to exercise an organised collective role. Militant school-teachers were in a position to mobilise their students for social and political action and some of the schools came to serve as fronts for revolutionary organisations during the turbulent first decade of the new century. The Nanyang Public Institute Patriotic Girls' School became the centre of anti-government activities in Shanghai during the years 1902 to 1903. The women teachers there held Sunday afternoon speeches in the local park and published a magazine for women.[43] The Tatung school in Zhejiang (Chekiang), where the women revolutionary leader Jiu Jin was principal, became a front for republican activities in 1906–7. There under the pretext of physical education classes, a girls' militia was formed.[44] The radicalising influence of the schools on both teachers and students was often immediate. In her autobiography, Soumay Cheng, remembered the impact of the new ideas at her school in Tientsin.

> The new idea of training young women to do more in the world of affairs than in the past had already stirred me and others of similar outlook . . . I could not and would not grow up in the traditional manner. I felt that I had a special role of my own to play in this transitional period which had already begun . . . the forces of the modern world drew me to them with an irresistible power.[45]

It was the new schools which produced and published the first women's magazines and were the centres of the patriotic, anti-dynastic and feminist activities which characterised the first decades of the twentieth century.

Most of the early magazines designed by and for women were published by teachers and students who saw the need to stir the opinion of their 'less-enlightened' sisters. The periodic press had become increasingly popular among the well educated, and every group, society and association soon maintained that it should have a periodic mouthpiece. The women's journals published and edited by women marked a radical departure in the history of the written word in China. An examination of the literature published for women in this first decade indicated that these magazines were the first attempt on any scale to raise the consciousness of women to an awareness of their narrow role in society and to educate and mobilise them to participate in public affairs. The influence from abroad was direct and many articles were translated which reported the position of women in foreign countries and especially the contemporary suffragette activities in Europe and America. The first magazine for the women of China was published by a Chinese woman student in Tokyo in 1901 to advocate women's rights and a 'social revolution'.[46] The first to be published in China itself was the *Women's Journal* edited by Chen Xiefen, a woman school-teacher at the Girl's Patriotic School in Shanghai. The contents, which had to do with women's status and education, partly consisted of specially written articles and partly of translations of foreign material.[47]. This journal began a vogue for exclusively women's magazines, for it was shortly afterwards followed by the publication of the *Women's Monthly World*, *New Women's World* and the *Women's World*. The first issue of the latter, published in Shanghai in 1903, contained articles on the lives of some American women and the biographies of a number of early women soldiers in China.[48] In 1906 a daily newspaper for women was edited by a Mrs Chang and published in Peking. This was said to probably form the first daily newspaper for women ever published in any country.[49] It was produced to publish news of special interest to women and to educate them in public affairs. It summarised the foreign and Chinese news reports of the day, provided education in arithmetic, physics, domestic science and hygiene and published short stories and fables. The Manchu princesses and various wives and daughters of Chinese officials wrote enthusiastically to Sarah Pike Conger, the wife of the former American Ambassador in Peking, to tell her about this first women's daily newspaper. It was popular, they said, thoroughly read and explained to others at special newspaper-reading meetings and it was included as a part of courses in school curriculums.[50] On its demise, two years later, it was followed by the publication of the *Women's Educational Daily* in Peking and similar dailies in Tientsin and elsewhere. These in time gave way to the more popular periodicals.

In 1906 two schoolteachers in Shanghai, Jiu Jin and Xu Zihua, published the *Chinese Women's Journal* which was devoted entirely to articles and short stories about patriotism and the emancipation of women. The paper was primarily produced for women students with articles exhorting them to both study and play an active role outside the home. In the first two issues Jiu Jin wrote:

> We want to unite our two hundred million sisters into a solid whole, so they can call to each other. Our journal will act as a mouthpiece for our women. It is meant to help our sisters by giving their life deeper meaning and hope, and to advance rapidly towards a bright new society. We Chinese women should become the vanguard in arousing women to welcome enlightenment.[51]

In common with Jiu Jin and Xu Zihua, other editors also wished to establish their new journals as a regular channel of communication among women in order to arouse their collective support for the issues of the day. In these new periodicals were also to be found the beginnings of an analysis of their oppression and its causes. An early issue of the *Peking Women's Journal* included a startling rejection of the cosmological basis of their inferior position and division of labour.

> O ye two hundred millions of Chinese, our sisters, listen! In China it is said that man is superior and women inferior; that man is noble and women vile, that men should command and women obey. . . . But we are not under the domination of man. The nature of men and women is the universal sense of heaven. How, then can one make distinctions and say that the nature of man is of one sort and that of woman another?[52]

Although these magazines were often short-lived and their circulation limited to the new schools and the small percentage of urban literate women, their appearance marked the first significant expression of a collective feminist consciousness—an awareness that women were oppressed and that they could constitute a potential force in influencing the direction of public affairs.

The new schools were also the centres of patriotic, revolutionary and feminist activities during this period. In spite of the early attempts of the early feminists to awaken their sisters there was very little attempt to organise women around their own special oppression. There are one or two tantalising references to clubs in

which young girls proclaimed themselves 'girls who follow their
own will'.[53] In 1907 women in different places were reported to
have formed societies for getting rid of the undue authority
usurped by the mother-in-law. It was reported that in many cases
their husbands became honorary members of this society![54] There
were a few scattered specific references to the equality of the sexes
in a number of associations, but on the whole these were few and
far between before 1911. Rather, the early feminists, who wrote the
first magazines, thought that no question was so urgent as the
threatened autonomy of China and the overthrow of the Manchu
dynasty and the foreign yoke of tyranny. What was feared above
all was the break-up of China among the scrambling foreign
powers. It is particularly apparent from the early women's
magazines and newspapers that the women contributors felt very
deeply for their country, and the issue around which women first
met, demonstrated and organised was that of 'national salvation'.
A number of nationalist issues brought individual women together
at public meetings, spontaneous demonstrations and into the
short-lived and school-centred patriotic associations. One foreign
observer noted that by 1911 mass meetings of women in Peking had
become such a common occurrence that they were no longer a
novelty.[55] What first stimulated women to act concertedly was a
series of national crises threatening China's sovereignty which
precipitated a wave of demonstrations of isolated and spontaneous
groups of patriotic and revolutionary women. Perhaps a collective
inheritance of the heroic strain displayed by Mulan and other
legendary women defenders of their country.

A number of Chinese girl students who were studying in Japan
formed a society for 'Universal Love' which intended its members
to volunteer as nurses in the event of a war between Russia and
China. *The Times* in England reported this event in 1903 and
commented that this proposal must have been enough to 'grey the
hair of many an old-fashioned Chinese gentleman'.[56] Later this
society moved to China itself. Each national crisis precipitated a
wave of patriotic activity among women. A limited number of
separately organised girls' patriotic societies like the 'National
Humiliation Society' in Canton were formed at the time of the
movement to boycott Japanese goods in 1908.[57] But there were only
a few separately organised patriotic societies for women which
sponsored sustained activity; more common in the cities was
individual, occasional and spasmodic attendance and participation
in the many spontaneous patriotic demonstrations. The girls of the

Methodist School in Fuzhou (Foochow) were 'the hostesses' at a mass meeting for women and girls called to share in a popular protest against a British loan for the building of a railroad in the Zhejiang province. This meeting, attended by Chinese ladies of the best families of the city, and pupils from the government as well as those from other missionary schools, was not against the new railroad itself, but they wished it to be built and owned by the Chinese.[58]

An issue which aroused strong national interest was the smoking of opium which, introduced into China by foreign powers, was not unnaturally a nationalist issue. Numbers of mass meetings for women were held to discuss this subject and various petitions in opposition to the practice were circulated. It was said that such meetings brought women together in larger numbers than had ever before assembled in Peking except perhaps for religious services. At one meeting 600 women representing 22 schools in Peking met, while another, called by the principal of a gentry school for girls, numbered 300, among whom were several princesses and wives of government officials. At these meetings, letters signed by a number of Chinese women were addressed and sent to the Secretary of the Anti-opium Society in England.[59] Women took part in street demonstrations during boycotts of American and Japanese goods in 1905 and 1908. In the latter economic boycott against Japan, arising from the case of the ship 'Tatsu Maru', thousands of girl students wearing mourning white and rings engraved 'National Humiliation' were reported to have marched out of their academies to hold meetings and join patriotic demonstrations.[60] In 1910 it was reported from Shanghai that the waves of militant nationalist demonstrations were well attended by well-disciplined schoolgirls and their teachers.[61] In their commitment to patriotic causes many women came to take up the anti-Manchu revolutionary cause of Republicanism. Without the fall of the decaying dynasty there could be no strong China able to withstand the demands of the foreign powers.

Prior to the overthrow of the Manchu regime a number of returned women students from abroad, particularly from Japan, and school students joined secret revolutionary societies and participated in many revolutionary incidents. There were no separate women's political organisations, but women joined revolutionary societies such as the 'Society for the Revival of China', the 'Restoration League' and the 'China Revival League' which later merged into the 'Revolutionary Alliance' associated

with Sun Yat-sen. Jiu Jin, one of the early feminists, and He
Xiangning, who later played a leading role in the women's
movement, were the first two women members of Sun Yat-sen's
revolutionary society. Another schoolteacher, Sophia Chang,
became a leader in the 'Revolutionary Alliance'. After she left her
native Hunan for Japan she took the name of the Russian
revolutionary heroine, Sophia Perovskaya, whose kerchief was
supposed to have given the signal to assassinate Alexander II in
1881. On her return to China after her student days in Japan she
organised the women in Shanghai in support of the Republican
cause. When ready money was urgently required she raised funds
by holding meetings at which hundreds of women poured their
jewels on to the platform. They organised street collections from
door to door and arranged benefit theatrical performances of plays
with revolutionary themes. The most popular was the 'Cycle of
the Three Revolutions' which featured first George Washington or
the American Revolution, second the French Revolution and the
Life of Napoleon and lastly the climax: the Heroes of the Chinese
Revolution.[62] Soumay Cheng, under the pretext of furthering her
education, went to Japan 'to look for the Revolutionary Alliance'.
She went to 'find their leaders and follow them, whatever the cost,
in their struggle to make China a Republic'. She tells how after
several secret meetings she was sworn into the Alliance by taking a
solemn oath to 'remain faithful and serve to the end, without
faltering, in the Cause which was to establish a democratic regime
in China and if necessary to give life should sacrifice be necessary'.
She returned to Peking as an agent, taking cover from, and using
the advantages of, her father's official position. Pretending to
found a society to open schools and further learning throughout
China, she established a regular revolutionary headquarters at her
father's house. Her main task was to organise the financial,
political and military activities of her fellow members in Peking
who included 'young and old, a few women, a few officers of the
Imperial Guard as well as some of the richest people in Peking'.[63] A
number of women organised and took part in the scattered
uprisings preliminary to the events of 1911. More than a few of
them were executed for allegedly smuggling arms and ammunition
and taking part in assassination attempts.

Women played a limited but conspicuous role in the events of
1911 to overthrow the Manchu dynasty. They went to the front as
nurses, conveyed messages and smuggled arms and ammunition
and some even donned military uniforms and organised themselves

into small fighting companies. When the fighting broke out in Wuchang, boatwomen from Canton travelled north to act as nurses to the revolutionary troops. One of the few Chinese women doctors called a meeting in Shanghai to encourage women to volunteer as Red Cross nurses. Nurses were needed urgently at the front. The meeting was called at a day's notice, yet almost 100 women attended it and next morning 30 to 40 of their number left for the front, but not as Red Cross nurses. 'Oh we were so angry,' the doctor later recalled, 'because the Red Cross in Shanghai said those men you call rebels are only thieves and robbers, bad men, they will not be grateful! But we knew, they were our brothers, our patriots, our homes. We *must* go help!' She started a new society, the 'White Heart Society' because 'they would not let me be Red Cross'. She recalled that despite the terrible things they were confronted with, they stayed, and became one of the first group of nurses to work at the war front.[64]

Women helped convey messages and smuggle arms and ammunition. The daughter of a wealthy merchant, who had died and left her all his fortune, devoted herself and her fortune to the cause.[65] Jin Jilan, a famous actress, was beheaded in 1911 for spreading rebellion among the people. It was discovered that after the murder of her husband she had for many years been dealing with 'confidential comrades' in the USA and devoting a large part of her income to the purchase and manufacture of ammunition.[66] During the Canton uprising of 1911, a Japanese journalist reported the arrests of girls whom he described as 'veritable walking arsenals'. He wrote that compared with 'modern Chinese women, the militant London suffragette is nothing. Daily she supplies arms and ammunition to her brother revolutionaries and is occasionally arrested with her tunic lined with dynamite.'[67] Soumay Cheng was a member of the newly formed 'Dare to Die Corps' in Peking which was attached to Sun Yat-sen's party and formed to carefully eliminate persons who were obstacles to the establishment of a new democratic government. The Corps were without any dynamite or bombs so she volunteered to be a carrier. She thought that as a girl she would excite less attention and for some months on an average of twice a week, she made the trip back and forth from Tientsin to Peking 'lugging suitcases of explosives'. Her description of her last trip on which she thought her luggage was about to prematurely explode illustrated the self-conceived romantic and heroic vision of her role.

Now I was convinced that my hour had come. The bombs were
getting ready to go off, and there wasn't a thing I could do about
it but sit there and wait. I was really frozen with fear, but in a
few moments my chaotic thoughts began to resolve themselves in
a heroic form. I had wonderful tragic visions of my friends and
family grieving for me ('she was so young to die') and of the
Guomindang in the South hearing the news of my sacrifice, in
my mind was a vivid picture of Dr Sun Yat-sen commemorating
a memorial to 'Soumay Cheng, Girl Patriot of Peking'.[68]

Despite much opposition many women formed themselves into
units to actually fight for the Republican cause. There was a clash
of wills in Fuzhou when the women in the Patriotic Society there
entertained ideas of going north as soldiers and fighting alongside
the men. A meeting was held at which the girls were told by a
well-known male speaker that women were weak and frail and
therefore useless in battle. The only means left to prove their true
patriotism was said to be the donation of their precious
possessions. Many women did give money, bracelets, rings and
other valuables, but feeling ran high at the meeting and a number
of young members of the Republican Society objected to the ban
on women soldiers. According to a missionary in Fuzhou these girls
were seized with such deep passion for their country that many
threatened suicide unless they were allowed to fight. Eventually the
authorities, thinking that the girls might be useful in caring for the
wounded, allowed eighteen to go to the front.[69] In spite of the
widespread opposition in many parts of China, women did
organise themselves into battalions with such names as the
Zhejiang Women's Army, the Women's National Army, the
Women's Suicide Squad, the Women's Murder Squad, the
Women's Military Squad and the Team for Military Drill.[70]
Another Chinese doctor in Nanchang who disapproved of such
'revolutionary rashness' reported how companies of women had
wanted to join the Amazon Corps of the Dare to Die Soldiers,
bevies of women had wanted to join the Red Cross as nurses. She
was so embarrassed to have to sit and receive mother after mother
who came to seek knowledge of her daughter's whereabouts.[71] In
Shanghai, the wife of a prominent revolutionary, organised a corps
of women soldiers and herself adopted the disguise of a poor pedlar
woman in order to throw a bomb at the viceroy to begin the
revolution there.[72] In Canton, armies of volunteers included
women and girls who adopted the same military dress as the men and

drilled in the same barrack yards. A foreigner who witnessed these extraordinary events observed that in common with the men soldiers, the women too were 'fired with a fanatical desire to fight to the death for the revolutionary cause'.[73]

The intensity of the patriotic and revolutionary activities had reached their climax in 1911. The actions of the schoolgirl and women revolutionaries of the educated classes had been all the more conspicuous because they had marked such a radical new step. This participation was recognised as a remarkable new phenomenon and became the subject of much comment. Astonished foreign observers noted with amazement how women activists were seized with deep passion for their country. One sympathetic woman missionary, though not sympathetic enough she said to align herself with their cause, commented that 'we saw the deep strong heart of the Chinese, touched and aroused again in their daughters.'[74] These astonishing exploits were recounted and widely circulated in the Chinese press and featured in later memoirs of the times:

> We heard for instance, of regiments of Chinese women getting measured for men's uniforms and going up to fight at Nanking and Hankou. We heard of turbulent crowds of women in enthusiastic meetings flinging their jewellery on the platform for the warchest of the revolutionary cause; we heard of women bomb throwers, of women spies, of women members of the 'Dare to Die' corps and of a dozen other picturesque and spirited activities.[75]

But the greatest acclaim of all was reserved for the woman revolutionary, Jiu Jin. Her exploits and reputation were to pass into folklore and legend and her career is interesting in that it personalises the struggle of women activists against traditional feudal restraints. In 1875 she was born into an official family in which she benefited from a classical education and was later married against her will to the son of a wealthy landlord who bought an official position in Peking. Peking was recovering from the Boxer Rebellion and foreign invasion and there was much talk of the partition of China. Jiu Jin took a keen interest in public affairs and was much influenced by the new books and tracts spreading ideas of democracy and national revolution. She was a talented poet and early resented the restraints surrounding her female role in Peking and her helplessness in the face of the Manchu dynasty's servility to foreign interests:

In vain in my dark room I grieve for my country;
There seems to be no way to exchange the kerchief for the
helmet.[76]

Her frustration with the corruption and luxury of official life in
Peking and her husband's attitudes increased until she found the
courage to break from her family and take up the revolutionary
cause.

In 1904 she sold her jewellery to provide funds for a trip to Japan
where she studied political science before entering a Training
College for Young Women. Here she came into contact with a
number of Chinese revolutionaries who were organising secret
groups and planning to overthrow the Manchu dynasty. She
founded a revolutionary society among women students and
applied to become a member of the Restoration League, later part
of Sun Yat-sen's 'Revolutionary Alliance'. At first her application
was refused on 'the grounds of her sex' for 'it would not be proper
for a woman to mix with the "working men" who were members
of the various secret societies affiliated with the League'; but
eventually, unable to resist her entreaties, they permitted her to
become the first woman member. She spoke at numerous meetings,
often wrote articles for the periodicals published by Chinese
students and was said to stir her audience with her passionate
patriotism and her clear analysis of events in China. In 1906 she
returned to China where she manufactured explosives and founded
a woman's magazine. Both projects were short lived and within a
few months she had returned to Zhejiang to take up an
appointment as principal of Tatung College of Physical Culture.
Here she founded a branch of the Revolutionary League, raised
funds, established contacts with secret societies and built up a
people's and separate women's army at her school. In league with
her cousin she helped to engineer a number of sporadic uprisings
which prematurely exploded and were put down. Her revolutionary
enthusiasm and strong feminism aroused hostility, and opposition
to her activities was such that within a year she had been arrested
and executed.

Jiu Jin through her personal struggle against the restraints
surrounding a feminine role became a conscious feminist. In her
personal life she often assumed the name 'Qinxiong' which means
'compete with men' and one photograph portrays her dressed as a
man in Western clothes with quite a jaunty cloth cap. Her poem

'Strive for Women Power' reveals her impatience with men's superiority and repression:

> We women love our freedom,
> Raise a cup of wine to our efforts for freedom;
> May Heaven bestow equal power on men, women.
> We would rise in flight yes! drag ourselves up. . . .
>
> Former practice was deeply humiliating:
> Maidens, young girls were actually mated like cows, mares.
> New light dawns in time of illustrious culture.
> Man's desire to stand alone, supreme, to enslave us
> Underlings must be torn up by the roots. . . .[77]

She made a number of calls to arouse women to a knowledge of their condition and to take the first steps in their own and the country's emancipation. She was a feminist who founded a women's association, a women's magazine and one of her favourite schemes was a women's army. In 1906 during a setback in revolutionary activities she concentrated on canvassing the support of women for the revolutionary cause. She published a women's magazine to stir feminine opinion. In the prospectus she set forth its aims and needs:

> Sad, downcast I grieve, moved by affection I rise, I run forward calling loudly to elder sisters, younger sisters, companions of the womb, begging them to establish a women's publication in the central State. Ah! slowly, slowly a thread of light is piercing the black darkness of our women's realm which, shut in on all sides, for four times one thousand years has existed until the present day. Ah! endless, endless, the long road, how shall we compass it? One hears of those who find the first impulse easy; those who find complete fulfilment hard . . . [we are] without definite direction, without psychological perception . . . my desire is that this malignant stirring [to follow men's footsteps to pass examinations on road to officialdom] shall not enter our women's realm, we must not climb these unworthy steps, pass these inglorious grades. . . . We who have passed the night in drunken stupor, who are not yet aroused, hear first movement of the sunrise bell. In Eastern quarter gleams the first clear light of dawn. Perception after awakening will not be long delayed. . . . If we lack whips with which to switch; builders' lines stretched taut with which to adjust; lack the swiftly moving

compass with which to set our course; perhaps, engulfed in their depths by mighty waves and whirling eddies, we shall drown. Therefore all to left, to right, should rouse the strength and power of public opinion to examine, carefully as does a supervisor, the country's people. What is charged with this official duty if it be not a newspaper?

I would now bind, twice ten thousand times ten thousand women in single indivisibility under our guidance; would at dawn and dusk penetrate women's realm throughout the country discussing general control of women's affairs; would provide women with dashing waves of independence in life's course; would rouse women's essence, spirit, to rise as birds in flight over fields, leaving swiftly earth's dust, that they may speedily cross frontiers into great world of light and brilliance. I desire that they be leaders, awakened lions; advance messengers of learning and intelligence; that they may serve as rafts crossing cloudy ferries; as lamps in dark chambers. That they may let shine, from the centre of women's realm in our country, bright light resplendent, glittering race in the beauty of its colour; that, on the whole earth ball, they startle the hearts, snatch the eyes of men, causing all to applaud, rejoice. I desire my companions of the womb, uniting to encourage themselves enthusiastically, to expend their strength, to pray that this magazine be established.[78]

She was convinced that women could serve as 'lamps in dark chambers' and lead the way in reform and revolution. After all, unlike men, they did not have centuries of conditioning in public life—as newly awakened they could use their untrammelled vision to light the way forward. Her magazine included a number of articles on the need to free women from a dependent and secluded role in order that they could play their part in public affairs. The feminist aims were means to achieve patriotic and revolutionary ends. Her primary aim in arousing women was to 'unite them with the scholars of the land to save China'. Her poem, 'Women's Rights' combines her feminist and patriotic sentiments and established her priorities—to follow in the footsteps of Joan of Arc.

We want our emancipation!
For our liberty we'll drink a cup,
Men and women are born equal,
Why should we let men hold sway?

We will rise and save ourselves,
Ridding the nation of all her shame.
In the steps of Joan of Arc,
With our own hands will we regain our land.[79]

She first and foremost dedicated herself to the revolutionary cause. In passionate writings she expressed her intense love for her country and determination to save China. In a letter to her friends she wrote: 'I will leave no stone unturned to strive for the early recovery of true China, so that we can meet in our own country. Although I am not quite sure whether I'll succeed, I shall stick to my mission as long as I live. Ever since the eight powers made war in China in 1900, my mind is made up to devote myself to the cause of the revolution.' Later in a poem she expressed similar thoughts with an increasing sense of urgency:

I cannot sit by and watch the maps change colour,
I cannot sit by and let our country turn to ashes.[80]

She placed herself at the foot of a long line of traditional patriotic heroes and heroines such as the warrior Mulan, Zhu Jia and Guo Xie. She was especially taken with Yo Fei who strove to prevent the Tartar forces conquering China in the twelfth century and often referred to herself as 'Jiannu Nuxia' (meaning the woman outlaw from Shaoxing) to show that she wanted to emulate ancient redressers of wrongs. In one of her photographs she is seen holding a small Japanese dagger which she apparently carried as proof of her determination to fight to free her country from humiliation and if necessary to die in the attempt. In the tradition of the scholar-rebels and bandit outlaws in Chinese history and popular fiction, she was imbued with the idea of individual self-sacrifice and heroism. She learned fencing, riding and sword play and single-handedly she wished to rescue women and China from the 'darkness' and 'blackness' of their condition. In these attitudes Jiu Jin was characteristic of her times. Her actions reflected the highly individualist strain in the revolutionary movement in which acts were often self-defeating and self-sacrificing in nature. But her struggle and deeds recorded in her poetry furnished a source of inspiration to later women. After her execution, Jiu Jin with her poetic and romantic image was instantly adopted as a martyr of the revolutionary cause and in China today she is still honoured as a patriot and a pioneer of the women's movement.

Like Jiu Jin the early feminists had made a beginning in the analysis of the causes of women's oppression and wrote to arouse their sisters to an awareness of their positions in society, but there was no doubt that their primary goal in mobilising women lay in encouraging them to save their country by contributing to the republican cause. But once the Republic was established in 1911, patriotism gave way to feminism and the right to vote became a prior cause. The collapse of the Manchu dynasty in the revolution of 1911 made way for a new form of government based on a constitution which attempted to introduce Anglo-Saxon democratic practice. Arrangements were made for Sun Yat-sen to be the new President of the Republic and to elect a new National Provisional Assembly to sit in Nanking. Many women began to form organisations to assert the rights of women to elect and be elected as representatives to the new National and Provisional Assemblies. After the Revolution many of the women's military fighting corps were disbanded and afterwards became associations to fight for equal rights and participation in the government. Many, inspired by the example of their Western counterparts, incorporated the title 'suffragette' into their association names. Western suffragette activities were widely recounted in the publications of these societies. The Chinese Women's Co-operative Association, led by Sophia Chang and based at a Shanghai school, put out a monthly magazine almost entirely devoted to translations of foreign articles and views of Western suffragettes. One American who visited a number of schools in Peking after the Revolution tells how the first question he met with was invariably 'Tell us about the suffragettes in England'. This would be followed by questions about militancy, hunger strikes, demonstrations and the firing of letter boxes.[81] The Chinese Suffragette Society in Peking was said to be directly modelled on its English equivalent.

Tang Junying, who had been a student in Japan and advocate of women's rights, founded the Chinese Suffragette Society in Peking. She said that this society had arisen out of her intense interest in the English militant suffragette movement. Her reputation as a woman of her word spread far and wife after it was reported that back in her home province in Hunan she had broken up a newspaper office single-handedly which had issued slanders against her good name. The Constitution of the Suffragette Society included ten points: the education of women, the abolition of footbinding, the prohibition of concubinage, child marriages and prostitution, the provision of social services for women in industry, the encouragement of modesty in dress, the introduction of better terms of marriage, the establishment of political rights, and the overall elevation of the position of women within the family.[82] In support of these aims the Society established a number of schools where the teaching staff were almost entirely composed of its members, and it published two papers—one written in the language of the educated classes and the other in the simple vernacular of the people. The papers contained a digest of news of the women's movements abroad, and a number of poems and articles on related subjects. The broad demands of the Society might be far-reaching in consequence, but their activities were mainly confined to agitation for a simple right—the vote.

Tang Junying was a frequent and vigorous platform speaker in Peking and Tientsin, and in person she led a body of women to demand the vote at the first meetings of the National Assembly in Nanking. When the National Assembly, debating the Provisional Constitution, made no provision for woman suffrage and refused to formally recognise the equality of men and women in the constitution, the Women's Suffrage Association joined to launch a three-day attack. On the first day women made known their demands and in a lengthy and heated controversy they resorted alternatively to persuasive and more agressive means to secure their rights. On the refusal of the Assembly to write the equality and political rights of women into the Constitution their members forced an entry into the House and after having vainly sought the attention of the President himself, broke out in violence, smashing window panes and other property and apparently even 'flooring' several of the constables on duty. The following day the Women's Suffragette Association from Peking mustered its numbers in strength, 'formed into marching order' and went to the Assembly House. The women demanded their rights and looked dangerously earnest and ready for a scuffle, so the Assembly had urgently to send for troops for protection.[83] In Peking a school of law and politics was established for suffragettes and according to the Chinese press, parties of suffragettes besieged the rival Provisional Assembly in Peking and threatened violent reprisals if the franchise laws were not so amended as to include votes for women.[84] The women of Canton also agitated for a share in the new democratic institutions. When the Provisional Provincial Assembly had first been established in Canton it had agreed to recognise women not only as voters, but also as members of the Assembly. Subsequently, however, the men seemed to have regretted their momentary enthusiasm and rash action, for very soon afterwards it was announced that women would have no part in the establishment or running of the permanent Provincial Assembly. Whereupon there was a large outcry from the suffragettes who formed an association to fight for their right to vote and be elected in the Provincial and National Assemblies. They made speeches, held meetings of a thousand or more women and sent deputations to the assembly which cited Queen Victoria and the last Empress, Zi Xi (Tzu Hsi), as examples of the efficiency of women citizens in their respective countries. They eventually resorted to a violent invasion of the provincial legislature itself. According to the *North China Herald*, the men of Canton were determined to withhold any rights to vote, and to prevent women from sharing in any aspect of the future government. When the permanent Assembly was elected in 1913 it comprised 120 members—all men.[85] With little success at home, some suffragettes began to take their crusade abroad. In 1913 word reached the Chinese press that a girl dressed as a youth had landed in Japan on behalf of the Chinese Women's Franchise Association for the purposes of agitating among prominent people there with a view to obtaining their assistance in favour of the enfranchisement of women.[86] The suffragette movement marked the first organised and collective expression of feminism in China.

The departure from tradition ensured maximum publicity for the activities of the feminists in these early years, but their activities were more conspicuous than widespread. The new era had given birth to the women's movement, but it was as yet limited in range of membership and scope of its activities. In these early stages the activists were mainly confined to a narrow social group consisting of the wives and daughters of reformers and revolutionaries and the students and teachers of the new schools. They had generally had the advantage of an intellectual-gentry background both in terms of education and wealth, in the form of personally possessed jewellery. The centres of their activity were mainly the schools in the urban centres and more especially in Peking and the large coastal cities such as Shanghai, Canton, and Tientsin. In these cities, and also in Japan, students were exposed to new and radical ideas in a more continuous and direct form. Neither urban-working nor peasant women were involved in the women's movement. The peasant because of the insularity of village life, well illustrated in the reminiscences of one of the literate inhabitants of Liuling village in remote northern Shanxi. He recalled being told that the Ching Dynasty was at an end and that now 'We were called the Republic of China. That was all. . . . He saw no evidence of any change and could not see that there was any difference at all. He remembered hearing about foreign countries and that there were now foreigners in China but they didn't bother themselves about that; for we lived in our village and everything else was remote.'[87] However, the growth of a manufacturing and industrial sector of the economy had drawn a number of women from the peasant and handicraft artisan households into social production in the new factories.

The growth of manufacturing industries in China was mainly reliant on foreign capital and a source of cheap labour. One newspaper report, extolling the virtues of investment in China, noted that there were no embarrassing factory acts limiting the hours and days per week of work.[88] In the silk filatures and cotton mills of Shanghai, Tientsin and Canton, women worked on a twelve-hour daily shift, seven days a week, for low wages ranging from 12 to 15 cents per day. There was little escape from these conditions, for the work force of the cotton mills in particular, was largely made up of indentured labour. Poor families, desperate for cash and the promise of a portion of their daughters' wages, contracted out their girls to the owners of the factory or his representative who in turn advanced their fares to the factory and undertook to provide board and lodgings of sorts. Despite the dependence of workers on their employers, women textile workers in Shanghai constituted one of the few categories of unskilled labour, alongside the miners and dockers, who dared to strike to better their conditions of work. The first Shanghai silk filature and cotton mill strikes occurred in the late 1890s. They arose out of disputes over reduction in wages during a short depression in these industries. The next wave of strikes occurred between 1904 and 1906. In 1904 women employees of a Chinese firm, which threatened to withhold back wages due to them, locked the staff in their offices while they 'da chang' or 'smashed the machinery' to pieces. Other strikes were called because of deductions in wages or projected reductions in the labour force. By far the largest strike wave occurred between 1909 and 1913, when women employed in the silk filatures came out at least twenty times. Twelve of these strikes were over arrears of pay, attempts to reduce wages and lengthen hours, and protest over their treatment by foremen. Some again involved the smashing of machines and almost all were described as riotous or very disturbing. The *North China Herald* noted that as a rule these disputes were characterised by riotous processions to the Mixed Law Court and a noisy interview with the magistrate. One cotton mill strike which soon spread to several

Chinese textile mills lasted for several days and on another occasion when their wages were withheld, 200 women employees of a silk filature invaded the British consulate.[89] According to one study, the strikes called over arrears of pay were generally successful, but only when the women had succeeded in causing so much trouble that magistrates or the police intervened for the sake of public peace and told the factory owners to pay up. The strikes were less the result of the impact of new ideas concerning women's rights than the result of their new economic position and the struggle of the wage-dependent for survival.

The new feminist associations had few real aims beyond the pursuit of the vote. This was seen to be a prerequisite to the entrance of women into public life, and it was the acquisition of public and political roles which constituted 'emancipation' at this time. Certain groups of women became aware, and then resentful of, the injustice of their being deprived of the right to vote or hold office and so to participate directly in the improvement of their own position and society through political channels. The shop run by the Chinese Women's Co-operative Assiciation in Shanghai offered for sale one article which was considered to be of 'striking revolutionary character'—a small round pill-box of a hat.[90] They said that the custom of staying in doors had hitherto denied them this object. The hat became the symbol of the 'new woman'. Soumay Cheng described her new knowledge of the modern world in terms of her attire:

> I did my hair now in the Occidental style of the day; in retrospect this seems to have been rather an unattractive cross between the pompadour and a bun at the nape of the neck. I dressed in what I thought was the latest and smartest style . . . I wore a hat—I think it was one of those high, flowing plates loaded with assorted trimmings. Since it was the first one I had ever had on my head, I was so taken with it that I could hardly be persuaded to take it off indoors.[91]

Others adopted the dress of either Western ladies, who represented the advanced model, or men, as the dominant social category in Chinese society. In the absence of a well-developed ideology and organisation there seems to have been a tendency for women to think that if they adopted the symbols of these two reference groups they would also acquire their status in society. A report to the World Conference of the YWCA in Berlin in 1910 described the 'liberty girls' of Peking by their clothing, foreign carriages and parties in the fashionable Wagon Lits hotel who were said to be quite in line with the 'smart sets' of New York and London.[92] Some of the young revolutionists caused quite a stir by wearing a man's suit, smoking a pipe or tucking a sword in at the belt. In inland areas such as the city of Chengdu in Sichuan came reports of schoolgirls dressed in boys' clothes.[93] Nor did the newly articulated rights of women extend into the domestic sphere. Within the family the early feminists conceived of no alternative to the subservient housebound domestic role which could be adopted as a platform. Instead many tended to avoid the dreaded institution altogether and used their newly acquired education or their jewellery or employment opportunities to escape from or avoid marriage altogether. This characteristic alienated many women and lost support for their cause. As one Chinese woman wrote in the Chinese press:

> [the Chinese women] do not rant nor clamour for the power to vote but a longing, hungering for knowledge, fills their hearts. They now realise what grandeur of the world is hidden from them, that the intellectual darkness of their own minds hinders them from filling satisfactorily the highest position given to mortals in this world, that of a parent—the mother. She pleads today for education that will qualify her to be truly a helpmate for her educated husband and an intelligent mother for her child.[94]

Despite the limited objectives of the women's movement, these first feminist stirrings were clearly recognised as a serious threat to traditional social relationships within the domestic sphere. Women's minds and feet should be unbound but no more, and even this programme was still resisted by or impracticable for the majority of social classes. The reformers themselves did not admire all aspects of Western social life, especially the nature of the family relationships and strove to avoid similar consequences. One way was to take a stand now and prevent their entrance into the public sphere which would inevitably influence their domestic position. Many believed like the government official, Zhang Zhidong, that suffrage for women would upset the balance of power in society and have repercussions in the home. As he put it 'if one recognises the importance of the bond between husband and wife, then the doctrine of legal rights between men and women is impracticable'.[95] The ideal of education but confinement to the domestic sphere was apparent in the following conversation between a Chinese gentleman and an American Professor of Sociology on the eve of the 1911 revolution:

> I admitted that the Chinese have better ideas than we do as to what children owed to their parents, 'still', I added, 'you'll admit, we have juster ideas as to the treatment of women'. 'Not at all', he replied. 'The place Confucius assigns to women is more favourable than that of the Christian West'. 'But why should women be so subservient?' 'Because women are very hard to control. You can never tell what they will be up to. At the bottom of every trouble, there is a woman'. 'Isn't that due,' I asked, 'to your depriving women of the educational opportunities they once enjoyed?' 'No, it was precisely experience of the difficulty of keeping women under control when they are educated that led our forefathers to lessen their schooling'. 'Then you would shut girls out of schools?' 'No, I wouldn't go so far', he replied. 'Let them be taught to read and write'. 'Nothing more?' 'Possibly, but it should be different from the education given to boys'. 'For example?' 'Why, teach the girl household arts and ethics so she will know her duties as daughter, wife and mother.' 'Would you teach her rights as well as her duties?' I insinuated. 'No, no! That is quite unnecessary'.[96]

One article in the Chinese press identified the problem for China, as for the West, as the maintenance of the traditional division of labour between the public and domestic spheres.

> Perhaps no nation has yet truly solved the great problem; for not even England and America, with all their magnificent educational systems and institutions, have arrived at the ideal point as to what female education ought to be. In their eager desire to promote the intellectual welfare of their women, they seem to have overlooked the one fundamental fact that whatever may be their mental capacity, Nature has by their very constitution intended a different sphere from that of men for them to move in.[97]

The author went on to say that unless precautions were taken, women in China, as in the West, could easily get out of hand and lose those 'finer sensibilities' and 'practical qualities which make them true women, a model housewife and an ideal mother'.

To counter these fears, the traditional position of women within the family and social structure was increasingly reinforced by legislation. On the occasion of the publication of an article in the Chinese press contrasting the 'courting swain' and marriage forms of the West with the 'garrulous go-between' of China, the Empress Dowager, on the advice of outraged officials, issued a code of punishments and penalties for breaking the rules of seclusion before marriage.[98] It was true that the Education Act of 1907 had recommended the establishment of new educational facilities for women, but at the same time it declared that women should remain subject to their fathers, mothers and husbands. Furthermore there was to be no 'free rapprochement between the sexes' or free choice of husbands.[99] Simultaneously the Ministry of Public Instruction forbade schoolgirls to take part in meetings held for the purposes of criticising the administration or in conferences organised by young men. They were forbidden from forming their own clubs or associations to produce journals or to write on any subject touching on 'social evolution'.[100] Any attempt by individual women to step outside the bounds of traditional behaviour were firmly dealt with. There were many cases similar to that reported in the *North China Herald* in 1912. A girl about to elope with a militiaman near Canton was arrested and publicly executed as a lesson to her peers. It was said that this was an example of the wild notions held by some Chinese women who had misinterpreted the new freedoms supported by the new Republic. These did not include 'the personal freedom to do what they like'.[101] In another case a married woman returned to visit her natal home where she became very friendly with a male cousin. She defended her behaviour as 'only ordinary freedom under the new regime'. She too was to meet an untimely death at the hands of her husband who went unpunished.[102] There was little support for the assertion of women's rights within the family structure. This earlier suppression of individuals who defended their behaviour on the basis of 'women's rights' was followed by the retrenchment of the women's movement itself in 1913.

The high expectations which had accompanied the flush of revolutionary success in 1911 was dashed by the rise of a new militarist government under the leadership of Yuan Shikai. The Guomindang Party under Sun Yat-sen and the new democratic institutions had themselves been weighed down with opportunists and conservative gentry who very often neither understood nor were willing to fight for the principles of democracy. They were never any match for the power of the northern military warlords of whom Yuan Shikai was the most senior. With the inauguration of

Yuan Shikai as President of the Republic in 1913, political and military power passed into the hands of these counter-revolutionary militarists. A period of reaction set in and the suffragette activities were quickly crushed by the conservative forces of Yuan Shikai. Tang Junying herself was arrested and for months rumours abounded that she had been secretly executed. A series of laws were passed in the year 1913 which repressed all political and social associations, their publications and, more specifically, forbade women to publish magazines and join in any political groups to attend meetings which included political discussions.[103] In Guangdong province a number of women found with weapons were executed as a lesson to their sisters and the Ministry of Education issued instructions that all suffragette unions throughout China were to be dissolved. These evidently had some effect for in December 1913 the *North China Herald* loudly proclaimed that 'China had shown the world the way in dealing with the suffragettes'.[104] Like the broader revolutionary movement, the visible women's movement came to a sudden end.

The new reforms had been responsible for arousing the expectations of a specific group of women many of whom began to dream or hope for a fate of more than a good marriage. The farewell letter of one such girl, written as she committed suicide because her husband's parents opposed her plan to unbind her feet and enter school, was widely circulated in the press. After explaining her predicament she closed with the following sentence.

> Indeed, there should be no sympathy for me, but the mere thought of the destruction of my ideals and my young children, who will without doubt be compelled to live in the old way, makes my heart almost break.[105]

By the close of the first stage in the history of the women's movement a certain section of Chinese women had begun to experience new public, social and economic activities on both an individual and collective basis. As one foreigner noted 'behind the manifestations and flamboyance of the early feminists, the activities of the leaders and pioneers, there was a steady movement towards the expansion of the public role of women in the cities and towns'.[106] Women had entered social production in the newly established factories of the cities and the pursuit of education and the rejection of bound feet had become accepted as a more or less legitimate pursuit around which women might organise. On these bases they had begun to attend public meetings and had sustained contact over a period of time with other women in associations and organisations and at their places of work. Women themselves began to be conscious of a new role and position in society, and the conservative *North China Herald*, albeit from its vantage point in Shanghai, thought few could be found to deny that:

> Among the tokens of progress that will have to be recorded for the first decade of this century in China, possibly the most marked so far has been the awakening of the Chinese women.[107]

The first feminists had above all challenged the traditional division of labour by claiming access to the public domain of activities and more specifically to the institutions of political decision-making. Their assertions and organisation marked the beginnings of a long debate on the foundations of the sexual division of labour and a long struggle by female solidarity groups to redefine the role and status of women in the public and domestic spheres.

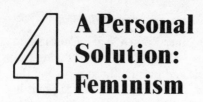

4 A Personal Solution: Feminism

Daughters of China, let the women in other lands be our guide,
Let us follow their sacrificial spirit to free ourselves.
Let us either live in liberty or die for our rights.

(Miss C. R. Chow, 1922)[1]

The 'new thought' of the Cultural Renaissance and the May Fourth movement injected a renewed social and political consciousness into the languishing women's movement. Once again the impetus came mainly from the intellectual reforms and from abroad. The 'woman's problem' was to become a *cause célèbre* of the Cultural Renaissance which began around the year 1916 and grew out of the general disillusionment with the stalemate and period of reaction which set in after the events of 1911. Hu Shi, a leading scholar in the Cultural Renaissance, was one who was stimulated into action by the disappointment of his high expectations of the Revolution which he soon decided 'had been a failure in all its constructive phases'. Far from China becoming a great modern state worthy of its potentialities he thought that what was needed was 'a completely revolutionised outlook on life, a new recognition of spiritual values and of the possibilities of modern civilisation'.[2] He and his fellow intellectuals set about to discredit the old Confucian ideals and social institutions and introduce new social values into China through the medium of the printed word. For this purpose they revived the periodic press.

The leaders of the new cultural movement recognised that there could be no popular movement for reform so long as they used the classical literary language of the scholar and gentry classes. They turned to the vernacular of the people to communicate the new ideas. Magazines, newspapers and books began to appear in their hundreds in this simpler and less esoteric language. One estimate for the single year of 1919 alone puts the number of new periodicals at 400.[3] The most popular, the *avant garde New Youth*, was eagerly awaited each week by students and teachers who flocked to the new bookstores which became the centres of discussion and intellectual activity. Hardly a periodical appeared which did not raise the 'woman's problem' or the 'woman question', as the issues surrounding the role and status of women were collectively referred to. Old practices such as the seclusion of women, the arrangement of marriage, concubinage, the double standard of morality and footbinding were severely criticised, and subjects such as the particular form of education desirable for women, their right to political participation, free love, monogamy, birth-control and the form of the nuclear family abroad were widely discussed, often advocated and sometimes practised. But the subjects under debate embraced a wide variety of complex ethical and philosophical questions. The list of contents taken at random from issues of two popular magazines gives some idea of the range of topics under discussion. The contents of one copy of the journal *The Renaissance* included the following articles:

The Christ before Jesus
The Foundations of Anarchy, and the Society of Anarchy
Opposed to the Life of Individualism
The Field of Psychology
Industry in Relation to Livelihood
Women's Rights and the Law
The Present-day Power of Democracy
The Building of Public Opinion
The Methods of Sociology[4]

and another entitled *La Jeunesse* included:

Pragmatism
The Foundations of Russian Revolutionary Philosophy
Work in Relation to Life
Discussing the Foundations of Electoral Franchise
Revolution in Thought
Men and Women's Social Life should be Free[5]

Indeed, the journalistic interest in the woman's problem increased so much during these years that in 1921 the *China Weekly Review* was led to comment that the media in China had 'devoted more space to matters concerning women than in any previous year—its columns were full of articles. . . . Birth control, matrimonial unhappiness, remarriage of widows, previously shunned, were now widely discussed.'[6] Whereas the women's movement in the past, resting on a narrow theoretical basis, had been almost completely preoccupied with claiming access to the public domain, now the movement broadened to include a redefinition of the role and status of its members in the public and domestic spheres.

The 'woman's problem' was usually viewed in terms of the

generalised emancipation or independence of the individual from traditional familial and societal restraints. This period marked the height of Western influence on its definition. The ideology of individualism brought in from the West stressed the status, rights and obligations of the individual. Lo Jialun in his article entitled 'Women's Liberation' clearly makes the point that women must become persons in their own right and not remain an 'attachment to men'. As he argued in this article, if social progress depended on the complete, free development of the entire body of individuals in society, how could women follow their free will and lead an individual public role while remaining confined to the household and with the Confucian tradition?[7] The Confucian ideology was firmly attacked as the single most important factor hindering the modernisation of social customs. The old ideas and practices were constantly contrasted with those thought to be characteristic of Europe and America. The article written by Chen Duxiu on 'The Way of Confucius and Modern Life' was typical of the tracts which rejected Confucianism as an outdated ideology, one that had abused womanhood for centuries and was now inappropriate in the modern age. An age which took Western practices as the yardstick by which to measure social progress. His article contrasted the division of labour in China and in the West:

> Sons and wives possess neither personal individuality nor personal property . . . [with] the woman . . . obeying not only her father and husband, but also her son, how can they form their own political party and make their own choice? The movement of women's participation in politics is also an aspect of women's life in modern civilisation. When they are bound by the Confucian teaching that 'To be a woman means to submit', that 'The wife's word should not travel beyond her own apartments', and that 'a woman should not discuss affairs outside the home', would it not be unusual if they participated in politics?
>
> Women [widows] have had no freedom and endured a most miserable life. Year after year these many promising young women have lived a physically and spiritually abnormal life. All this is the result of Confucian teachings of decorum.
>
> In today's civilised society, social intercourse between men and women is a common practice. . . . In the way of Confucian teaching however 'men and women do not sit on the same mat'. . . .

Western women make their own living in various professions such as that of lawyer, physician and store employee. But in the Confucian Way . . . the husband is the standard of the wife. Thus the wife is naturally supported by the husband and needs no independent livelihood. . . .

In the West parents and children usually do not live together, and daughters-in-law, particularly, have no obligation to serve parents-in-law. But in the way of Confucius, a woman . . . 'never should disobey or be lazy in carrying out the orders of parents and parents-in-law. . . .' This is the reason why the tragedy of cruelty to daughters-in-law has never ceased in Chinese society.[8]

Articles such as these were written to inspire the younger generation to rebel. Chen Duxiu, an eloquent spokesman of the new ideas, called on the new generation to 'fight Confucianism, the old tradition of virtue and rituals, the old ethics and the old politics . . . the old learning and the old literature'. He hoped that the young would be self-conscious and aware of their responsibilities to struggle to change society.[9] One of the clauses of the Manifesto of the magazine *New Youth* specifically called on women to take up their own cause. It stated that: 'We believe that to respect women's personality and rights is a practical need for the social progress at present, and we hope that they themselves will be completely aware of their duty to society.'[10] Women were to respond to this challenge and many took up the pen in the cause of women's emancipation.

These women declared their intention as writers and journalists to make the most of every opportunity provided by a revived women's press to arouse women to a consciousness of their position. In an interview one of their number said that she thought women should analyse their position in society and draw attention to their subordination:

Now is the time to call attention of Chinese women to the gloomy and unwholesome aspects of their social life. They should immediately be brought to the full realisation that they constitute a nucleus of society and that as such they should fully co-operate and insist on their right of co-operation with men for the advancement of the general social welfare. It is only through a diffusion of new learning and new knowledge, accompanied by an elevation of their thoughts and the enlightenment of their views on life, that they can be awakened to the fullest sense of their responsibility.[11]

In the maiden issue of *Girls' Daily of Canton*, its journalists elaborated on their self-appointed task:

> To oversee the government and to lead society into an enlightened path is the duty of journalists. A few words from their pen constitutes a criticism which in effect will criticise the actions of society and reform their misdemeanours in the course of time. . . . As to human beings in the world, it is impossible to neglect entirely the welfare of the female sex; yet our parents have adopted such an idea as to despise the female sex and ignorant citizens have echoed with the ancients the saying that 'Virtue lies within a girl who possesses no education or ability'. Hence at the mercy of the male sex our two hundred million sisters have been condemned to a hall of darkness. Why? Are females not also human beings? Why then should they receive such treatment in society? On this point the writer is inclined to think that we, the female sex, are partly responsible for such consequences, since we did not assert our rights and never struggled for our own welfare. . . . In order to preserve our position in society, we must have a definite plan—namely, through journalism and newspaper propaganda to attain the necessary result. . . . To educate the ignorant and strengthen the weaker ones will be the duty of this paper. Therefore we, the publishers of the *Girls' Daily*, propose to support and carry out the following points as our aims:
> 1 All things, which will preserve the dignity and virtues of a woman, we will advocate in our columns.
> 2 All things which are beneficial to womanhood we will agitate.
> 3 All those who are in sympathy with our cause, we will manifest.
> 4 All those who are working contrary to our cause, we'll fight to the last.[12]

The aim of the *Women's Bell* was to educate women and enable them to take part in the progress of society towards liberty and equality through the solution of the woman's problem by women.[13] The *New Woman* was published with the object of arousing women to reform the old society and give birth to a new society in which the 'new woman' was 'complete in personality, was joyful in spirit, had an honest occupation, was equal, free, independent and mutually helpful'. This aim was reflected in its manifesto in which the declared objectives were:

1 To sweep away all obstacles which hinder the new woman from self-realisation.
2 To investigate the best methods of progress and take action along those lines.
3 To select and commend the latest American and European literature on the new woman.
4 To investigate properly present labour conditions among the women of China.[14]

Even the first section of each issue of the *Ladies' Home Journal* was given over to advertising women's rights.[15]

In analysing the causes of women's oppression the new women's magazines, perhaps taking their cue from radical intellectuals like Chen Duxiu and Hu Shi, were unanimous in airing the opinion that it was the Confucian ideology rather than economic factors which had been responsible for their downtrodden position, not only in the public sphere but also in the domestic sphere. An article entitled 'The Revolution in Thought', which stated that before any further changes could occur the old thought that exalted the male sex and despised the female must be rejected, recommended the examination of Confucian texts to show up the sexist nature of his writings.[16] One article did just this under the heading of 'Confucius' Views on Women'. The author first notes that the introduction into China of Nietzsche's theory of re-evaluation should immediately set the thinking Chinese in an inquisitive and somewhat critical attitude towards their established institutions. She pointed out that even devoted followers of the most revered Chinese sage, Confucius, had begun to doubt the value of his teachings. Although some went as far as holding him wholly responsible for China's backwardness in science and thought, she would not go so far, she said, for some of his moral and ethical codes such as 'do unto others what you would want done unto you' were of inestimable value. Unfortunately however Confucius did not apply this doctrine to the relationship between men and women. She went on to say that Confucius

failed to see that what ought to be done to men also ought to be done to women. The result of this failure is and has been disastrous for the women. For thousands of years Chinese women have been maltreated, disregarded and despised so that the deep-rooted anomalous conception of women created through his teaching presents, even down to the present, *a persistent obstacle in the way of working out the just principle of equality between men and women* [my emphasis].

'Women and villians are the only people that are hard to deal with', Confucius once said. The fact that he treated women in the same category as villains affords a good testimonial of his contempt for them. Perhaps this remark was made for specific application under peculiar circumstances, but let us look further. 'Women are those who breed contempt from intimacy and complain at the slightest inattention. They are hard to get along with because they are seldom satisfied, whether or not men are close to or away from them.' Such utterances as this shed further light on his views concerning women that have been upheld by men ever since his time. But this is not all. What is of greater social and political significance is his condemnation of women in public affairs. During the reign of Zhou Wuwong, in the Zhou dynasty, there was a political revolution in which a woman with nine other officials at Zhou Wuwong's court took part. It has not been known who she was, but the fact that she participated in the plot was established. When Confucius wrote his 'Book of Spring and Autumn', he remarked thus: 'There were only nine that took part in the revolt, because there was a woman, who could not be counted.' Thus at the stroke of his pen, women were disqualified for, and debarred from, political activities.

It is true that Confucius recognised women as an important unit of society, for in his interpretation of the 'Book of Changes', he said: 'There must be men and women in order that there may be husbands and wives; there must be husbands and wives in order that there may be fathers and sons; there must be father and sons in order that there may be kings and their magistrates.' But his conception of the duties of women was unnecessarily narrow even for his time. He considered the task of bringing up children as their only duty. He treated women as servants and slaves of men who can sell and buy them like commodities. If he had only known that women are capable of exercising their five senses as well as men are . . . he would have saved Chinese women the unjust and undeserved sufferings at the hands of men for the last two thousand years.[17]

In the revolt against feudal customs, the women's and other radical magazines provided a forum for the discussion of new ideas and the source of many of the new ideas was Europe and

America. Foreign literature enjoyed a certain prestige and literary characters like Nora in Ibsen's *A Doll's House* became popular heroines. Great numbers of articles in the Chinese press continued to be translations of foreign material and the suffragette movement especially still attracted the attention of women's magazines. Readers never tired of hearing about the activities of the Pankhurst family and other suffragettes who were often much admired. The *Women's Monthly*, one of the most popular of women's magazines, and noted for its translations of English articles, was known to have heartily applauded the destruction of public buildings, property and pillar boxes by militant suffragettes in England.[18] The visits of prominent Westerners to China prompted reports of their speeches or reviews of their writings. Articles on the subject of birth control were stimulated by the visit of the American, Margaret Sanger, and the visit of Ellen Key from Sweden prompted an examination of the whole idea of motherhood. This period was marked by the impact of foreign ideas and the mere fact that ideas originated from abroad was sometimes enough to recommend their adoption. Ding Ling, a novelist who was still at school in Changsha city when John Dewey and Bertrand Russell went there to lecture, recalled how although they did not make much of an impression on her directly, she knew their ideas must be good—for were they not from the outside world?[19] A woman-club member in Shanghai spoke of the debt of Chinese women to the example set by American women:

> It is not flattery to say that Chinese women look for feminist ideals and inspiration from America. From American missionaries Chinese girls first imbibed the sense of human personality which their menfolk for ages past had all but denied them. From American schools they learned the comforting strength of an independent mind and the sweetness of real freedom; from American homes they drank in the wholesome atmosphere of domestic harmony with which they are making normal the Chinese household; from the high-spirited and achieving American woman they have received the lesson of self-respecting and self-reliant character, whether it be in taking up a professional career, or entering the ranks of breadwinners, or home-building.[20]

Whereas the previous period of intellectual turmoil had been notable for its unwillingness to take the struggle for women's rights beyond some improvements in their position in the public sphere, this period was notable for the criticism and rejection of the patriarchal family structure whose members were ranked by age and sex. There was a growing contempt among the urban literate for the domestic tyranny of the 'ten thousand evil' society, and the undesirable traits of traditional intra-family relations were catalogued to provide ample ammunition in support of change in the most radical of debates and articles. The most compelling contemporary concern of the rebellious younger generation was with the institution of marriage. Many young students rejected 'fate' and avoided a predestined marriage. Cai Zhang (Tsai Chang), later a leader of the national women's movement, tells how at this time she hated the idea of marriage because of the unhappy experiences of her mother and elder sister, and in the society around her she saw only unhappiness in the lives of most married couples. She tells how she, her brother and Mao Zedong all made vows to remain single.[21] Many girls took a similar vow to 'show the world that Chinese girls were dissatisfied with their existing social positions'. Celibacy was the subject of many an article. One, 'The Awakening of Chinese Women and Celibacy', discusses this state as a form of protest:

> In recent years there has been an ever-increasing chorus of women avowing to live single. Though this may be due to new conditions which more or less provide women with opportunities to earn an independent living, their awakening to the horror and undesirability of their social and family life contributes in no small measure to this result. It shows their reaction to the age-long oppression by men. It expresses their discontent with the present family system. It is a sign of their progress in thought and in ideals of life. Celibacy may not be desirable in itself, but in China it is a good index to the abhorrence which women entertain towards married life.[22]

Others rejected the elaborate ceremonial but not the institution itself. For them the freedom to choose their own marriage partner was all important, and a brief romantic courtship 'à la Western style' was an essential '*rite de passage*' in joining the ranks of the modern young. Notices such as the following appeared in the newspapers:

> T.L.K. of Zhili province and S.J.S. of Zhejiang province, having agreed to be married to each other, are today, the 28th of June 1918, united in wedlock before the witness T.Y.P. The

affections of the two are overflowing and will continue though their hairs turn grey.

signed T.Y.P., T.L.K., S.J.S., S.C.[23]

The women's magazines featured advice columns on items such as the selection of a marriage partner, on ceremonies appropriate to the new form of marriage and on other related topics. One of the most comprehensive of these appeared in the *Chinese Ladies' Journal* which ran a series of articles on 'Selecting a Husband'. These began by listing the miseries of the past when parents cared very little for the 'elements of love' between young people. 'Now that Western civilisation has come to China,' it said, 'parents no longer have the right to interfere.' However, the article also warns that many young lovers have misused the term 'free marriage' and much immorality and unhappiness have been caused. It was because 'there is nothing so fine as lifelong love' and 'to avoid these pitfalls' that the journal planned to print a number of articles on the subject. The first proceeded to advise young girls on the appropriate criteria by which to judge future husbands. It was desirable to investigate their habits and character with great care and the *Ladies' Home Journal* discussed a list of suitable qualifications under headings which appeared in the following order: appearance and knowledge, age, occupation, property, relations, health, living habits, temper, character, purpose and general considerations. Young girls were told that these points were of the greatest importance to lifelong happiness and could either be elicited from interview, correspondence or in the last resort by getting information from his neighbours.[24] Articles such as these were widely read and discussed by school, or college, students and the urban literate. They were influential in inducing widespread revolt by these groups against parental restraints.

It was not unknown for the new periodic press to enter into arguments between families and daughters, often taking sides and using the opportunity to criticise the old, and advocate and advertise new trends. Perhaps the best known example and the one often quoted by observers was the public debate stimulated by the publication of a girl's letter in the daily papers in Tientsin and Peking. She wrote that, in view of the national chaos and social order, it was necessary for modern Chinese girls to acquire the highest education possible in order to face the problems of life. As for her, her education had been cut short by conservative parents who despite her pleadings had refused to give way. In these circumstances she saw no alternative but to 'cut all her connections with her family'. The editor of the paper invited readers to send in their opinions concerning this case. The flood of letters which poured in were so strongly in favour of the girl that her father, a well-known scholar of the old school, was forced to compromise and the editor of the paper acted as mediator. He compiled a treaty of peace which, based on the letters written in the girl's support, contained the following stipulations:

1 The parents promised to support the girl and her sister in school.
2 In case the girls felt it wise to go to a boarding-school, the parents promised to make no objections.
3 The daughters were to be free to choose their own courses of study.
4 The daughters were to be allowed to buy and read any decent books, magazines and newspapers.
5 The daughters were to have freedom of correspondence, but were to report their movements to their parents.
6 The parents were to promise to support their daughters in case they wished to study abroad.
7 The girls were not to be betrothed before the age of twenty-five. If they should then have their own views on matrimony, they were to be free to lay them before their parents. There should be no betrothal without the consent of the girls.[25]

It was the latter demand which contributed more than anything else to the ever-increasing generation gap. Not a few women committed suicide when the right to choose their own marriage partner was denied them. One case in particular was said to illustrate the immense influence of the new literature on female emancipation. Li Zhao died three days after she had jumped from the upper storey of her Shanghai home on the morning of 18 September 1919. There was tremendous public concern over her case, and her correspondence was assembled and published immediately after her death. It revealed how profoundly she had been concerned with the 'woman's problem' and affected by current articles on the subject. As a result of reading the latter, she had totally opposed her parents' attempt to marry her off in the conventional manner and she rejected the traditional family structure in general.[26] The new literature was influential among its readers in inciting revolt against old customs and once again the new schools and educational institutions with their concentrations of literate and articulate girl students provided the institutional basis for separate women's patriotic and women's rights organisations.

School and university students were particularly susceptible to the influx of the new ideas. Ding Ling tells how even in old-fashioned schools such as the Girls' Normal School she attended in Changsha, the girls were 'energetic, enthusiastic and unrestrained.' As soon as they heard of a new idea they wanted to put it into practice. No sooner had the students learned of bobbed hair than they had a secret cutting session at which, despite the extreme prejudice against it, 80 students cut their hair. To show their concern over the future of China, they went out on the streets and wept over the humiliation of China at the hands of the foreign powers.[27] Although the number of government, private and mission schools for girls increased (see Table 1) and became more and more and more popular, there were still many barriers preventing equality of opportunity in education and full participation in

Table 1

	1910	1914	1917	1919
No. of schools	42,444	59,796	128,048	134,000
No. of teachers	185,566	200,000	326,417	326,000
No. of students	1,625,534	3,849,554	4,269,197	4,500,000

(Source: M. T. Z. Tyau, *China Awakened*, London, 1922, p. 4)

student affairs. Despite the increasing popularity of the schools, women still only formed just over 12 per cent of the students in Peking and it was not until 1920 that girls were first permitted to enter most branches of higher education. In that year a number of higher normal schools and leading universities admitted women on an equal footing with men. Simultaneously many schools and colleges became co-educational. Some young girl students were determined to avoid a cloistered education primarily devoted to preparing them for their roles as wives and mothers which was characteristic of some girls' schools. In *The Family*, a very influential novel among students which was set in this time, one young girl announces to her boy cousin how she intends to enrol at a co-educational school. Moreover she was determined to withstand any parental opposition: 'It doesn't matter whether Ma agrees or not. I can make my own decisions. I'm a person, the same as the rest of you.' 'Well said, Bravo,' said her cousin, 'spoken like a true New Woman.'[28] Ding Ling describes the scandal she and five other girls caused in Changsha when they sought entrance to the boys' school there. They had wanted to attend a boys' school because the courses were much better and the other girls' schools were either too expensive or backward politically and culturally. Their entrance caused a disturbance, although many boys were good to them and helped them in their schoolwork, others were angry, jealous and wrote letters accusing them of this or that. However, the girls won their case and one boy was even expelled for his uncompromising attitudes.[29] These new opportunities were not won without a struggle but once won, girl students began to participate in the new 'study societies' and the student unions.

In study societies students gathered to discuss ideas and written materials not taught in the schools. Girls sometimes formed their own separate societies, for instance, a 'Girls' Society for Work and Study,' of which many later leaders of the women's movement were members, was established to encourage women to discuss new ideas and eventually many of its members went to France on a part-work and part-study programme. Girls were among the earliest members of the 'New People's Study Society' which devoted much time to the woman's problem and particularly with instilling in women a consciousness of their potential social and political roles.[30] For many of the girl students these societies and the discussion of theoretical problems with men was a new experience. Cai Zhang remembers how she learned a great deal from listening to conversations and participating in the society's activities.[31] The free mixing of ideas and of the sexes aroused suspicions. Zhu De, later a commander of the Red Armies and member of the government after 1949, participated in a study group at this time. He told his biographer that the groups discussed new ideas, books and magazines, and men brought their wives and sisters who, for the first time, learned to discuss ideas with men who were not members of their immediate families. He remembered that their disregard for social customs and the meeting of men and women as social equals meant that they were thought of as wild and immoral by 'old feudal forces'.[32]

The two sexes began to meet freely in the student unions which were established on a permanent basis first in individual schools, in cities and in provinces, and later the Student Union of the Republic of China, with its headquarters in Shanghai was active and influential. Girls' schools organised themselves into alliances among which were the Alliance of Girl Students in Changsha, made up of members of eleven schools mostly girls' middle schools, and the Progressive Association of Girl Students.[33] Girls' schools individually and in alliances were affiliated to the National Union of Students. At an inaugural meeting of a city-wide student organisation in Tientsin, a girl leader from the city's first Girls' Normal School remarked on the significance of the occasion:

> Conditions are very dark. Some lay all the blame on our unenlightened government. I, little sister, say that the most unenlightened of all are our Chinese women. First, we bind our feet; second, our minds are bound; third, we are inferiors and servants of our husbands. Today, in the amalgamation of our women's society with the Students' Union, we are unbinding ancient restrictions.[34]

The Ministry of Education attempted to curb these activities of girl students, but despite the fears of parents and opposition from the authorities, they began to participate in the students' organisations. The leadership positions of the various committees of the student unions were nearly always shared by one boy and one girl student. It was sometimes found that at first the girls tended to take their cues from the boys, but it was not long before they initiated activities themselves.

In addition to the student population there was by the May Fourth period a substantial number of school graduates who had entered the profession, government and private business concerns upon leaving school and before marriage. Teaching, nursing and medicine formed the most popular professions, but some women took the unprecedented step of entering business. In Canton there were said to be forty factories owned and operated by women and in Nanchang women owned and operated both the city's electric light and telephone plants. A school was opened to train girls in the banking business and some staffed the new savings banks specially established to encourage women to become economically independent. There was a growing feeling among this group that women could not hope to depart from traditional role-patterns unless they had found a source of economic support alternative to the family and the provision of some form of economic independence or security had been one of the aims of establishing separate women's banks in Peking and Shanghai. The founder of the Peking Women's Bank sent canvassers to call upon wealthy women in their homes, explain the principles of banking and told them what rights they had and how they could control their money, or at least safeguard it. These visits set many women thinking and the lists of bank depositors grew. She also hoped to establish a savings department for lesser incomes. Her aim was to generally educate women along progressive lines as well as to make it pay—'it is not only the commercial side that interests me but the great opportunity it gives women to become independent.'[35] The Chinese Women's Bank in Shanghai, formed in 1922, managed the financial affairs of a large school for girls and allowed the girl students to open an account. However, it was chiefly for the more affluent of Chinese women for it possessed safety vaults for their jewels on which loans could be raised. The head woman accountant there also did a good deal of house-to-house visiting for she believed it to be very important for Chinese women to become financially self-supporting and independent.[36]

Photographs of these young women pioneering in the business and professional world show a certain air of sophistication and they are almost always clad in Western fashions and had acquired a Western name. Their hair was bobbed and waved and they led a gay social life, but as pioneers in their chosen field they frequently faced professional and business discrimination. In job opportunities, rates of pay and promotion prospects, their sex was at a disadvantage and many were automatically dismissed on marriage. They too, as members of women's patriotic and women's rights associations, school alumnae associations, 'returned students from abroad' clubs and professional and business women's clubs, joined in the patriotic and feminist activities of the May Fourth movement.

As in the years before the 1911 revolution the first preoccupation of the literate and articulate was with the fate of their country. The heightened patriotic and political atmosphere and activities of the period of the May Fourth incident heightened national consciousness and brought many women into public meetings and patriotic associations, on to the streets in demonstrations and out on strike. The occasion was the Treaty of Versailles. In 1914 Japan had seized the German concessions in Shandong and a year later made the infamous 21 demands regarding special rights in Shandong province. During the Conference held at the end of the First World War at Versailles, the indignant Chinese entertained hopes that the previous German and now Japanese-held concessions would be returned to China. The terms of the Treaty, which gave them to Japan, and the new revelations that the Japanese had all along acted with the compliance of weak and feuding warlords in Peking, sparked off a wave of demonstrations, the establishment of patriotic associations and a boycott of Japanese goods. In this renewed nationalist activity which swept China in the wake of the Versailles settlement, women played no small part. They formed their own patriotic organisations or associations 'to save the nation'. In one girls' school, for example, several hundreds of students with the help of their principal organised themselves into 'Committees of Ten to Save the Nation'. Each was despatched to various areas of the city to give lectures of which the following was typical:

> Dear compatriots, everyone must awaken to the fact that China is about to be lost and we shall become enslaved just as happened to the Koreans, and our women will suffer extreme humiliation. Taiwan is another example [of Japanese colonialism]. Let us all be aware of China's predicaments and support native products.[37]

The pupils of Zhounan Middle School were similarly motivated. They organised themselves into groups set up for 'discussion, investigation and communications'. Every day discussion groups of four to five students went out to public places to lecture to women and girls about the persecution of China at the hands of Japan and how it was their responsibility to boycott foreign goods and to promote national industries. The committee groups distributed posters and leaflets for the purpose of spreading this message as widely as possible.[38] Other groups such as the Progressive Association of Girl Students in Changsha campaigned in the Chamber of Commerce among the merchants to promote the sale of native goods.[39]

In the large cities women participated in the massive demonstrations which were held during the months of May and June 1919. Upon the arrests of students in Peking, 100 girl students went to make speeches in Peking and the next day 1,000 of them from 15 girls' schools assembled in Peking and marched to the President's Palace to protest against this treatment of the students. The Ministry of Education attempted to curb the freedom of girl students ruling that 'she shall not leave school premises without good reasons or band herself with other girl students to go out and waste time on the streets'.[40] In one county seat where the girls were locked behind closed schoolgates, they took matters into their own hands and held their own ceremony within the school confines:

> While we heard the drums and bugles, and the shouting of the slogan 'Down with Imperialism' from outside, we also wanted to do the same thing on the same lines. We wrote our slogans on pieces of paper torn from our exercise books and pasted them on our chopsticks. We organised a parade in the playground. . . .[41]

Women from all classes attended specially held women's demonstrations. On one occasion in Canton approximately 10,000 women marched through pouring rain to listen to vigorous speeches and pledge themselves to a boycott of all Japanese goods.[42] A foreign observer of the protest in Tientsin noted that:

> China's womanhood, thanks to the action of the Paris Conference over the Shandong question, is as active as its rising manhood in discussing publicly the burning politics of the day. . . . The new woman is therefore abroad in the land. She is patriotic and public-spirited.[43]

Overall the newspapers of the time concluded that one of the most remarkable features of patriotism was the large part taken by the women of China. Indeed, they were seen to be as keen as their brothers in the desire for the betterment of their country's welfare and were devoting much time trying to work out ways and means for her national salvation.[44]

Although many separate women's organisations, such as the Tientsin Patriotic Women's Association, were immediately concerned with arousing women to do something for their country, they also planned in the long term to improve the position of women in society. After the events of 1919, women's rights associations were formed to specifically improve women's public and domestic status in Peking, Tientsin, Shanghai, Canton, Changsha and a few other cities. The women of Hunan province led the way. The Hunan Women's Association was founded in Changsha in 1921 to co-ordinate action around their 5 demands of property inheritance, to vote and hold office, for education, equal rights to work and free marriage. This association became known as the 'five-proposal movement', and according to a Chinese newspaper, 'it strenuously contended the status quo' in order to improve the legal status of women.[45] A group of Zhounan Middle School students led in a protest to demand the equality of women and their right to inherit property as the Hunan Provincial Council, and a number of women demonstrated in the streets of Changsha in favour of 'self-determination' in marriage. Taking advantage of the current sessions of the revision committee of the Hunan Provincial Constitution, the Women's Association sent a delegate to state their case for the right to vote and be elected. During the debates, she was able to fight several issues to a favourable conclusion in the face of the opposing parties.[46] In the new provincial constitution women suffrage was granted and Hunan became the first province to recognise equal rights for women in the constitution. The success of this local suffragette movement provoked similar campaigns elsewhere.

The women in Guangdong secured the right to vote after several public demonstrations demanding equal rights. While the Provincial Assembly in Canton was debating a bill for the election of district magistrates, 700 women demanded entrance and the right to vote. In the disorderly scenes that were said to follow several suffragettes were injured and a number were knocked down unconscious. After Sun Yat-sen and the governor of the province promised that the women of Canton should be given the right to vote, jubilant processions of women shouting 'Victory, Victory' marched to a public meeting. Here 1,000 enthusiastic women, beneath banners inscribed with 'Equality for our Sex', 'Long live Sun Yat-sen', 'Give us the Vote' and 'Woman Suffrage for China' made plans for securing further equality for their sex. Later a large demonstration, singing *en route*, marched to a Provincial Assembly and offices of the Military government to express their appreciation of the sympathy shown by the officials there for their cause.[47] In Zhejiang province, too, the Feminine League for Equal Rights won the right for women to vote and hold office in the Provincial Government.

In Peking two rival organisations were formed to fight for the rights of representation there. The Women's Suffrage Association was founded in July 1922 by girl students of the Women's Higher Normal School and the Peking Law College. It had three aims:

1 For the purpose of protecting women's rights, all the articles of the constitution partial to men should be abolished.
2 In order to secure economic independence for women, the limiting of inheritance rights to men should be abolished.
3 In demanding equality of opportunity in education, the old system of giving women a limited education adapted only to domestic affairs should be abolished.[48]

The organisation spread rapidly, but from the first it encountered official opposition to its main platform of suffrage. The Peking authorities interfered with their activities because 'women had no rights and no understanding of political questions'. As the Premier stated women must first be educated before they could possibly take a hand in the governing of the country.[49] The continued resistance of officials convinced a group of young women at the Peking Women's College that simply to demand suffrage would not solve the 'woman's problem'; there were many other rights necessary to the development of women's personality, hence they formed the Women's Rights League which had seven demands:

1 The opening of all educational institutions in the country to women.
2 Adoption of universal suffrage and the granting to women of all constitutional rights and privileges given to men.
3 Revision in accordance with the principle of equality of those provisions in the Chinese Civil Code pertaining to relations between husband and wife, and mother and son, and to property rights, disposing capacity and the right of succession to women.
4 The drafting of regulations giving equal rights to women in matter of marriage.
5 Prohibition of licensed prostitution, girl slavery and footbinding.
6 Addition of a new provision to the Criminal Code to the effect that anyone who keeps a concubine shall be considered guilty of bigamy.
7 Enactment of a law governing the protection of female labour in accordance with the principles of 'Equal work, equal pay' and 'A woman is entitled to full pay during the time that she is unable to work owing to childbirth'.[50]

A petition incorporating these demands and signed by 500 or so signatures was presented to Parliament. Branches of these two associations were also established in Shanghai by representatives from the Shanghai Business Women's Club, the Shanghai Women's Club, the Women's Christian Temperance Union, Young Women's Christian Association and a large number of girl students.

In 1924 when a National Congress was called in Peking by Sun Yat-sen to abolish the unequal treaties and prepare a permanent national constitution, women were not invited to attend or send representatives. This omission caused various women's organisations, including the Women's Suffrage Associations and the Women's Rights Leagues to send representatives to constitute a national women's rights association to fight for women's representation and rights at a national level. It was explained that this single new national movement was formed both to fight the general impression among men that women could be overlooked and treated with disdain, and to uphold and protect the rights of women to work alongside, but not compete with, men:

> We are not fighting for official positions, we only want to be placed on terms of equality with men and to uplift China in civilisation and character.
>
> We also want to be independent financially. We are not out for individual aggrandisement or selfish ends but as women and as citizens. We want to take an interest in politics. We want voting powers, but we do not want to make politics our line of business or as a source of power for ourselves. We want to work for the future of China.[51]

They unanimously opposed the provision on suffrage as it was written into the draft regulations for the National Congress. This read: 'All men of the Republic of China over 25 years of age and with a proper education shall have the right to elect and be elected.' They organised demonstrations through the streets of Peking under the slogans of 'Down with imperialism', 'Down with militarism', 'Same pay for equal work', 'Monogamy to prevail', 'Absolute freedom of marriage and divorce', 'Opposition to one-sided hypocritical chastity', 'Freedom for women to choose occupations', 'Abolition of prostitution', 'Prohibition of slave trade', etc.[52] When the women began to march the military forces as well as the police were ordered to prevent any demonstrations and prohibit further public meetings. This order, together with the promulgation of unequal laws in which the rights of women were overlooked altogether, was to mark the beginning of another period of suppression.

Despite the breadth of some of the platforms of the Women's Rights Associations their membership and activities were very limited. A report issued by the Peking Society of International Education noted the important part taken by educated women in organised movements to obtain equal rights.[53] The wives of intellectual reformers, businessmen and men of the government continued to play an active role. On one occasion the *North China Herald* listed the leaders of the National Women's Rights Association: the wife of an ex-Premier and leader in social and educational activities, the wife of a veteran diplomat and statesman, the wife of a former Minister of Justice, the daughter of the reformer Kang Yuwei and the wife of a former revolutionary leader who had herself been a member of the 1911 'Dare to Die Corps'.[54] The exclusive characteristic of the organisations is fully reflected in the social make-up and demands of the Tientsin Women's Patriotic Association.[55] According to a contemporary observer in Tientsin, the members of this association included several hundred educated ladies and wives of the most influential families of the city. In addition to their immediate aim of arousing women to do something for their country, they planned in the long term to abolish any part of the social system which was detrimental to the position of Chinese women. The part of the social system which they seized upon as the most detrimental to the position of Chinese women was the system of concubinage. In a declaration on the subject they explained their position:

> One of the most painful and horrible sufferings which women have been experiencing during the last several thousand years is the system of concubinage. Once women become concubines, their fate is sealed . . . and numberless women have in consequence become degraded. The status of Chinese women as a result has been lowered. . . . One man, if he is wealthy enough, may take from three to ten concubines. Many corrupt officials, merchants and national traitors, usually keep a host of them in their homes.
> Unless concubinage is abolished, our family system and finally our nation will be destroyed. We modern women cannot refrain from paying attention to this question. . . .

Concubinage was to be abolished, but not by the 'poor unfortunate women' placed in this degrading position—the concubines themselves. They were banned from becoming members of the Association and in a statement the Association gave its reasons:

1 Although the promoters of the association are teachers and students of girls' schools, they are more than pleased to have wives and members of *reputable* families to join them so that they may be able to render greater services to the country. Why not take in concubines who are also Chinese women and are none the less patriotic . . .? Our object in organising the association was to arouse our sisters to do something for their country. Our future plan is to reform the family, to reform society and to abolish any social system which is detrimental

to Chinese women. These concubines who desire to join us will probably fail to understand these ultimate objects of the association. They would be offended should we in future discuss the question of the abolition of concubinage. Such a disagreement of views will result in hindrance to the progress of the association.

2 Such being our principle, we cannot admit the right of concubines to exist as part of the society and consequently cannot allow them to become members; otherwise our task of uprooting the evil will be increased ten-fold. However, we are not looking down upon them or considering them not as our equals. On the contrary, *we are devising means of their salvation from their present deplorable state*.

3 There are three classes of concubines in China. Some are ambitious women belonging to good families. Some are sold into slavery as a result of calamity or misfortune, some are women without principle, not knowing the sin they have committed, and are satisfied with worldly comforts and luxuries. Still others are prostitutes who are impudent and proud of their degraded position. If we take in as our members any concubines at all, *the good name of the association will surely be compromised*. Furthermore, this is the first time that Chinese women have tried to do something for their country, and we are consequently passing through a trying period.

4 Ninety-nine out of every hundred women in China are not free. We are now sending eighty or ninety women to speak on public questions. These lecturers include teachers, students, matrons and young women. We have now completed our patriotic work inside the city and will continue our campaign outside it. We are grateful to our parents for their support and sympathy, which will be withdrawn if they discover that we are not living up to our principles. *Our parents will dislike our association with degraded women*. These are the four reasons why we exclude concubines from the Association. [my emphasis]

That the good name of the Association should not be tarnished or the reputation of its members sullied were the primary reasons given for their exclusion. This was despite the fact that many concubines were unusually wealthy and could have contributed handsomely to the society's funds. The society's members were probably more interested in abolishing the custom in order to prevent the intrusion of concubines into their own homes than in the fate of the concubines themselves. For these ladies, although they could rarely attain the status of a wife in the home, the custom provided a means of social mobility and access to unaccustomed riches and leisure. Concubinage was primarily a problem of the richer urban classes and this interest of the society very much a reflection of the class bias of its members.

Demands such as the right to vote or the campaign against concubinage seemed hardly relevant to the majority of women. Indeed the suffragettes complained of the lack of interest in their cause. When the women teachers in Peking went beyond their circle and sent out several appeals for attendance at meetings to solicit support for equal rights, they found that the response was often dispiriting.[56] In a report the Shanghai Women's Club criticised its members for the small attendance at its meetings. This was put down to the fact that a club for women was still a novel idea and although it was an innovation that appealed to them in the abstract, they were as yet unaccustomed to activities outside the home and still thought their presence to be undesirable unless some point in which they were vitally interested was under consideration. Yet in the industrial cities themselves, the primary location of some of the most active women's rights associations, there was on their doorstep a growing concentration of women factory workers whose vulnerable and dependent position in the work force demanded that they organise and mobilise wider support.

The growth of national industries during the First World War, when foreign powers were otherwise engaged, had led to an increase in the number of Chinese-owned factories in the cities of Shanghai, Canton, Tientsin and Hankou. The need for cheap and unskilled labour in Chinese and foreign-owned industrial enterprises in large cities created new openings for impoverished urban and peasant women from the rural areas. Textiles formed the main components of the new industrial complex and it was the cotton and silk mills which were the major employers of women. The number of cotton mills alone jumped from 49 to 102 between 1919 and 1922. In Shanghai, between 1914 and 1920, 47 to 65 per cent of workers in textile factories, 31 to 43 per cent of workers in service industries and 11 to 23 per cent of other industrial workers were women.[57] The employment of female labour was not just predominant in the Shanghai textile industries for in Guangdong province a total of 160 silk filatures each employed around 600 women workers,[58] and women formed the backbone of the silk and cotton factories of Wuxi and the cotton mills of Wuhan and Tientsin. The women worked long hours, usually a seven-day week for 12 hours a day and their wages consisted of a few cents daily. Indeed, it was the long hours and low wages of the labour force which was one of the incentives encouraging foreigners to set up an industry in China. These very favourable circumstances were outlined in the following report from a contemporary trade journal:

The profits of the ———— factory again surpass
$1,000,000. To those who bestow thought on the progress
of textile industries in China, the following particulars
concerning this concern might be of interest. The company was
started in 1904 with a paid-up capital of $600,000 . . . [which]
was increased to $900,000 in 1916 . . . for the past two years it
has been running night and day without intermission. . . . The
working hours are from 5.30 am to 5.30 pm and from 5.30 pm to
5.30 am respectively. No meals are supplied by the factory. Most
of the cotton is produced locally. It will be seen that the
company is in an exceptionally favourable position. With the
raw product at its door, an abundant and absurdly cheap labour
supply to draw on, and no vexatious factory laws to observe, it is
not surprising that its annual profits should have exceeded its
total capital on at least three occasions.[59]

In practice this meant low wages, cramped working conditions and the neglect of welfare and safety standards. When one foreign lady was taken to look at the conditions under which factory women worked in Shanghai, she said she was at a loss for words to describe her visit to a silk filature:

What shall I say about that silk filature where women and little
girl children wear out their lives in steam and heat and long
hours of incessant toil that some of us may be clothed in silk and
others may make a profit out of their life force? Even babies
rolled around on the filthy floor because there was no place for
the mothers to leave them. There was no welfare work in this
factory, no creche, no rest room, no lunch room, not even stools
for the 'feeders' so that they might sit part of the time. These
'feeders' from six to sixteen toss the cocoon in steaming, boiling
water to start the thread.
For 25 cents Mexican (13 cents of gold) a day, those minors

work through a twelve hour day. The older girls and women, the spinners get 50 cents Mexican (25 cents gold) a day. The thick steamy vapour shrouded the room in haze. The air was stifling and vitiated.[60]

The stifling atmosphere was the prevailing impression of another visitor who likened it to that of a Turkish bath. 'Imagine', she said, 'a large room with a vapour atmosphere like the hot room of a Turkish bath, through which long rows of women could be dimly discerned, each woman seated before a metal bowl of steaming water. . . .'[61] The wages of the women were not only low but they were lower than those of the men workers (see Table 2) and even where women formed the bulk of the labour force they were supervised by men who often took advantage of the vulnerable and dependent positions of the women workers. Factory women were increasingly compelled to unite and organise against their employers.

Table 2 Average Wages in Textiles, 1920 (based on 291 days' work)

	Daily wages		Yearly Wages	
	Max.	Min.	Max.	Min.
Men	$0.77	$0.16	$210.00	$43.85
Women	$0.52	$0.14	$149.00	$43.67

(Source: Lin Tung-hai, *The Labour Movement and Labour Legislation in China*, Shanghai, 1933, p. 68)

The bid to improve their economic conditions stimulated labour demonstrations, the organisation of labour unions and strikes among the women. Women's labour unions made their first public appearance. In the cotton industry in one district in Guangdong where the women workers were fairly well organised, the local union had a reading room which was also a meeting place for general discussions.[62] With the increase in numbers of workers and the worsening of economic conditions, the number of unions and strikes increased in the 1920s. In the Shanghai silk industry the unions made considerable headway when the local Chinese authorities and the Provincial Assembly did nothing in response to repeated requests by workers' representatives to improve the conditions of labour in the factories.[63] In May 1922 the silk workers submitted a petition to the Provincial Assembly of Jiangsu asking for a ten-hour day, an increase in 5 cents a day and provision for an unconditional weekly and monthly bonus. No satisfactory settlement was reached and the situation there became very tense and as a result Shanghai saw its first city-wide strike by the women in the silk filatures in August 1922. It involved seventy filatures and the number of participants was variously estimated from 20,000 to 60,000 persons. They had been organised by a society bearing the camouflage title of 'The Society for Promoting the Welfare of Working Women'. Despite the employers' opposition it had a considerable membership within a few weeks of its foundation. The immediate cause of the strike was the action of the employers, who, in response to the Americans' increasing demand for silk, decided to increase the working hours of the silk filatures. The strike was organised by a few women of the society under the leadership of Mo Ziyin. On 5 August the society women, bearing banners with the slogans 'World for democracy', 'Equality of women with men', 'Promote women's welfare', and 'Give us our rights', marched in procession to various mills. According to the newspapers all the women left their work and joined in a parade in the streets of the Chabei area of Shanghai. The banners they carried were to 'make the world know of their harsh conditions'. Their demands were fourfold:

1 Non-interference of mill owners with the organisation of the Society for Promoting the Welfare of Women Workers.
2 Ten-hour working day as the limit.
3 An increase of five cents in the daily wage.
4 One day of rest every two weeks.

The mill owners immediately retaliated by closing the mills, thus exerting all the economic power in their hands to force their employees to withdraw their demands. They indignantly claimed that they on their part had been more than fair to the girls by allowing them up to fifteen minutes for unavoidable delays in reporting to work. In addition, wages had been raised in the past from 32 to 40 cents per day and they had paid periodic dividends to the girls. 'What more could they be expected to do?' By 12 August the workers were forced to return to work with only the promise of wage increases. It was said that 'the necessity to earn the daily bean curd forced them to give up the struggle'. The strikers had neither the cash reserves, nor the organisational leadership to hold out against mill owners. Contemporary economists thought that the failure of the strike was partly due to the ignorance and inexperience of the workers, their lack of educational advantages,

and to the looseness of the organisation of the women's union
which was not able to concentrate or co-ordinate its efforts in the
emergency. The strike was unsuccessful, but the strikers benefited
from their experience in the defeat and, despite mass arrests of
strikers for the violation of the martial law then in force and the
closing down of the women's union office, the union was
re-formed. It promulgated new regulations and solicited new
members in order to strengthen itself in the event of future
disputes. The strike was said to 'begin in earnest the strife between
capital and labour in China', and the fact that it should have been
begun by women workers was said to open a new phase in the
movement for women's rights in China. The *North China Herald*
drew attention to its significance:

> That a number of women, and those of the poorer and most
> ignorant class should challenge the power of such an extremely
> wealthy organisation as the silk guild indicates a consciousness
> of their own importance and determination to assert their rights
> . . . we call attention to their strike merely to indicate that a new
> phase of the women's rights movement is opening in China.[64]

The *North China Herald* might use the term 'women's rights
movement' to refer to these labour struggles, but social divisions
and class interests were such that in this period there remained two
quite separate movements. Women workers, too, demonstrated
alongside women's patriotic associations and as employees in the
foreign-owned industries they had a unique contribution to make
to the national effort. For instance women workers in Japanese-
owned factories walked out on strike on more than one occasion in
order to express their patriotic disaffection for their employers.
The effect of their strike action was not lost upon other groups of
women, but on one occasion when the two groups did come
together in support of strike action one woman student recalled the
difficulties in communication:

> We went from one group of the girl-workers to another but it
> was hard to talk with them because of the different dialects and
> some of us had to have an interpreter. The girl workers were
> surprised to get support from the students and much interested
> in us.[65]

The social make-up of the two groups and their prior causes were
such that even a common national interest was unlikely to make for
the combining of their different interests and activities.

The May Fourth period was important for a whole new generation that experienced, for the first time, organised and collective activity. The political and economic development of this period had given great impetus to the development of organisations among students, urban workers and women, and for the first time continuing struggle was believed to be more effective in the face of opposition than the traditional outlet of suicide which was diagnosed by intellectuals, such as the young Mao Zedong, to be a social phenomenon resulting from the overwhelming force of social pressures which finally crushed the individual. He thought that there are always people in society who want to commit suicide because society itself seizes their 'hopes' and utterly destroys them, with the result that they are left 'completely without hope'. He went on to urge that the fearless spirit of resisting tyranny should rather manifest itself in struggle against evil forces rather than in suicide.[66] A spate of articles discussed the rights and wrongs of suicide. An example was that written by Chi Xi which was entitled 'Does Youth Commit Suicide or Does Society Murder Youth?' The story of one girl, Li Jicun, who ran away from home in Changsha on the eve of an arranged marriage and joined in the Work and Study programme at Peking and her father's public outrage at her revolt and flight became so notorious as to arouse the interest of the media. The student press applauded Li Jicun's action for she exemplified the new spirit of 'struggle' against the traditional social environment.[67]

By the end of the May Fourth period, however, it seemed to many that in the individual and collective struggle against social, economic and political traditions the strength of the traditional social environment remained overwhelming. The women's movement did not guarantee the strength of its individual members. The extension of the women's rights into the domestic sphere brought individual feminists into direct conflict with their families. Against individual women were marshalled all the time-honoured arguments, and the old ideas did not die easily, even among the members of the economically independent and so-called 'modern generation'. The argument which follows, taken from the autobiography of a young girl student, must have been typical of the family tension generated by issues such as the freedom to choose a marriage partner.

Father: '[Your] reasons for breaking off this [arranged] engagement are chiefly these two: first, there is no love between you and second your ideas are different. Let me answer you very frankly. First, love can only be created between husband and wife after marriage. To have love before they are married is ridiculous. As you have not yet married Guang, how can you expect to have love for him? The second point is his ideas. Now that term can only be applied to revolutionary people, and has nothing to do with man and wife. *Your marriage into the Xiao family is not a revolutionary affair, but is to fulfil your duty as a woman.* The best you can do is to follow our ancient teaching so that you can have a family in which when the husband sings, the wife shall join in. Since this is not a revolutionary affair, what do you care about ideas?'

Daughter: 'Father, to have love only after the wedding is your philosophy of love. That was a special characteristic of the old-fashioned society, which is dead. Now, to have a happy union, men and women must know each other and must have agreeable feelings for each other first . . . as for their having the same ideas that is even more important . . . the modern marriage is directly connected with the reforming of society. Those concerned should not only think of their own happiness but also of the good of society. As well as being husband and wife, they should also think of the good of society. As well as being husband and wife, they should also be good friends and trusting comrades. As Xiao Guang's ideas are entirely different from mine, we haven't the slightest chance of being friends with each other and the fundamental condition of our marriage is gone.'

Father: 'M'm! Ideas? Why should women have such dangerous things? . . .'

Mother: (shouting to father): 'Please stop arguing with her. This beast cannot be considered a human being! Doesn't she realise that father and mother are greater than heaven? How dare she oppose our wishes? I sent you to school hoping that you would learn propriety, righteousness, temperance and purity, but who would have thought education would turn you into a beast without respect for your

mother and father. . . . Schools are not much better
than hell! Anybody who has been to school can act
just like a devil. When they come home, no matter
what happens they must break their matrimonial
engagement carefully arranged by their parents.'[68]
(my emphasis)

Although many individual women had acquired the new ideals of
feminism or economic independence, or both, they found it
difficult to actually take the unfilial step and actively disobey or
ignore parental opposition. The student press in 1920 argued that
too many girls and boys, though they talked about struggle, were
more often than not crushed by their social environment.[69] The
adoption of new norms of behaviour was not enough. This was the
lesson drawn from the case of Miss Li Zhao who according to press
reports ran away from home to study in Peking on the eve of an
arranged marriage. Her family refused to send her any money for
living expenses or school fees, and although her girl friends gave
her money from time to time, she was scarcely able to make ends
meet. Prolonged hardship so weakened her that eventually she
contracted tuberculosis and died.[70] Wealth was almost a prerequisite to the negotiation of some form of personal solution.
Deng Yingzhao (Teng Ying Chao) recalled the uncertainty of this
era: she hated the old Chinese customs of arranged marriage and
unfair treatment of women but she had no constructive ideas
beyond recognising the necessity of economic independence.[71] But
even where some form of economic independence was accessible
there was still the tendency to subscribe to the new ideas and
practise the old customs. Soumay Cheng describes how she arrived
home from studying in Paris to find her grandmother just a few
hours dead. It was said by her family that her independence and
'violent activities' had been more than the old lady could stand. She
recalled that from a commonsense point of view she could easily
have reasoned that this was not true, or at least that she had
another side to the argument, 'but to defend herself then would
have been out of place'. For centuries Chinese families had been
such inviolable units; the old mother occupying a position of
almost sacred importance, that she now found she fell prey to a
flood of atavistic emotion. She later described the remorse and
grief which engulfed her as she participated in the elaborate and
prolonged funeral ceremonies:

> For many nights I took part in the ceremonies, watching the
> monks circling the body, wailing and chanting, until towards
> dawn I would fall into an exhausted sleep.
>
> It is extraordinary to me today to see how quickly I reverted to
> the old customs at that time. The years in which I had been
> engaged in various forms of revolutionary activity, completely
> absorbed in seeking Western knowledge, and had thought and
> talked in foreign languages, all slipped away from me; however
> it must be remembered that I was only 21 at the time and my
> modernity was still largely skin-deep. But there must have been
> considerable conflict within me: a part of me must have
> rebelled against this orgy of useless emotion, because at the end
> of the official period of mourning, I fell violently ill with fever,
> overwhelmed, no doubt, by the tug-of-war between two
> different worlds which was going on inside me.[72]

The conflict was largely seen in terms of deviant individualism and
without a well-developed analysis of oppression and organisation
the individual struggle left feminists, even among the privileged
educationally and economically, exhausted and isolated.

It seemed to many that the women's movement was no nearer a
solution. With suppressive measures and their continued exclusion
from most political institutions there was some disillusionment
with contemporary political structures and their ability and will to
improve the position of women. This mood of disillusionment is
evident in a declaration issued by the National Women's
Association. It stated that:

> The Government has consistently ignored their suggestions and
> demands. The Government also promulgated unequal laws
> under which rights of women were overlooked and sometimes
> suppressed altogether. . . . Since the establishment of the
> Republic and even before Chinese women did a great deal for the
> country but this Government has not recognised this.[73]

This disillusionment led to the development of two opposing
tendencies within the women's movement based on the relevance or
irrelevance of political structures and processes to the goals of the
women's movement. On the one hand many of the women's
organisations rejected political structures and turned instead for a
solution to the self-help activities and organisations of women
themselves. They promoted social welfare and reform activities to
provide for the economic independence of women and especially of

poorer women. This interest in social welfare had been fostered by the separate girls' educational institutions on the grounds that it utilised 'special feminine talents'. The Chinese National Association for the Advancement of Education noted that:

> With means for such education and training, women's contribution in the world of thought and deed will be incalculable, in building up China's new social structure. Such problems as child labour, women's employment, long hours and low wages and poor working conditions should be analysed and, if possible, solved. To meet such needs schools, colleges, universities should offer girls and women courses in theoretical and applied . . . techniques of social service. In the community, the improvement of housing, diet, and public health should engage the most serious attention of social workers.[74]

In this respect a young schoolgirl later recalled the influence of the dean of the girls' department of a commercial school which she attended. The teacher was Cantonese, had taken a social science degree in the USA and had a special interest in social welfare:

> She was fond of social work and took us to visit factories and plants in Shanghai. After this, I received high marks because I took a real interest in the subject and wanted to improve the terrible lives of the workers. At the Nanyang Tobacco Company, I saw young girls and old women pale and yellow, almost too tired to pick up the dirty leaves, and in the stocking factories conditions were even worse. I felt very sorry for them.[75]

Most of the social welfare projects for working girls and women were undertaken by clubs of women and wealthy patrons. Many students, returned students, professional and business women, previously members of women's rights associations, joined women's and business girls' clubs, the YWCA, the Women's Social League or National Council of Women. Like their American counterparts on which they were modelled, social reform became one of their main interests. The founder of one of the first of these clubs to appear in China, the Chinese Women's Club of Shanghai, was impressed by the growth of clubs in America:

> This is the first woman's club that has been formed in China of the same nature as those in America. When we think of the early days there, not so very long ago, when the first woman's club emerged out of the sewing-circle, and now when we read of the

vast projects, the all-absorbing programmes of the conference
recently held by the American Federation of Woman's Clubs we
feel encouraged and know that we too have made our humble
beginning.[76]

These organisations were greatly concerned with women's
conditions of work in the factories. Miss Zong Weizong, a
secretary of the YWCA, conducted a column in the leading Chinese
daily newspaper in Shanghai publicising the working conditions of
women and children in the mills and factories of that city.[77] In
Shanghai a joint committee made up of representatives from the
YWCA and American, British and Chinese Women's Clubs was set
up to make study of conditions in factories and promote industrial
and social reforms. Upon her return from an American College,
Song Meiling, daughter of the wealthy Song family and later
known to the world as Chiang Kai-shek's wife, interested herself in
social work and especially in the interests of women. She acted as
secretary for the joint committee of the American, Chinese and
British Women's Clubs formed in 1921 to study factory conditions.
Others like Xia Fujin set up small-scale experimental projects to
better the social lot of small groups of the unfortunate. She
established a school for knitting and crocheting to help girls
become well-mannered and self-supporting. Twenty girls, ages
ranging from 14 to 25, were taught to knit and crochet bootees,
sweaters and caps in special designs ordered by interested patrons.
All materials were furnished as well as free lunches at 11.30 of
'mutton, fruit, cakes—real nourishment'. Six days a week she gave
this enterprise her personal attention, not even neglecting social
manners in the girls' training. Paper serviettes were furnished as
handkerchiefs and person neatness emphasised.[78] It seemed to
many observers that the new social conscience of the fortunate was
such that they could no longer stand by and look on the plight of
the women workers and the poor with indifference.

There are signs multiplying that it is the educated women of
China who are going to shoulder much of the responsibility for
the amending of conditions so inimical to health as those in the
silk filatures and in the workers' poorest dwellings.[79]

Most saw their work solely in terms of altruism, they did not
support strike action, women's rights as such or see their work as in
any way 'political'. The president of the YWCA expressed her
opinions:

I do not believe in a struggle for equality or for rights. I believe that by showing what they are willing to give to their country, women will get more opportunities to serve than they can manage.[80]

The women's representative of the National Christian Council thought women should undertake no activities that would separate them from their menfolk.[81] At the opening meeting of the National Council of Women in China it was stressed that the primary purpose of this organisation was social service and it was in no way associated with politics.[82]

For another smaller group of women their experience of the May Fourth movement encouraged them to search for alternative political structures which would provide a broader political solution to the 'woman's problem'. They turned to the newly established Communist Party which alone seemed to offer an analysis and opportunity to combine nationalism and feminism. Many future leaders of the wider revolutionary movement and the women's movement served their political apprenticeship in the patriotic movement which often had aroused their initial interest in politics and in women's rights. Cai Zhang told Helen Foster Snow that she became interested in nationalism because of the Japanese invasion of Shandong and the 21 demands.[83] She and a friend founded the Women's Work and Study Group in Changsha and helped organise the activities of the Students' Union and the teachers' anti-Japanese association. Xiang Jingyu organised girl students of the Zhounan Girls' School and addressed many meetings calling on the people to unite and save the country. The May Fourth incident interrupted the calm student life of Deng Yingzhao and caused her to set aside her studies temporarily. She was director of the public-speaking department in a combined organisation of girl and boy students and organised the girl students and housewives of Tientsin into a patriotic society. She later recalled that this period 'prepared the ground for later activity, and the confusion of new thought at least taught us to hate the old social system of China and to struggle to change it. For myself it was a good training ground.'[84] In each case these future leaders concluded that the redefinition of the role and status of women required changes in the total socio-economic structure of society which in turn required the unity of China and above all the ousting of the foreign powers. Their experience of the May Fourth movement led them to reject the Western model for the Chinese women's movement.

This period had seen the height of Western influence but it also witnessed the beginning of a general awareness that solutions current in the West were not necessarily appropriate to social, economic and political conditions in China. The decline of both Western and Christian influences on the more radical groups such as the supporters for women's rights was marked. The pursuit of the vote seemed to be an increasingly inappropriate demand. After 1920 the potential of the democratic institutions established by the 1911 constitution seemed infinitesimal. The country was rapidly becoming an arena for competing warlords. Moreover the missionaries who had once been a more radicalising influence were proving to be a more conservative force in the atmosphere of the May Fourth movement. The activist girl students were predominantly from the government and private schools not the mission schools. The *North China Herald* was not alone in noting that it did seem as if the mission girls' schools were all too slow to join a progressive movement such as the Women's Rights League.[85] The representatives of the YWCA and WCTU might speak at their meetings and express support for their demands, but they were primarily concerned with teaching the proper care of babies, child welfare, home hygiene, home economics and inculcating the ideals of Christian love and beliefs. Mission schools and Christian organisations had been a radicalising influence but one of their explicit aims was to supply new behavioural restraints in the vacuum resulting from the breakdown of old social codes. Many students began to have a great dislike for the hypocrisy of Christians who, it was said, believed in words of kindness and charity instead of action, in prayers instead of programmes or who did a great deal of charity work among beggars and others, but ignored the Chinese who wanted to fight for their own rights.[86] There was one exception. The *North China Herald*, expressing foreign commercial interests, noted that the present women's movement should appeal to businessmen for once Chinese women get some of their rights there will be a demand for better clothes which England could provide so much better than anyone else. Merchants and manufacturers could foresee a profitable time ahead and it was deemed 'obvious that from this point of view the women's movement is to be encouraged'.[87]

There was a strong feeling amongst the Chinese that many foreign teachers misunderstood the problems of China and there was a growing realisation that they gave expression to foreign interests not only inappropriate to China but actually counter-productive to her interests. The following is an account of two schoolgirls' conversation on National Humiliation Day, the anniversary of the Japanese presentation of the 21 demands of China:

'Why don't we close the school for the day?' I asked one of my schoolmates when I heard the morning bell.
'Why?' She really had forgotten what day it was.
'Don't you know it is the day of National Shame?'
'This school never joins in such things.'
'Are we not going to join the [public] parade?'
'Of course not.'
'Why?'
'You must realise that Norway is also one of the imperialist countries. One of the slogans of the paraders is "Down with Imperialism!" Do you think the authorities would allow their students to shout "down with themselves"?'
'We must all go, no matter what happens', I shouted.
'Yes, let us all go. . . .'
'We must ask the school authorities to close the school for the day and let us remember the day of our National Shame.'[88]

For the more radical in the student, women's and labour organisations the future of their movements began to lie elsewhere than in following the example set in Western countries.

By 1925 it seemed to a small number of women activists that the future of the women's movement lay in co-operation with the new nationalist and revolutionary movement emerging in Canton. It seemed to provide the only hope of both uniting China and standing up to foreign demands and redefining the position of women. The new revolutionary movement in Canton aimed at the achievement not only of a unified and independent China, but also of an independent and emancipated womankind. After the example of the Soviet Union the revolutionary movement in Canton turned its attention not just to the status of women within society but to the socio-economic structures responsible for maintaining their dependent position. The Shanghai Women's Rights Association was one group which passed a number of resolutions in support of this new nationalist movement. One of these stated that in view of the breakdown of China by the forces of imperialism and militarism a great responsibility devolved on the women in the present national crisis. National unity was of paramount importance. The victory of the Nationalists in Canton over one of the warlord cliques, the Fengtien militarists, was viewed by the Shanghai Women's Rights Association as a victory for autonomous governments and weak and small nations. They sent a telegram to the new nationalist revolutionary movement in Canton in which they rejoiced at these victories. They said they placed their hopes for the future in the Canton movement's struggle to implement the principles of the late Dr Sun Yat-sen.[89] At the same time the Shanghai Women's Union issued a Manifesto urging women to play an active role in the new movement:

> Dear Sisters, [it said] if we really wish to free China and throw off the yoke of slavery, we must join in the grand revolutionary movement. We must not be passers-by and act in a lady-like manner of the old style. We should take notice of the present conditions of the country and of society. Current conditions make us parasites of militarism and imperialism. We must consider ourselves crusaders in the overthrow of imperialism and militarism and release our nation from slavery. Dear sisters be quick and join our revolutionary army. . . .[90]

The Manifesto concluded with the cries of 'Long Live China' and 'Long Live the Women of China'. Feminism, patriotism or nationalism and labour movements hitherto separated were to be brought together in the one analysis and struggle. Indeed the Nationalist Revolution of 1925–7 was to mark a turning point in the history of the women's movement and set it on a new path of development.

An Uneasy Alliance: Feminism and Socialism

Train quickly to become the vanguard of the people,
To wipe away the old ways and down with love.
Accomplish the Socialist Revolution, you great women!
(Revolutionary Chorus, 1926)[1]

The formation of a new revolutionary movement in Canton in the early 1920s to work for national reunification, independence and later the construction of a socialist society marked a watershed in the history of the women's movement in China. Henceforth two identifiable and interlinked forces explicitly worked towards the redefinition of the role and status of women. One was the nationalist and later socialist revolutionary movement and the other the separately organised women's movement. The combined attempts of the two movements at work among women were brought to a sudden halt in 1927, but the initial attempt to integrate the two movements is important because the theoretical basis for their integration was elaborated and a strategy marked out for the future achievement of their combined goals. On this basis the women's movement expanded to include rural and urban working women and for the first time it advocated a political solution to the 'woman's problem'. In the integration of the two movements, feminism became linked to a social alternative and the platforms and activities of the movement reflected its wider social base, but it was also apparent that the new theoretical basis and combined strategy had certain implications for the construction of the women's movement itself and its relations with the wider revolutionary movement.

The first steps in the structural integration of the women's movement into the nationalist revolutionary movement occurred during what is called the Nationalist Revolution of the mid-1920s. This step was largely inspired by the policies of the newly formed Chinese Communist Party (CCP). During the May Fourth movement several leading intellectuals had become increasingly interested in Marxism and the events of 1917 in Russia. They saw in these a possible solution to the problems facing their own country. A number of study groups were formed and discussion articles, written in radical periodicals, began to arouse popular interest among students. The First National Congress of the CCP was held in Shanghai in 1921. Here twelve delegates, representing a total of fifty or so party members, resolved that the party should be guided by Marxism-Leninism and take Bolshevism in Russia as its model. When they came to consider the position of women in China they were also influenced by analyses in European socialist literature and the separate organisation of women in the Soviet Union.

In the tradition of Marx, Engels and Bebel, Chinese Marxists turned their attention to the economic foundations of the oppression and exploitation of women and began to link their struggle to that of the proletariat against the forces of capitalism. In an article published in 1919, Li Dazhao tried to show that the oppressed condition of Chinese women was inexorably 'determined' by economic relations.[2] He thought China could learn from events in Europe during and after the First World War when circumstances had forced women into employment outside the home and then into competition with men on the job market. He found this experience to be instructive for China for it showed how women at work were compelled to unite in their own interest and how employment had brought them into direct economic relations and the struggle against capitalism. Other intellectuals such as Dai Jitao in his article 'Similarities between the Emancipation of Workers and the Women's Emancipation Movement',[3] and Chen Duxiu in 'The Woman Problem and Socialism'[4] began to identify the liberation of women and that of the urban workers as the two greatest problems in contemporary Chinese society. They linked the two. They saw that the problem of women had two sides for not only were women generally oppressed by men but women workers also shared the oppression of the men of their class. Not only did they view women as one of a number of oppressed groups from whom they could draw support, but the changing position of women was to be an index or symbol of the general historical and social progress. They quoted the words of Marx: 'the degree of the emancipation of women is the natural measure of general emancipation.'[5]

The Communist Party was founded at a time when the Soviet leaders in Russia were giving considerable attention to the legal rights and organisation of women there. In 1918 a new law had provided for free choice of marriage partner, the legal equality of husband and wife in all spheres and the right to divorce. Alexandra Kollontai who for many years devoted herself to improving the position of women in Russia had long advocated the creation of a separate women's section within the Communist Party.[6] After twelve years of struggle her efforts were realised when the first Congress of Peasant and Working Women was held in November 1918 and attended by 1,000 delegates. Here, in a much-quoted speech, Lenin formally assessed the role of women in the revolutionary struggle in Russia. He argued that:

> There can be no socialist revolution, unless a vast section of the toiling women takes an important part in it. . . . It has been observed in the experience of all liberation movements that the success of a revolution depends on the extent to which women take part in it. The Soviet Government is doing everything to enable women to carry on their proletarian socialist activity independently.[7]

Here he emphasised one aim of the Soviet Republic which was to abolish all restrictions on the rights of women and establish socialism in order that women might be 'fully free and emancipated'. At the Congress, too, a special committee was set up to help women to understand their new rights and to teach them how to use them. The task of the newly founded working women's movement was to make 'politics available to every working woman and bring women into general productive labour'. In establishing a special and separate organisation to change the 'unpolitical, unsocial, backward psychology of women, their isolated sphere of activity and the entire manner of their life', the Communist Party of the Soviet Union was setting a precedent.[8]

From the first the Chinese Communist Party made the emancipation of women one of its policy platforms. Its First Manifesto on the 'Current Situation in China' issued in 1922 made 'equality in the rights of men and women' one of its immediate aims.[9] A year later the Party formally recognised the unlimited right of all to vote regardless of sex, the need for protection of female labour and the necessity to abolish all legislation restricting to women.[10] Above all the CCP thought that it was the social structure resting on a particular economic base which was responsible for their present position. Hence the need to organise women as a part of the wider revolutionary movement. In 1923 the Women's Section of the CCP was established to recruit women to work in their own and in the wider revolutionary movement. This marked the first attempt by a political party in China to arouse and *organise* women as a separate social category. The task of establishing a women's section was largely delegated to Xiang

Jingyu who was the ninth of twelve children born into a big merchant family in the province of Hunan. In 1915 she had graduated from one of the most progressive girls' schools in China, the Zhounan Girls' School in Hunan, where she was an active leader in the May Fourth movement.[11] She had made numerous public speeches calling upon people to 'unite and save the country' and according to one of her friends 'always completely forgot herself in her work' and consequently suffered from overwork and exhaustion. She had founded and taught at a co-educational primary school, led an anti-footbinding campaign, and she and Cai Zhang organised a women's work-study group in Changsha. In 1919 she and several of her friends from this group went to France on a 'part work, part study' programme. Xiang Jingyu simul- taneously attended a French-language school and worked first in a rubber plant and later in a textile mill. She joined a student discussion group to study Marx and Lenin, anarchism, socialism and the events in Russia. On her return to China in 1922 she joined the Communist Party, and at the Party's Second National Congress in May 1922 she was elected a member of the Central Committee and head of the Women's Department.

She outlined her views in articles such as 'Three Types of Women Intellectuals in China', 'Recent Developments in the Chinese Women's Movement' and 'Three Points for the Shanghai Society for Women's Rights'. In these she published her critique of the previous isolated and 'feminist only' tendencies of the women's movement.[12] She saw no future in a movement which conceived of the struggle as primarily that of women versus men or the pursuit of individual happiness within a monogamous family and had for its platforms the 'vote', 'individual liberty' and 'free love'. She noted that organisations with these platforms generally lacked wider support and their activities were largely confined to holding meetings, passing motions, sending circular telegrams and petition- ing the government. She argued that to demand women's rights without fighting to change the social system and safeguard the future of the country would lead nowhere. She thought that a few women participating in the government could not of itself bring about change. Women would still remain exploited and oppressed by domestic reactionaries and imperialists and remain without legal protection of their rights. The present social position of women was founded in the existing social system, and only change in the latter could improve the position of the former. She therefore advocated making the women's movement a part of the overall political movement, calling on women to join in the struggle to overthrow imperialist and reactionary rule as a first step in their emancipation. She sharply criticised the suffragettes for not having 'the courage to take part in the real political movement—the national revolutionary movement—the prerequisite to the movement for women's rights and suffrage'.[13] On the contrary, she said, they collude in the politics which are the obstacle to their own goals. She held study meetings for a 'group of professional and independent women who were willing to work for society' at which she spent much time explaining the teachings of Marx and Lenin. One of her friends remembers how she often talked of the oppression of women and especially that of the women workers. She usually concluded the meetings with the reminder that only when intellectual women combine with women workers will they be able to understand their position and the women's movement become a movement of all women.[14]

A number of magazines were published by the Communist Party for female factory workers to interest them in their own struggle. Among them were *Labour and Women* and the more vigorous *Women's Voice*. The goal of the latter was the liberation of women of the oppressed classes and their recruitment into the labour movement. Its patience with those who dwelt on the topics of love, hairbobs and styles of dress was short. The journal often called on the 'awakened intellectual women' to arouse female workers and stressed the need for consciousness and organisation among them. 'No matter what the conditions, organisation is necessary. Before you have control and power you must have organisation.'[15] A newspaper article noted that Bolshevism appeared not to be unwelcome among the women of Guangdong province and the Women's Association of the CCP increased in numbers from 100,000 in 1925 to 300,000 in 1927.[16] Although the Women's Association of the Communist Party remained a tightly knit and separate organisation of women party members, it worked alongside and within the Women's Department of the Guomindang Party from 1923.

When in 1923 the Guomindang Party under the leadership of Sun Yat-sen entered into an alliance with the emerging Communist Party, both parties agreed that 'the chief and immediate aim of China is the achievement of national unity and national independence'.[17] The Communists thought that the working class in China was not as yet 'sufficiently differentiated as an absolutely independent force' and therefore it was necessary to combine the activities of the Guomindang with those of the newly established Communist Party.[18] Sun Yat-sen on his part was hopeful that by working alongside the Communist Party his party would secure Soviet aid in the arduous and urgent task of eliminating warlordism. Individual Communists joined the Guomindang Party and they, with the help of Russian advisers, convinced Sun Yat-sen that what the Guomindang Party needed was a disciplined party organisation and a popular movement of support among peasants, workers and women. The new nationalist alliance favoured a greatly accelerated growth of the women's movement in China. As one foreign observer noted this was in no small degree due to the attitude of the new revolutionary leaders towards women 'for they seem to feel that the problem of improving the conditions of Chinese womanhood is one of the most important problems of the Revolution'.[19] At the First National Party Congress held in Canton in 1924, several women were elected to the Central Executive Committee of the Guomindang Party (GMD). The Manifesto issued at this First Congress clearly stated that 'in law, in commerce, in education and in society, the principle of equality between the two sexes shall be recognised and the development of rights of women was to be promoted.'[20] In the same year, the GMD at a second Representative Congress adopted several resolutions. The first group were legal:

1 To enact laws regarding equality between the two sexes.
2 To fix the right for women to inherit property.
3 To prohibit trade in persons.
4 To protect women who escape from marriage because of oppression.
5 To enact marriage laws based on the principles of free marriage and free divorce.
6 To enact labour laws for women based on the principles of same pay for same work, of protection of womanhood and of child labour.

The second group were headed 'political':

1 To elevate the standard of female education.
2 To emphasise education for women labourers and peasant women.
3 To admit women for employment into government organisations.
4 To admit women for employment into business organisations.

5 To establish nationwide day nurseries and orphanages for children.[21]

Two women, He Xiangning and Song Qingling (Soong Chingling), who had worked for the Guomindang Party since its early days, were both elected to its Central Executive Committee. They were both especially committed to improving the position of women. Soong Qingling, one of the three Song sisters, was married to Sun Yat-sen and was herself an enthusiastic worker in support of the Nationalist Alliance. For several years she had pointed out that the fight for the vote as waged by women in Europe and America was largely irrelevant in China. She had worked in Shanghai among factory women and thought that women should participate in the national revolution for two reasons: first to work together with the men of China for an independent nation, and second to work for their own freedom.[22] The exclusive struggle between the sexes only ignored the class differences among women. In one of her early speeches she noted that:

> Women must fight not only against male oppression, but against female oppression also. It is incongruous for us to be fighting against oppression from men and at the same time oppress other members of our own sex. As long as there are slave girls in China, women must join together to work for their emancipation. And as long as the working women are oppressed, the fight for women's freedom must be carried on. These oppressions grind down the women of China as much as do the injustices that are 'women's lot' because they find themselves today in a man-made world.[23]

He Xiangning was the wife of Sun Yat-sen's closest and most trusted friend, Liao Zhongkai. She had been one of the first woman workers in the old Guomindang Party and after a prolonged exile of some years in Japan she and her husband returned to Canton in 1923. He Xiangning headed the Women's Department of the Guomindang Party which was established in Canton in 1923.

After the alliance of the two parties, women from both the CCP and Guomindang Parties worked together in the Women's Department or Section of the Guomindang to organise women in support of agreed demands. He Xiangning described the purpose of the Women's Department as drawing women into active participation in the Revolution and to obtain from the Nationalist Government recognition of the rights of women. The priorities were clear. Revolution and a unified China first and women's freedom second.[24] The main task of the Department seems to have been the education and training of women leaders. The Women's Department established a special girls' school to train women to establish and lead the organisations of women. The schools usually offered a three-month preparation course, and on the completion of training, girls were appointed as special delegates or propagandists and sent out to the various provinces and districts to arouse the interest of women in their rights and organise women's unions. To aid the creation of women's collective consciousness and build up solidarity among women, 8 March was set aside as Women's Day. This date had originally been declared 'International Working Women's Day' in 1910 at the suggestion of Clara Zetkin at the International Conference of Socialist Women in Copenhagen. It was to be a day for women the world over to unite and fight for their emancipation. In 1924 the Women's Department for the Guomindang organised a parade and rally in the First Park in Canton. In celebration of Women's Day a small band mostly of women students and workers assembled to shout 'Down with imperialism', 'Down with warlords', 'Same work, same pay', 'Prohibit the buying of slave girls', 'Abolish polygamy' and 'Equal education'.[25] By 1927 it was estimated that the Women's Day Parade in Canton had swollen to 25,000 women.[26] It was demonstrations such as these which caused the Canton-based *China Weekly Review* to remark that women seemed to be one of several special groups, alongside students, factory workers, and peasants, who were being organised by the nationalist revolutionary movement.[27]

Although the women representatives of the two parties in the Women's Section worked together in support of similar goals some differences in the orientation of their strategies were apparent. An American journalist attended a meeting of the Executive Committee of the Women's Section and noticed some disagreement between the representatives of the Communist Party and Guomindang on the role of mass meetings and women's organisations in 'swiftly educating women to take a part in politics with their husbands in building up a new government'.[28] She noted that the younger members, mostly Communists, tended to be impatient with the caution of the older women who felt that women could not be awakened quickly for custom is 'three thousand years strong'. He Xiangning thought that the best way to arouse women outside Canton was to organise Women's Red Cross for 'every women knows her duty to care for the wounded, raise money for hospitals and open factories for disabled soldiers'. She thought that 'to these needs even women of ancient customs will be responsive'. The Communist girls disagreed. They thought that the oppression of peasant and working women was such that they would quickly respond and be active in working to forward their rights. They tended to concentrate on organising the peasant and factory women workers into local women's associations while the women members of the Guomindang (Kuomintang) Party tended to concentrate on formulating the demands, the education of women and co-ordinating the activities of the Guangdong Women's Association.

According to the Manifesto of the Guangdong Provincial Women's Association it was formed 'to unite women of all walks of life in the province and to articulate their strength for the thorough emancipation of women, and to participate in the revolution of the people for China's true freedom and democracy.'[29] A visitor to Canton, after attending one of its meetings, tells how greatly impressed she was by the 'order and efficiency with which the meeting was conducted'.[30] There were 100 delegates representing some 65 women's organisations. They included workers, students, teachers, physicians, nurses, telephone operators, business women and soldiers' wives. They were discussing a petition which was to be presented to the Guangdong Provincial Assembly. The petition reflected the interests of a wide-ranging section of the population. They demanded equal rights for women in law, politics, economics, education and property inheritance. Women were to be granted freedom of marriage and divorce, equal opportunities to enter government organisations and concubinage was to be prohibited. Equal pay and equal treatment, protection of women workers and the establishment of nurseries were demanded in the interests of the factory women. A women's educational institute and mass education programmes were especially demanded for peasant women and prostitution was to be abolished. Prostitutes were to be given the opportunity to train for an occupation. The Women's Provincial Association gave its support to a petition presented by the Women's Department of the Guomindang calling on the Party to admit women to a greater share in the posts at central, provincial and municipal levels. The Provincial Assembly was later to grant all the points in both petitions.

It seemed to one foreign observer that 'perhaps for the first time the real importance of the industrial and peasant women is being recognised',[31] and one area in which women workers of the Communist Party worked among the peasant and factory-working women was in the Hailofeng area of Guangdong province.[32] There they had some success in organising a General Women's Union for the district. After some months it was estimated to have more than 1,000 peasants, students, teachers and factory-worker members whose ages ranged from 12 to 30 years. The concubines of rich men, who though sharing in their wealth had no rights or protection, were said to be prominent in the leadership of the union, but it was the factory girls who were described as the most determined members. They brought the benefits of their previous experience of collective organisation in the trade unions to the women's unions and took the lead in its activities. For some time trade unions had been organised in the small private factories for weaving, papermaking, umbrella-making and other small industries which had been established by the governor of the province. In some of the textile industries nearly all the workers were women and they had organised separately in support of better working conditions. The general women's unions undertook the defence of the newly stated rights of women as defined by the nationalist revolutionary movement, investigated petitions for divorce and organised women to aid the Nationalist armies in first-aid, transportation and intelligence. Individual members could call on the union to intervene in cases of cruel treatment from their families or husbands and according to one committed participant this mediation was effective in attracting wider support. In the rural areas of Hailofeng district, women tended to join the peasant unions which were unusual in that they were made up of separate men's and women's unions. In fact, the Hailofeng Women's Peasant Union was said to be the first such union in China and about a quarter of the 7,000 members of the joint union were estimated to be women. Their experience in Hailofeng and other rural areas led the Communist Party to formally adopt its own resolutions on the women's movement:

1 In Party work among women emphasis must be laid on carrying the activities to the common people.
2 Though women workers constitute the backbone of the women's movement, women students are also important, for they are the bridge between the party and women workers, and an equally important influence in breaking up thoughts

and habits of the traditional familistic society.

3 Peasant women occupy a very important position in China's women's movement and it is necessary to train leaders for this branch of work.

4 Women's publications must be in simple and popular style, emphasising the intimate experience of women's own suffering and practical needs.

5 Efforts must be made to increase women Party members and to develop leaders for the women's movement.[33]

To expand the women's movement beyond the boundaries of the Guangdong province, girl students were trained in special schools to join the 'propagandist teams'. The teams were attached to the Nationalist armies which were formed to break the power of the regional warlords in central and northern China. Their northwards march from Canton to the great central valley of the Yangtze river in 1926 is usually known as the Northern Expedition. It was led by the young military commander, Chiang Kai-shek, but it was not just a military manoeuvre for it was also to be a carefully prepared and planned political movement to arouse peasants, workers and women in support of its wider objectives. In the wake of the Northern Expedition to the Yangtze valley women's unions were organised in the villages and the towns. Three or four hundred girl propagandists travelled with the army on its northward march from Canton. They had bobbed hair, wore trousers, military jackets, belts and caps. A few of the girls were interviewed by the American journalist, Anna Louise Strong, about their work. 'We travel behind the army,' one of them said, 'but we take no part in fighting. Nor do we work among the soldiers; they have men propagandists for such work. Of course, when we see wounded men, we do all we can to help them for they are our brothers. We give them a fan or a towel; we urge peasants to carry them to hospitals, sometimes we go to the local hospitals, if there are any, to get places for them.' But this they admitted was not their real work. 'We are attached to the Political Department of the army, which organises the first provisional civil government in the new territory. Our work is to organise the women. For this we go into the homes and markets, wherever women are to be found, and talk with them.' They told her how they approached peasant women:

We explain first the difference between the northern troops and our revolutionary forces. We tell them we came to save them

from oppression and to bring a new way of thinking. We explain
that men and women are now equal. Even though you are a
woman you are still a person. We say they have a duty to society
and not only to husbands. It is a good thing to ask advice of
parents about your marriage, but not to let parents decide
everything concerning it. We explain the new doctrine of free
choice in marriage, that young folks have the right to select their
own life partners. We also explain that, by the new law, women
may inherit property, and we say that the feet of young girls
must not be bound.[34]

As soon as they had aroused a few score women in their support
they formed a local women's union, and left the task of further
organisation to the Women's Department and provincial women's
associations.

In Hunan province a wide network of women's unions were
established in this manner.[35] The Liling county association of
women was reported to have at least fifty branch unions with more
than 6,000 members by December 1926. Special classes to train
women cadres in the women's movement were soon established in
some of the counties of the province. Participants in the 35-day
courses heard lectures on problems related to the peasant
movement and women's liberation and were at the same time given
some military training. Some county associations of women
published their own text books. *Problems of Women in China*
was one of the books published in Liling county. Its main aim was
to draw attention to the influence of ancient ethical codes on the
lives of women which had kept them 'from achieving political and
economic independence'. The women's unions in several counties in
Hunan drew public attention to their cause on Women's Day in
1927. The *Hunan People's Gazette* reported the demonstrations and
meetings. In describing a meeting in one county it wrote that 'after
the speeches, women from many walks of life demonstrated in the
streets shouting the following slogans: Women Unite; The Rural
Women's Movement is the Core of the Women's Movement;
Absolute Freedom for Women in Marriage and Divorce; Smash the
Old Ethical Code; Promote a National Women's Organisation;
and Long Live Women's Liberation'. 'Most outstanding,' the
paper observed, was the fact that the demonstration was held in the
rain on muddy, slippery streets, 'with the demonstrators all
wearing straw sandals'—a far cry from the bound feet of the
past.

The girl propagandists and armies of the Northern Expedition were also welcomed by some women of the large cities of Wuchang and Hankou in neighbouring Hubei province. A poster pasted on the city wall of Wuchang city illustrated the reputation which the nationalist revolutionary movement had acquired and expressed the rising hopes and expectations of at least one group of women in that city:

> We women of Hubei for several thousand years have suffered under political, economic and legal oppression. Propriety, traditions, and all sorts of social conventions and customs have bound us. Long ago we lost our rights as humans. From whom has this suffering come? It was because we ourselves didn't apply ourselves, we didn't know how to unite and strive and fight for our rights as humans. At the same time the sphere of darkness meant oppression for us, like a deep root that couldn't be budged. So for several thousand years we were mere things, useless things in society.
>
> Now that the revolution has extended to Hubei, and the national government committees have come, we want to welcome them, because they are the people's officials, because they have given the people freedom from suffering, and because they seek the people's good. Our suffering was so very deep that we have limitless hope in these officials, we believe that they will give us economic and political equality with the men, that they will revise the unequal laws, and that they will do away with all laws that harm or hinder women, and will protect the rights of women; that they will rid us of the terrible bondage of traditions and customs, and all the bad things that have bound women. We especially believe that, following the plans of the Guomindang, this government can help women to have utter equality, economically, politically and legally with the men.
>
> Fellow women of Hubei! This is our chance to seek freedom and equality. A thousand times over we don't want to lose this opportunity. In the midst of this political freedom we want to spread our organisation. We want to foster our ability so that we can stand under our banner of the Women's Movement. . . .'[36]

Song Qingling (Soong Chingling) later related how, during the first fortnight she was in nearby Hankou, groups of young women students came to her to ask how they could aid the work of the Guomindang and help their sisters in developing a new woman-hood in China that 'would be cognizant of the new temper of the times, politically conscious and free'.[37] However, the girl propagandists did not meet with the same reception everywhere.

In the rural areas away from the influence of the larger cities, the girl propagandists met with a cooler reception. In the villages of Honan province the uniformed, bob-haired and natural-footed girls contrasted strongly with the peasant women who were confined to the domestic domain, their feet still bound and who could still be exchanged with impunity. After two months of intensive campaigning only 2,000 members were enrolled in the women's unions and ultimately the girl propagandists had to be withdrawn because of the reaction their 'scandalous' appearance aroused.[38] Women leaders active in Henan deplored the situation there. In contrast with the progress of women elsewhere in China over the past twenty years they thought that:

> This Henan of ours is an interior province and unresponsive to popular opinion. The literate, and those men in authority, are still imbued with the age-long prejudice against women having any standing in society, and lord it over us as in the bad old days. The women, on their part, only take thought for study and manage their personal affairs and care nothing for such questions as the enfranchisement of their sisters. Those of us who advocate women's rights are like a voice crying to the clouds, and Honan, drugged by old customs, neither listens or hears.[39]

They went on to deplore the small progress that had been made despite a certain amount of propaganda and the fact that work among women was not altogether neglected. 'We honor the pioneers in this movement, but as a great house cannot be built with one beam, and no great work can be accomplished by one person, neither can the great task that has fallen to our lot be successfully carried on by a minority of the female population.'

During the Northern Expedition it was Hankou, a city on the Yangtze River in Hubei province, which became the base of the more radical elements of the nationalist revolutionary movement after the Communists and left-wing of the Guomindang Party separated from the Guomindang Party led by Chiang Kai-shek. After Hankou was taken by the Nationalist armies in September 1926 a women's department for the province of Hubei was established there and soon a flourishing women's movement was in evidence. This department set out to initiate a number of reforms, train women leaders, organise a network of local unions in Hubei and send girl propagandists into the neighbouring provinces of Hunan and Henan. Not long after its establishment, regulations were passed providing that women should be included among the jurors in all cases where female prisoners were tried. It drafted and promulgated a comprehensive list of radical reforms similar to those passed previously at the Second Congress of the Guomindang Party. Their provisions included the right of women to petition for a divorce, to obtain alimony in divorce proceedings initiated by the husband, protection for oppressed daughters-in-law and maid-servants, the emancipation of prostitutes, the rights of inheritance and prohibitions against the selling of women.[40] To direct the activities and channel the energies of eager but unprepared women, a girls' school for politics was opened at which the curriculum consisted of studies in the history of the Guomindang Party, 'revolutionary techniques' and the women's movement. The course was attended by 100–150 girls who were mostly middle-school graduates, lasted six months and was intended to prepare revolutionary leaders and organisers of the women's movement.[41] A new military college was established for girls in Wuchang across the river from Hankou. This school offered a twelve-month course for girl 'propagandists' who travelled with the army. Many of the girls escaped from intolerable domestic situations to attend either the political school and become workers in the women's movement or the military school with a view to becoming girl propagandists. Xie Bingying was one such girl who escaped from such a 'fate' and entered the military school for girls. She kept a diary which was later published in serial form in the newspapers.[42]

Xie Bingying was the daughter of an official who had been educated in Changsha, a centre of progressive ideas during the May Fourth movement. She had been much taken with the idea of the freedom of the individual to love and the concept of romance until her second elder brother sternly brought her to task. His words were to linger long in her memory:

'You woman, what a worthless creature you are! The bloody bell of the time has been sounded, and you are still snoring loudly in your dreams. Such stories of handsome young men and beautiful maidens should have been thrown away long ago, there is no meaning in them. The one is just like the other. You are an awakened woman and you used to like the new literature. Why don't you read some revolutionary works?'[43]

He gave her *The A.B.C. of Communism*, and an *Elementary*

Treatise on Socialism to read and under their influence and the urgent need to leave the city of Changsha to escape from the near prospect of an arranged marriage, she left her home town determined to enter the military school in Wuchang. She described her sentiments on arrival at the school. It seemed to mark the beginning of a new life, of a bright new future. 'Every one of us was crazy, intoxicated, singing and jumping about.' Later at night she wrote, 'When a person becomes too happy or too excited, she is unable to go to sleep all night. Her mind is full of thoughts, just like millions of sparks dancing around her—in the quiet of the night I would have liked to shout and jump about!'[44] Her motives for entering the school had been mixed. She supported the aims of the revolutionary movement but at the same time she saw it as the solution to all her personal problems. It had enabled her to escape from an arranged marriage. 'Where could she go, a girl under twenty years of age and without half a piece of cash to bless herself with?' She thought that nine out of every ten of the girl students at the college had initially wanted to join the army to get away from family situations. They had all searched for an avenue of escape. But she also thought that the moment they came to school and put on their uniforms of grey cotton, their ideas became less self-centred. They became aware of the 1,250 million oppressed people, the responsibility for whom they were taking on their shoulders. The dual aims were reflected in a speech made at a parade by one of her class-mates:

> My schoolmates and my sisters, when we decided to join the army, we decided to sacrifice ourselves. We severed relations with our families to serve the Revolution. Our aim was not only to save our suffering selves but also the oppressed masses. Especially when we girls joined the army it was a history-making event without any precedent. Since the Government gave an equal chance to the girls, enabling us to work for the nation and for society, it has been a blessing to women.[45]

The sense of urgency and enthusiasm with which she describes their new single-minded devotion to the Nationalist cause is typical of the writings of the participants. 'As soon as we had learned to sing the chorus of the Revolutionary song called "Struggle", everyone of us liked to hum the chorus:

> Train quickly to become the vanguard of the people,
> To wipe away the old ways, and down with love,
> Accomplish the Socialist Revolution, you great women.[46]

Every time they sang the phrase, 'Down with love', she said, 'we would always shout especially loudly, as if we wanted to warn all our friends that during the time of our mission we were not going to give any thought to love.' Indeed they considered personal love to be a private and selfish affair, a plaything entirely belonging to the idle rich and of no consequence. They felt their most urgent task was revolution in which they had placed their future and happiness. She said they were ready to sacrifice their lives in order to create a future society which could be enjoyed by all members of society. For 'unless the old system was completely shattered, womankind could never be freed'.[47]

The Hankou Women's Union undertook the protection of women's rights and the organisation of women in their support within that city's boundaries. An American journalist visited the Hankou Women's Union in 1927. She was received by two pink-and-white costumed girls of about twenty-five years of age who were the secretaries of the union. There were ten such secretaries, all unpaid except for one 'recording secretary' who got $5 (gold) a month and her board and room for being constantly on duty. There were six departments of work: administration, social recreation, propaganda, organisation and the treasury. Departments co-operated to launch special campaigns. They had a budget of $50 (gold) a month from which to pay rent, servants, handbills and food for the secretaries. There were seven district women's unions in Hankou, with a total membership of more than 3,000 women though fewer actually paid their dues.[48] The union undertook a campaign to provide educational opportunities for women. The demands in this respect included the following goals:

1 To give relief to ignorant women and educate them.
2 To organise reading committees and to give vocational education to ignorant women if possible.
3 To educate ignorant women until they can read and write.
4 To ask for funds for the work from the educational organs of various places.
5 Those interested in educational affairs are expected to open schools for women, or write to the Women's Union, which may urge the government to open the schools.

This educational campaign was closely followed by the proclamation of a radical bill of rights for women. It sought to protect women's rights and prevent their sale and exchange:

Art. 1 With reference to divorce, the decision of the court
       should be based on the following points:

1 If a wife seeks divorce, and the husband is unwilling to break
the marriage contract, she may, if she has proper grounds,
secure a decree, and remarry in accordance with the resolution
adopted by the Second National Delegates' Conference. She
may ask the local court to base its decision on this principle.

2 If a husband seeks to divorce a wife who cannot support
herself, the man must continue to support his divorced wife
until such time as she may remarry or no longer need his
assistance.

3 The wives and concubines of the wealthy who are often
mistreated, may appeal for legal release and secure alimony
if the decree is granted.

Art. 2 A young daughter-in-law who is cared for by her
       husband's parents, may ask the local Women's Union to
       make an investigation in case of ill-treatment. The
       local court may give her legal aid by fining her husband's
       parents or by censuring them.

Art. 3 With reference to the emancipation of oppressed
       maidservants there are three regulations, as follows:

1 If a maidservant is cruelly treated by her master, the local
peasants' union may ask the local court to cancel the contract
so that she may return to her family or her guardians, or the
local court may find a better master for her—one who can pay
her for services.

2 If a maidservant is beaten or injured by her master, the judge
of the court should order the master to pay the medical fees.

3 A master cannot take his maidservant as his concubine. If the
maidservant is under the age of fifteen, the master may choose
a husband for her if she agrees with his choice.

Art. 4 Prostitutes should be emancipated from the oppression
       of their procuresses. In order to extend legal assistance to
       them, the local court may fine the oppressor or cancel the
       slavish contract so that the oppressed may marry or find
       some other work.

Art. 5 With reference to the selling of an oppressed woman as a
       wife or to a house of prostitution, when such cases are
       detected by the Women's Union, the unscrupulous sellers
       will be severely punished by the court. Similar
       punishment shall be given to those who sell widows or
       orphan girls.

Art. 6

1 The right of inheritance in acquiring property of deceased persons should be extended to women as announced by the administrative organs.
2 The only daughter has the right of inheritance in acquiring the property of her deceased father. None other can acquire it unless he has obtained the will of the deceased.
3 The son or the daughter of a widow has the full right to acquire his or her mother's property. If a widow does not want to remarry, the family of her deceased husband should give her a pension, if they can afford to.[49]

The women's union in Hankou gave practical support to women in support of these rights and constituted itself the protector of women in all kinds of difficulties. There were numerous cases of young girls sold into prostitution by their parents, of newly wedded or widowed daughters-in-law and ill-treated slave girls who ran away to the women's union for protection. One young prostitute who wanted to leave the brothel and marry the man of her choice was thwarted in her attempts by the 'matron of the house'. Under old Chinese custom the owner's rights would have been supported by the police, but the women's union to whom she fled, took the case into court and secured her legal release.[50] Another case involved a widowed daughter-in-law who, learning of the intention of her deceased husband's parents to sell her, ran away to the women's union.[51] Others escaped to the union offices on the eve of an arranged marriage. The unions often investigated cases of alleged ill-treatment of slave girls who turned to them for protection. While Anna Louise Strong was visiting the union headquarters she found six slave girls, all suffering from physical blows, sheltering there. The women's unions formed a new avenue of escape and their influence came to be feared. One of the slave girls recounted a conversation with her mistress before she ran away. Her mistress who beat her every day had accused the slave girl of going about and telling people of her ill-treatment: 'she tied me up and beat me all over my body. I said: I will go for help to the women's union. . . . My mistress said: If you shame me before the women's union, I will get you back and cut you in little pieces.'[52] In the cases where wives were ill-treated, the union would generally try and persuade the husband to be more considerate and kind, but if a husband refused to mend his ways the union supported a divorce petition. The unions supported many women in divorce proceedings and divorce announcements began to appear in the public press. For example, Dang Yu inserted a notice informing that:

> Under the pressure of family autocracy I married Lo Shangding, to whom I never bowed my head. Happily the Nationalist armies have come and raised women's rights so I hereby announce that I have secured judgment from their courts for a permanent divorce. I announce this in order to stop any interference with my liberty from the relatives of my husband.[53]

The women's union in Hankou adopted a quasi-judicial role and held divorce hearings on its own authority and granted divorces without formal court trials. The women's union also assumed the right to punish husbands and mothers-in-law for cruelty to wives and such punishments sometimes took a very public form. On one occasion the guilty partner was forced to take part in a degrading procession through the streets. He was compelled to wear a dunce-cap and shout slogans advocating women's freedom. Erring husbands were sometimes publicly humiliated in the streets by local women's unions while their families stood by angry, desperate, helpless before the powerful women's unions.

At the height of the Nationalist Revolution more than $1\frac{1}{2}$ million women in over ten provinces were estimated to be members of some association under the leadership of the Nationalists,[54] and the open and collective rejection of past taboos seems to have generated a powerful sisterhood. The deliberate break with ancient customs long revered by the rest of the community separated off and bound these girls into one and isolated them from the rest of the community. The rejection of old values required courage, energy and resolution and it was these characteristics which were commented on by contemporary observers of events in the larger cities, and especially in Hankou, in 1926–7. The more conservative *North China Herald* reported the exhilaration and optimism of the women celebrating Women's Day in 1927 in Hankou.[55] It described the thousands of bound-footed factory women and 7- to 9-year-old girls from the local mills dressed in blue cotton coolie cloth and wearing union badges who hobbled in procession alongside students and women representatives from public bodies. Nationalist and feminist banners were held aloft throughout the women's ranks with slogans calling for freedom for women, equal rights and wages with men and pledging support for the Guomindang and Nationalist movement. In the afternoon a women's mass meeting was attended by thousands of women workers, students and representatives of all classes who were described by the newspaper as 'eager, enthusiastic and almost inspired'. A conference of women delegates in Hubei province was held in Hankou at the same time. The conference speakers spoke of the 'tide of emancipation from age-long oppression' and compared their struggle to that of feminists the world over for equality and freedom. Foreign observers certainly felt themselves to be in the presence of a movement of extraordinary momentum and of far-reaching consequences. Anna Louise Strong, who was greatly impressed by the spirit of the women's movement, noted that there was such enthusiasm against footbinding in one cotton mill in the British concession in Hankou that the streets were at one time littered with bandages which the women in their haste had torn off there and then.[56] Another observer forecast that 'the year 1927 will probably go down in Chinese history as a record year of the women's movement',[57] and one witness of events in Hankou described the streets there as 'full of women imbued with the new spirit of independence and enthusiasm'.[58] He wrote with some foresight that:

> The success of the Nationalist Revolution is not yet by any means assured, and the progress of the women's movement will surely be hindered; at intervals it may be temporarily arrested; but it cannot be reversed—the ideals conceived cannot be obliterated. Whatever the fate in store for the Nationalist government, it may be that historians of the future will find that the greatest and most permanent achievement to its credit has been the promotion of the women's movement.[59]

The combined strategy worked out by the women's movement and the wider revolutionary movement to redefine the position of women was shortlived in the mid-1920s, but the structured integration of the women's movement into the wider revolutionary movement affected the internal development of the women's movement and its relations with the wider revolutionary movement. The expansion of the women's movement into rural areas and factories was applauded for broadening its social base, but it also raised a number of problems for the leaders of the women's movement in the cities. Many of them found it hard not to be dismayed or discouraged by the very magnitude of the task facing them. There were times when it seemed to the women leaders that the weight of tradition and custom was almost overpowering. Song Qingling spoke of the difficulties facing women leaders in 1927:

Today Chinese women are emerging. To the outsider it seems wholly miraculous. But although we, who are working for the emancipation of Chinese women, recognise the miracle that makes this rebirth at all possible at the same time we recognise the stupendous difficulties involved. The whole weight of traditional forces is against us, traditional international forces, traditional economic forces, and, in addition, traditional social and family forces. It is not easy to be a leader of Chinese women today! We are beset not only by the obstacles in the way of national and economic emancipation, but also disapproval of the conservative classes who feel that a woman's life should be spent as it has been always spent, either in the drawing room or in the kitchen of the house of her lord. [60]

The platforms of the women's movement raised fundamental and sensitive questions involving traditional and intimate relations within the family and their mere proclamation was often enough to arouse strong opposition from both men and women. Above all the establishment of a network of mutually supportive women's unions relied primarily on the participation and commitment of the women themselves in each city, town and village. Beyond the cities and their near environs the women's movement found itself for the first time face-to-face with the problems of arousing women's consciousness to an awareness of their real position in society. In the villages of Honan such had been the initial antagonism that the strategy of the girl propagandists engendered, that they had had to be withdrawn after a few months of intensive work. There was a new awareness of the immense challenge facing the women's movement and the need to work out a variety of approaches in arousing women to a consciousness of a wider social role and recognition of their rights. There was to be no easy or quick solution to the problem of redefining the position of women. Moreover the members of the women's movement, defined initially on the basis of their sex, did not form a unified social category, rather they were divided by class and generation.

The expansion of the women's movement often brought many young educated girls and professional women into contact with factory and peasant working women, slave girls and prostitutes. They often had to overcome their own class prejudices and cope with the considerable opposition of their parents and teachers. Four young girl propagandists asked the American journalist Anna Louise Strong more than once if she shared the disapproval of their former mission schoolteachers who opposed their contacts with peasant women. One of them said, 'Tell me, do you think it is right for us, as forerunners of the women's movement, to give special emphasis to women of the very lowest classes, since they are the most oppressed?' They went on to specifically mention prostitutes rescued from houses into which they had been sold and slave girls who escaped to the women's union for protection. 'Our parents and teachers all say,' they continued, 'that it is wrong for us to walk alone in the streets like men, and to talk with such people and fight for them. They say that because we do these things we also are "lost women".'[61] They were torn between shame from customary censures and the knowledge that it was precisely these types of girls who needed help more than anyone else. The enthusiasm for the revolutionary and women's movements was not always shared by the older women and there was a tendency for the women's union to become the monopoly of the young. The members of the Hailofeng Women's Union were all under 30.[62] Not surprisingly, the older generation, the mothers-in-law who had at last gained a position of relative respect and authority in the household, felt threatened by the women's union to whom defiant daughters-in-law, slave girls, and concubines could turn for protection. The establishment of a power base alternative to the household threatened the hegemony of the mother-in-law and the enthusiasm with which the young members embraced the cause of the women's movement tended to widen the generation gap. Notions of love and free choice of marriage partner directly threatened the position of the elder generation and horrified them beyond all bounds.

The tactics or strategy adopted by the younger members of the women's movement often ignored the whole process of education and they prematurely forced the symbols of emancipation on other women. In the 1920s bobbed hair, the symbol of the 'new woman', was sometimes imposed on unsuspecting older women. According to the dean of the Women's School for Revolution in Hankou this action was greatly resented by the older women and was the cause of complaints which poured in from the country districts.[63] It was reported that women even committed suicide as a result of the ensuing shame. Time and again the women's union in Hankou sent word to all the local women's unions that the question of cutting hair was purely a personal matter and no one had the right to cut another's hair by force. It was pointed out to the culprits that their action was, in fact, counter-productive to the development of the women's movement and they would be better occupied in encouraging the unbinding of feet and identifying the sources of women's oppression. But again consciousness-raising in itself did not offer viable solutions to those women who sought to subsequently and actively redefine their position in society.

It had soon become clear that it was not enough to set up unions to help women to understand their own oppression and position without establishing a refuge or facilities to support their role in the protection of women and their rights. The women's union in so many cases became an avenue of escape from intolerable domestic situations, a role for which it was rarely equipped. Many girls landed on the doorstep of the women's union expecting shelter and support, but in fact there were few facilities for the refuge of, say, run-away slave girls. They needed an alternative source of economic support. A few entered the Schools of Politics and of the army in Hankou, but there were almost no alternative opportunities. The women's union in Hankou would have liked to have given them all an education and it did consider starting a combined work-shop and school where they might work half-time and study half-time. Most of these plans had to be laid aside for in these early stages of the war the Nationalist movement needed all its funds for the expedition against the warlords. In the town of Siangtan in Hunan, the women's union did try to open a trade school for sewing, weaving, cooking and making stockings, but this did not go well for lack of capital.[64] The women's union usually had no alternative but to return them to their owners and protect them from further cruelty as best they could. They feared that if word got around that the women's union provided a home plus an education they would have been inundated not only by run-away slave girls but also by factory girls. The women's unions were very often caught in a dilemma between their ability to live up to their ideals and the expectations of the newly conscious, and the resources at their disposal in present social conditions.

For the first time the feminists had entered into an alliance with socialism and their joint aims had demanded that women in working for their own interests should respond to all forms of oppression and enter the wider revolutionary movement. Within the wider revolutionary movement the separate organisation of women, as opposed to the organisation of other social categories or class associations, was founded on the basis of their special history of oppression and the necessity to form an independent power base from which women could negotiate a new role and status in local villages, urban neighbourhoods, factories and other institutions.

Within their own organisation women were to be encouraged to form their own solidarity groups to break down their traditional social isolation and evolve a collective sense of identity and translate the individual experience of oppression into a coherent analysis of oppression. In these female solidarity groups women were encouraged to articulate their oppression or 'speak bitterness' and 'exchange experiences'. From the beginning, however, the alliance between the women's movement and the Nationalists was uneasy. In its bill of rights the Hankou Women's Union agreed to accept the general direction and supervision of the Women's Department of the Guomindang (Kuomintang) Party, but it also added a clause stating that in certain circumstances the women's union maintained the right to act as an independent organ.[65] The joint aims of the two movements demanded that women, besides being made aware of their own oppression, should also be made conscious of their class interests. Hence they were encouraged not only to join their own unions but also to join the peasant and the labour unions in factories as well. Article 7 of the Manifesto issued by the Hankou Women's Union set out the principles upon which the relationships between the women's union and the peasant, labour and student unions were to be based: the women's unions were to be primarily responsible for the personal interests of women and the peasant and labour unions for their class interests:

1 A village woman who is a concurrent member of the peasants' union and under the direction of the women's department of the peasants' unions, may ask the peasants' union to protect her when she is oppressed by landowners, local rowdies or the gentry.
2 Any woman who is a concurrent member of the labour union may ask the labour union to protect her if she is oppressed by her employer.
3 Any woman who is a concurrent member of the students' union may ask the latter to support her if she is not satisfied with her school.[66]

The exact form of the relationship between the women's and the class-based unions continued to worry some of the girl leaders. Should sexual or class oppression take first place in their work among women? Some of the girl propagandists talked to Anna Louise Strong about their priorities. They explained that there was much difference of opinion regarding the organisation of women in the country districts. This was reflected in the controversy of whether there should be separate women's unions or women's sections of peasants' unions. These girls themselves had worked in the peasant unions because they thought that the problem of women was closely related to that of the peasants and the first problem was the economic welfare of the entire peasant family, for, after all, 'if the peasant cannot find peace and welfare the women will by no means find it'.[67]

Factory women sometimes joined separate women's unions, but very often they were organised in women's sections of the labour unions under the joint direction of the Labour and Women's Departments of the Guomindang. The Guomindang trained potential leaders of the factory workers in special schools established to teach the principles operative in both the women's movement and the labour movement: both openly encouraged girl workers to organise and fight for better conditions.[68] After the Nationalists took over Hankou and Shanghai, women's labour unions were established in nearly every factory and women were often seen performing the same services as men in picket lines and women workers with union badges were to be seen in large numbers in both the frequent labour demonstrations of protest and special women's parades held in celebration of Women's Day in the cities under Nationalist rule. In Shanghai the unions sent teachers into the factories at lunch hours to give the girls reading lessons. In Wuxi, Liu Jianxian described how women workers began to take a great interest in the labour movement once the unions were able to take an open stand under the Nationalist rule. Union leaders were very busy because workers from all kinds of factories sent requests to the union headquarters for organisers to come and help form local unions. Liu Jianxian herself was in charge of the organisation of the women in the silk factories.[69] Women delegates to the All-China Labour Conference were forthright in stating that there had been no liberty at all for women of their class until the Nationalist armies had taught them to organise. Without the Nationalist armies the unions had always been suppressed and their leaders imprisoned. It was evident that they felt the problem of women workers to be of central importance within the labour union. At the Conference a number of the women workers attended a luncheon given in their honour by a foreign correspondent. Here they stated that although the union was for everybody it was especially needed for women, who:

are the most oppressed of all living beings. Not only must the women work twelve or sixteen hours in the factory, but she must wash and sweep and cook at home, and also comb her hair and look after herself. How could she manage herself with such long hours?

With union help they hoped to improve their conditions of work.

We expect the Nationalist Government to make the factories have schools for us to learn in and also a special room to feed babies in. And hospital care when we are sick, because we are too poor to pay a doctor. And also vacation with pay before and after babies are born.[70]

Under the Nationalist government the conditions of some women workers were improved. In Wuchang and Hankou some slight gains were made. In the match factories, for instance, the hours of work were reduced from eighteen to twelve and the wages raised from 16 or 17 coppers a day to 40 coppers.[71] Six weeks' rest at confinement had been approved by the unions and this ruling was enforced in a number of plants. In Shanghai the unions protected women threatened by fines and beatings, some working hours were reduced and wages raised. The union abolished humiliating punishments such as forcing girl workers to stand all night in a small cage because of a bad mistake.[72] In Wuxi delegates of the women silk workers, led by Liu Jianxian, negotiated with their employers for one whole day and many of their demands were accepted. The workers got increased wages and shortened hours so that work began at 5.00 a.m. instead of 4.30 a.m. and a rest period was given for meals. They successfully opposed the withdrawal of bonuses of 40 cents per month for 'good work'. Some of the women workers were very impressed with the results of their negotiations and at the time felt that 'the factories belonged to the workers at last',[73] but they also felt that the importance of the rights of working women was underestimated within the labour unions. Some women workers felt that their class interests were neglected by the male-dominated joint unions. Some of the girl delegates at the Labour Conference held in Hankou felt that their sections of the unions were still weak. They might be treated better by foremen but their more concrete demand for an eight-hour day had met with little support from the union and little response from employers. One factory girl from Canton thought from her own experience that the problem of women was the most difficult question in China and as yet she had benefited little from the new government.[74] In Shanghai, some strikes by women workers were considered to be the exclusive affair of women and as such were left without appropriate union leadership and support.[75] These tendencies were apparent at the time and the subject of later complaints that women did not at this time always get the support of the joint organisations waging class struggle. As a result women were often confined to the women's section and isolated from the rest of the movement giving rise to a situation in which the women's section was left without adequate union support.

If the woman's movement was sometimes isolated by the lack of support of union men, it was also true that feminist pursuits of the women's movement potentially cut across the class interests of the joint organisations, with the danger that it would divide the classes which formed the backbone of the nationalist revolutionary movement. The enthusiasm of the women for their own cause raised a number of problems, not least of which was the tremendous adversity and opposition they aroused within the revolutionary movement itself. The very organisation of women antagonised the men of their families. In rural areas cases were reported where women were beaten for attending public meetings and in the *North China Herald*, Reuter News Service reported a street demonstration in Hankou by the 'husbands of emancipated wives'.[76] The demonstrators, mostly labourers, assembled before the General Labour Union headquarters and shouted 'Down with the women's union'. They were protesting against the frequent meetings and 'new freedoms' which were disrupting their home life and claimed that since the arrival of the Nationalists, who preached freedom of women, free love and emancipation of womanhood, their wives no longer returned home to their bed and board, but spent their nights out in the same manner as 'alley cats'. The husbands demanded the return of their wives to the old customs. In one area the women's union from a city visited a nearby village and cut off the hair of women, one of whom tried to drown herself afterwards. Whereupon the men inhabitants of this village armed themselves and wrathfully descended on the city crying, 'If we want our women's hair cut we can do it ourselves.'[77] But there was no doubt that the question of divorce both posed the most difficult problem for the women's movement and aroused the sharpest of protests within the wider movement.

The question of divorce took the revolution into every home and directly affected family life. The opposition was particularly strong among labourers and peasants, many of whom had struggled for years to afford a wife. They could ill-afford to lose her and with no servants they were especially dependent on their wives in domestic affairs and for the care of their children. Even in Hailofeng where the men were considered to be more sympathetic to the cause than most, some hated the women's union. They nicknamed it the 'Bureau of Divorce and Remarriage' because it defended the rights of women and took care of the divorce problem.[78] In one incident in the Yangtze valley the 1,000 men of the peasants' union were so incensed when the women's union granted a divorce to the wife of one of their members that they all began sending their wives home to their parents as a strike against the women's union. 'If even a woman can put away her husband, how much more can we men.'[79] This caused such a scandal in the neighbourhood that eventually the women's union was forced to beg the original divorcee to return to her husband in the interests of the peace of the community. The women's union found itself in a dilemma. If it did not live up to its promises and grant the appeals of its members, women would lose faith in the unions and in the whole ideal of women's freedom and rights. They would be seen to be weak. Powerful unions might adopt extreme methods to humiliate the husband and his family. In Changsha, a woman complained to the union about the ill-treatment which she had suffered at the hands of her husband. He was given a hearing, found guilty and was punished by being made to parade through the streets where he was ridiculed by the crowds. After returning home he committed suicide leaving a very indignant family who held the women's union to be singularly responsible.[80] There seemed to be some danger that the widespread resentment against the new freedoms for women, which tended to set sex against sex, might divide the revolutionary forces when they were on the defensive, and solidarity most important. Problems such as these were recognised by the leaders of the women's movement themselves,[81] but before any modifications to their strategy could be decided upon and introduced the women's movement was suppressed. The growth of the women's movement was temporarily arrested in 1927.

The open and collective rejection of past prohibitions and taboos potentially affected the interests of the men of every household, the interests of village elders and of the employers of labour thus causing widespread resentment among large sections of the population. In villages the members of the women's unions attempted to attack time-honoured customs and the habits of generations. In one county town in Hunan province the activities of the women's union aroused much opposition.[82] It was led by Wang Suzhen, the daughter of a well-off, but not rich, peasant. She was a Christian girl with unbound feet and had been sent away to an American Mission school. Shortly before the Nationalist armies marched into Hunan she returned to her home town where she caused a sensation. Instead of long wide trousers and a long coat with long sleeves, as was the custom, she wore a long full skirt with the smallest hidden trousers, 'practically no trousers at all' complained the old-fashioned country women. Her necklace with a watch on it and her fountain pen, usually found only in Shanghai, Canton and Hankou, also aroused comment. To add insult to injury she chose her own fiancé in line with the recommendations of the women's unions and soon became the president of the local women's union. Under her direction it apparently expanded to include hundreds of members. Her success led her to hold 'head high in the wind' and almost take on an attitude of reckless confidence. A friend described her almost glad defiance: 'She was happy, she was drunk with being happy, as she swept more and more women, even old women into her women's union.' The women's union was described as undertaking 'very wild things':

> they went into the streets with scissors, speaking to strangers, telling women to cut their hair off. They cut their hair off right there in the streets. They say that once or twice women, who were over-persuaded, or maybe compelled to cut their hair off, went home and strangled themselves. The women's unions go into the houses, searching for bound-feet women. If they find a bound-foot woman under thirty, they give her a little time to get her feet unbound, so that it will not hurt too much. After this they fine her. . . . These women make parades in the streets; they shout slogans. They hold mass meetings together with men; they talk with strange men. They proclaim the new laws of the Guomindang, that a wife may get a divorce if she is much tormented, or even if her husband takes a concubine.[83]

The women's union, the first ever in Lingxiang, introduced a new code of behaviour for women and Wang Suzhen openly encouraged other girls to follow her example by choosing their own marriage partners. She soon became a danger to the established morality and people grew to hate her very much.

If the rural and small-town women's unions aroused the

opposition of its residents the organisation of women factory labourers likewise aroused the opposition of their employers and owners of factories. In Wuxi, girl-worker Liu Jianxian was harassed as a result of her work among fellow workers.[84] She was a member of the women's division of the department of Labour. Before she joined the women's union she had spent several years working in silk and cotton factories. She describes how she used to wonder why they had to begin work while the city was asleep in order to get no more than enough to eat. They never saw the sky for months and some never saw the sun for years. She describes how she hated the factory and its owner, wondered why he was so rich and often asked herself 'when will this hard life stop?' She found that any disruptive action they took was spontaneous, short-lived and without any long-term goal or political meaning. The risk of dismissal was great as she had often learnt to her cost. As workers they understood little of the economic relationships and although they had a union of sorts, it was not always very effective. Some Communists came into the factories and held secret meetings in the women workers' dormitories and said to them 'You are not even as good as cows or horses because they at least get rest, but you work sixteen hours a day. Why is your life so hard? It is not fate, but capitalist oppression. We workers must unite and fight against the capitalists.' They heard a lot about the Guomindang (Kuomintang), the Communists and their Nationalist armies. After each secret meeting she herself felt excited and felt earnestly that every word they said was right. She joined the Party and concentrated on working among the factory girls. She talked to them as often as she dared and every Sunday persuaded as many as possible to join in the secret meetings. At first some had to wash their clothes, or go home or had no time and she was often frustrated. Sometimes only a few would come, but they were keen and often agreed with her ideas and were happy to support the union. She worked hard on behalf of the Communist Party in the cotton mill and soon some of the 5,000 workers joined the union and the Party. The latter was secret and had some hundred members. She began to spend short spells in factories where she was usually dismissed after the secret meetings were discovered. She frequently called on the capitalists to negotiate with her to improve the working conditions of women employees and she became a well-known leader of the labour movement in Wuxi.

Opponents of the radical section of the National Revolutionary movement used the 'new freedoms' of women, the peasants and labourers and the activities of their unions to build up popular opposition. The rivalries within the party coalition increased in 1926 and 1927. One of the issues which divided the Communist Party and left-wing Guomindang from the remainder of the Guomindang Party concerned the role of the mass movements of peasants, workers and women. The right wing of the Guomindang viewed these militant organisations with suspicion for they were ranged against the interests of their supporters, bankers, merchants, landlords and employers. The organisation of workers, peasants and women, had alienated large sections of the population, but it was the women's freedoms and unions, whose activities affected the balance of power in every household and village, which became a potent weapon and target of the opposition. The real and rumoured 'new freedoms' of women were used as a means to denigrate the radical wing of the revolutionary movement. Given the strength of the customs, bonds and taboos which they attacked, the policies and programmes of the women's unions were sure to arouse opposition and there was no doubt that the enthusiasm of the young activists was sometimes responsible for hasty tactics which often alarmed and alienated as much sympathy and support as the issues themselves. But more were imagined, cited in the most provocative of sexual imagery and expressed in almost hysterical terms. National newspapers reported events from Hankou, Hubei and Hunan so as to give an impression of almost total licence and immorality. The natural mingling of the sexes and free choice of marriage partner stimulated wild tales of immorality and free love.

An article on the School of Politics was entitled 'The Wild, Wild Women' and other articles drew the headlines 'Former Restraints Violently Resented', 'Old Standards of Morality Breaking Down' and 'Women Going to Pieces under the Nationalists'.[85] The most spectacular of the rumours that were telegraphed down the line from Hankou was the story of the 'naked women's parade'.[86] It was said that the women of Hankou were intending to march naked through the streets to celebrate their 'new free will and independence of action'. The rumour was increasingly embellished in detail. At one time it was reported that officers were to be appointed to inspect the candidates and accept only those who were physically fit for display! The women's unions subsequently denied the reports and stated publicly in newsprint that they had now found the fabricators of the rumours and intended to punish them and the editor of the offending paper which had first reported the rumours. Correspondence letters said to originate in Hunan were duplicated and sent to newspapers as evidence that 'by a law, all girls over sixteen must be married within one month or the government will provide husbands for them'.[87] Members of the gentry class, who normally held as many concubines as they could afford and were often patrons of brothels, fled from Hunan and Hubei to the cities where they spread reports that within six months all wives and sisters would be Communised. Pictures of immodest scanty bathing costumes were published as an example of those said to be worn by the girl propagandists who travelled with the armies.[88] Later Han Suyin was to note that the only accusation which the 'conservative forces could fling at the CCP was, of course, sex. Their greatest crime was "free love", they preached equality of women and appalling crimes which threatened the salvation of China! Rabid anti-Red newspapers accused the CCP of practising orgies.'[89] During the Nationalist Revolution rumours and wild tales fell on willing ears and fed the wave of retribution which was to follow the eventual split between the Guomindang and CCP Parties.

The rivalries within the party coalition came to a head in 1927. Chiang Kai-shek and the more right-wing of the Guomindang Party which had its headquarters in Nanking, decided to open a military offensive against the CCP and left-wing Guomindang in Hankou. The activities of the women's unions, alongside those of the peasants and labourers, were brought to a standstill. The separate Women's Department of the Guomindang in Hankou was closed down, and from the towns and villages came reports that women's associations and unions had been summarily disbanded on the charge of being 'Red'.[90] The agony of disbandment for those who had experienced new expectations and a new way of life was well expressed by the girl soldier Xie Bingying. In her diaries she described her feelings on receiving the news that the school for army propagandists was about to close. She and her friends had been called to a special assembly held at very short notice.

'My schoolmates'—strange, this was not his usual salutation to us. Even his voice was different. Before he went on any further we seemed to feel he was trembling. We feared that something very unfortunate had happened, and sure enough he was proclaiming our unlucky fate. Indeed he was reading out our sentence.

'First of all, I want you to be calm, to be brave, to be prepared for the worst.'

F

'What, are we going to the front again? But what is there to be afraid of?' This was in my thoughts.

'It is very unfortunate news that I am going to tell you, but I want you not to be heartbroken. A revolutionary must be prepared for setbacks and obstacles. They are quite common. We should never give up and never be despairing.' What was he going to say?

'Because the reactionary force is so great and because we want to preserve our revolutionary forces for a better time under better circumstances, and because the present conditions are pressing upon us, we have to demobilise for the time being.'

This was a thunderbolt from the blue, a bombshell in the night! It had almost knocked the life out of all of us. We were almost unconscious, but the lieutenant's voice went on heroically.

'Of course, this is not because we are afraid, not because we do not want to resist, for we are determined to have the final struggle. Those of you who are very robust and can run very fast may follow the Eleventh Army to fight. Otherwise you should all return to your own homes and suffer for the time being. In the very near future perhaps you will have a freer and happier life. Now each of you will receive ten silver dollars for your expenses and I advise you to get some civilian clothes to disguise yourselves. The uniforms you must destroy.'

Heavens, what was all this about? Why should we be demobilised? Our hopes, our ideals, were they finished after such a short appearance? After the lieutenant's report all the other four officers gave us some further advice. . . . These words were as knives piercing into our hearts and many of us were shedding tears. So we were to leave the school tomorrow! Tomorrow was the time when we should go into hell, for going back to our old-fashioned homes was as bad as going to hell. Alas, who wanted to go there?[91]

Not only did they not want to return to their old way of life, but the opposition was such that their very lives were endangered.

Their most immediate problem was one of survival. In the 'anti-Red' reaction any girl with the tell-tale bobbed hair was under suspicion. It was regarded as an almost infallible evidence of radicalism and on this pretext alone thousands of girls were shot and otherwise killed after being subjected to gross indignities. That passions of the time ran high is evidenced by both the force of the extremist reaction which set in and the forms of reprisals which were taken against young women activists. The newspaper, *Ta Kung-pao*, reported that the most common form of punishment for girl Communists in Canton was to wrap them up in cotton padded blankets soaked in gasoline and then burn them alive.[92] Others who had worn boys' clothes were stripped to the waist and exposed to public gaze so that 'every man in town may see she is in reality a woman' before being killed.[93] Many met an awful end. The prevailing mood of retribution is well indicated in the town of Lingxiang where Wang Suzhen met a swift and crashing end at the hands of the militarists with the support of the local population. One of her friends described the scene after the soldiers had entered the town. Wang Suzhen's own neighbours, for the hate they bore her, brought the soldiers to her and shouted to urge them on. He went on to tell how she had no chance of escape for:

> the soldiers were all about her, men soldiers and one girl
> agitator. That was what everyone called Wang Suzhen now. The
> soldiers shouted many bad words at her till they stirred their rage
> up. Then they cut her to pieces with knives and bayonets. They
> began with her breasts then they cut off her arms, they cut off
> many pieces. By and by they fired seventeen shots into what was
> left. The shots were to show how much they hated her.[94]

The *China Weekly Review* noted in August 1927 that for four months a systematic massacre had been going on in the territory controlled by Chiang Kai-shek which had resulted in the smashing of people's organisations and the execution of leaders.[95] The ruthless campaign spread from Hankou to Peking and from Shanghai to Canton and lasted until 1930. During these years thousands of women activists were killed including the young Communist leader, Xiang Jingyu.[96] For those that survived it must have seemed a bleak, low and hopeless moment in the history of the women's movement.

Despite the suppression the initial union of socialism and feminism had proved to some activists in the women's movement that their struggle was one between differing political, economic and social interests. This formed the gist of a poem by Zhang Jianzhen who wrote the following poem on the eve of her execution; although not all would have shared her optimism at the final outcome:

They say I'm a Communist girl
and I dying know that at least
I will not be given to Zhang Jiu*
Red and White will ever be divided
and we shall see who has victory,
who defeat; the white flowers now
are fading as our scarlet ones
burst into eager bloom.[97]

The split within the nationalist revolutionary movement in 1927 and the subsequent division of China into two areas—one governed by Chiang Kai-shek and the Guomindang Party and the other by Mao Zedong and the Communist Party—provides a unique opportunity to follow the contrasting development and fate of a women's movement allied to each of these differing political, social and economic interests.

---

* Zhang Jiuhua was a local Guomindang warlord.

'The Feminine Mystique': Guomindang China * 6

For the modern Chinese woman, let her freedom be restrained by self-control, her self-realisation be coupled with self-sacrifice, and her individualism be circumscribed by family duty. Such is our new ideal of womanhood and to realise this is our supreme problem.

(Zeng Baosun)[1]

Despite the repression of the women's, peasants' and workers' movements, the reputation of the Guomindang (Kuomintang) Party, as a nationalist revolutionary party dedicated to the rebuilding of a united China and the emancipation of women, largely remained intact. The Guomindang Party never ceased to talk about revolution and emancipation, it simply redefined the terms. Revolution became reform within an urban capitalist and rural semi-feudal structure, and emancipation included the often contradictory demands for a return to the virtues of traditional femininity and domesticity and new opportunites for professional employment. New economic relations and traditional ideals of womanhood proved difficult to accommodate within a single structure, and the growing irrelevance of the traditional ideology in the contemporary social and economic conditions was eventually to contribute to the rapid demise of the Guomindang Party in the late 1940s. In 1928, however, Chiang Kai-shek had emerged as the strong man and the leading architect of the new China. Nanking became the new capital and with the support of his armies and the landed, industrial and commercial aristocracy, Chiang Kai-shek set about the establishment of a strong central government in China. The country was more unified than previously, new plans were afoot to erect a modern state and it seemed as if the national dignity of the country was about to be reasserted. The Guomindang government under Chiang Kai-shek was recognised by the foreign powers as the legitimate government of all China and respectability

* Quite by coincidence both Norma Diamond and myself have chosen the title 'The Feminine Mystique', first used by Betty Freidan to describe the situation in America after the Second World War, to characterise the areas ruled by the Guomindang Party and Chiang Kai-shek. See N. Diamond, 'Women under Kuomintang Rule: Variations on the Feminine Mystique', *Modern China*, vol. 1, no. 1, January 1975.

followed hot on the heels of legitimacy. It was the initial aim of the Guomindang to restore the women's movement to its previous respectability by rescuing it from the militant and 'immoral' influences of the extremists—the Communists. It first set about separating feminism from socialism, and second it redefined feminism.

Many were persuaded that the Communists had influenced the women's movement for the worst and that the revolution could continue, but with less violence, under the direction of the Guomindang. On Women's Day in 1928 when more than 1,000 women and girls gathered together to celebrate at a public meeting, the slogan 'Execute the CCP' was to be seen among the banners advocating 'Equal Pay', 'Equal Education' and 'Women Participate in the People's Revolution'.[2] The committee rooms of the new government commission on the women's movement displayed the posters: 'Attack Illiteracy', 'Protect Women's Labour', 'Reform the Home' and 'Down with the Communists'.[3] According to an American journalist who had been sympathetic to the approach of the girl propagandists, the well-heeled members of the new women's commission (the old one which had included some CCP members had been forced to resign) shut their eyes to the terrorism, preferring to interpret it as restoring order.[4] Within the women's movement, 'restoring order' meant rescuing it from the militancy, 'the wild excesses and the Red revolutionary fervour' which had inspired the girl propagandists of the Nationalist armies. In a number of new pamphlets which were published on Women's Day in 1928, the clearest of distinctions was drawn between the disruptive influence of the CCP and the constructive role of the GMD. The former had led the women's movement along an abortive and diversionary path and was considered to have done great harm to the cause. Only if the CCP was suppressed was a great step forward in the women's movement considered to be possible. The GMD, on the other hand, had made preparations to give women their 'freedom', and as the 'true leader and saviour of the movement' it was said to be deserving of their active support. The new pamphlets represented the orientation of the new women's movement. Militarism was condemned by nearly all the writers of the pamphlets who advocated moderation and morality. Emancipation was expressed in terms of personal development and education of the individual. One writer indicated these new directions when she wrote that:

The meaning of the women's movement is not to annihilate masculine strength, men's valour, nor is it to put an end to the grace of women's nature or evade the function of motherhood. . . . The women's movement [from now on] must cut out, root and branch, this attitude of antagonism of the sexes.[5]

Other writers were concerned with rescuing concubines and prostitutes from the immorality of their fate, while others saw women's emancipation and women's rights solely in terms of the personal qualities of education and professionalism by advocating increased schooling and job opportunities.[6] Politics was an inappropriate interest for women and as a subject was carefully avoided. Edith Pye, an English member of the Women's International League for Peace and Freedom delegation which toured China in the late 1920s, found no sign of any active political work among women in Shanghai, Hankou or Peking after the split between the two parties.[7] Political work smacked of Communist influence and was strongly suppressed.

The belief that the Guomindang was responsible for setting the women's movement on a new path of development and had the interests of women at heart was fostered when they incorporated their long-fought-for rights into the law of the land. The first hints of the shape of the new law appeared in *The China Critic* which quoted a government order in 1928 to the effect that the Guomindang 'intended to ensure the emancipation of women's rights in China on the principle of equality between men and women in law, in economics, in education and in society'.[8] Soumay Cheng, a woman lawyer, described her excitement when she was appointed to the commission to draft the new civil code of China. It was the 'realisation of a dream, or part of it'. She felt it symbolised the progress of her country and she worked to embody within the civil code the principle of absolute equality for women. In fact, the drafting of the law proved to be a long and difficult task, for not only was the new law supposed to provide for rights of women, but the commission was also charged with the duty of preserving the essence of 'those customs, traditions and moral principles under which Chinese people have lived for centuries'.[9] When the new Civil Code was finally issued in December 1930 it formed a compromise between the forces of tradition and the call for modernity. Yet for all its concessions to custom it greatly improved the legal position of women.

The code assumed a patrilineal and patriarchal family, but the authority of the head of the family was diminished vis-à-vis the women and children of the household. Women were entitled to choose their own husband, and in the matter of divorce, their rights became more symmetrical with those of men. Daughters, both married and single, were granted the same legal rights as sons to property inheritance and rights of ownership, and the laws governing matrimonial property protected married women's property rights. Women were not to be excluded from acting in the position of the formal head of the household, and in making adultery an offence equally punishable for men and women the law did away with the old double standard. A year later the new Factory Law precluded women from certain kinds of work and allowed them, where they performed the same kinds of work as efficiently as men, to be paid the same wages. Simultaneously the new Penal Law was revised to recognise that both husband and wife had a mutual obligation to be chaste. On the other hand, men under the statutory system governing matrimonial property retained managerial rights and their position as heads of the conjugal family gave them the decisive voice in the event of conflict with their wives. Although the idea of equality of women was not carried through with absolute consistency, the new laws profoundly affected the legal status of 50 per cent of the population. In theory the laws were capable of changing the domestic and public, economic, social and political relations between men and women, but the traditional social and economic position of women was not given due consideration. Indeed, the benefits of the law were confined to a small articulate section of self-supporting and independent women. There was little attempt to widely and effectively implement the new law, but its very existence did affect the history of the women's movement. It was as if the passing of the new laws signalled the achievement of all the goals of the women's movement. Their continued struggle was hardly necessary.

On the basis of the new constitutional gains, the leading feminists proclaimed the emancipation of women. This is what the women's movement had been fighting for. What need was there for the further organisation of women in pursuit of these same ideals? Many echoed the sentiments of a leading feminist, Wu Liande, when she applauded the GMD for their 'marvellous emancipation' of the womenfolk of China.[10] Many disregarded the previous struggle of the last decades and credited the emancipation of women to the stroke of the pen of the government. Ren Tai noted that women had broken down the old conventions and institutions 'without much effort'.[11] Dr Wu Yifang observed that now economic independence was within easy reach of the modern Chinese lady. If she was well trained and qualified she might compete equally with the men for any position from the highest government office downwards. 'Unlike her American and European sisters, she does not have to battle against opposition from members of the other sex.'[12] The spokeswoman for women educationalists, Dr Zeng Baosun, President of the Girls' College in Changsha, made a widely publicised and often quoted speech commenting on the ease with which the emancipation of Chinese women had been achieved. She thought that: 'compared with the women of the West who had to fight hard for their rights of education, profession and suffrage, the women of China gained theirs at very little cost.'[13] Most of the leading feminists were intellectuals who were college educated, more often Christian than not, and were now professional women in the fields of education, law and medicine. They were less outraged by the economic fate of their sisters of other classes than the threat to the 'feminine' qualities traditional to Chinese women. Their speeches continually contrasted the Amazonian qualities of the radical girl students during the Nationalist Revolution to the competence and lasting influence of those who practised the traditional arts of home-makers.

The leading feminists publicly voiced their fears that women of most classes were not fit and ready for the acquisition of the new legal rights. One foreign observer recorded in his impressions of the time that many of the women leaders began to experience certain misgivings about the rise in status, the new freedoms which women had acquired, and the efficacy of extending these to all masses of Chinese women.[14] What was to become of the home and traditional family life? It was said that if marriage and divorce were made easy there was a danger that those without the appropriate education would confuse liberty and licence. There was an even greater danger that the ensuing destruction of the home and the erosion of old forms of family life would result in the ruination of the entire younger generation. Articles illustrating the terrible temptations in the way of the modern Chinese girls forecast a continuing downhill path of immorality.[15] To forestall this downfall and counteract the fears that old virtues were being discarded and family life destroyed, a new ideal of womanhood was proclaimed.

To many of the feminists in search of a new code of standards, the only solution for women seemed to lie in a combination of traditional ideals befitting wives and mothers and a Western professional training. They advocated a way of life based on a mixture of Confucian rules of conduct and forms of behaviour required for the development of modern capitalism. Dr Wu Yifang, President of Ginling College for Women in Nanking, believed that the future generation of women would combine the rich heritage of Confucian virtues with the advantages of a modern vocational education.[16] Dr Zeng Baosun analysed the present dilemmas facing a modern woman and described her ideal qualities. She believed that this period was critical for the development of womanhood in that a Chinese woman

> is at the cross-roads; it is difficult to say which road she will take. Will she revert to the old as the pendulum swings back? Or will she throw over all her heritage and become a totally new person unknown to her land and alien to her civilisation? Or will she retain what is best in China and supplement it with the best from the West? The third alternative is naturally what we want. To achieve this it is necessary for the modern Chinese woman not to be de-nationalised but to have such a thorough knowledge of the culture and civilisation of her own country that she will personify what is best in them. For then, and not until then, will she be able to re-evaluate and make the best use of those desirable old Chinese ideals such as maternal love and wifely devotion. With a foundation like this she can build a superstructure of Western training in arts, science and philosophy, or anything else she chooses. Therefore, for the modern Chinese woman, let her freedom be restrained by self-control, her self-realisation be coupled with self-sacrifice, and her individualism be circumscribed with family duty. Such is our new ideal of womanhood and to realise this is our supreme problem.[17]

The return to the old Chinese ideals of maternal love and wifely devotion, as recommended by the feminists, was also taken up by the government as part of a nationwide campaign called the New Life Movement.

The New Life Movement, launched in 1934, was aimed at the social and moral rejuvenation or spiritual reform of the Chinese people through the application of Confucianism, mingled with a little Christianity, to the modern problems of China. To maintain social stability, popular discipline and to promote morality, the ancient Confucian virtues of propriety, loyalty, integrity and honour, which had been responsible for the greatness of the country in 'remote times', were re-acclaimed. To assist in the revival of these moral tenets Confucius was recanonised, Confucian ceremonies were re-enacted and a flood of books and articles on traditional virtues were published. The aim of the movement was to revive the habit of behaving in accordance with fixed and unquestioned rules which traditionally defined correct relationships between the rulers and ruled, the generations, and the sexes. Song Meiling who with her husband Chiang Kai-shek sponsored the New Life Movement, observed that its purpose was 'to help the people, to train them to take their rightful places in society and to enable them to become useful citizens in a modern democracy'.[18] She established and directed the Women's Department of the New Life Movement. Song Meiling thought that there was one unquestionable basic principle which the traditional code of ethics had laid down for women and that time would never shake. It was that 'virtue is more important than learning'. 'To my mind,' she said, 'if one has to choose between virtue and learning, virtue is the more to be cherished. There is, however, no reason why a woman should not be both virtuous and learned. This must be indelibly stamped on the minds of young girls. . . .'[19]

Far from analysing the causes of their oppression women were encouraged to believe that they had not been oppressed at all. In the writings of the times the traditional relationships between the sexes was reinterpreted to raise women to a previously unimaginable and elevated position and the traditional suppression of women was belittled by the foremost men scholars of the day, including Hu Shi,[20] Tang Leang-li[21] and Lin Yutang.[22] They fastened upon the small minority of outstanding women poets and scholars such as Ban Zhao, who on the death of her father and brother took over the compilation of the histories of the Han dynasty, as proof of traditional women's access to power and status. It was emphasised that the women of the wealthier classes had shared the benefits of a rudimentary literary education. As the wives and mothers of the nation's sons they were said to have held a privileged position of much status in China. It was admitted that although the traditional mothers may have been ignorant and superstitious, their very sacrificing life had inspired many a son to perform noble deeds and develop an exceptionally fine character. Indeed, China owed them an obligation for raising such 'pillars of

Chinese civilisation'. The very absence of legal rights in the past was held to be responsible for the power a woman wielded in the home. According to Tang Leang-li no country in the world could compete with China for the distinction of being a nation of hen-pecked husbands. 'Women in China', he says, 'built up their strong social position because a wife could not be dislodged from her position.' The conditions under which divorce was impossible, was said to work to their advantage and give them power and protection.[23] The emphasis on the sexually determined roles of women prompted the revival of the cult of domesticity. Not only Mother's Day but 'Good Mother's Day' was celebrated.[24] Women were urged to return to the kitchen. As men provided for their families, this movement thought that their husbands had the right to see their homes well managed by their wives. A pressure group was formed to support a new Draft Contract Law which in effect recognised the right of a husband to cancel his wife's employment should her work prove detrimental to the welfare of the family.[25]

Girls and women were encouraged to improve their standards of housekeeping as part of the New Life Movement. Song Meiling threw herself heart and soul into the reform of domestic habits. Along with her husband, Chiang Kai-shek, she travelled to many parts of China to explain the principles of the New Life Movement and encourage orderliness, cleanliness, simplicity and frugality. Cleanliness, much to the amusement of some foreign observers, was for Song Meiling symbolic of all that must be done to remove the age-old dirt that had reigned supreme before her coming! At schools of the New Life Movement which were established and directed by Song Meiling, girl students were trained to go out and help strangers, supervise people's conduct in the parks and theatres, and visit homes and advise housewives as to how to keep their homes clean and sanitary. Numerous organisations (like the Village Reconstruction Movement, the Mass Education Movement, and other agencies) were created in the 1930s by the government, universities, missions and private societies. They sent representatives, often graduates and students from the cities, into the interior of China to teach the women literacy, public health and technical skills. The training programmes mainly fell within the rubric of the New Life Movement, and re-emphasised the traditional virtues of wives, mothers and household arts as well as the acquisition of new skills. Rarely were the new legal rights part of the curriculum. Yi Fangwu wrote in 1940 that the traditions re-emphasised by the New Life Movement were so well known that these teams sometimes accomplished things without much special effort;[26] it was fondly imagined in the cities that:

> In the mud-floored chambers of a rural middle school or the great three-walled chambers of some old Chinese house anywhere in 'Free China' a class of small children and worn farmer women, who have been working in the fields all day and can spare only the twilight hours, chant after the teacher the simple truths about hygiene, moral philosophy and nine divided by three.[27]

The traditional division of labour between the sexes was once again sanctioned and this time by the feminists themselves. They thought that the right kind of education for girls should emphasise sexual differences and prevent the unthinking appropriation of male standards of thought. They urged that reforms be introduced into girls' curriculum to foster their homemaking role. Zeng Baosun, of Changsha Girls' College, criticised the form of education in girls' schools which tended to duplicate that characteristic of boys' schools with a few additional subjects such as needlework, cookery and theoretical domestic science haphazardly thrown in for good measure. It was feared that these important subjects had been relegated to an insignificant position in the school. They were allowed the minimum of time, were neglected by the teachers and usually despised by the students. The girl students had been encouraged to shun these subjects in favour of men's work in the professions. Not only did this mean that girls left school without any idea of homemaking, child welfare or nursing, but they were said to also develop a 'wrong notion of the equality of the sexes'. As Zeng Baosun said, 'Instead of realising that true equality lies in each developing its own line, they try to approximate the male standard of thought and life, thus turning themselves into pseudo-males.' What was lacking and what was needed, she said, was a 'thorough study of girls' requirements in life'.[28]

The most eloquent exultant of the 'feminine mystique' of this period in China was the philosopher and writer Lin Yutang. He extolled the virtues of the maternal role which alone were enough to sanction the traditional division of labour and override class divisions.

> There are talented women as there are talented men, but their number is actually less than democracy would have us believe.

> For those women, self-expression has a more important meaning than just bearing children. But for the common people, whose number is legion, let the men earn the bread to feed the family and let the women bear children. . . . Of all the rights of women, the greatest is to be a mother. . . . A curly headed child [is] her triumph and her delight, more surprising than the greatest book she has ever written and saturating her with more real satisfaction than the moment of her greatest triumph on the stage . . . so nature has ordained, so let men and women live.[29]

He subscribed to the new ideal of a wife as one 'with new knowledge but old character', but in the event of conflict he knew where his sympathies lay.

> While I regard the increased knowledge and education as an improvement and approaching the ideal of womanhood, I wager that we are not going to find, as we have not yet found, a world-renowned lady pianist or lady painter. I feel confident that her soup will still be better than her poetry and that her real masterpiece will be her chubby-faced boy.[30]

He held that this image of womankind was true for all classes. Take the salesgirls in the department stores of Shanghai who 'look with eyes of envy on the married women with their fat handbags and wish they were buying instead of selling'. 'Sometimes', he continued,

> they wish they were knitting sweaters for their babies instead of counting the change, and standing for a stretch of eight hours. . . . Most of them know instinctively which is the better thing. Some of them prefer their independence, but the so-called independence in a man-ruled society does not amount to much. The cynical ones laugh a little at this 'independence'. The primeval urge of motherhood—formless, wordless and vague and strong—fills their whole beings. . . . Their instinct is right. What is wrong with marriage? What is wrong in protected motherhood?[31]

The last question was in response to those who maintained that women in the roles of wives and mothers were 'dependent beings'. If society decreed that women's place was in the home, the woman who left it was by definition aberrant. Lin Yutang abhorred the politically prominent women who courted publicity. In contrast to those who disappeared into good homes, the former were 'the worst scoundrels of their sex' and did not represent modern Chinese womanhood. For him modern Chinese womanhood was represented by the 'wise, gentle and firm mother'.

In addition to fulfilling mystified domestic roles, women were also encouraged to play a limited social and economic public role. They were encouraged, at least while they were young and single, to obtain professional qualifications and enter employment, while social work was advocated for the leisured. Women in the professions and colleges were exhorted to set an example to the rest of the nation by assuming a spirit of service for others and Song Meiling more than once criticised the narrow interests of middle- and upper-class women, especially after they were married and had children, and begged them to develop a sense of social responsibility and found local movements for 'New Life'. At her behest the number of clubs and organisations which aimed to direct the public energies of women into social, philanthropic and charitable activities expanded in the large coastal and inland cities. These included professional and business women's clubs as well as Christian and 'Returned Students from Abroad' associations. The organisations, some more and some less affiliated with other groups, met the desire of professional, business and returned girl students to both meet together and to do something to improve their society. Individually they were often appalled by the increasing menace of poverty which threatened the future of the bulk of China's people with the result that the associations often adopted programmes of work to educate and aid stricken women and children by establishing child orphanages, beggar settlements, and running classes on literacy, mother-training and home-reform. Even the most fashionable of women devoted themselves to fund-raising or social and welfare services in one form or another. This was indeed the age of the women's club and the doyen of them all was the Chinese Women's Club in Shanghai.

This club, which was to set an example and later encourage the establishment of local women's clubs both in Shanghai and elsewhere, had a chequered beginning to its career. The club had been founded in 1918 at the suggestion of some public men in order that it might help entertain the wives of distinguished foreign guests. At the same time, they also embarked upon an ambitious social service programme, but because virtually all the members had little or no previous contact with the practical business of running a club and experienced leadership was wanting, the original group more or less disintegrated within a very short time of its founding. In the late 1920s and early 1930s the club was revived by graduates of colleges and middle schools in China and returned students from abroad. A report presented by the chairperson in 1936[32] said it existed to attract educated women who found it easy to fall into the leisured class or engross themselves in the old-style family 'with all the latter's complicated human and social programmes' and younger 'society women', who like their counterparts in New York or London, were easily led into an aimless whirl of dinners, dances and parties becoming mere 'social butterflies and parasites'. The President of the Club was sure that the leisure class needed only to be guided to become interested in some form of welfare and help in the great cause of 'social betterment'. The Club annually collected sufficient funds to make donations to various charities whose numbers grew with the expansion of the Club's resources. It also co-operated with other like women's organisations to promote common interests and allied objectives, and was a member of the joint Committee of Shanghai Women's Organisations which was a loose federation of some eighteen or nineteen local groups.

Although women were encouraged to play a public role, it was a public role of a very limited kind. Political activity was in no way encouraged. Song Meiling, in a speech, was to emphasise that: 'It is harmful for every woman to strive to take part in politics . . . work in the women's movement should be concerned with general education, vocational training, women's service and welfare and family problems.'[33] Women were involved in the New Life Movement but it was made abundantly clear that it was in no way meant to be a political movement.[34] The President of the Chinese Women's Club in Shanghai expressly stated that women's clubs had no avowed political aim.[35] Although a number of women were employed in the central government organs, they held about 3 per cent of the available jobs and this was said to give cause for congratulations to the government.[36] Women continued to be excluded from the Congress of Representatives. In the Draft of a Constitution for the Republic of China, which was published on 5 May 1936, there was no provision for their representation at the National Congress of the Representatives of the People, and further there was no woman elected in any of the countrywide local elections which took place at that time.[37] In education institutions, outspoken girl 'agitators' were accused of being Communists and were expelled from their school and colleges.[38] While for political and ideological reasons there was a movement to close co-educational schools and return to middle schools of a single-sex type.

As early as 1928 a National Education Conference in Nanking proposed the end of co-education in middle schools and colleges,[39] and the Commissioner of the Canton Department of Education began a campaign for separate education. He accused the girl students of flirtatious behaviour and generally interfering in boys' studies.[40] Another reason put forward in support of the campaign was the said Communist practice of sending 'cute girl agents to the schools to encourage the boy students to become fully-fledged Reds'.[41] This was despite the fact that girls in co-educational schools were reported to be of a 'quiet, shy and conservative type' in comparison to the single-sex normal schools where girls appeared to escape from the normal inferiority complex and 'blossom unhindered into full-grown radicals and leaders away from the numerical and ideological domination of the boy students'.[42] Whenever women participated in political activities which were at all reminiscent of those that had occurred during the Nationalist Revolution, repressive measures were taken. Strict precautionary measures were taken by the authorities each Women's Day to prevent demonstrations in the streets.

The ideal image of womanhood combining traditional qualities, limited interests and some form of economic independence refused to accommodate changing socio-economic patterns. Contemporary economic and political developments threatened the sources of economic independence available to two new classes of urban women. The expansion of education (in 1935 there were 106,075 girls enrolled in the high schools (about 20 per cent of the total number of pupils), several thousand in the normal and vocational schools, and 6,272 (16 per cent) in colleges, universities, teachers' colleges, and technical high schools),[43] of industry and of commerce in the 1930s and 1940s created a class of women conscious of both the advantages of an education and its consequent opportunities for economic and individual independence. This group of foreign and China-educated students, business girls and professional women, reached sizeable proportions in the old and new capitals, the ports and the important cities of the interior. In 1949 it was calculated that there were approximately 300 to 400 thousand career women in the country, most of whom were elementary and high school teachers, civil service workers or nurses. A few were qualified doctors, dentists, lawyers, social workers or journalists. There were also a number of women self-employed in business, and a few managers and executives in the many industrial and business enterprises. Many were employed as clerks, book-keepers, stenographers and typists in these establishments. As the rate of inflation and unemployment rose in the cities and the economy became more and more depressed, the first to be made redundant were always the women employees. Government departments, and numbers of national and provincial banks laid off many of their women employees.[44] In 1940 the Post Office suddenly declared that it would no longer employ married women.[45] Women in employment whether they were teachers in Shanghai or the dance-hall girls in Shanghai and Canton were equally threatened by discrimination and unemployment.[46]

The average Chinese woman factory worker was reported to be unmarried, nineteen, illiterate and earned the equivalent of $4.83 US dollars per month. This was the conclusion drawn from a survey conducted in 1937 of 102 Shanghai factories, encompassing 19 different industries. Forty-two point four per cent of the women were 18–21 years, 25.3 per cent were 14–17 years old, and 16.6 per cent were 22–5 years; 83 per cent were single and 17 per cent married.[47] They were often of peasant origins and tended to retain close ties with their home villages, but as long as they stayed in the cities they were entirely reliant on their wages for support. Their numbers were always increasing, but there was a high turnover and with long lines of unemployed outside the factory gate they were vulnerable to the threat of dismissal. Only in the largest factories and cities did they dare to organise and protest at their working conditions. In 1945 women textile workers in Shanghai surrounded the city branch of the GMD and demanded that the government alleviate all the kinds of oppression in their lives,[48] and a year later they paraded on Women's Day to demand more control of their work conditions and 'Equal Pay for Equal Work' (see Table 3).[49]

Table 3 Average Monthly Income of Chinese Workers

	1938	1940
Men: Hourly	22,352 yuan	43,607
Women: Hourly	12,648	22,024
Men: Piecework	26,551	51,884
Women: Piecework	16,426	34,670

(Source: *China Year Book*, 1943, p. 1018)

The effect of the deteriorating rural economy on the status of peasant women all too often reduced their bargaining power in the exchange of their productive and reproductive capacities. Observers in China throughout the 1930s and 1940s spoke unanimously of the deteriorating economic conditions in the countryside. Several forces worked towards increasing penury among the peasants who formed at least 85 per cent of the population in the 1930s. A rise in population coincided with the increasing fragmentation of the land which, together with the decline in government public works and effective flood control, led to a serious depletion of the food reserves. Public granary stores for relief fell into disuse, and with the decline of central power, local and regional overlords began to increase taxes and impose their own levies which could number up to 80 or so items. The introduction of cash crops and the commercialisation of land affected land leases, prices, tenure conditions and rent charges. Prices for land doubled in some areas and tripled in others, and secure tenure was often replaced by short-term contracts. In the late 1930s it was estimated that landlords, 2–4 per cent of the population, owned 20–30 per cent of land in the north and 30–50 per cent in the south.[50] With increasing inflation competition for land increased as city dwellers found land the only stable form of investment. The growth of cheap and plentiful industrial products, domestic and foreign produce, threatened traditional rural industries and handicrafts which the peasants had hitherto relied upon to supplement their incomes. The peasants could still be classified into the landed and landless, but gradual impoverishment was almost universal and the ravages of famine, flood and war took their toll during these decades. Those who were pushed off the land migrated to the cities or took to banditry where their livelihood was even more precarious. Economic pressures, which reduced the margin between subsistence and starvation in many areas, exacerbated the practice, already common in some rural areas, of buying and selling women. They were bought and sold as domestic slaves, additional wives or concubines, potential prostitutes or as indentured industrial labour. Rich men measured and advertised their wealth by their number of wives, with some landlords accumulating tens of women. The literature of the period is scattered with examples of daughters, wives and widows who were sold in return for food, money or services. Jia Yinglan of Liuling village in northern Shanxi, sold twice, recollected the circumstances of each sale.

> When I was twenty-two I was sold. He [my husband] came one
> day and fetched me and my daughter and took us to a slave
> dealer called Yang. . . . When I had been two days with Yang,
> the slave dealer, he sold me. He sold me and my daughter for 220
> dollars to a farmer called He Nangang.

She was very unhappy, he was an old man, but she was thankful
that he did not ill-treat her, and she had the additional fortune of
bearing him a son. But this fortune was short-lived. Her husband
died and again she was sold.

> I was, of course, a widow and a burden to the village. The
> landlord wanted to marry me off. My husband's relatives, that is
> Mr He's relatives, wanted to marry me off, too, in order to get
> the house and my children. There was a man in the village who
> was willing to buy me. I don't know how they arranged it, and I
> don't know who he was. But I didn't want to live any longer. I
> just wanted to be with my children. [51]

Women were used to make good debts or rent arrears. The old
ideas of chastity, and life-long loyalty of women, already less
common among the very poor, were further outmoded by
worsening economic conditions in which women were exchanged
with impunity. For many village women the only means of escape
from poverty, forced exchange and traditional village sanctions,
like gossip, was employment in the cities.

In each of these three groups, individual educated and
professional, peasant and factory working women found it
increasingly difficult to come to terms with the contemporary
economic developments. Those best able to combine Confucian
virtues and a modern vocational training belonged to the urban
wealthy and middle classes, but they faced increasing discrimination in employment, and conflicting ideologies, traditional,
modern and Western, were particularly apparent within their
family life and inevitably involved them in some form of
compromise. In common, they had been exposed, to a greater or
lesser extent, to Western ideas and life-styles. Some of these girls
and women had experienced life abroad and others were much
influenced by what they heard, read and saw of the West in China.
European dress, the perm, make-up, bare legs, jazz and free and
romantic love continued to hold their attraction at least before the
days when the new patriotic spirit of the war called for frugality
and a return to things 'Chinese'. It was among this group that

foreign authors and the Chinese authors of liberal and progressive views held the most influence. Ba Jin's *The Family*, a critique of traditional gentry family life and spokesman for the rights of youth and women, was a popular book.[52] Lu Xun was by far the most influential author in these years. His short stories criticising repressive features of the old society were widely read.[53] The very multiplicity of ideas which abounded meant that this group inevitably experienced some form of confusion and soul-searching, even among those who set the greatest store by economic independence and modern ideals.

Han Suyin, an independent-minded foreign-trained doctor determined to earn her own keep, recalled in a vivid account her reactions to the fixed and unquestioned rules of behaviour advocated by the New Life Movement.[54] On her marriage, her husband, one of Chiang Kai-shek's staff in Chungking, determined to eradicate 'the foreigner' in her and reimpose Confucian feudal traditions. 'You have been abroad too long . . . you must be all Chinese, you must write down your resolution . . . your resolution to be a virtuous, true Chinese woman.' She was to recall that little did she know then what those words in all their degradation meant. Her husband constantly repeated the ancient sayings 'a woman of talent is not a virtuous woman', 'to contradict your husband is a sign of immorality' and 'a woman should be a virtuous wife and an exemplary mother', and read aloud extracts from *The Thousand Virtuous and Chaste Widows* who preferred death to dishonour. He once told her that the women he most admired were those who committed suicide when their husbands died, for 'the chastity of a woman is the only worth that a woman has'. If she dared to offer a political opinion and question the policies of the government her husband retorted 'What do you know of such things? Why don't you care about womanly things instead of bothering about political issues?' As a midwife she witnessed the fear, disappointment and rejection of mothers who bore daughter after daughter. 'So many lives,' she exclaimed,

> each the life of a woman, a mother, or so many mothers
> throughout the centuries; sometimes my skin seemed to burst off
> me with awareness of injustice, with the burden of this collective
> wrong, fashioned into the very marrow of society, an era, lauded
> by pompous Confucian precepts as Destiny, Heaven-ordained.[55]

Han Suyin wrote with vehemence about the more obvious effects of the traditional ideology, but she also remembers how that ideology had a more insidious effect of eroding newly found confidence and consciousness. She recalls how she was full of zeal, ardour and the will to do well—'of course I wanted to be Chinese, of course I wanted to have noble thoughts, and now guilt began to creep upon me . . . a moral Confucian guilt'. She began to feel shameful and unworthy by the weight of the knowledge that she had 'lost her honour' before her marriage. It became difficult for her 'not to feel guilty about such a thing despite all her previous conditioning of sexual freedom and equality for women and the rejection of the double standards for men and women.'

The well-known Song sisters also did not escape the contradictions of the time. They had been brought up in a Christian home by a progressive and American-educated father and an educated mother devoted to Christianity and social service. They were educated first at the famous foreign-style school for Chinese girls, the McTyeire Girls' School in Shanghai, before spending several years in America at school and college. On their return to China each became very interested in social reform and made a fortuitous marriage to the present and future political leaders of China. Eling, the eldest, married H. H. Kung, a recognised descendant of Confucius and later chief financial adviser to the Guomindang government; Qingling married Sun Yat-sen and Meiling married Chiang Kai-shek, neither of whom need further introduction. Their very social positions attracted attention and they were perpetually advertised as representatives of the ideal of the times—active in social and patriotic works, devoted wives, with Qingling a devoted widow and Eling a devoted mother. Headlines such as 'They Stand in the Forefront of the Women's Movement' repeatedly appeared.[56] Their raising of funds and sponsorship of social projects won them much acclaim, and according to their friend and biographer, Emily Hahn, 'even the smallest child in China is well aware that Mesdames Kung, Sun and Chiang are excellent wives and helpmates'.[57]

In reality each found it difficult to combine domestic and public roles. To many the advocation of traditional norms of behaviour seemed a most unlikely pursuit for the foreign-educated, much travelled and Western-oriented Mme Chiang. She was accused many times of not practising what she preached. Her sternest critics were to be found among Chiang Kai-shek's advisers. They thought all modern women were a dangerous threat to social stability and domestic tranquillity, and that Mme Chiang was too outspoken and had too much influence in the government. According to her biographer she was aware that she trod a narrow path, and a sense of insecurity and strain eventually affected her health.[58] Eling, more shy and retiring, also found it difficult to combine tradition and modernity in her own life. In line with the teachings of the New Life Movement she thought that the old-fashioned virtues of modesty and anonymity for women were best, though her family background and American training caused her to make a reservation to the effect that women must also be financially independent.[59] However she herself attracted considerable criticism from all sides, chiefly because she accumulated more property than was thought proper for a woman. The third sister, Madame Sun, took a different line from her sisters and refused to pay lip-service to the old values. She rejected the reimposition of Confucianism and spoke out strongly against the co-option of the Women's Movement to government service. She had been horrified by the events of 1927–8 and subsequently refused to associate herself with the policies of the Guomindang government. She left China in 1927 and in her farewell message she dissociated herself:

> from active participation in carrying out the new policies of the [GMD] Party. In the last analysis, all revolutions must be social revolutions, based upon fundamental changes in society; otherwise it is not revolution, but merely a change of government.[60]

With certain limitations it was the young and single women of this class who, requiring few social facilities to combine domestic and public roles, could afford to pay lip-service to the old ideals but maintain their economic independence. An American journalist thought that the single career-women in Shanghai, Peking and Hong Kong had 'freedoms of movement' approaching those possessed by American women.[61] But Lu Xun, the writer, thought these apparent freedoms were misleading. 'In point of fact', he concluded, 'nothing has really changed' for:

> If you let a small bird which has been shut up in a cage stand on a pole, its status appears to have changed; but actually it is still the plaything of men. . . . We should not rest content with the present position, but fight unceasingly for emancipation—*in ideas* and in our economy. (my emphasis)[62]

If the professional and educated women were deluded into thinking that their position had changed appreciably, the peasant and factory working women had no such illusions. In rural areas peasant women were deprived of any source of economic independence. The decline in handicraft production took what could have been the sole form of economic independence available to peasant women. In diversely situated villages, studied by anthropologists and sociologists in the 1940s, it was evident that in most of the countryside the traditional ideology lay more or less intact. Olga Lang found that it was absolutely impossible for the young people of the villages to choose their own marriage partners. Her team investigated 360 marriages in 170 families in villages in North China and in Fujian and Jiangsu provinces. In only one case did the parents ask the consent of a young man and he was a college student. Out of 170 rural inhabitants interviewed only 3 women admitted ever having heard of 'modern marriages'.[63] Lang's findings coincided with those of other investigators.[64] It was presumed that women still knew nothing of outside affairs. In 11 of the 85 peasant families of North China and Fujian from whom information was secured, Olga Lang found that the wife's advice was an important factor in the husband's decision about business problems because of her cleverness and capabilities. In 29 cases the husbands made a show of consulting their wives in order to keep peace in the family. 'I talk things over with my wife, but the women understand very little about such matters', said a 36-year-old peasant from Fujian, expressing the opinion of many other peasants. Other peasants and their sons did not hesitate to state that they never considered consulting their wives. Lang found that within most households the husbands were the managers, sometimes consulting their wives and sometimes giving them orders.[65]

Women had little if any idea that there were new laws guaranteeing new social, political and economic rights. Fei Hsiao-tung found that in the villages he studied in the provinces of Yunnan and in the Yangtze valley in the late 1930s and early 1940s, women continued to be regarded as inferior to the men in all respects, they were excluded from all public affairs and they certainly had no knowledge of their new legal rights. In these areas wives had no rights of divorce and there was no indication of any likely change in the unilateral principle of inheritance though the law had been on the statute books for the last seven years. The villagers in Yunnan explained to him that land, the most valuable asset and the economic basis of survival in the countryside, can be of no concern to women because they bring none into the household on marriage.[66] In 1945 the anthropologist Martin Yang found in his native village of Taitou, in Shantung province, that filial piety and feminine loyalty were the two most treasured virtues. Divorce was out of the question.[67] Even in 1948–9, C. K. Yang found in Nanchang, located on the outskirts of the bustling city of Canton, a centre of law and government, that legal protection for the individual was not well developed. The village school was now open to girls, if only for one to two years, but the customs which he described were those which for centuries had circumscribed the role of women.[68] Altogether, few modern books and newspapers had found their way into the majority of villages and when they did their influence was marginal. For the greater part peasants remained illiterate. Dr Buck's investigation of literacy in the 1930s among 46,601 rural families in different parts of China revealed that 69.3 per cent of the men and 98.7 per cent of the women were illiterate. Even those classified as knowing how to read and write were for the most part unable to read a newspaper or a book.[69]

It seemed to many peasant women that old sayings polished through long centuries of use no longer seemed sufficient to deal with new situations. Zu Yuji was one of the girl students at Ginling College in Nanking who was sent to the small market town of Zhong Hechang in Sichuan to establish a rural service station. City born, bred and educated she had no idea what countrywomen should be taught, but her conversations with them revealed their predicament and fears:

> they were not familiar with the flood of paper money that was sweeping away their household earnings, they could not understand the registration which the police were undertaking, they could not read the contract for a house or farm that the family was engaged in renting, they wanted reasons for their babies dying within a week after they were born, and how to keep their children's faces from being pocked by dread disease. They wanted to learn to teach their children not to bother them, and they wanted to acquire a handicraft and the art of managing a garden.[70]

Working women in the big cities were somewhat better informed and influenced by the modern trends than the peasants in the countryside, but they still tended to see them as the prerogative of the rich. There were a few modern marriages among the industrial workers in Tientsin, Shanghai and Wuxi, but on the whole Olga Lang found that although parents in the cities were less conservative in theory, they were unlikely to practise the new ideas.

Many would say that new ideas were 'something for the rich people, like modern dress and automobiles'. Olga Lang also found that many of the factory workers she interviewed in Tientsin and Shanghai had used their position at the factory to escape from an impossible family situation caused by economic conditions or oppressive domestic relationships.[71] Employment in the foreign and Chinese-owned factories had given these women a source of economic independence, but interviews and studies reveal that many would have given up their new independence in order to escape the hardship of factory work. The majority took the view that to be a housewife was preferable to factory work with the harsh and demanding foremen, the long hours and enforced family separations.[72] New authority in the family alone was not attractive enough to tempt them to work in the factories. Although their employment was financially necessary, most clung to the old ideas approving the traditional division of labour and distribution of authority. The women workers Olga Lang interviewed had not consciously sought to change their position, but change had in fact been imposed upon them by new economic roles.

The most detailed study of the origins of factory girls showed that the factory had provided an outlet from the restraints imposed by the old ideology.[73] In one cotton mill the fieldworker found that with few exceptions, the 578 unmarried workers and the 56 married workers desired to escape from the chains which social traditions imposed on women. The following were cited as the most common family troubles: girls who had lost both parents often felt themselves despised by other relatives; girls whose mothers had died complained of maltreatment by stepmothers; girls who lived with brothers and their wives felt miserable because of the antagonistic attitude of their sister-in-law; girls who had been married and had continuous quarrels with their parents-in-law, their sisters-in-law, or with their husbands, and some had been deserted by their husbands. One nineteen-year-old girl had run away from her home and her cousin introduced her to work in the factory where her co-workers helped to protect her from the wrath of her husband who had taken up a vigil at the factory gate. Most of the workers had come to the factory through private contacts with their relatives or friends who were established workers in the factory. There was a high turnover and at the time of the investigation only one third of the work force had been at the factory for more than a year. Some of the girls were forced to return home, others left the factory when conditions at home promised to take a turn for the better and others came to hate the factory more than their home conditions. Complaints about the behaviour of the supervisors, the petty rules governing their living and working lives and the complete disinterest of the employers in the welfare of their employees were common. Many of them appreciated the alternative economic support which the factory provided, but their ideal remained a warm and secure family life. There were several substitute or surrogate 'families' formed within the factory. In one of the dormitories twelve girls had created imaginary, extensive and intricate family relationships. The women workers had sought to escape from oppressive family relations but still consciously retained the old ideals of family life. As soon as their position at home was seen to improve they tended to return to their domestic roles.

For each class, the gap between new social and economic roles and old ideals widened still further as the result of the outbreak of war. Once the Japanese armies crossed the borders into China in September 1931 the government's manipulation of ideological factors was severely threatened by the rising patriotic movement. At first the Guomindang government, unable or unwilling to check Japan's aggression, pursued an appeasement policy which only served to strengthen the hands of the invader. The Guomindang government was much more interested in suppressing the Communists, and as the Japanese troops moved further into North China a rising patriotic movement demanded positive preventative measures. At first these took indirect forms. In 1933, for example, Japanese and other foreign goods were boycotted. Four popular bodies in Shanghai decreed that 1934 should be 'Women's National Products Year' in order that their Chinese goods might compete with the foreign products which were flooding the Chinese markets. In that year Women's Day meetings were organised by the Chinese Women's Committee for the promotion of Chinese Goods. 'Buy Chinese' was the theme of the speeches and several of the local factory owners distributed samples of their manufactures at the meetings.[74] But as the Japanese armies approached Peking, the government could not check the resurgence of the political wing of the women's movement. From 1935 onwards anti-Japanese sentiment abounded in the cities where many girl and boy students came on to the streets, especially in the threatened city of Peking, to demonstrate in protest against the government policy of 'wiping out' the Communists before national resistance in the face of continued Japanese encroachment. In 1935, students in Peking launched the National Salvation Movement, and within a few weeks hundreds of National Salvation Associations (NSA) had been launched in all parts of the country and among all groups of the population including women. On the day of the founding of the Women's NSA in Shanghai, a thousand new members paraded through the city with slogans of a political nature such as 'Stop Civil War', 'Chinese must not fight Chinese', 'Form a united front against Japan to save the nation' and 'Women can emancipate themselves only through participation in resistance'.[75] The new women's organisation soon formed many separate occupational sections for professional women, teachers, students, workers and housewives.

More than anything else the war with Japan revealed the ambivalent attitude of the Guomindang government towards the organisation of women and the women's movement. With the outbreak of war, women were mobilised on a large scale to meet the needs of the national war of resistance. Not only were they exhorted to encourage sons, husbands and fathers to take up arms to defend the heritage handed down by their ancestors,[76] but they were persuaded to take an active part themselves. Mme Chiang broadcast the first of a number of calls to the women of China:

> We women are citizens just as much as are our men. Our positions, our capabilities and our lines of usefulness may be different, but we can contribute our share. . . . Today in Spain, women are standing in the fighting lines with their men; and during the Great War in every country they gave their best to aid in the realisation of victory. We Chinese women are not one bit less patriotic or less courageous or less capable of physical endurance than our sisters of other lands, and that we shall now show the world.[77]

Chinese women did indeed respond to the new national crisis. From the outbreak of war women participated fully in the war work both at the front and in supporting activities. A number of women formed their own fighting battalions. In many provinces women's War Service Corps accompanied military units providing auxiliary services and additional fighting forces. The Hunan War Service Corps, for instance, accompanied one military detachment through a battle-studded march from Shanghai to Hankou.[78] The Yunnan Woman's Battlefield Service Unit started from that remote southwestern province and proceeded by foot almost two thousand miles to the Central China Front.[79] The most famous of the girls' military units was the Guangxi Women's Battalion made up of 500 girl students.[80] Indeed, the Japanese were often surprised to find that their combatants were in fact women. A United Press message from Shanghai of September 1937 noted that thousands of Chinese girls were fighting alongside regular army forces in the front lines and many others were engaged in militia duties in the rear or were assisting in first aid relief in the battle zones.[81] More generally though women were mobilised not for front-line services, but for supporting work in the rear. Mme Chiang, who doubted whether the physical strength and endurance of women could equal that of men destined to face the enemy, recommended that the real task of women at this time was to 'stay behind the lines'.[82] In one of her speeches she outlined the duties of women during the war as carrying on men's work at the rear so that they could go to the front, or to assist in 'upholding the morale and obeying implicitly the orders of the Government'.[83] During the war she devoted herself to encouraging women to undertake these and other areas of war work.

Shortly after the outbreak of the war Mme Chiang called the wives and daughters of the leaders of the New Life Movement and proposed that women combine the principles of that movement with resistance and war work. At the same time she established two national organisations to specifically encourage women to participate in war work. The Women's Association for War Relief was established in August 1937 and soon had thirty-five branches raising funds, providing medical supplies and clothing for the army.[84] Early the next year the Association for Care and Education of War Orphans was established to provide orphanages for the increasing number of war orphans. Numerous small organisations worked alongside the National-government-sponsored organisations, the Christian organisations and the National Salvation Associations. It was reported that in Shanghai alone twenty-eight women's organisations were working feverishly for the war effort in 1937.[85] It was soon evident that the proliferation of separate organisations all working for the same end resulted either in unnecessary duplication or in the neglect of large areas of work. The growing need for an active national organisation of women to plan, co-ordinate and correlate women's work was increasingly recognised. The Eastern Miscellany published an article by Wang Xiaoyin called 'What Women Should do during National Crises'. She considered it was imperative that women should be trained for various types of war work including transportation, nursing, air-defence, child-care and propaganda. She quoted the example of the Soviet Union where 'women receive training just like men', and called for further rationalisation and organisation of womanpower.

> Together with more education, there should be more well-organised activities, as organisation is just as important as education. Foreigners always laugh at us for being in a state of disorganisation, and they are right to a great extent. In these critical years women should organise to work for liberty in political, economic and social standing. We require organisation among the women in towns, rural districts and in different vocations as well as in homes, so that every woman can have a part in the work of saving the nation.[86]

In response to this demand for a national and all-inclusive organisation of women, Mme Chiang called a national women's conference in Kuling in May 1938. In addition to delegates from each province, all the prominent women leaders of the country were invited—writers, professional women, government officials, student leaders and heads of organisations. Long-established organisations such as the YWCA, the new political organisations like the NSA and the new wartime products like the National Women's Relief Associations sent representatives. At this time the GMD had temporarily given up the pursuit of the CCP and they were co-operating to fight against the Japanese so that there were also a limited number of Communist women present. They represented the women of the Soviet base areas in the north of China. In her opening speech Mme Chiang defined the broad objective of the women's conference:

> We, who are gathered here today, are the so-called intellectual leaders of Chinese womanhood. Each of us has been invited to attend this meeting because we have a definite contribution to make to the ultimate goal. Upon us, therefore, rests a gigantic responsibility of leading our fellow women in every stratum of society.[87]

She went on to talk of the need to devise a national programme for women's war work. The machinery was established to reach women of all classes and sections of society. The Women's Advisory Council of the New Life Movement, with Mme Chiang as chairwoman, was appointed as an organising and co-ordinating agency whose main functions were to inform, advise, liaise and train leaders for expanded war work. Nine departments of work covering Co-ordination, Training, War Area Service, Rural Service, Livelihood, Cultural, War Relief, Refugee Children, and Production were established. The conference covered a wide range of subjects and problems in formal and informal discussion groups. This was the first time that women delegates from the entire country had met together and they were greatly excited by the spirit of the conference.[88]

There was a tremendous burst of enthusiasm for war work among the women. By 1941 there were more than 317 women's organisations spread throughout 21 provinces participating in war work, their activities ranging from raising funds, nursing, making garments for soldiers' entertainments, caring for refugees and orphans, to stretcher duties and informing on spies and infiltrators.[89] Newspaper article after newspaper article praised the contribution of the women to the war effort. Photographs showed women, who barely a year ago had been confined to their homes, working in hospitals, in sewing circles or at some courageous war deed. Women were taught the principles of the New Life Movement, literacy skills, public health and hygiene, new methods of production, and handicraft skills were revived. The most interesting projects established were Industrial Co-operatives in which evacuated factory girls, soldier wives, refugee and peasant women whose lives had been dislocated by the war were taught skills and given materials to become economically self-sufficient. They established their own literacy groups, clinics and vocational training schools within the Co-operatives.[90] The greatest difficulty in establishing the various projects discussed at Kuling was the lack of trained leadership and organisers. Mme Chiang herself wrote in 1941 that it would be an exaggeration to say that the mobilisation of women was widespread because of the enormous need for trained personnel.[91] She founded a number of training schools where college students and young high-school girls were taught to give instructions in character-building, improve the standard of living of the people, safeguard the interests of the people and to promote wholehearted support for the winning of the war. They were sent into the country in 'teams' of twenty or thirty and from their headquarters they established, in temples or any public building available, classes in sanitation, rural economics, the three Rs, and first and foremost in the war and its significance. There is no doubt that the women who attended these and other like courses benefited from the acquisition of new skills, but these courses were not widespread and few directly questioned traditional relations between men and women or the economic relations which were responsible for so much misery in the 1930s and 1940s. The aim of Mme Chiang and the Women's National Advisory Council to establish a national working organisation of women and to accomplish the social regeneration of Chinese women through 'economic reconstruction, education and especially the ideals embodied in the New Life Movement' floundered.

The Guomindang government's continuous calls on women to contribute to the war effort and the mistrust of the spontaneous organisations which arose in their wake reflected the ambivalent attitude of the government towards popular organisations in general. It was very difficult to limit their field of manoeuvre to one that was acceptable to its conservative supporters. Practical classes in literacy and rural self-help for example were very likely to inadvertently touch on real grievances, and questions of political import such as the system of land tenure and the nature of local politics. At these points the gradualist approach of the social worker and educator of the women's movement ran into the vested interests of local power-holders. Even the harmless enough social clubs gave women new collective experiences, the impact of which was recognised by the president of the Women's Club in Shanghai:

> These social affairs make club women conscious of their organising and co-operative ability, develop leadership through assumption of responsibility of all sorts and furnish them an experience previously denied them. The membership fees are merely nominal, but even this creates a band of unity and sense of organisation that endures to their benefit.[92]

Under the banner of patriotism women came to experience new political and social activities which brought them face to face with old prohibitions.[93]

In the movement to save the country many of the old taboos came to be questioned. The record of a meeting at a university in Peking to celebrate Women's Day in 1936 illustrates the reaction which set in against the old traditions reiterated by the New Life Movement.[94] Wall newspapers on the campus included drawings showing women under pressure from 'li' or old rules and customs in the family such as the demands of chastity; others portrayed the history of Women's Day, and the position of women under Fascism in Germany and Italy where they had to 'go back to the kitchen' was contrasted with their role in Soviet Russia. The slogans centred around the theme of 'down with feudalism' and 'the family circle' and 'into society to take up national liberation work', and university and middle-school students sang the special March 8 song about never returning home and fighting oppression. The chairwoman, Gong Busheng, impressed upon the audience that the problem of women was part of the national problem. She tried to show that it was not an individual problem or a psychological one, but was bound up with the whole social system. Their problem, she argued, could only be solved if women contributed to the war effort to save China from degradation and Fascist suppression. Another woman spoke about the origins of Women's Day and how women now have their one day a year as opposed to the 364 days belonging to men. A famous doctor in Peking got up and advocated the cultivation of the family, and the rearing of healthy children and upright youths by women as a panacea to the country's problems. His speech was strongly opposed and the audience hit back with a number of arguments. One girl got up and spoke about Engels's theory of the family and private property. But this was apparently too academic to elicit the popular response produced by the less sophisticated arguments, such as that most children were brought up by servants anyway and that the problem facing China now could not await the arrival of a new generation.

In Shanghai and Qingdao when women workers walked out of Japanese-owned textile mills on strike the National Salvation Associations of Women formed committees to mobilise support for them.[95] In one of the cotton mills in Shanghai ten women workers organised themselves into a 'Sister Group' to arouse support for underground resistance against the Japanese. Soon the interests of the Sister Group expanded. They met in the evenings and on Sundays to study and discuss marriage, the different aspects of women's position in society, social evils, state affairs, and to read newspapers.[96] The goals of the National Salvation Associations brought women into the prohibited political arena and if the Guomindang needed any convincing of the likely dangers of this move they had only to look to the Soviet bases of the Communists for substantiation of their fears. It was reported that the Communists 'encouraged slave girls and concubines to revolt against their masters and they incited the peasant women to stand up and denounce their husbands' misdeeds!'[97]

To counteract any such activities the government continued to circumscribe the activities of women. The government-sponsored organisations of women rested not so much on a well-developed ideology or organisation as on the foundations of personal loyalty to Mme Chiang herself. As in the New Life Movement, so in the National Women's programme, Mme Chiang relied in the main on the help of wives and daughters of trusted Guomindang officials, a handful of professional women and foreign missionaries. In the provinces, the wives of the provincial chairmen were usually directly responsible to her national standing committee. According to Mme Chiang, the most notable example of good work was that undertaken by Madame Wu Dingzhan, wife of the chairman of Guizhou province, who was a 'typical old-fashioned lady and mother of the most conservative type'. Madame Wu was said to arrive at her office punctually every day and rule the office with an iron hand which was a 'sight delightful to behold and to be emulated'. Madame Zhu Shaoling of Gansu and Madame Ma Bufang of Qinghai provinces were also considered noteworthy examples of wives of Provincial chairmen who though 'of the old school' had cast aside their reserve and spurred on the women of their native provinces to participate in war work.[98] Mme Chiang herself supervised the training of new leaders. Emily Hahn, the friend and biographer of Mme Chiang, concluded that in the training schools, it was her personality that 'worked the miracle of turning these representatives of the middle-class women from what was formerly the most sheltered group of femininity in the world, into young Amazons of civilisation.' She went on to describe how Mme Chiang went every day to their classes and 'talked as only she can talk', nervously, burning, eagerly, sincerely, until in a burst of young enthusiasm mixed inextricably with hero-worship 'the girls made themselves over into what they knew she would want them to be'. Apparently even the smallest details of the training school reflected her personality and particularly her preoccupation with cleanliness. She noted that one of the problems which emerged as new centres of training were established was her inability to give so much time to individual groups.[99]

Peasant and working women largely remained outside any organisation for women. One of the delegates at the 1938 Conference told Nym Wales that the one attempt to organise women of all classes was short lived because there was no base network of mass organisations.[100] Song Qingling, a critic of the government, observed in 1941 that the work of organising the peasants remained unaccomplished for lack of any concrete organisation.[101] There was no organisational network which reached into the villages and poorer urban areas and through which the majority of women could contribute to the patriotic movement, let alone fight for their political, social and economic rights. Any attempt was firmly suppressed. In 1940 a meeting of delegates from the women's organisations in the capital, which was called by the Women's Advisory Council to devise measures of self-protection, attracted the attention of the secret police.[102] Political activity smacked of Communist influence and a wave of arrests followed the New Fourth Army incident in 1941 when once again Guomindang troops fought in battle with Communist forces. Many participants in women's organisations were arrested including one member of the highest co-ordinating body. Many of the most active organisers were compelled to either leave the country or flee to the Communist bases in northwest China. Notices, such as:

> It is learned that Miss Chen Zizhui, well-known left-wing authoress and head of the Cultural Affairs Department of the National Women's Supervisory Committee under Mme Chiang has resigned; it is understood she has joined the New Fourth Army in Eastern China.[103]

can be found in the personal and news columns of contemporary newspapers. Women who joined in the increasing resistance to the rising economic inflation and continuing civil war were harassed. For instance many girl students were wounded in student demonstrations against inflation and hunger when soldiers surrounded and arrested students at the National Women's Teachers' College in Chungking.[104] A year later more than 6,000 Shan Chui 'rebellious' textile factory workers were surrounded and attacked by the police and army. They fought back regardless of the tear gas and armoured cavalry, and many were fined, arrested or killed.[105]

Many women had become increasingly frustrated with the prolonged state of war and civil war, first with the Japanese and then with the Communists, the growing state of economic disarray and the repression of their organisations. After the Nationalist Revolution of the 1920s women activists were given the choice between the limited reforms advocated by the Guomindang Party or taking the path of revolution with the Communist Party. The majority had chosen reform and redefined feminism accordingly. But like the body of Guomindang supporters as a whole, the women's movement, after its expansion in the 1920s, had gradually contracted to an urban middle- and upper-class movement which attempted reforms on the basis of altruism, benevolence and patronage. Any systematic attempt to organise women in their own specific and class interests aroused the antagonism of the ruling classes. Like Eling Song, wife of the financial adviser to the government, its supporters believed in a voluntary form of social contract. She had always wondered 'why labour and capital could not be friends'. She had placed her hopes in the evolution of a happy family relationship in which capital played 'big brother' and labour the 'little brother'.[106] Faced with increasing internal opposition and civil war the Guomindang fell into rapid disrepute. Their response to any kind of protest or disruption was always the same—they blamed the interference of outside forces, namely that of the Communists. The Guomindang never recognised or understood the real grievances of the rural and urban working classes upon whose labour power the profits of their supporters rested. Certainly in Guomindang China outmoded ideological constructs and increasing inflation and impoverishment had by the late 1940s caused some women to appreciate the limits that the organisation of society itself placed on their wider aspirations.[107] Throughout the 1940s small numbers of women had opted to follow in the revolutionary tradition of the Nationalist Movement of the 1920s and join the Communists in their Soviet Bases.

'Woman Work': Communist China 7

Realise the slogan of women's liberation.
(CCP Resolution on Women's Movement, 1928)[1]

Following the split between the Guomindang and Communist Parties in 1927, the CCP continued to nurture the women's movement as part of an overall strategy to build anew a nationalist and revolutionary movement in China. In the next twenty years the CCP once more attempted to integrate the goals of the two movements by first mobilising women to participate in the long political and military struggle that lay ahead, and then using this mobilisation as a means of improving the status of women in social, political and economic spheres of activity. To realise the slogan of women's liberation the Communists planned to educate and organise women for struggle against their double oppression: the oppression shared by the men of their own class, and the oppression at the hands of their menfolk. First the impasse resulting from the severe setback and repression following the rupture with the Guomindang provided an opportunity for the CCP to analyse the history of the women's movement during the Nationalist Revolution and its relation to other oppressed groups and their organisations. A summary of this analysis can be found in a Resolution on the CCP and the women's liberation movement which was passed at the Sixth CCP Congress held in Moscow in 1928.[2]

It was apparent that the CCP had not found it easy in the 1920s to balance the demands of the women's and class associations. The resolution reiterated the fundamental principle that though women shared the same class oppression and therefore class organisations and struggle as men, their special oppression also demanded a separate organisation and separate struggle. It criticised the 'feminist women's movement', or one that is divorced from politics and revolution, and which seeks to liberate women by peaceful means and propaganda, 'as sheer illusion and fantasy'. Furthermore the resolution noted that while the reformist women's movement predominantly influenced the 'petty bourgeois intellectuals' there was always the possibility that this kind of movement which opposed class struggle would also attract and deceive the working and peasant women. Yet with the nationalist revolutionary movement itself there had been a very real threat that the work among women might conflict with the activities of the wider revolutionary movement and thereby become a divisive force setting men against women or women against men and disrupting the revolutionary forces. The women's movement was criticised for following its own independent line. On the other hand there was also the threat that the male-dominated class organisations and Party would ignore the interests of women and cause their special organisations to take on the traditional status accorded to individual women, and thereby become a second-class organisation to which women were confined. The male domination of village affairs, the neglect of woman work and the relegation of the women's associations to a secondary place in the revolutionary struggle might mean that the women's association was no longer in a position to protect the newly won rights of its members. It also ran the risk of becoming isolated from the class struggle. In the Resolution, the Party was criticised for elements of 'negligence and opportunism'. 'Negligence' in that the Party had not paid enough attention to the concrete demands of the women's movement or recognised its importance by promoting women to Party membership or leadership positions. 'Opportunistic' in that the Party had found it politic to rely on the urban middle-class or bourgeois women, who had already improved their position somewhat, rather than the often less conscious working and peasant women. The support of these middle-class women had proved to be unreliable and had faded away with the split between the two Parties and the subsequent repression. They had opted for the reformist programme of the Guomindang that offered to recognise the equality of men and women before the law. The Resolution suggested that the nature of the links between the two movements was primarily determined by the social composition of the women's movement itself. The main recommendation of the Resolution was that top priority should be given to work among peasant and urban working women, and in keeping with the Marxist tradition, especially the latter. It recommended that the platforms of the women's movement should be revised to reflect this emphasis.

Demands were drawn up which would improve the working conditions of factory women workers. These were to include the realisation of the eight-hour work day; prohibition of night labour by children, pregnant women and nursing mothers; a shortening of the night-hour shift, equal pay for the same kind of work;

protection of mothers; prohibition of women from engaging in excessive and dangerous work; a regular weekly day of rest; prohibition of small children working in factories; organisation of kindergartens and nurseries. Help was to be given to organisations already in existence such as the mutual aid associations and 'sister leagues' of the women workers in textile and silk factories who daily struggled to improve the conditions of their work. In this way trade unions would eventually be able to unify the demands and organisations of, for example, the various sister leagues. The special oppression of peasant women was also considered, and the spontaneity with which they had entered the Peasant Associations in the past recognised.

> The experiences of the peasant movement in many areas in the past show that peasant women are the bravest participants among the struggling peasants. Seeming to absorb the peasant women into the movement will definitely result in the failure of the agrarian revolution.[3]

The concrete demands proposed which would directly affect their interests included rights of inheritance, rights to land, opposition to the custom of having several wives, opposition to the practice of adopting child-brides, opposition to imposing marriage on girls, the rights to divorce, and protection for the labour of women farmhands. The Resolution finally went on to consider the role of middle-class women and came to the conclusion that women of the petty-bourgeois class—the urban poor, handicraftsmen, small merchants and the intellectuals who identified with the goals of the revolutionary struggle—should not be ignored for 'during critical moments of the revolution, the attitude of the petty bourgeois can determine victory or defeat for revolution or for counter-revolution'. Although their importance was recognised, the role of petty-bourgeois women was given less consideration than working and peasant women, who were to form the backbone of the new women's movement and, with their menfolk, of the revolutionary movement. The primacy accorded to either of these two groups, the peasant or urban working women, at any one time reflected internal divisions within the CCP itself.

The emphasis on the role of urban working-class women was in line with the general policy of the CCP, following on from Marx and Lenin, that the progress of the revolution was determined by the degree of preparation of the urban working classes or urban proletariat. This policy, associated in China at this time with the name of Li Lisan, propelled the Party towards concentrating its main work in the industrial centres. Although on the one hand, places such as Shanghai, Tientsin, Canton and Wuhan sheltered large numbers of workers, they were also the centres of the political and military forces of the Guomindang. In Shanghai, where Liu Jianxian was head of the Department of Women Workers in the CCP Trade Union, workers' demonstrations and strikes usually resulted in large numbers of arrests. The atmosphere of fear and suspicion which followed made it difficult for them to expand their influence and many even left the CCP trade unions to join the influential Guomindang or Yellow trade unions which, having legal and monetary advantages on their side, sometimes brought results, however meagre.[4] In a number of the industrial centres a series of abortive uprisings ended in defeat and dispersal, and in the urban areas the repression and persistence of the GMD rendered the open, and even underground, existence of the CCP almost impossible. In this situation a number of Party members began to search for alternative ways of continuing the revolutionary tradition of the years 1925–7. The number and nature of peasant uprisings in these years had caused one member, Mao Zedong, to recognise the revolutionary potential of the peasantry in China.

The decreasing arena of revolutionary struggle in the cities and the rapid defeat of a number of autumn harvest uprisings in the countryside forced the remnant military forces of the CCP to withdraw to the isolated and rugged mountain stronghold of Jinggangshan on the Hunan–Jiangxi (Kiangsi) border. Here their leaders, Mao Zedong and Zhu De, began the painstaking task of building up a Red Army recruited from the rural inhabitants of these and surrounding areas. The next few years witnessed a major reorientation of the CCP in which the policies of Li Lisan and his followers lost credence, and the efficacy of establishing bases in rural areas and winning the support of the peasantry increasingly won the support of Party members. With these changes, peasant women rather than urban women workers became the backbone of the new women's movement.

In his essay on the 'Autumn Harvest Uprising' in Hunan Mao Zedong analysed the oppression of peasant women and inextricably linked their liberation with the fortunes of the peasants' revolutionary struggle. He wrote that:

A man in China is usually subjected to the domination of three systems of authority [political authority, clan authority and religious authority]. . . . As for women, in addition to being dominated by these three systems of authority, they are also dominated by men [the authority of the husband].[5]

Mao Zedong considered these four authorities to be the 'four thick ropes' binding the Chinese women, especially those of peasant origins. He thought the political authority of the landlord underlay the three other systems of authority, for with the overturning of the power of the landlord 'the clan authority, the religious authority, and the authority of the husband all begin to totter'. 'In a word,' he said, 'the whole feudal-patriarchal ideology and system is tottering with the growth of the Peasants' power'.[6] His analysis perceived there to be a close connection between the productive relationships in agriculture and the system of landownership on the one hand, and the hierarchical relations between the sexes on the other. He forecast that the breakdown of the economic relations would be followed by the breakdown of the social relations between the sexes. On this basis the women's and the wider revolutionary movement were intimately linked, and the importance of both movements in improving the position of women was to form the guiding principle of woman work in the rural Soviet Bases. The balancing of the demands and interests of the two movements was to exercise the CCP in the ensuing decades, but in the late 1920s the first priority was to secure a base of some stability and gain the support of peasant men and women.

It was some years before a women's movement was re-established on any large scale. Although the CCP at its annual executive meetings continued to affirm its support of the working and peasant women's movement, woman work remained limited in scope. Until the establishment of a base of at least minimal stability it was confined to generally arousing women to an awareness of their situation and forming women's unions in the wake of the movements of the mobile Red Armies. A few young propagandists continued to travel with the Red Armies. Kang Keqing, later to become a noted woman commander of the Red Army, ran away from her native village in Jiangxi to join the Red Army in 1928. She had been a member of the Women's Union organised during the Nationalist Revolution in 1926 and now she was escaping from an arranged marriage to a shop clerk. She was one of a hundred or so women based in Jinggangshan who approached the villagers, explained the policies of the Red Army and organised partisan movements in its wake.[7] Agnes Smedley, an American woman travelling with the Red Armies, described the formation of a women's union in the district of Ningkang near the military stronghold of Jinggangshan. The day the Red Army entered the district, mass meetings were held and Committees appointed to found women's, peasants' and labourers' associations which were to elect delegates to represent their interests on the Revolutionary Committee ruling the district. In the Ningkang district there were many women agricultural labourers who were eligible to become members of the Agricultural Labourers' Union. Smedley noted that these women quickly joined it and soon took charge of that association. Their activities aroused the curiosity and interest of other women of the district. Before a week was out 3,000 or so women workers of the market town had demanded a union of their own. In response to this demand a general women's union was organised and many also joined the Red Guards, an organisation formed to defend each village and town.[8]

Although the education and organisation of women was the responsibility of one of the Departments attached to the central executive and the district revolutionary committees, the still precarious position of the Red Army and the suppression of the pursuing GMD armies made it difficult to undertake any long-term programmes. Zhu De, one of the leaders of the Red Army, felt that while the new Women's Associations tended to lead to the first break in the ancient subjugation of women to men, woman work was on the whole rather neglected in these early years.[9] A Resolution of the CCP passed in 1930 noted that the present tendency to neglect the women's movement was a grave political error.[10] Soon the situation began to improve. From 1929 the Red Armies had begun to abandon the stronghold of Jinggangshan in favour of a new base in rural southern Jiangxi and it was here that the first Chinese Soviet Republic was founded. For the first time the Party acquired formalised control over a domain which enabled them to embark on a series of programmes to implement a combined strategy which would redefine the position of women as part of the establishment of a new economic, political and social system.

The women's movement, or what was known as woman work, was formally acclaimed an important aspect of revolutionary activity. The constitution proclaimed by the first All-China Congress in Juichin, Jiangxi, guaranteed the thorough emancipation of women.

It is the purpose of the Soviet government of China to guarantee
the thorough emancipation of women; it recognises freedom of
marriage and will put into operation various measures for the
protection of women, to enable women gradually to attain to the
material base required for their emancipation from the bondage
of domestic work and to give them the possibility of
participating in the social, economic, political and cultural life
of the entire society.[11]

These principles of equality in status and participation were
incorporated into several laws which specifically affected the
position of women in marriage and the family, and in their
relationship to the land, the factory and new political institutions.
As important a factor as the passing of the new laws was the
establishment of special Women's Departments in all Party
organisations, and in each district local women's congresses
presided over work among women and elected representatives to
defend their interests in the locally elected peasant and worker
soviets. A 'Plan for Work Among the Women' was drawn up by
the Special Committee for Northern Jiangxi of the Central
Committee of the CCP in 1931.[12] In it emphasis was placed on the
implementation of the new laws in practice, especially among
peasant women and working women of the towns. It was stressed
that it was not enough just to introduce new legislation, it had to
be put into practice. The Plan also included a warning that some
issues caused the women's movement to be 'led away from the
general movement and become isolated'. The Plan suggested that
when this happened there was no connection with the overall
revolutionary and class struggle and the integration of the women's
movement into the wider revolutionary movement was hampered.
To prevent this the women's movement was to encourage its
members to participate in class associations and political
institutions.

A most important organisational goal of the Party was the
establishment of elected peasant and worker soviets that would
maximise the involvement of the population in local government.
To break down the traditional division of labour and give women
every opportunity to participate in political affairs and represent
their interests in sufficient numbers, it was laid down that at least
one or two of every five of the leaders of each soviet should be
of women. A report published in the early 1930s revealed that a
number of village and regional soviets were presided over by

chairwomen, and practically every soviet consisting of five members included one to two women who participated in the general work of the soviet and in committees for improving the position of women.[13] In 1934 it was recorded that in the majority of city and village soviets, women delegates constituted more than 25 per cent of the deputies.[14] In an investigation of one exceptionally advanced district, Mao Zedong found that the number of women's representatives in the lower district congress rose from 30 per cent in 1931 to 62 per cent in 1932 and by a further 2 per cent in the following year.[15] Agnes Smedley was impressed by the number of women speakers at meetings and by the calibre of the fifty or so women who attended the first Congress of the Soviet Areas. She cited the case of one old peasant woman who, though she was nearly sixty years of age, had walked for six weeks to reach the Congress.[16] However, there are also instances of villages attempting to limit the voting power of the women and interfere with their work in the soviets. But on the whole in Jiangxi it may be that there was a relatively low level of resistance to women's participation in public affairs because of the absence of men away with the Red Army. The continuing civil war which characterised much of the period of the Jiangxi Soviet was not without its effect on the position of women in political and economic activities. Though in these southern provinces peasant women were not unused to labouring in the fields, they were encouraged to take a larger part in agricultural labour. A speech on 'Our Economic Policy' in 1934 recognised that the participation of women in agriculture was crucial to the maintenance of the economy of the Soviet Base. It went on to say that 'our fundamental task is to adjust the use of labour power in an organised way and to encourage women to do farmwork.'[17] It was a similar policy in the industrial sector of the economy. Women in the towns were encouraged to take employment and there were upwards of 10,000 women workers in the 310,000 strong Trade Union movement.[18] Liu Jianxian, a worker from Wuxi and Shanghai who moved to the Jiangxi Soviet was in charge of the women workers' movement. Special laws were introduced to give protection to female and child labour. They were not allowed to undertake heavy jobs and women were to receive two months' leave with full pay before and after confinement.

To enable women to participate in political and economic activities, literacy classes were held at which texts such as 'Woman Work' or 'Talks with Women' were studied. Women were encouraged to attend schools and in some evening courses more than two thirds of the pupils were women.[19] Efforts were made to explain the policies behind the popular slogans: 'Extinguish the feudal forces', 'Struggle for the freedom of marriage', 'Prohibit the practice of foster daughters-in-law', 'Cut the hair short and unbind the feet' and 'Oppose the Three Commands of Obedience and Four Virtues'. Training courses were established to train women activists in leadership techniques. But as in nearly all spheres of activity in this period it is difficult to judge the degree of success of these policies. It is clear, however, that the period of the Jiangxi Soviet was an important stage in the developing and testing of practical policies. The Communists found that the offensives of the GMD often forced these policies into taking second place to the war effort.

An all-out effort was made to absorb women into the war effort. As one of the women's songs, 'Sending my brother or lover to war . . .' suggests, women were exhorted to encourage their menfolk to enlist in the Red Armies. But active service was not only limited to men. There were some women in the Red Army and more belonged to its supportive organisations. A few like Kang Keqing attended classes at the military academy and later led troops in battle. Kang Keqing was made a detachment commander of the Women Volunteers. The estimates of the detachment's number range from 200 to 500 and all were peasant women. Kang Keqing told Nym Wales that although after good training, intellectuals and students might be able to do this kind of work, peasant girls had a much greater endurance and were more determined and unwavering. 'Even with thorough training the intellectual's social background asserts itself in actual fighting. Theoretical understanding of the revolution is not enough to overcome this background.'[20] Some women were attached to the Red Army to do political work among the soldiers. The vast majority of active women over the age of eighteen joined the Red Guards and those under eighteen joined the Youth Volunteers. These two groups worked in the rear nursing the wounded, carrying supplies, guarding villages and towns, and with the Women's Aid Corps organised laundries, kitchens, intelligence units and sewing corps. A poem written by a young girl in Juichin, Jiangxi called 'Midnight and Still Making Shoes' became a popular folksong:

Moths fly into the lamp
because of the light, bees
search out flowers for sweetness;

lass half through the night
still making shoes for the fighters
helping brothers to go out
kill the enemy that come like wolves.[21]

A contemporary report on the Soviet Areas describes the contribution of women to the defence of the bases against the Guomindang forces in glowing terms.[22] But if the Communist Party and the women's movement co-operated to break down the traditional division of labour and defend their territory, the hostility aroused by the freedoms of marriage and divorce tended to once again separate one from the other.

The freedom of marriage and divorce had been an important principle to the early Communist leaders. It formed part of their more general opposition to the hierarchical relations within the family. The Provisional Marriage Relations discussed in the first session of the Central Executive Committee of the Chinese Soviet Republic in Jiangxi (28 January 1931) opened with the words: 'Under feudal domination, marriage is a barbaric and inhuman institution. The oppression and suffering borne by the women is far greater than that of men.'[23] It was proposed that marriages should be contracted in Soviet Areas on an 'absolutely free basis'. 'Freedom', it said, 'must be the basic principle of every marriage.' Regarding divorce, they felt that because of the traditional handicaps still affecting women, such as bound feet, lack of education and opportunities for economic independence, it was necessary 'to deviate in the direction of protecting the women until they have gained economic independence and place the greater part of the obligations and responsibilities entailed by divorce upon men'. Hence the new economic guarantees for the women and provision for children on the dissolution of marriage. It is difficult from the evidence in the material available for this period to draw conclusions as to the extent to which the provisions of this law were adopted. According to one early report the freedom of marriage and divorce was the most difficult problem to solve and was certainly nowhere near being solved in many areas.[24]

The experience in several districts illustrates the range of difficulties encountered. At a mass meeting in Yunsi district, where differences broke out between women and both the Red Army soldiers and men peasants, a resolution was passed which, though approving freedom of marriage in principle, limited the conditions of divorce.[25] In another district the peasants demanded the death penalty for those women who attempted to take advantage of the law proposing freedom of marriage and divorce.[26] In some districts in southwest Jiangxi women interpreted the new rights of divorce to include the murder of their husbands.[27] Freedom of marriage was mistakenly interpreted by some, including cadres, to mean sexual licence[28] and many women were themselves also opposed to the new principles and firmly obstructed any attempts to implement them.[29] It seems likely that the misinterpretation of and opposition to the provisional law by peasants of either sex were responsible for the modifications in the law which soon began to appear in Party documents and were incorporated into the Marriage Regulations at the end of 1931. The Communists found themselves torn between their beliefs in the principles of the freedom of marriage, with their obvious attraction to some women, and the opposition they aroused when implemented in practice. Hence the new distinction between 'freedom' and 'absolute freedom'. A Party document illustrated the juxtaposition: 'We must not only refrain from imposing limitations on the freedom of marriage . . . but we must resolutely oppose the idea of absolute freedom of marriage as it creates chaotic conditions in society and antagonises the peasants and the Red Army.'[30] Another document resolutely opposed the absolute freedom of marriage and firmly believed that women will be able to win freedom of marriage but by a less direct approach. There must be some kind of mechanism by which marriage and divorce could be contracted and formalised. This was exclusively to be a function of the Soviet government, which was designated the only organ which could guarantee freedom of marriage and divorce. In other words, it was not a matter to be decided by the villagers themselves or the women's movement on a spontaneous basis.[31]

The implementation of the marriage laws was taken up by the women's movement and the Party. At repeated intervals the Party reiterated its goals and discussed the problems of implementing their policies; Deng Yingzhao later recalled that the introduction of free marriage accounted for much of the work among women in the Jiangxi Soviet.[32] Zhu De observed that women were the most militant advocates of the equality of the sexes and often adopted their own methods of dealing with those of their menfold who proved recalcitrant.[33] It was the apparent preoccupation of the women's movement with this single problem which caused concern to the Party. It tended to isolate the women's movement and separate it from class associations and the wider revolutionary movement. The immediate participation of women in the wider political movement was said to be hampered and obscured by the single issue of freedom of marriage. For instance when 'they [the leaders of the women's movement] concentrated on marriage problems', they facilitated 'the emergence of a contradiction between the sexes which could obstruct the land reform'.[34] The women's movement was warned by the leaders of the wider revolutionary movement against neglecting other elements of social and economic organisation without which freedom of marriage or any other improvement in the position of women could not take place. Mao Zedong, in his report to the Executive Committee published at the Second National Congress of Representatives of the Soviets held in March 1934, clearly made the point that the disappearance of the

feudal marriage system was dependent on the wider programme to institute a new social, political and economic system. Only when, after the overthrow of the dictatorship of the landlords and the capitalists, the toiling masses of men and women—in particular the women—have acquired political freedom in the first place, and economic freedom in the second, can freedom of marriage obtain its final guarantee.[35]

During the Jiangxi Soviet, however, the mobilisation of women for military and allied purposes increasingly tended towards the neglect of other facets of woman work. Attention to marriage regulations, land reform regulations, labour regulations and the establishment of creches was either neglected or subordinated to the demands of the military struggle and survival. Although in the first five years of the Soviet it was proudly noted that in southwestern Jiangxi there were upwards of 300,000 women members of the peasant unions, trade unions and the Red Army,[36] by 1934 the CCP leaders were more critical of their record in woman work. Mao Zedong concluded from his investigation of woman work in the Zhongyang district that the specific interests of women were being lost in the concern for the more general policies, and insufficient attention was given to education and the explanation of the new policies to peasant and working women. He called on the women's movement to modify its approach to women and improve its work style. He recommended that meetings of representatives of women workers and peasant women should:

first of all attend to problems which affect the close interests of the masses of women, and following mobilisation in connection with such problems, associate it with the mobilisation in connection with all political problems. The attention which many areas are now paying to this point is very inadequate.[37]

But there was no opportunity to put this new approach into practice. At this juncture the most urgent problem became less the expansion, than the very survival of the Communist base. The combined pressure of the economic blockade and the fifth military encirclement by the Guomindang increasingly undermined the position of the CCP in Jiangxi. The Red Army was eventually left with no alternative, but to break its way out of the Guomindang stranglehold by abandoning the Jiangxi base. Thus began one of the greatest physical feats of the twentieth century—the Long March.

The Long March was a 6,000 to 8,000 mile circuitous trek from the southern to the northern provinces of China. In the course of a year the Red Army traversed on foot almost inaccessible mountains, some of the longest rivers of China and treacherous marshy grasslands. They were under constant daily and ground attack by the pursuing Nationalist forces. Among the marchers were 50 women: 30 CCP members who had worked for many years in the women's and the wider revolutionary movement and 20 others. Several were past and future leaders of the women's movement and many have described their experiences. Apart from constant warfare, food shortage and ill-health presented the biggest problems during the Long March. Some women were stronger than others. Kang Keqing, the strong woman commander, recalled 'It was as easy for me as taking a stroll every day. Sometimes I rode a horse and sometimes I walked with others and carried my own belongings and those of others who were in a weaker state.'[38] She was said to have carried a man on her back on two or three occasions and always carried three or four rifles to encourage the others. Liu Jianxian found the first few weeks very exhausting.

> At first the marching was difficult. Our feet were so sore we had to wash them with hot water every night. Many lagged behind and could not keep up. Only a few women joined the Red Army on the Long March because it was so difficult. . . . Death seemed to lie in wait everywhere.[39]

Deng Yingzhao, an activist in the women's movement, recalled a year of unbelievable hardship. In 1934 she had had a serious relapse of tuberculosis and for the first four months she lay on a stretcher unable to walk. 'Only my belief in what we were trying to do and my willpower enabled me to triumph over the suffering of the first months.'[40] Later she was able to walk or ride a horse. 'I shall never forget the hardships and difficulties of these months. We were constantly pursued and attacked by the Guomindang troops.'[41] She described to the Australian author Dymph Cusack how they often had to march at night and make great detours to shake off their pursuers. Lightly clad they passed over snow-covered trackless mountain regions and 'the rarefied air made it difficult for us to breathe, and for me with my sick lungs, it was particularly hard. . . . As we progressed things got worse. It was difficult to get food, difficult to cook it when obtained.'[42] To deal with the shortage of food and to forestall complaints of physical weakness the fifty women formed a special women's detachment to carry and arrange for their own food.

Despite the arduous route and the physical difficulties which they faced, the women undertook political and educational work, nursing duties and collected provisions from the peasants in the villages where they stopped and rested en route. Kang Keqing said she was so busy organising meetings when they stopped that she hardly had time to wash her own clothes.[43] Their task was to explain to the peasants 'what we were' and 'what we stood for'. Usually the peasants fled from their villages on the approach of the Red Army, but they soon returned once they saw that the Red Army kept the strictest of discipline and paid for all its provisions. Several times they made surveys of the landlords' land and goods and helped in their redistribution. In Tsunyi, Guizhou, where they stopped for ten days, Liu Jianxian helped organise the women silk workers to secure salary increases from their employers.[44] The CCP personnel and Red Army passed on, but they left behind a reputation which entered into the local folklores of the villages. The very dimensions of the Long March were destined to become a legend with all the qualities of the traditional popular epics, and referring to it, Mao Zedong is said to have afterwards offered the opinion that the women had been more courageous than the men![45] In October 1935 the Red Army finally reached northern Shanxi where local communist leaders with a small Red Army had established a Soviet District. The area administered by the CCP gradually expanded and just more than three years later the Shanxi–Hebei–Chahe and Shanxi–Hebei–Shandong–Henan border region governments were established. Henceforth the regions under Communist government are referred to as the Soviet Areas or the Liberated Areas. Once more the CCP governed an area of some stability and set about the introduction of laws similar to those instituted in Jiangxi and the establishment of peasants', labourers' and women's organisations.

From small beginnings the women leaders and the Party set about constructing the women's movement. They adopted a procedure of approaching peasant women individually, then encouraging them to form their own solidarity groups. The awakening of women in the rural bases in the north of China was to prove a much more difficult task than in the cities and the south. Shanxi and Shaanxi were especially poor and custom-steeped provinces where large numbers of women still had bound feet, where all but 5 per cent of the women were illiterate and where female infanticide was widely practised. Peasant wives were even more downtrodden than their oppressed and embittered husbands. Their position had been further degraded during the Great Northwest Famine of the early 1930s when thousands of women and children had been sold into servitude. In this atmosphere the very sight of the young uniformed and free-striding girl soldiers was enough to frighten local women indoors. 'Here come the terrible women soldiers,' they were said to mumble to each other in awe and fear.[46] The ladies of the gentry families refused to receive them, sending their menfolk instead and thus suggesting by implication to others that the girls were of the order of prostitutes.[47] It was only after the young girls discarded their uniforms, donned peasant clothing and at first contented themselves with offers to help with washing and babysitting that the peasant women could be encouraged to talk about their lives and perhaps come to identify the sources of their suffering and oppression.

One young girl student, Xu Guang, described the initial difficulties of establishing personal links between young intellectuals and the women of the villages.

> We intellectuals had had little contact with the peasants and when we first walked through the village in our Chinese gowns or skirts the people would just stare at us and talk behind our backs. When the village head beat gongs to call out the women to the meetings we were holding for them, only men and old women came, but no young ones. Later we found out that the

landlords and rich peasants had spread slanders among the masses saying 'They're a pack of wild women. Their words are not for young brides to hear'.[48]

Xu Guang herself found that it was many visits before the women of even one peasant family would chat with her. It was only after she described the fate of families in Japanese-occupied territories and the story of her own life that the mother-in-law in the peasant family became sympathetic and communicative. Xu Guang described how she too came from a poor family which had been persecuted by the Guomindang and that her own mother had died when she was fifteen. 'As we talked I would help her with whatever she was doing, like cooking or feeding the pig, and when she was spinning I would prepare cotton for her.' The mother-in-law gradually came to admit that 'these women have heads on their shoulders. They are also downtrodden people and are of one heart and mind with us.' Xu Guang also found that 'we students changed in the course of our work among village women. We discarded our city dress and put on peasant clothes. We became very close to the local people and many of the elderly women "adopted" us as "daughters".' One village woman, Guo Hengde, who was later a local leader in the women's movement, described how she first came into contact with girl propagandists. In 1938 a young woman Communist cadre, Guo Jing, came to stay in her house. She ate the same food of husks and wild herbs, wore the same coarse homespun cloth and spoke in the same homely language as Guo Hengde. 'We were soon like sisters', said Guo Hengde as she went on to acknowledge the influence of Guo Jing and her ideas on her own life. Her influence had set it on a new course.[49]

Individual peasant girls might be persuaded to unbind their feet, the terms of the new marriage law were publicised and, most important, women might be encouraged to think of themselves as individuals who could take an active role in society rather than passively accepting their fate. But it was a process of long and slow persuasion. At first peasant women responded to the new ideas with a certain amount of scepticism. They agreed that it would be wonderful if women were the equals of men, but what chance did they have if from ancient times till now 'man has been the Heaven and women the Earth'? Early slogans such as 'Let both men and women take part in our revolution', 'You are workers like your men' and 'Women can do revolutionary work and contribute their share to the strength of our country just as men', were aimed at changing the self-image and expectations of women as much as overcoming male resistance. In Liuling village in Shanxi the first CCP leader, Li Yiuhua, remembered that in the early years when women weren't worth anything, the emancipation of women was one of their main platforms. Thirty years later he could still remember some of the songs and slogans which they had used.[50] The Party found that bureaucratic methods had little effect. In a local footbinding campaign in one of the border regions, the order fining the family of any woman with bound feet was soon withdrawn in favour of a further educational programme which encouraged people to emancipate their feet by themselves.[51] On the other hand meetings for education were not supposed to become mere 'shop-windows' dissipating the precious energy of women by merely subjecting them to speeches which were difficult for them to understand or reciting certain abstract slogans on every available occasion.[52] Deng Yingzhao noted in these early years that the fight to conquer the idea that women knew nothing but household affairs was particularly difficult. 'Our job wasn't easy: giving them a sense of their importance and an awareness of what we wanted our country to be.'[53] In many areas of Shanxi it was many months before even separate organisations for women could be established. A Resolution of the Party's organisation department published in September 1936 makes clear that little had as yet been accomplished in the women's movement.[54]

Gradually, however, women were persuaded to meet together outside their homes and articulate and share their personal experiences. Women cadres stressed the need to gather together to speak of their bitterness and share their experiences in order to better understand their own position.[55] They were persuaded that it was only when they found they had common grievances and formed a group would they be able collectively to introduce and defend their new rights. By 'speaking bitterness' and 'exchanging experiences' the members of the group learned that their own experiences were not unique. Years of consecutive incidents of degradation and humiliation were vividly etched into the consciousness and had made for much repressed bitterness. Leaders like Deng Yingzhao found that once awakened to the realities of their position, peasant women struggled for their new rights with impressive courage and conviction.[56] Out of their shared oppression women began to think of themselves as a separate social category and establish Women's Associations. In Longbow village Hinton observed that within the Women's Association

brave wives and daughters-in-law, untrammelled by the
presence of their menfolk, could voice their own bitterness
. . . encourage their poor sisters to do likewise, and thus
eventually bring to the village-wide gatherings the strength of
'half of China' as the more enlightened women, very much in
earnest, like to call themselves. By 'speaking pains to recall
pains', the women found that they had as many if not more
grievances than the men, and that given a chance to speak in
public, they were as good at it as their fathers and
husbands.[57]

The separate Associations aimed at safeguarding women's new
rights and drawing them into new public, social, political and
economic activities. The position of each individual was strengthened by the presence of the Women's Association in the village,
but it was quite clearly stated that at this time a cautious policy was
to be adopted in developing a movement to work exclusively for
women's rights in view of its potentially divisive effects. The
Communist Party also adopted a limited policy in respect of
peasant land ownership and class struggle. Instead of full-scale
redistribution of land they contented themselves with reducing
rents during the period of the anti-Japanese War. Women's
Associations were encouraged to devote themselves to practical
tasks which would both directly meet the needs of the village
women and win widespread popular support. The main work of the
women's movement in the northwest Soviet Areas was to be the
mobilisation of women to take part in social production, the war
effort and political institutions, and through these activities to
forward their own new economic, social and political interests. It
was forecast that each of the former activities would contribute to
the improvement of the position of women in the rural bases and
the redefinition of their former roles. The struggle for women's
rights was to be indirect rather than direct during the period of the
anti-Japanese War.

The involvement of women in individual and collective
production was considered to be the most appropriate contribution
women could make to the economy and anti-Japanese war effort in
the Soviet Areas. At the same time it was stated that the inclusion of
women in social production was 'the most important link in the
chain that protects women's own vital interests'.[58] It would enable
women on the basis of their improved material conditions to
overthrow feudal oppression politically, socially and economically.

Therefore the active participation of women in production was to be the central task of the women's movement with the small co-operative production units becoming the basic organisations of the women's movement. The main areas of production in which women could participate were in agriculture—the cultivation of land, the raising of livestock and silkworms, and in spinning and weaving. The potential contribution of women to agricultural production, which was more of an innovation in north China, was outlined in a document published in 1936. Women with natural feet were to be mobilised to clear land and partake in the main tasks of agricultural tasks such as ploughing and the skills of spinning and help in weed-pulling, collecting dung and other auxiliary tasks.[59] Classes were set up to teach women some of the more skilled agricultural tasks such as plowing and the skills of spinning and weaving. There was an acute shortage of cloth in the liberated areas, but the availability of factory-produced cloth from the textile mills in the cities had in recent years all but replaced the rural handicraft industries.

Peasant women had often forgotten the techniques of spinning and weaving and no longer had the necessary implements at hand. The Women's Association set up small co-operatives in which women spun, wove and made quilts, clothes and cloth shoes. In Ten Mile Inn village each of the 22 small co-operative groups of ten women, into which the Women's Association had been divided, met regularly every day and night. In the daytime group members would help each other in the elaborate process of laying out the yarns in preparation for setting it on the loom. In the evenings they would gather together to spin, reel yarn and wind it on to the bobbins.[60] The resultant agricultural and industrial production contributed to the economic development of the Liberated Areas. At the beginning of 1943 the number of women weaving in village textile co-operatives had reached 13,500. Following a campaign in this area of production in 1943, the number had increased to 41,540[61] and by the end of that same year, their production had far outstripped that of the factories in the towns of the Liberated Areas. In one village at first only 6 women had been persuaded to participate in 1940, but within five years, 70 had become members of the Women's Association production groups in the village.[62] By 1948 between 50 per cent to 70 per cent of the women in the Liberated Areas were said to take part in farm production.[63]

These new activities were not only a necessary contribution to the war economy, but they also revolutionised the economic value of women, contributed to the redefinition of their domestic roles and elevated their status in village society. Instead of remaining an economic burden to the family, individual women became economically productive and were enabled to contribute to the household budget. As contributors to the family income they commanded more respect than when they toiled only at unpaid housework. Many an antagonistic oppressive husband or mother-in-law, who objected to this extension of their wife's or daughter-in-law's activities outside the home, was often mollified by the wages which they brought home. Isabel and David Crooks who lived in Ten Mile Inn village, where women had in the past been forced into unemployment by lack of capital and by urban machine competition, thought that the improvement in their economic position was the most powerful factor in the beginning of the emancipation of the women of Ten Mile Inn.[64] The women themselves began to realise their new worth and became aware of the implications of their new economic independence. 'Now a woman can earn a living through her own work. Why should I suffer at the hands of my husband all day long?'[65] The natural association of women in co-operatives fortified women's individual morale and collective strength and with this new-found confidence they emerged to participate in other activities outside the home.

The story of Zhan Shuying illustrates the new identity and position achieved by some women. As a consequence of joining the Women's Association, against the wishes of her husband and mother-in-law, she continued to be very badly treated at home until a year later her position began to improve as the result of the government's production drive. Through Zhan Shuying's earnings and her industry, the economic position of the family was greatly improved and because of her production efforts she was elected a chairwoman of the Women's Association, she was sent to further her education and training in political work and became a mediator in village affairs and disputes. As a result of her increased status, Zhan Shuying's mother-in-law began to boast of her achievements, and finding that he was married to a woman of great local prestige her husband too began to respect her.[66] The production drive was primarily the responsibility of the Women's Association which consequently shared the new status accorded its members. In one village, where the Women's Association had taught the girls of the village a number of productive skills, the village elders, seeing the girls make good use of their spare time, began to think differently about women 'taking up politics'. Some of them even admitted 'That the Women's Association doesn't seem so bad after all! They're learning quite a lot that's useful there.'[67] In another district where no woman had previously been engaged in spinning and weaving, relations within the individual families of the 220 woman producers were said to have improved. Apparently the beating of women became less frequent. There was a new saying that if a 'husband and wife both go one way, sand and earth will turn to gold'.[68] In another village where nearly all the men were away in the Red Army and women had recently taken their place in the fields, an old peasant man expressed his new appreciation of the role of women in the village: 'This year our food comes from the women. We have always believed women were no good, but now for the first time in our lives we will live on food produced by women.'[69]

Women also directly contributed to the war effort, first in the anti-Japanese war and second from 1946 in the civil war against the Guomindang. Women were encouraged both to support their husband's enlistment in the Red Army and participate in the guerilla war themselves. The co-operation of the women in the guerilla war was essential and they were encouraged to play a large part in the war operations. Young women joined fighting corps and self-defence detachments to fight the enemy themselves. Girls of 15 to 25 years of age normally joined the Women's Militia which co-operated with the Men's Militia in mine-laying and similar work. Classes were held for women which covered espionage and sabotage methods. In intelligence work they were urged to become the 'eyes and the ears of the army'. They took turns at guarding the villages and crossroads, tearing down walls or destroying roads before the oncoming army, nursing the wounded, carrying stretchers, acting as secret messengers and hiding food supplies from the enemy. Groups from the Women's Associations led the guerilla corps when their villages were occupied by the Guomindang. To confuse and frighten the enemy, so they dared not remain long in the village, they took 'pot shots' at them and threw hand grenades. When ammunition was in short supply they lit firecrackers in kerosene tins. Women worked at the rear of the forces administering first aid, undertaking supply work and preparing food provisions. For the most part uniforms, shoes and such equipment were made by the women of the villages. One phrase covered all such activities: 'Guarding the rear of our armies.'

The behaviour of the Red Army towards the villagers and especially towards the women was in vivid contrast to that of the GMD and Japanese armies who were known to loot and rape[70] and was an important factor in the identification of the women with the cause of the Red Army. Nearly all observers who visited the Liberated Areas in the 1930s and 1940s reported the tremendous war effort and courage of the women. Many lost their lives and are still remembered for their brave support of the Red Armies and their defiance of their Guomindang captors. Liu Hulan is perhaps one of the best-known war-heroines in China today. Liu Hulan was a young peasant girl who was a member of the Anti-Japanese Children's League before she attended a forty-day women's study course in a neighbouring village on her own. Soon after she graduated from the training class she was elected secretary of her village branch of the Women's National Salvation Association. She was conscientious and enthusiastic in her work for the welfare of its members. Working long hours, she mobilised the women to help carry food to the village fighters, make shoes for them or care for the wounded. She undertook important work for the Party and Red Armies and provided a constant stream of valuable information on the movements of the enemy armies. She made many enemies among the landlords of the village and when the GMD re-occupied the village she was arrested as an accomplice of the Eighth Route Army and a leader of the Women's Association. In front of the whole village she was interrogated under threat of decapitation and after refusing to give any information she was executed.[71] Her courage, defiance and loyalty has long since been remembered along with that of other revolutionary heroines by the people of China.

The mobilisation of women to participate in the war effort brought home the importance of the women to the welfare of the local community and it was also linked to the campaign to further the rights of women. When women such as Liu Suying, a leader of a village Women's Defence Corps, were asked why they had wanted to join the fighting forces their two reasons were: 'For the defence of our country against Japanese aggression and the emancipation of women.'[72] An example from the south shores of the Yangtze, where the New Fourth Army was engaged in guerilla activities, shows how the Women's Association there lost no opportunity to simultaneously forward women's rights alongside war work. In one valley, occasions such as the presentation of pillow cases to the soldiers in hospital were made with a 'fiery speech on women's rights'. On Festival days, members of the Women's Associations went to hospitals to visit and talk with the soldiers. Speeches were delivered in each ward, and Mother Cai, the 68-year-old leader of the women of the valley never closed a speech without telling the soldiers about women's rights or urging them to induce their own womenfolk to join the Association. At a very successful mass meeting held on Women's Day in the great courtyard of an old ancestral temple, men leaders were invited to say a few words of greeting, but all the major speeches and front seats were reserved for women. Soldiers, officers and civilian men had been invited to sit at the back, and listen to Mother Cai speak on the women's part in the war and women's social, economic and political rights.[73]

Women were encouraged to join inclusive class organisations and to play a full part in the political institutions of the liberated areas. It had been suggested by the Party that one of the causes underlying male neglect of women's class interests was the separation of the organisations and the lack of contact between the two sexes. Thus women were exhorted not just to join their own exclusive organisations but also to participate in joint peasant and labour organisations which were designed primarily to look after class interests. In this way unnecessary sex segregation was prevented and the class consciousness of women was nurtured. All men and women were given full suffrage rights and in the Liberated Areas women were encouraged to vote and take part in the administration of their villages. An important feature of the 1941 elections was its co-ordination with a campaign for women's rights. A front page editorial in one of the newspapers urged women to play an active role in the election both as candidates and voters.[74] In 1939 the CCP had issued an important policy statement recommending that the Party should pay particular attention to recruiting to its membership more women of worker, peasant, intellectual and petty-bourgeois origins.

> Women constitute half of the population of China. Without women's participation in the revolution, the revolution cannot succeed. The number of women workers in the Party is too small at present, primarily because not enough attention has been paid by the Party. . . . All CCP members, especially women workers, must regard the expansion of female membership as one of their important tasks. The Party must today emphasise the task of absorbing into its ranks revolutionary peasant women and

women intellectuals in great numbers. The Party must regard
this as part of its regular activity and see to it that the political
consciousness and the cultural level of its women members are
enhanced through training and work.[75]

The Women's University in Yenan and local educational projects
were established to train women to lead in the women's movement
and in other political organisations. About 400 students from
widely ranging backgrounds were admitted to the university.
Among the entrance requirements was a specific commitment to
fight for the emancipation of women. Special attention was given
to local education projects to train peasant women to take part in
political institutions. In Ten Mile Inn village the committee
members of the Women's Association, none of whom had any
previous experience in leadership positions, were sent on a
fifteen-day course run by the county for training women leaders.
They returned to their village greatly inspired by the course, for not
only were they encouraged to discuss their past sufferings but they
were urged to express their opinions on policies and even offer
criticisms of the course and those who ran it. It was the fact that
their opinions were solicited that impressed them.[76] In the first
election of local representatives in the Shanxi–Chahe–Hebei
border region in 1940 it was estimated that 85 per cent of the
eligible women cast votes, and 20 per cent of the representatives at
the region, county, and village levels were women. By 1941 in north
Shanxi alone some 2,000 women were elected to positions in local
administration. In many districts there were a number of elected
women heads of villages.[77] In 1937 in the townships which served as
local headquarters of revolutionary activity in the Shen-Kan-Ning
border areas, women might form as many as a quarter of the local
Party membership.[78] In the border areas as a whole though, women
formed from 2 per cent to 3 per cent of the Party membership and
in some areas it was still rare to find women members.[79] One of the
chief problems was their previous confinement to the domestic
sphere, and their lack of confidence and experience in dealing with
public affairs.

For this reason literacy classes in the winter schools were
established in rural villages. Text books were produced which
identified customs and beliefs which had prevented women from
holding formal public roles. The following passage from a school
book in the Shanxi–Hebei–Shandong–Henan border region contrasts the position of men and women in the old society and

highlights some of the repercussions of the traditional division of labour.

> The old society is too dark; men and women are treated
> differently. The man goes to an office, the woman stops within
> the compound. The man wears new clothes, the woman dresses
> in rags. The man eats white flour, the woman, husks and chaff.
> The man can scold until heaven bursts, the woman seldom opens
> her mouth. The man reads books, the woman stands at the side
> of the cauldron. The man three times changes his temperament,
> the woman swallows into her stomach the words she has to say.[80]

The text goes on to outline the opportunities now available to women in the new society provided the traditional divisions of labour and attitudes of deference can be overcome. The Women's Association put on productions of plays which portrayed women's struggle to survive in the old society and their struggle to change their position in the new society. Women as much as men were portrayed as revolutionary heroes and leaders. As Wu Guangwei, an actress in Yenan, told Nym Wales, the American journalist, plays were an ideal medium for raising consciousness because of the widespread illiteracy.[81] More than one foreign observer found it a moving experience to see women with bound feet who had hitherto not been allowed outside the home, toddling around the stage acting out the part of the 'emancipated woman'!

A particularly popular play in the Liberated Areas was that of the 'White-Haired Girl' which was first performed in this period. It is the story of a daughter of a peasant who was forced to become a slave in the landlord's household when her father was unable to pay his rent. Ill-used and rebellious she flees to the mountains where scarce food resources turn her hair white. She is finally found by the Red Armies and returns to her home village now liberated from the feudal forces. She joins the Red Army and takes a part in the political activities of the village. Jack Belden, an American journalist, describes a performance of this play which was attended by the women and girls of several villages on the eve of Women's Day. On a bitterly cold night an audience of at least 2,000 attended the play including country officials, workers from the local potteries, clerks from the co-operatives, old peasant women in shawls, girls in uniform and young farm girls in simple jackets and trousers—all were crowded in a great semi-circle around an improvised stage lit by a glaring pressure lamp. The bitter reality of the play was not lost on the women in the audience many of whom shared similar backgrounds to the heroine. 'At several points in the play I saw women, old and young, peasant and intellectual, wiping tears from their eyes with the sleeves of their jackets.'[82] His impressions were substantiated by David and Isabel Crooks in Ten Mile Inn village. Even an old upper-middle-peasant woman, whose life had been far more comfortable that most, wept throughout the play and tearfully spoke of herself afterwards as another white-haired girl when she recalled her ill-treatment as a young daughter-in-law. On poor peasants the impact was still more powerful.[83] By these means peasant women came to contrast their old and and new positions, and the classes that were held enabled them to recognise and analyse the causes of their oppression and the foundations of the traditional division of labour. As a result the number of local women administrative leaders increased. By 1946 one quarter to one third of the Party members were women.[84] In this way women began to participate in policy-making decisions and at the same time forward the interests of women.

The involvement of women in production, war and political activities were the chief means of improving the position of women during the years of the anti-Japanese war (up to 1945). These policies directly or explicitly served the needs of the wider revolutionary movement and also indirectly and implicitly worked towards the redefinition of the role and status of women. The combined strategy was based on the principle of 'unity' and any conflicts between the sexes, generations and classes affecting the orientation of the women's movement and its relations with the wider revolutionary movement were submerged beneath the demands for unity in the face of a common enemy—the Japanese invaders. Yet it proved impossible to completely eliminate conflict between the sexes, generations and classes within the villages of the Soviet Areas. Many women, either individually within the family or collectively within the village, found it difficult to counter the resistance of the men when they tried to extend their activities beyond the domestic sphere. Husbands, fearing their wives might go astray, objected to their attending public meetings and many young wives who insisted on attending women's meetings braved the inevitable domestic crises on their return—usually a beating or scraps of food instead of the usual meal. Many a young daughter-in-law had painful memories of her first steps into public life. Dong Yulan recalled 'the road was rough with stones'.

First, the elders of my family didn't approve. They said it shamed the family for a woman to show her face so brazenly at public meetings. And sometimes when I'd try to rouse the women to take part in public work, I'd be roundly abused for my pains by some cross-grained old stick-in-the-mud. Then I'd feel dispirited.[85]

The women in Longbow village found that as they organised themselves into a separate association, attended public meetings and entered public life they encountered more and more opposition. Hinton observed that opposition from the men within their own households, most of whom regarded any activity by their wives or daughters-in-law outside the home as 'steps leading directly to adultery', took a particularly virulent form.[86] In Ten Mile Inn village, some cadres forbade their wives to attend the Women's Association which they nicknamed the 'Prostitutes' meetings'.[87] In this same village, members of the local branch of the Party took few steps to involve members of the Women's Association in the central organisation of village affairs. One of them cited their reasons:

We felt that militant women weren't virtuous and the virtuous women weren't militant. So though we knew we ought to recruit some women members into the branch, we couldn't find any who seemed suitable. But of course if the branch had really paid enough attention to the problem of recruiting members, we could have solved it.[88]

Examples can be cited where Women's Associations were relegated to the position of a second-class organisation for second-class citizens, and women were initially excluded from the affairs of the village such as village elections.[89] The male domination of village affairs, the neglect of woman work and the relegation of Women's Associations to a secondary place, might mean the Women's Association found itself unable to forward the interests of its members. In Longbow village for example when the vice-chairman of the Peasants' Association forced an under-age girl to marry his son because he had bought and paid for her, the Women's Association, afraid of his power, refrained from interference.[90]

The opposition of mothers-in-law was often as adamant as that of their sons. The leading activists in the women's movement tended to be young wives who had been adopted into their husband's families at an early age. They carried a heavy household workload and often had no near natal family to protect them from the ill-treatment meted out by their mothers-in-law. The mothers-in-law, unlike the daughters-in-law, felt they had little to gain from the Women's Association. While the younger women were very concerned with free-choice marriage, elder women saw this as a threat to their control over daughters and daughters-in-law. While younger women opposed all family beatings, older women tended to countenance beatings just so long as mothers-in-law administered them. Their privilege after years of subjugation! One short story written at the time illustrated the tensions between the elder generation and the new Women's Associations. Meng Xiangying's mother-in-law had long been against her meeting with outsiders, particularly with other young married women. In her experience, when young wives got together it was always to compare the faults of their mothers-in-law. When her curiosity got the better of her and she attended a Women's Association meeting to find out what the young women talked about, she was shocked. The women wanted emancipation; they were against being beaten and sworn at by their mothers-in-law and husbands; they were for ending footbinding; they wanted to gather firewood, fetch water and till the fields; they wanted to do the same work and eat the same food as men; they wanted to go to winter school. In her view this was rebellion. If mothers-in-law and husbands could not beat young wives who could? Surely someone had to beat them, surely they would not have the nerve to demand natural feet? Would women who gathered firewood and fetched water still be women? She thought Meng Xiangying was obstinate enough while illiterate, but if she learned to read and write she'd be even more high and mighty. 'What was the world coming to?' She mounted a campaign to counter every new activity Meng Xiangying initiated in the village.[91]

There was little direct class struggle in any form before 1946. Although the poor peasant women (the peasantry was subdivided into rich, middle and poor peasants according to the amount of land and other possessions they owned and according to whether or not they worked their own land or hired labour) had the most to gain, the traditional power structure of the village was sometimes reflected in the social make-up of the leadership of local Women's Associations. In Ten Mile Inn, for example, the great majority of the twenty-two group leaders and committee members of the production groups were drawn from the relatively wealthy middle-peasant class. The main reason for this was that leadership of the woman work as a whole was taken over by those qualified to lead its most important aspect—production. The poor peasant women, lacking capital in the past, had not learned the skills of spinning and weaving. It was the women of the old middle-peasant families who in the past had learned the skills and had enough capital for the wheels, looms and other equipment and the raw materials. In Ten Mile Inn the Women's Association had become an expression of the interests of those older middle-peasant women who, while they could see the advantages of earning an income through production, had no further interests in the social and political emancipation of women. They tended to view production as an end in itself rather than as a means for improving the political status of women, advancing their cultural level and their complete emancipation.[92] In limiting the activities of the Association to production enterprises, the special problems of the poorer peasant women who were mostly adopted-in daughters-in-law were neglected.

There is evidence that some members of the women's movement became impatient with the combined strategy based on the principle of 'unity' and the resulting ambivalence of their individual and collective position. They pushed for more direct recognition of the conflicting interests of men and women, mothers-in-law and daughters-in-law and rich and poor peasant women. They thought that because women were bullied by men and by parents-in-law, women must win their due rights from the men and directly and actively fight for freedom in the home. One of the most outspoken critics of the policy of 'unity' was Ding Ling, a novelist and short-story writer resident in Yenan who publicly lamented the fate of women in the Soviet Areas. She wrote an essay entitled 'Thoughts on March 8' which appeared on the literary page of *The Liberation Daily* on 9 March 1942. In it she expressed a certain amount of discontent with women's present position. In theory she thought they were supposed to be emancipated, but in reality they were still subject to contempt and misery:

If women did not marry, they were ridiculed; if they did and had children, they were chastised for holding political posts rather than being at home with their families; if they remained at home with their families they were slandered as backward. Whereas in the old society they were pitied, in the new one they were condemned for a predicament not of their making.[93]

H

Xu Guang, a village women's leader, had doubts about policies of a less than direct nature. She felt women would never gain any rights unless they took the initiative and directly struggled for them against their husbands and against their families. Many young members of the Women's Association in her village agreed with her and wanted to hold meetings to publicly criticise tyrannical husbands and mothers-in-law. This they felt would strengthen the women's determination and give vent to their anger.[94] The Communist leaders seem to have been aware that women were often caught between the old and the new ideas and practices and came up against competing expectations on all sides, but they thought that at this time national unity was more important than direct action to resolve these problems and also that only a long-term political solution would improve the position of all women. Both the views of Ding Ling and Xu Guang were criticised.

Ding Ling was criticised for her invective, not so much because of the nature of the frustrations she was expressing, but because of her narrow feminist standpoint as a 'liberated woman intellectual'. This viewpoint was said to ignore the formidable problems of redefining the social and economic role of women in this remote area of China and in a war situation. The women's problem could not be solved in isolation. As a result of public criticism she herself later admitted that she had been convinced that the continued emphasis on narrow feminism by women intellectuals was outdated and harmful to the nationalist cause. She later confessed to Gunther Stein in an interview that for the sake of national unity and victory, the first priority of both men and women was to co-operate and work for the whole revolution.[95] In Xu Guang's village, those who took a 'feminism first' stand were persuaded to modify their views. It was pointed out that at present Japanese imperialism was the enemy of the whole Chinese people and to divide the people, one sex against the other, would undermine their strength. They acknowledged that victory in the war could only be won by uniting all those willing to fight the Japanese. Xu Guang wrote that 'Without National liberation and the establishment of a new society women's liberation would have no meaning.' As a result they went from house to house explaining the present situation and suggesting that in the meantime they be content with reasoning patiently with their stubborn mothers-in-law and husbands.[96]

It was not until the withdrawal of the Japanese troops in 1945 that Communist leaders felt it was feasible, and no longer against the interests of the wider revolutionary movement, to allow the women's movement to take a more independent policy involving more direct forms of struggle between the sexes. At the same time they introduced policies of land reform which allowed for more direct struggle between the classes. Land reform was the first step in breaking the economic power of the landlords and richer peasants. According to the Agrarian Reform Law promulgated by the CCP in 1947, land in rural areas was to be equally distributed to the peasants irrespective of age and sex. Women were entitled to separate land deeds. Sometimes this entitlement remained more abstract than real as much because of certain practical difficulties as any chauvinism. Problems ranged from questions such as what should a girl do with her land on marriage, should engaged girls have their land at their father's or their future husband's property and on what basis should land be distributed to new widows, to discussions and resolutions of problems concerning the location of separate wives' and daughters' plots. Many women settled for joint ownership of land, but even this was an important step. In Chaojia village every poor peasant, man or woman, was allotted a piece of land. To emphasise the fact that women had economic equality with men, each woman was given a land certificate in her own name or wrote her name alongside that of her husband's on one certificate. Before women had always been referred to by others as 'so-and-so's wife' or 'so-and-so's mother'. Now for the first time in their lives they said they heard their own names spoken in public.[97] They had acquired a name alongside a share of the land.

Some women were quick to realise the implications of land reform for their own lives. In the most oppressive situations women could immediately become independent of the husband's family. The women William Hinton interviewed had acquired a new spirit of independence, typically expressed as: 'When I get my share, I'll separate from my husband. Then he won't oppress me any more.' 'If he divorces me, never mind, I'll get my share and the children will get theirs. We can live a good life without him.' 'When I get my share I'll never look for a husband again. A husband is a terrible thing.'[98] For most women, however, the ownership of land meant they would at least be able to stand up for their own rights from a position of comparative strength. Women not only acquired land and a new economic position, but they learned of the class nature of society at first hand and achieved a certain class consciousness as a result of their participation in the village meetings held to criticise landlords and redistribute land. In Litun village, a public meeting was held to criticise Liu Guozhen, the landlord. Women too voiced their accusations. When the moment came, some shrank back tongue-tied before their old oppressor whose shadow still hung over them. Others remembered how their whole family had slaved, how they went hungry and ragged on account of him. He had often forced the peasants to work without payment and organised raiders to waylay and rob the peasants as they came home from market. He had been much feared. The first woman speaker stood up boldly and poured out the tale of his cruelties. Then other women followed and denounced him for his hitherto unspeakable crimes. Throughout the criticism-meetings they began to realise 'why we peasants suffered so much in the old days'.[99] Poor peasant women were encouraged to form their own separate group within the poor Peasant Associations to concentrate on their particular problems. They derived a separate strength from their own collective organisation which tended to act as a radical core within the broader Women's Association.

The acquisition of women's rights affected every household and where husbands and mothers-in-law persisted in their opposition and ill-treatment a certain amount of direct and responsible struggle between the sexes was condoned. Theoretically education still remained the most important means through which to criticise the feudal ideology and inherited customs, but when required by circumstances, the 'backward elements' who wanted to maintain the old feudal customs and who constantly tormented and oppressed women could now be directly criticised and reformed. This type of confrontation, however, was to be regarded as an 'internal thought struggle' within the peasant class and was to be rigorously distinguished from the form of struggle used against the landlord class during land reform.[100] In many villages it was not uncommon for an errant husband to be brought before the village Women's Association to confess his misdeeds and promise to change his ways. Sometimes, in the face of persistent obstinacy, bitterness and anger long repressed surged to the surface and the acutely felt collective sense of injustice was physically expressed, although it was said such incidents usually resulted in no more than a bruise, a cut and a 'red-faced bowed-headed' husband. In Longbow village the wife of the poor peasant Man Zang registered a complaint against her husband to the Women's Association. A meeting was called by the women of the village which demanded that Man Zang explain his actions. Arrogant and 'unbowed' he told how he beat his wife because she went to meetings and 'the only reason women go to meetings is to gain a free hand for flirtation and seduction'. It was the latter remark which aroused a furious protest from the women. Blows followed upon words and under their influence Man Zang promised to change his ways. With the threat of a repeat performance if he did not, it was said that Man Zang never dared to beat his wife again.[101]

In another incident, the woman concerned described the proceedings to an American journalist. Her father-in-law had been held a prisoner for two days in a room in the building of the Women's Association. A meeting of the women in the village was called to decide what to do with him. Many of the fifty or so women wished to have him beaten immediately, but they were influenced by the more cautious of their sisters:

> Sisters! We must take our meeting to be a serious business so that it should not be shameful to the people and so that we should get a good result from our actions. As it is we have been treated unjustly enough by men, but we should not fall into the same error. We must have respect for our Women's Association so that everyone shall respect it. Let us first discuss how we shall treat the old man before we decide on anything.

The meeting finally decided to call in the old man. He refused to admit he had done anything wrong and called on his daughter-in-law as a witness. Strengthened by the presence of the other women, Gold Flower outlined the causes of her past suffering.

> 'I married into your family—yes! But there's been no millet for me to eat. No clothes in the winter. Are these not facts? Do you remember how badly you treated me in the past five years? Have you forgotten the time my mother was sick and you made me kneel in the courtyard for half a day? In the past I suffered from you. But I shall never suffer again. I must turn over now. I have all my sisters behind me and I have the Eighth Route Army.'

As she shouted these words his face grew dark and red. A few women spat at him as a mark of their disrespect. 'Are you ready to reform yourself?' they asked. 'I will change' said the old man in a low and subdued voice. 'Will you torture your daughter any more?' 'No,' he replied. 'All women unite,' 'Women unite' echoed the women. Gold Flower responded to their support: 'My turning over is all due to you, I know now you are powerful. I know, too, that the Eighth Route Army has done something for me.' That night when she went home, her father-in-law was so ashamed he could not hold up his head. 'Was this overturning movement your doing?' he asked. 'No, it was not my doing,' Gold Flower replied. 'There are sister groups in the village which investigate the bad treatment of women. They know everything.' The old man looked at his daughter-in-law in fright and Gold Flower smiled to herself. 'At that moment the future seemed sweet and full of promise.'[102]

In both villages a few examples were said to have taught peasant men to be more circumspect in the treatment of their wives. Having once shown their power the women did not have to beat every man in order to make progress on this question. Thereafter, a serious talk with a strong-armed husband was usually enough to make him change his ways. In this way the women had demonstrated their collective power and proved to themselves, and the inhabitants of the village, the strength of the Women's Association. After a life-time of submission they too felt they had 'stood up', or 'fanshen', which meant literally 'to turn the body' or 'to turn over' and enter a new world. But from the interviews recorded with those women there seems to have been no pretence that such direct action or struggle alone could win them equality. This form of struggle was largely seen to be meaningless without an equivalent improvement in their economic position.[103]

The aim of the CCP leadership in the Soviet Areas was to begin to improve the social position of all women through economic and political measures and juxtaposing policies of 'unity' and 'struggle'. The development of their separate organisation within the overall revolutionary movement was designed to further the goals of both the women's movement and the wider movement for national independence and unity. This combined strategy was certainly successful in encouraging women to contribute to the wider nationalist revolutionary movement. Historians have given much consideration to the role of peasants in the wider nationalist and revolutionary struggle of the 1930s and 1940s but the special contribution of peasant and other women has largely been ignored until more recent studies. Yet nearly all the foreign journalists and observers who travelled in the Liberated Areas reported at length on the very significant role of peasant women through their enthusiastic and practical support of the Red Armies. Two American journalists, Jack Belden and William Hinton, who wrote the two classic accounts of life in the Soviet Areas in the 1940s, were both left in no doubt as to the contribution of the women to the victory of the Nationalist and revolutionary forces. Hinton, who lived in Longbow village, observed that in the Taihang mountain area, the Women's Association was, in addition to being a measure for achieving equality, an instrument for mobilising the women behind the revolution in all its aspects. He thought that many women realised, as if by intuition, that it was impossible to talk of the liberation of women without the defence of the Soviet Areas against the GMD armies and without the successful transformation of society. He concluded that if the demand on the part of women, that they should no longer be treated as chattels, alarmed the men 'the all out support which they [the women] gave to the overall revolutionary goals disarmed them and won from them a grudging admiration. In their hearts they had to admit that they could not win without the help of "half of China".'[104] Belden, finding that in many villages women were the most passionate supporters of the Eighth Route Army, concluded that 'in the women of China, the CCP possessed, almost ready made, one of the greatest masses of disinherited human beings the world has ever seen. And because they found the keys to the heart of these women, they also found the keys to victory over Chiang.' Belden is not alone in thinking that the substitution of the pain, anguish and despair of Chinese womanhood by joy, pride and hope was a phenomenon of the most tremendous significance.[105]

That the women also brought benefits to themselves is evident from interviews in which individual women expressed their gratitude to the new government. They felt they had a vested interest in the victory of the Red Armies and CCP. For example, Wang Zhoude had experienced both poverty and oppression and her father and husband had both been killed by the Japanese. Through the Women's Association she had learned new skills and begun to participate in village affairs. These new opportunities caused her to exclaim 'The Eighth Route Army opened heaven and earth.'[106] Time and time again Gold Flower of Li Jia Zhuang village turned to her local Women's Association for help in solving her personal problems of domestic subjugation and like Gold Flower, it seems that many individual women made up their own minds that 'the old society would never return'. They personally would not let it![107] In many cases it was the local Women's Association which on behalf of its members was able to take the shared experience of women, translate it into collective needs and fight for their collective causes.

The experience of the Liberated Areas had proved that within the wider revolutionary movement the women's movement had a very important part to play. It articulated the personal immediate resentments of individual women against particular aspects of their own oppression, and taught them the value of collective action and mutual support. The value of separate organisations in raising the confidence of women was reiterated in a document published in 1948 which, after reporting the results of an experiment conducted in one county in the Liberated Areas, recommended the establishment of separate organisations for women as a matter of course. It found that in areas where women had only joined the mixed Peasant Associations they had felt uncomfortable in the presence of men and few had spoken at any of the meetings. The women themselves had admitted that: 'If we're speaking with men present those who ought to say a lot say very little.' Of the experiments reported, only in areas where women already belonged to their own separate organisations did they attend meetings enthusiastically, lose their reserve in speaking publicly and participate fully in forms of revolutionary struggle.[108] It was out of this newly acquired confidence that women found the strength to exercise their collective will. Individually, oppressed women turned to the village Women's Associations for help in solving personal and domestic problems. Without the support of their sisters few women would personally have dared to take the struggle into their own families. The Association defended the newly won rights of women in village affairs. In one village where women were excluded from the first village elections, the Women's Association refused to recognise the newly elected head of the village. They only gained recognition of their voting rights after the Women's Association encouraged all its members not to sleep with their husbands. In the repeat election a woman was elected deputy-head of the village.[109] At a meeting of the Peasants' Union held to discuss land reform in another village, the Women's Union was not invited to participate. The all-male meeting decided that girls under the age of eighteen years should not be eligible for their share of the land. It was the Women's Association which drew attention to the law and demanded a fresh discussion at which they be present. The old decision was rescinded.[110]

The unmistakable value of the women's movement was recognised by both the Party and the women themselves in 1949 when it was institutionalised on a national basis. The membership of the Women's Associations expanded during the 1940s. In 1943 it was estimated that the Women's Association, which had numbered 173,800 members in 1938,[111] had reached 2½ million.[112] In 1946, the same year that the Women's National Salvation Association was renamed the Women's or Peasant Women's Association, the membership had risen to 7 million[113] and within a further two years the expansion of the newly liberated areas had almost tripled this number, to reach 20 million women.[114] The only figures available which give the proportion of women who were members of the Association in any one village are those for Bien Jia village which was 'liberated' in 1940. By 1945 three quarters of the women had joined the Women's Association.[115] By 1948 the rapid expansion of the women's movement into newly liberated areas made necessary an all-embracing organisation to unify policy, and systematise and co-ordinate women's work. As Deng Yingzhao noted, with the approaching nationwide victory and the urgent, enormous and difficult construction of a new China, new tasks awaited the women's movement. If women were to attain equality in all spheres, the women's movement had to make every effort to improve the position of its members, support their struggles and contribute to the building of a new socialist society.

> It was necessary [she said] to overcome the weakness we inherited from the old generations such as narrow-mindedness, frailty, triviality, a sense of reliance on others, susceptibility to sentiment, vagueness in political conceptions and lack of principles.[116]

The women's movement, with the support of the Party, proposed to convene a nationwide congress of representatives of all local associations of women in the spring of 1949 with the aim of establishing the All-China Democratic Women's Federation as the central organising body of the women's movement.

By 1949 new rights of women had been guaranteed by law, a new ideology and material conditions had laid the foundations for their individual economic independence and their own organisation had been formally empowered to forward their own interests. In the pursuit of common goals, many in the women's movement began to acknowledge the interdependence between their own women's and the nationalist revolutionary movement. Xu Guang came to this conclusion as a result of her experiences in woman work in Xiaowang village during the war of liberation. She thought that the contribution of women to the struggle to repel the Japanese had not only given them encouragement, but also educated the men and people as a whole. In the course of that struggle the feudal thinking and customs discriminating against women began to break down.

Moreover:

> Reality also educated those of us doing woman work. We came
> to understand more clearly that the women's movement was an
> integral part of the revolutionary movement. We saw that if the
> women's movement had been divorced from the revolution as a
> whole, and had fought solely for women's rights—thus
> becoming a struggle to wrest rights from men and making men
> the target of their struggle—it would have split the revolutionary
> ranks. Endless conflicts between the men and women, and
> between the young women and the old women would have
> resulted. This would have been harmful to the struggle for
> national liberation and that for the liberation of all oppressed
> classes; it would have turned society against the women's
> struggle and put obstacles in its way. [117]

Yet despite the value attached to this principle of interdependence,
the alliance between the two movements remained uneasy. A
Resolution on Woman Work in 1948 summarised the work of the
alliance and pointed to two tendencies that had to be guarded
against: one was to think that all would be well with women so long
as general revolutionary aims were fulfilled and that there was no
need to pay special attention to women's problems or to have
separate women's organisations; the other was to think that
women's liberation was a cause in itself and not part of the wider
revolution. [118] What had tended to keep these tensions under
control, or to a minimum, was the overriding demands of a
nationalist struggle.

A New Society: New Standards

[The] emancipation of women is first and foremost the business of women . . . it is important that the full realisation of their rights must depend upon their own struggle and can never be bestowed upon them by others.

(Deng Yingzhao, 14 March 1950.)[1]

On the first day of October 1949, the People's Republic of China was proclaimed after a near century of disunity, civil war and foreign invasion. The leader of the new government, Mao Zedong, announcing the birth of a new age, declared that 'The Chinese people, one quarter of the human race, have now stood up.'[2] One half of the population were women and they too were to be given every opportunity to 'stand up'. The new government was explicitly committed to redefining and improving the position of women in society. The Common Programme, new China's basic law of development adopted by the People's Political Consultative Conference which was made up of national representatives, provided for the 'full emancipation of women'. It stated that

> The People's Republic of China shall abolish the feudal system which holds women in bondage. Women shall enjoy equal rights with men in political, economic, cultural, educational and social life. Freedom of marriage for men and women shall be put into effect. (Article 6)

> The special interests of juvenile and women workers shall be safeguarded. (Article 32)

> Public health and medical work shall be expanded and attention shall be paid to the protection of the health of mothers, infants and children. (Article 48)[3]

Although these provisions safeguarding the rights of women had been proclaimed in the Soviet Bases and by the Guomindang government they were now to be extended to the women of the whole country. Within the new programmes of socio-economic construction including Land Reform, the implementation of the new Marriage Law, the founding of modern industry and the gradual displacement of individualised peasant production with collectivised agriculture, the government planned to create material conditions and new opportunities favourable to their emancipation. But the CCP also forecast that while a government could provide the legal and material conditions favourable to improvements in female status, it was the women themselves who must individually and collectively negotiate a new role and status. As one local leader of woman work said at the time: 'It's easy enough to talk about the freeing of women. But it isn't a thing that happens of itself, even when we have a government that makes laws to give women equality with men.' She went on to say that 'we have to make an effort ourselves'.[4] Deng Yingzhao, a vice-president of the Women's Federation, made a similar statement at a national level when she said that the emancipation of women is first and foremost the business of women. For 'it is important that the full realisation of their rights must depend upon their own struggle and can never be bestowed upon them by others'.[5] Their special and separate organisation, the All-China Democratic Women's Federation (ACDWF) was to play a key role in encouraging women to redefine their domestic and public roles, in converting new rights into standards of social behaviour.

The nationwide separate organisation of women, the ACDWF, was founded in Peking on 3 April 1949—six months before the People's Republic was proclaimed—to co-ordinate and give direction to woman work throughout the whole country. All earlier organisations of women, including the Young Women's Christian Association and the Women's Christian Temperance Union, were absorbed into this single national organisation. The Federation accepted group membership only and the national organisation operated on the principle of indirect representation. It was described in 1949 as a 'united front organisation of democratic women of all social strata and professions'.[6] This all-inclusive nature meant that all women who came within the category of 'the people' were eligible for membership. Briefly, the category of 'the people' as defined by Mao Zedong in 'The People's Democratic Dictatorship' included 95 per cent of the population or all those classes or strata or social groups in Chinese society (the peasants, urban proletariat, petty and national bourgeoisie) 'which favour support and work for the cause of socialist construction' in opposition to 'those social forces and groups which resist socialist revolution'. The latter, the 'enemies' of the people, included those of the landlord or bureaucratic bourgeoisie and the women of these groups were to be excluded from the activities of the Women's Federation. Like the People's Democratic Dictatorship, the Women's Federation was to be largely based on working and peasant women, but was to establish close connections with and include those of other classes such as the wives of small shopkeepers, managers of factories and intellectuals. Although these latter groups were serviced by others in the old society, there was the possibility that they would come to serve the new society.[7] In Shanghai in 1951 for instance there were among the total number of organised women (301,412 or roughly 22 per cent of the female population), 162,563 women workers in various occupations, 70,000 peasant women in suburban villages, 32,030 women students, 8,240 women teachers, 4,266 women employees in the government, 20,573 family women and 3,753 members of different democratic groups.[8]

Local women's groups were centred on a variety of social institutions such as schools, factories and other places of work or in the residential communities of the village or urban neighbourhood. Local groups took various forms. Many of the groups were first established to encourage literacy among their members. Others were formed as newspaper reading groups or to study Marxist writings. In each, special consideration was given to government policies, local social and economic conditions, and the special implications of each of these for women. Local consciousness-raising groups, especially in the newly liberated areas of south China might take the form of practical work teams in the fields or in the factories, and would usually play a supportive role in meeting the practical and emotional problems of its members. The two functions often went hand in hand. In Liuling village, the local group of women combined study, labour and consciousness-raising.[9] Their leader Li Guiying had attended a Party school in 1951 and had learned to read and write. On her return to her village she formed a local group of women to teach them her new skills. Many came to the winter classes and learned to read and write enough characters to write simple accounts, receipts and to keep notes. The group became a labour group in 1953 and learned to make shoes and clothes and improve their agricultural tools, feed poultry and spin. But Li Guiying still felt that they had not really broken away from the past, hence she encouraged the village women to meet together for discussions after winter school. 'We tried to get the women to tell us themselves what things had been like before, how it was now and how it ought to be in the future.' They contrasted the old practices of seclusion, arranged marriage and bound feet with the new opportunities. The question of equality posed more problems. 'We discussed whether women are men's equals or not, and most felt that within the family, men and women are equal. We help the men when they work in the fields and they should help us in the house.' But many of the older women relaxed in the belief that 'women are born to attend to the household'. 'A woman cannot work in the fields! That can't be helped. It is just that men and women are born different. A person is born either a man or a woman. To work in the fields or in the house.' She said that they had long discussions on these and similar questions. Similarly in factory workshops or their subdivisions, women met to study or discuss their mutual work and personal problems. A representative from each sat on the woman work committee of the factory which either constituted a local branch of the Women's Federation or of the Women's Section of the Trade Union.

Local groups or committees of women, be they textile factories, co-operatives, or those based on the street or neighbourhood, directly elected representatives to women's councils or 'representative conferences' which met in the larger villages, rural districts or city wards. In 1949 the 'representative conference' or congress had been designated the local and basic form of organisation most suited to the conditions of rural and urban China and the conference or congress of representatives was to play an important role at every administrative level, from local to national, in discussing past achievements, analysing present problems and determining the future policies of the Women's Federation in the area represented. It was to meet at regular intervals and in the intervening period an elected 'representative committee' (or council) was responsible for carrying out resolutions, attending to the daily routine matters and convening further conferences at regular intervals.[10] In the newly liberated areas of central and south China it was often some time before the representative conferences took the initiative in establishing the new rights of women. In Nanchang village in the newly liberated Guangdong province, where the anthropologist C. K. Yang was resident in 1950–1, the local Women's Association sent several representatives to conferences in a near-by village. At this early stage the representative conference did little more than meet and discuss current political campaigns, but as he says 'the very presence of an independent organisation of women dealing with public affairs was in itself a new phenomenon of considerable importance, something entirely out of context with the traditional social order based on sex segregation and the exclusion of women from public affairs.'[11] Others in the older liberated areas and cities took more initiative. In almost 50 per cent of the townships in one county, the local women's representative congress held regular meetings and took much initiative in their work.[12] In one of the wards of Peking, particularly noted for its woman work, women from some 3,400 households, mostly those of workers and small handicraftsmen, businessmen or industrialists, elected a representative for every thirty households. The newly elected conference or council of representatives elected a chairperson, several vice-chairpersons and other officials all of whom were unpaid. The work of the council or congress was roughly divided into four categories. It publicised as widely as possible the Marriage Law; helped women to take part in handicraft production either individually or in co-operatives, it kept an eye on the welfare of women and children in the ward and saw to it that the women were kept well informed on current happenings so that they could take an active part in them. In these ways the council claimed to maintain close contact with the women of the ward.[13]

Each city ward, township and rural district congress or conference sent representatives to meet and work at the county, city or at urban district level in the larger cities, and it was reported that by 1952 Women's Federation branches had been formed in 80 per cent of the counties or equivalent administrative units.[14] The following schedule of activities was recommended by a county committee of the Women's Federation: the committee of the County Women's Federation should hold a conference every month; the County Women's Representative Conference should be held once a year; it should arrange for a number of joint meetings of leaders of woman work of the various administrative levels within the county and keep in touch with them through the circulation of reciprocal reports and letters.[15] Representatives from the counties and cities met in the Women's Federations formed in each province, municipality and autonomous region. For instance the Peking Municipal Democratic Women's Federation included representatives of thirteen District Women's Federations each of which in turn represented a dozen ward women's conferences, congresses and councils. When Tie Lianli interviewed the secretary of the Peking Women's Federation in the early 1950s she said that every village and every street within the Peking environs had a women's representative who attended conferences and reported back to them. In Shanghai she found that there were fifteen sub-branches of the Women's Federation and at the Shanghai headquarters of the Women's Federation there were 115 staff. They were divided between departments responsible for administration and the organisation of women within Shanghai; general education and publicity; women's social welfare, including ante-natal and child care; literacy; women's education in agricultural and other skills; and a department responsible for liaison with other joint organisations outside the women's movement.[16] The highest body of the Federation was the All-China Women's Congress which met every few years to draw up the policy and programme of the women's movement all over the country. The First National Congress was held after liberation in 1949, the second of the National Congresses was held in 1953 and the third in 1957. The Second Congress in 1953 was attended by more than 900 delegates. In the view of Xu Guang, one of the leaders of the women's movement, the main purpose of the conference was 'to review the achievements and experiences of the women's movement during the past four years since the last congress and to define our future tasks in relation to the requirements of the present situation'.[17] Between meetings of the National Congress, the officers and executive committee were elected to carry out the work of the Federation, to put the decisions of the conference into effect and generally give guidance in the work of all the women's organisations. In 1949 the officers elected were those who had had a long history of participation and experience in the women's movement. The honorary presidents were Song Qingling and He Xiangning; the president, Cai Zhang, and the vice-presidents numbered five: Deng Yingzhao, Li Dezhuan, Xu Guang, Shiliang and Zheng Yun. Through this national network the Federation was said to be in contact with some 76 million women.

The formal aims of the Women's Federation were to strengthen the unity of women of all nationalities and classes in order to protect the newly won rights of women, give expression to their new aspirations, break down their traditional social isolation and raise their levels of political understanding and vocational ability. In sum to redefine the role and position of women. The attempted redefinition of sex roles assumed a new definition of sex-role differentiation, and now the traditional division of labour and evaluation of sexes into superior and inferior categories were interpreted as culturally rather than biologically determined phenomena. That is, it was in terms of ideologies and value systems that physiological differences were interpreted. This belief in cultural determinants allowed for the possibility of change and the alteration of social institutions and norms supporting biological differences. A documentary study of the women's movement reveals that after 1949 it operated on the assumption that women were now living in a new age in which the old definitions of women's 'duties' and 'rights' were no longer appropriate. New questions required the working out of new solutions, the setting of new standards and the introduction of new behavioural norms. An open letter addressed to the readers of a Chinese magazine refers to the questions facing women in this new age. 'The women of China', it said

> won the right to dignity and equality only recently, after long years of tremendous struggle. Now they are energetically transforming these rights into deeper reality. In every walk of life, in cities and villages all over the country, they are asking: how shall we act to use our freedom well for our children, for our country and ourselves? With steady purpose, they are expunging the effects of their age-long feudal oppression from their lives and learning how to take their new position in society.
>
> Such knowledge does not come of itself. Discussion, analysis and exchange of experience show the way forward. Serious questions which affect great numbers of women are debated in the national press and in women's magazines, in forums and in meetings large and small. Should housewives go out to work? Should educated women stay at home and care for their children after they become mothers? Is a weekly nursery better than a day nursery for the children of busy parents? Should women try to do 'men's jobs'? What should be the grounds for seeking and granting a divorce? What is the best way to bring up children to be good citizens of the new socialist country that is coming into being? Even very simple everyday problems like 'What shall we wear?' . . . have come up for wide discussion, and men as well as women have joined in. This is a new age, and the old standards of women's 'duties' and women's 'rights' no longer prevail. The liberation has opened all roads. The new standards have to be thought out and established by women themselves.[18]

In learning how to take new positions in society it was assumed that such knowledge did not come of itself, but required constant discussion and analysis. In other words it was a conscious learning process which was to be participated in by all. A women's magazine, *Women in China* (*Zhongguo Funu*), was established by the Federation to act as a forum for the discussion and analysis of the new standards. It was published monthly to introduce women to the new egalitarian ideology and to facilitate a nationwide 'exchange of experiences' in its implementation in practice. It provided an avenue of communication between groups and branches, it publicised conference reports, discussed mutual problems and reported the results of research. General principles and the individual choices facing women in their own lives were debated at great length and individuals and collectives reported at length on their own experiences in selected fields of activity. The life histories of those who had succeeded in solving problems, rejecting the old ideology and adopting new standards of behaviour and learning new skills were published to encourage women to believe that change in their own lives was possible.

The newly organised women's movement set out to redefine the traditional division of labour within the household and between the public and domestic spheres. It encouraged its members to implement the new legal and material conditions favourable to the redefinition of their role and status.

The traditional family institution was identified as one of the main vehicles of the perpetuation of women's inferior position and it came under wide attack. In particular, the Marriage Law, which was published in May 1950, was designed to form a new basis for intra-family relations. The first law to be passed by the new government, it was jointly formulated by them and the Women's Federation. It was based on the study of Marx and Engels, the experiences of the Soviet Union in this sphere, and influenced by previous legislation passed in the Soviet Areas and by the Guomindang. Compilation of the new law took about eighteen months and there was constant discussion in the Women's Federation and other groups before it was revised, adopted by the government and became law. The new law opened with the unequivocal statement that the arbitrary and compulsory feudal marriage system which was based on the idea of superiority of man over woman and which ignores the interests of children shall be abolished.[19] It was to be replaced by a new marriage system based on the free choice of partners, on monogamy, on equal rights for women, and the protection of the lawful interests of women and children. The new type of family viewed the relationship between husband and wife as a full and equal partnership based on the recognition that women have an equal right with men to develop their knowledge and skills, an equal right to independence, and freedom for full participation in economic, social and political life. The provisions go on to prohibit bigamy, concubinage, child betrothal, interference with the remarriage of widows and the exaction of money or gifts in connection with marriage. Divorce was to be granted when both husband and wife desired it, while in those cases where either the husband or the wife alone sought divorce, it could be granted only when mediation had failed to bring about a reconciliation. A number of Articles of the Marriage Law dealt with property and the maintenance of women and the care and education of children after divorce. The law was far-reaching in its consequences for women, but the limitations of legislation alone in effecting change in this sphere had been all too evident in Guomindang China. Hence the first concern of the women's movement was the implementation of the new law. Shiliang, a lawyer and one of the vice-presidents of the Women's Federation, was aware of the magnitude of the task and while acknowledging the deep-rooted influence of the feudal marriage system, she also expressed their determination to change it.

> We must use and are using every possible means to implement
> the Marriage Law thoroughly. We regard this as a constant,
> serious, political task and are determined to achieve complete
> victory in this important social reform.[20]

The Women's Federation was partly responsible for the widespread advertisement of the provisions of the Marriage Law and it played a supportive role in counselling and practically assisting women to exercise their new rights.

Shiliang wrote that the main purpose of the publicity drive was 'to make the fundamental spirit of the law—equality of men and women, and freedom of choice in marriage—known to every household in the city or village, from the centre of the country to the remotest areas, so that every man or woman should abide by the law and observe it as the new social morality.'[21] Much of the material distributed by the ACDWF was in the pictorial form of posters, cartoon strips and mobile exhibitions. Many could not read and write. One very colourful poster set out in a series of 30 pictures the main provisions of the new law. There could be seen a disgruntled merchant foiled in his attempt to take a concubine, an angry mother being told that she cannot demand a dowry, a modern girl refusing to allow her mother to betroth her little sister, the People's Court trying to bring about a marriage reconciliation, parents co-operating to run the home and care for the children and so on.[22] A wall newspaper observed in Anshan showed up the thoughtless husband. Mother and father are shown returning from work, mother carries the baby and the shopping bag while father strides ahead burying his nose in the newspaper.[23] Exhibitions which displayed pictures and drawings illustrating the contrast between the old and new forms of marriage and family life were held in both urban and rural areas in large numbers in the early 1950s. Some exhibits included commentaries by speakers who themselves had suffered in the old society and facilities were sometimes provided where individuals could raise their problems privately with counsellors. An exhibition in Shaoxing, a rural town in Zhejiang province, drew over 10,000 visitors in five days, and an exhibition sponsored by the local Women's Federation in Shanghai which lasted for ten days in December 1951 drew 160,000 visitors.[24]

Numerous new stage plays, films, folk tales, rhymes and songs were centred around the themes underlying the new law. In Wu village for example, one young girl whose own free choice of a husband had aroused her family's anger, encouraged the girls in the village to act in a play called 'This Way is Better'. It was about a village girl who made her own choice of a husband and had a very happy life.[25] One of the new operas was based on a story of an eighteen-year-old girl who had been forced to marry a ten-year-old boy. After 1949 she had been able to get a divorce and marry a young man of her own choice. Many folksongs and rhymes rejecting feudal customs originated during these early years. A rice-planting song from Dingxian

Only a horse that accepts two saddles is a good horse
If a woman marries eight times she is still virtuous,[26]

was written to replace its feudal counterpart: 'A good horse won't accept two saddles, a good woman doesn't marry twice.' Another from Hunan, advocating resolution in the face of opposition to free marriage, opens with the line: 'If the boy is resolute and the girl is resolute, why fear the mountains being high and the rivers deep?'[27] Another on the same theme originated in Shandong province:

The water bubbles in the stream
I ask you, who will arrange your marriage?

Will it be your father, will it be your mother?
Will it be your elder brother or his wife?
It is better to choose for oneself, arrange the marriage oneself!
There is no need for the go-between and her boasting to both
parties.[28]

There were articles especially written for the press, periodicals and
wall newspapers, copies of the Marriage Law were widely
distributed and pamphlets on the subject were to form the central
theme for discussion meetings and study groups held in factories,
villages, organisations, government agencies, army units, schools
and street committees. In Lingxien county, Pingyuan province, a
group of young women studied the Marriage Law and as a result
put forward a set of conditions to their betrothed or husbands. 'We
hope our partners agree', they declared, 'to our entering spare-time
schools, joining in winter study and participating in meetings and
mutual aid groups.'[29] In Chungking the Marriage Law was studied
by the workers of several factories and afterwards it was said that
the majority of husbands were persuaded that it was against the law
to interfere unreasonably with the activities of their wives.[30]

   The Women's Federation gave practical support to its members.
Speaking of their problems or past lives in 'speak bitterness' or
'recall the past' meetings was a first step towards defining their
present position. Many women with the support of their groups
found the courage to not just talk, but to act and fight for the right
to choose their own marriage partner, to remarry if they had been
widowed or to divorce. Jie Yun found the courage to marry again
in the face of considerable opposition.[31] Wang Shu, a concubine,
turned to women from the Federation for help in getting a divorce
and in finding work to support herself.[32] The Women's Federation
acquainted women with legal procedures and assisted them
practically in taking divorce cases to court, but the initial
implementation of the Marriage Law was not easy. It affected each
home, each family and in much of China new practices were
introduced which were totally at odds with the long experience of
generations of the majority of the population. This was especially
so in the newly liberated provinces of southern China. A woman
leader in a village there told the Australian author, Dymph Cusack,
that change didn't come easily in their village, there was much
opposition from the older generation and the village was often
deeply divided on many of its provisions.[33] The free choice of
marriage partner, the remarriage of widows and the practice of

divorce particularly seemed to have aroused suspicions, opposition and caused bitter struggles.

The older generation, particularly, felt their control of family affairs to be threatened by the ending of the old practice of arranged marriages. Many a story from villages reported parental opposition not so much to the new partner as to the fact that they had not been responsible for the match. When one girl told her family that she had chosen her own marriage partner, her father had replied 'What is this free love business—it's losing face business.' But his daughter would not yield for had not the nation passed a law which said he was not supposed to interfere.[34] Although women were still forced into marriages not of their own choice,[35] many arrangements became a form of compromise where the parents might introduce the young couple who now met and gave their consent before the ceremony.[36] In areas where continued segregation of the sexes reduced the chances of mixing and mating, parental pressure usually retained considerable force. In many areas the families of widows continued to view their remarriages as bringing shame to the whole family and ruining its reputation in the village. One widow of eight years' standing in Huai Yang district, Henan province, had never dared remarry until after the Marriage Law was proclaimed by the new government. Encouraged by the new law she married the village head 'of her own free will'. She was at once denounced by her uncle, brother-in-law and brother in turn for bringing 'disgrace to the family name', through a 'violation of all conventions' and one which could only be resolved by her death.[37]

Such brutal negation of the freedom of widows to remarry was not uncommon, but the most formidable problem arousing the strongest social resistance was that of divorce. The stability of the family institution seemed to be at stake, even though divorce had never been freely advocated as a panacea for all ills. Where both partners in marriages which had been 'arranged in the old arbitrary way or resulted from sale or purchase or were bigamous and suffered from strained relations and subsequent cruelty' desired divorce, it was granted.[38] Case histories relating the fate of strained partners often concluded of these cases that upon divorce 'one unhappy couple has been turned into two loving pairs'. Between 1950 and 1957 large numbers of divorces were granted and divorce cases formed the largest proportion of all marriage disputes brought to the courts. Many of the suits were initiated by women,[39] the new significance of which was not lost on the village population. Women claimants used the new law in the support of their cases and such was the impact of the new law that it was often dubbed 'the divorce law'. Although the new Marriage Law in theory, and sometimes in practice, gave women a new weapon with which to bargain to improve their position *vis-à-vis* their families, suspicions, fears and opposition abounded sometimes resulting in their death or suicide, especially in the more conservative rural areas.

It was the Women's Federation which brought the increasingly evident resistance against the new law to public notice through the media. Not only did they cite cases where those whose traditional authority was threatened were forceful and violent in their opposition or where there was a genuine misunderstanding of the law, but they also cited cases in support of their argument that it was often the attitude of the local Party leaders and cadres themselves that was at fault. From their new positions of authority, many cadres, victims of their own conditioning, either interfered on behalf of the forces of conservatism, suppressed or ignored the new demands of women or actively abused the provisions of the law. These cases were more common in the southern provinces where the local political leaders were less experienced and had received less training than their counterparts in the longer liberated areas of the north. They were also accused of unscrupulous behaviour in dealing with their own domestic situations, in treating their wives as personal belongings and women generally as 'inferior beings'. The Women's Federation noted in a report on the state of affairs in southern China that to get a divorce, there were three obstacles to overcome: the obstacle of the husband, of the mother-in-law and of the cadres. Apparently it was the latter which was often the hardest to overcome.[40] There was no doubt in their minds that the behaviour of certain of the cadres was responsible for some of the problems in implementation of the new law, and the cause of much suffering of women caught between the old and new ideals.

It was these problems which caused the government to investigate the situation towards the end of 1952, two years after the promulgation of the new law. It was found that the nationwide implementation of the law had been uneven. In many localities the people and the government workers either misunderstood the law and made many mistakes as a result of too little preparation and education in its provisions. There were instances of resistance to the provisions of the law and the number of suicides and murders warranted serious attention and investigation. It was estimated by

Shiliang, Minister of Justice and a vice-president of the Women's Federation, that investigation revealed three types of areas according to levels of understanding and stages in the implementation of the law. Those areas still in the minority where the publicisation and implementation of the law was satisfactory, the majority of China where some suspicion and distrust of the law still existed, and the areas where old customs and misconceptions surrounding the new law were responsible for the continued widespread suffering of women.[41] It was the very real difficulties and problems involved in introducing reform in this intimate area of family life which prompted a new campaign in March 1953.

The new nationwide campaign was launched to re-publicise and enforce the provisions of the Marriage Law. Before launching it on a nationwide scale, the campaign was carried out experimentally in sample villages, factories and streets to clarify the problems likely to be encountered in each area and discover suitable methods of work. When the Marriage Law team arrived in one village in Sichuan province, they found that domestic relationships there had changed little from the age-old patterns.[42] The team first set about training the representatives from the village Women's and Peasant's Associations, the Party and the Young Communist League and the village administrators. The local leaders were keen to attend the lectures on the law and its implementation, but when it came to the panel discussions in which they were invited to illustrate points from their personal experience and knowledge they were reluctant. The tendency was to mention only small things that had happened in the remote past. Some of the men insisted that wives had to be 'punished' occasionally, and there were women present with such an inferiority complex that they agreed! This attempt to expose feudal practices was abandoned in favour of a public meeting in the village at which a few actual cases were brought to public notice. This was the prelude to a village-wide campaign after which small group discussions were innovated. As a first experiment, they called family meetings at which wives were encouraged to reveal any ill-treatment by husbands or mothers-in-law. But this was soon abandoned because it only caused quarrels. Instead, the people of different categories met separately to discuss mutual problems. Mothers-in-law were asked to recall how they had suffered from family tyranny when they themselves were young brides, wives were encouraged to overcome their sense of inferiority and husbands to discard feudal ideas of male supremacy.

In another case in Hebei province, a committee member of a

village Women's Association reported on her own change of attitude as a result of the visitation of a Marriage Law team.[43] The evening of the day after the team arrived, the women of the village decided to meet and study the Marriage Law every evening. After two nights of study, the visiting team suggested that each speak from her own experience and take the opportunity to discuss any of their individual problems. 'Then we can see if old feudal ideas are still holding any of us prisoner and how we can deal with the matter.' Several of the women responded and told of the problems of their married life or offered advice based on their own experience, but Zhang Xiuying, a committee member of the village Women's Association, was strangely silent when it came to personal matters. She had been divorced by her husband and, influenced by the contempt expressed by her family and village for those who had remarried, she had resigned herself to a lonesome life. After learning of her problem the team had talks with her mother and a mothers' meeting was held to discuss the problem of remarriage following divorce and widowhood. Family pressure soon ceased. At a later discussion meeting Zhang Xiuying talked about how she had for a long time remained 'an uncomplaining and uncritical' prisoner of feudal ideas despite her position in the local Women's Federation. She promised to remedy her own thoughts before helping other women in the village 'to free themselves from the tyranny of old, worn-out ideas that kept women in subjection and unhappiness'. It was the nationwide persistence of old customs, old ideas and the problems associated with the implementation of the new law in the early 1950s that convinced the government that a long period of painstaking and patient work would be necessary before the new practices were fully accepted.

The implementation of the Marriage Law was one of the first priorities of the new government but the methods of its implementation brought the government and the women's movement into conflict. A general directive of the government in 1953 criticised the work methods used by many local female solidarity groups in their support of the new Marriage Law.[44] They were accused of viewing the Marriage Law exclusively in terms of women's rights or as an instrument for the oppression of men by women and its implementation as the exclusive responsibility of the women's movement. In some areas the Marriage Law had consequently become known as the 'Women's Law' or as an 'unequal teaty against the men'. The result was often a backlash or reaction in which the new Marriage Law became unpopular with both men and some women thus isolating the leaders and activists in Women's Associations from the rest of the village. The directive recognised that some initial conflict between men and women in the implementation of the new policies was inevitable, but it made it clear that the methods of class struggle were not appropriate to the struggle between the two sexes. Mao Zedong's teaching on the different types of contradictions in society was quoted: 'Contradictions of different character can only be solved by methods of different character.'[45] Class struggle at this time was that between the 'people' or the 95 per cent of the population who 'favour, support and work for the cause of socialist construction' and the 'enemies' or all those 'social forces and groups which resist the socialist revolution'. Struggle between the sexes was described as a non-antagonistic contradiction which was defined as an internal thought struggle among the 'people' to be resolved through long and patient education. The people themselves, on the basis of a new social consciousness would correct their mistakes and reform their relationships. To this end the government recommended that henceforth on the one hand the provisions of the Marriage Law should be continuously publicised and enforced through the long-term process of education, and on the other, women should be encouraged to enter social production. The achievement of reform within the domestic sphere was directly linked to the movement to transform the mode of production and involve women in social production.

When the CCP became the National Government of China in 1949, it predicted that improvement in female status would closely follow participation in production. The expansion of the national economy and the reorganisation of industry and agriculture had been planned on the assumption that China was uniquely rich in labour power and that women formed one of the most underdeveloped of China's resources available for economic development. In the mid-1950s Mao Zedong said of the role of women in socialist construction and the economic development of the countryside, that they 'form a vast reserve of labour power which should be tapped in the struggle to build a great socialist country'.[46] However, government policy assumed not only that the involvement of women in social production was necessary for the economic development of the country, but that involvement in production was of the utmost importance to women themselves as a precondition to their liberation. After Engels the government and the women's movement emphasised that the first premise for the emancipation of women was the reintroduction of the entire female sex into public industry, and the following passage from Lenin was often quoted:

> In order to emancipate women thoroughly and to realise real equality between women and men, it is necessary to have public economy to let women participate in joint production and labour, and then women would stand in the same position as men.[47]

It would enable women on the basis of their improved material conditions to overthrow feudal oppression and attain equal status with men in the domestic and public spheres. Through employment they would acquire economic independence and access to social resources which they could use in bargaining to improve their position. The saying, 'Marry a man. Marry a man, clothes to wear, food to eat', would no longer hold true. Since 1949 the recommendation of Mao Zedong to 'unite and take part in production and political activity to improve the economic and political status of women' has been widely quoted.[48] On these grounds successive government policies of land reform, the collectivisation of agriculture and the expansion of the industrial and rural sectors of the economy have been supported by the women's movement. It has encouraged women to take advantage of the new opportunities to take a full and wide-ranging role in production and each new policy has been celebrated as a new stage in the emancipation of women.

In rural areas the position of women was first improved by the redistribution of land. Deng Yingzhao concluded in 1952 that: 'land reform has a most far-reaching effect on the political, economic, social and domestic status of women and of course, on their outlook as well. . . .'[49] In the southern provinces land reform took place in the early 1950s and, as in the old liberated areas, women were given their own land certificates or their names were placed alongside their husband's on a joint certificate. This was sometimes more a formality than a reality, but women had an unprecedented sense of their importance and they could potentially appropriate and take their share of land out of the family on the occasion of their divorce, widowhood or remarriage. No longer did the old proverb: 'If you come, I shall feed you. If you go, you can't take anything with you'[50] apply. However land ownership alone didn't improve the position of women. Men still said 'Ten stars are not as bright as one moon.' Women seldom worked their own land, but the first steps in the movement from individualised to collectivised agriculture did encourage them to do so. In Wu village in north China, six widows and divorcees were encouraged by the local Women's Association to form their own mutual-aid team. They drew up a set of rules for the team, ways of measuring labour and checking output. In 1951 their team cultivated 26 mu of land and their cotton crop averaged the same amount as any mutual-aid team in the village. One of the women, Han Jinlan, also chairman of the local Women's Federation, was convinced that the pooling of their efforts in co-operation was better than the sole reliance on two hands. 'To co-operate', she said, 'stone becomes jade' and 'to unite sand becomes gold'.[51]

Where there were men in the family there was often a less obvious need for women to work in the fields. Once co-operatives were formed however the expansion of the local economy often demanded the inclusion of women in the work force. Co-operatives, made up of 100 to 300 or so households which pooled their labour, land and implements, planned collective production programmes and its members were paid according to the amount of the family's capital investment and time worked. These new institutions widened the scope for women's participation and the Democratic Women's Federation in Xingtai County, particularly active in its work among women, reported on its work there as an example for others to follow.[52] The Women's Federation in Xingtai County drew up plans which included programmes to explain the co-operative system of organisation, to encourage women to give up the idea that production was exclusively a man's job, to undertake part-time or full-time agricultural and other productive work, to overcome men's 'usual contempt for women's working ability' and to teach women agricultural techniques. In one of the co-operatives in poorest Shanxi the chairman had a good talk with the men to persuade them that they would have to help give the women a confidence in their capabilities and teach them skills. 'If we don't,' he said, 'then the co-operative will be like a cart with one wheel off. It'll go round in circles and never move ahead!'[53] The local Women's Association persuaded the women to take up new jobs. Most responded, but a few of the women from the better off families, who had normally led lives of leisure, were reluctant to discard their dependent role. They were doing very nicely as they were. As one said, 'Whoever wants to be emancipated can be emancipated; as for me, I'd rather remain as I am.'[54] It was not always easy to persuade women of the benefits of entry into social production.

In one of the nationally famous agricultural producers' co-operatives, the deputy chairperson, Shen Jilan was responsible for mobilising women in her village to take part in agricultural production. She described how difficult it was to persuade the women.[55] In the second spring after the co-operative was organised, plans were drawn up not only to increase agricultural output, but also to take up forestation and animal husbandry. But the success of this plan was reliant on the inclusion of women in the co-operative's work schedule. 'You'd think it was easy,' said Shen Jilan, 'but it wasn't.' Her village of Xikou had a good record in the implementation of the Marriage Law, but 'this didn't mean that all feudal ideas had disappeared or that every man regarded a woman as an equal. Not at all.' Women still had no independent source of income thus 'if a young wife wanted to make herself a new dress, she still had to get the consent of her parents-in-law or her husband. At table, the men still got the best food, and the women served them.' Her own mother-in-law had said to her: 'Jilan, we all live from your father-in-law's labour. He should eat well. For us, anything will do.' Shen Jilan found it hard at first to encourage women to work in the fields. The men declared 'women are not farmers'. The older women said: 'We can cook, make beds and hull grain. We're no good in the fields.' Some of the younger women also said they lacked the skills. 'I began step by step,' said Shen Jilan. 'First of all, I called on all the women and explained that only active work could liberate them. This brought more than ten of the younger women out. Then I tried the older ones.' Her plan was to first attract one woman, Mrs Jin, who was despised by her husband and was by reputation conservative and idle. This was to shame the other women into work. Patiently Shen Jilan worked to win the confidence of Mrs Jin. She said to her, 'We'll never be emancipated if we don't do farm work like the men.' But Mrs Jin only replied. 'I'm too old, I don't care whether we are emancipated or not.' Shen Jilan made the issue more personal. 'Your husband looks down on you and you haven't any decent clothes. If you come out, there'll be more earnings in the family and your husband will respect you.' Eventually more and more women, including Mrs Jin, worked in the fields, but with a low morale. The women only received half the wages of the men who themselves defended this discrimination by saying 'Let the women prove their ability before they ask for more.' Only after women attended classes to learn agricultural techniques and challenged the men for the same jobs, did they begin to be awarded similar pay for similar work. In 1953 Shen Jilan reported that all talk of women being unfit for this and that stopped, and women were integrated into the newly established co-operative. 'Everything changed for us after this,' Shen Jilan said happily. 'Instead of three women officers of the co-operative there were now eight and everyone in the village and in the home treats us with a new respect.' By 1955 the widespread establishment of rural co-operatives was in full swing and with it the movement by the Women's Federation to encourage and help women to enter into agricultural production.

In the urban areas women were also encouraged to take up new occupations in industry, and training schools were set up to equip women with the requisite literacy and technical skills. The heavy industry sector of the economy was expanding fast in the early 1950s and new and spectacular occupations for women such as those of pilots, train drivers, lathe operators, rail despatchers, iron and steel workers, attracted a lot of attention. The example of Dian Guiying, a young girl of twenty who became the first woman train driver in China, was written up to inspire young girls to make a radical break with the past. Dian Guiying's struggle to be accepted was said to typify the obstacles in front of Chinese women who began to carve out new careers for themselves.[56] She had begun her career by selling meal tickets in the workers' dining room at the Dairen City Railway depot and for long her sole aim was to escape from this menial task by finding a husband. She had even begun to embroider a trousseau in anticipation of setting up a new home in the near future. The turning point in her aspirations came when she attended a lecture on the role of women in the new society and learned of their traditional oppression when confined to the household. Her dream burst. She had always thought of marriage as an escape to a newer and happier life, but she realised 'it had all been a dream, nothing but a dream of slavery in another form'. She remembered the theme of the lecture 'to become really free, women must take part in social labour. Only when women are economically free can they find true political and social freedom.' She began to change her attitude towards work and after visiting an exhibition illustrating the role of women train drivers in Russia she made up her mind to become a woman train driver. She applied for entrance to a new training programme which had been set up for women. It was then that she had to face the considerable opposition.

A major handicap was her supposed lack of physical strength and stamina which composed the butt of male prejudice. Her father objected to her chosen occupation and said 'Remain where you are a little longer and then it will be time to marry you off.' Her father's reaction was enforced by the response of the men of the factory. 'The locomotive section must be making a joke,' said the doctor who gave her the prerequisite medical examination. 'Well, if women can do this work, why should there be men at all?' said an experienced engine driver. 'If you women wait until you break down from exhaustion before you give up this crazy notion, it will be too late then,' a stoker said with mock concern. But Guiying and her classmates would not be deterred. They vowed not to give up before their training was completed. Many were the times they remembered this vow as they suffered perpetual exhaustion from continually stoking their engines and struggled with their limited education to master the technicalities involved in their new occupation. In the initial programmes designed to gradually help them build up their strength the extra consideration they received often antagonised the men train drivers. The rumblings of discontent finally forced the factory to call a meeting to educate the railwaymen: 'if you are indifferent or opposed to women becoming skilled locomotive workers, you just don't know where your interests lie. Are you better off when you keep the women in your families in idleness and have seven or eight mouths to feed? Of course not. If your womenfolk earn their living they free both themselves and you.' The men were asked to help Guiying and her friends become the first all-woman train-drivers' team in China. Their progress had been frequently described in the newspapers and it was evident that throughout their course, the girls themselves were fully conscious of their importance as pioneers in this particular job and in the economic liberation of women.

Those already trained and in occupations were encouraged to improve their productive skills and try new jobs and those professional women who had skills, but who now confined their attentions to the affairs of the household, were persuaded to once again put their skills to social use. Intellectuals like Bu Junshen were persuaded to return to work. Bu Junshen was a housewife who was a graduate of Yenjing University who had taught a little, got married and had two children. She had shut herself up in her home and turned housekeeper. 'I only looked after the children, put the house straight and made it a cosy home.' She had not bothered much with outside events until, influenced by the achievements of other women, she began to take up her studies again and resumed teaching. She described how she had began to share more than just household interests with her husband and children. 'Three-and-a-half years ago,' she recalled, 'I led the inactive life of a hibernating insect, buried deep in the soil, and quite unaware that spring is near.'[57] Another group with some socially useful skills were the wives of capitalists and businessmen who had often had the benefit of an education and professional training. First though, their social attitudes of superiority had to be changed. It was pointed out that before 1949 this group had shared their husband's parasitic extravagant and easygoing life, and as wives they had also been reliant on their husbands, thus having a dependent status politically and economically. Although the material standards of their class were superior to those of the rest of society, they suffered the same relative sexual suppression as the women of poorer families. Moreover, after 1949 the basis of their economic position had been seriously undermined by the replacement of private ownership with joint state–private enterprises in which former owners became joint managers receiving an upper limit of 5 per cent interest on their capital investment. The national and local Women's Federation held conferences for the women of this class to help them to understand the true nature of their position in society in the past and aid them to adjust to the ways of the new society. For many the first step was just to undertake their own housework after a life-time's habit of being waited upon by servants. This in itself was a radical change. They were encouraged to participate in community activities, social production and social service work. Dymph Cusack talked to the wife of a banker in Tientsin. She had attended a conference of capitalists' wives in Peking and had come away with the feeling that she had wasted much of her time in the past in idleness at tea parties and at mah-jong. Now she and many of her friends were learning to take part in the new society.[58] Some were helping in nurseries, many were active workers on their street committees and others took on jobs, where according to their fellow workers, they were beginning to 'drop half their arrogance'.[59]

To enable women to take a full and wide-ranging part in social production the government and the women's movement combined to reduce the number of structural constraints derived from women's biological functions, their traditional role of child-rearing and their previous lack of educational and other opportunities to exercise their talents, all of which continued to work against the redefinition of their role in society. The government and the Women's Federation worked together to establish new facilities to allow them to combine a public role with family life. To provide for women's child-bearing role, the Labour Insurance Law guaranteed working mothers 56 days' maternity leave with full pay, and women workers and workers' wives were entitled to maternity benefits. Pregnant women and nursing mothers worked reduced hours and where they worked in heavy industry or on night shifts, they were moved to lighter work or day shifts. A network of midwifery health clinics was established to improve the hygiene of childbirth and the health of the mothers and infants during the pre- and post-natal period. The Health Department and the Women's Federation co-operated to retrain old-type midwives in modern methods of child delivery. They were given a basic knowledge of the hygiene required and were shown the futility of such superstitious practices as opening all doors and cupboards if the birth was delayed—not to mention those that were more harmful in their effect. Despite exhibitions of mother and child care it was some time before the women, and peasant women especially, accepted the newly trained midwives. Many still believed in the methods of the old peasant midwives, even though their unsterilised instruments and habits had caused nearly a third of all newborn infants to die of tetanus.

Many a new and enthusiastic midwife was disappointed at the reception which she received in a village and she found that the support of the local Women's Federation went a long way in forwarding the acceptance of her work, and where branches were strong, meetings were held to explain the process of childbirth and contrast the dangers of the age-old customs with the benefits of the new methods of delivery. Many of the older women remained sceptical, but some of the young mothers were ready to give the new methods a try. The guinea pig in one village was Li Xiuying. Of ten children already born to her, seven had died of tetanus. At first she was dubious. 'Could these young girls with their pigtails really deliver her eleventh child safely?' Then she remembered that the landlord used to send his pregnant wife and concubines to the hospital and there they had their babies safely. These girls had also been trained in the hospital. She decided to try the new method and watched by the whole village with the keenest of interest, she gave birth safely to her eleventh child. Thus the modern methods of midwifery began to win the peasants' confidence.[60] In rural areas infant mortality dropped to one third of its former figure. Common childhood diseases, formerly rampant, were reduced with the establishment of child health clinics, improved sanitation and inoculation. Not only were the facilities for childbearing improved, but women were to be given the freedom to plan and space their families.

In the past constant childbearing had taken a terrible toll of women's health and strength. When Han Suyin was working in an obstetric hospital in the city of Chungking in the 1940s, she had been appalled by the wastage of women and children.[61] In 1954 the new government made plans to introduce the subject of birth control to the people. It had been a subject of heated debate in the early 1950s. Many had opposed the introduction of birth control in their country. The population of China was seen to be its greatest strength and China was 600 million strong only because the knowledge of birth control had never been propagated. In 1952, in the national newspaper *Renmin Ribao* (*People's Daily*), birth control had been condemned as being simply 'a means of killing the Chinese people without shedding blood'.[62] Others held out against the demand saying that since liberation, industrial production had risen by about 10 per cent a year, agricultural production by 5 per cent and the population by only 2.2 per cent.[63] There was no need therefore to resort to birth control to gain a better livelihood. Others still, considered the question immoral and unethical—a taboo subject. Against this battery of opposition, popular organisations, especially the Women's Federation, worked to show that there was a demand for birth control.

The women's organisations argued that birth control was not meant to reduce the population, rather it was in interests of women that they should be offered the means to space their children and limit their families to manageable size. They said that to make the equality between men and women a 'real and living' practice, women must have the opportunities to study, acquire skills and take part in political and economic activities. This meant that they must be able to plan and space their families to protect their health and strength from too many and too close births. The age of marriage was so low before 1949 that many women still in their early twenties had 4 or 5 children and 7 or 8 by the time they reached thirty. 'This is a heavy burden on them and it was from such considerations that the question of birth control arises.'[64] The Women's Federation published a survey carried out in Peking which showed that the majority of people wanted information on birth control.[65] In response to such pressures the government began to popularise and promote the practice of birth control in 1955. The monthly women's magazines in January and March 1955 gave detailed instructions on the different methods of birth control. Pamphlets, posters, slides, exhibitions, meetings and lectures helped explain both the techniques and significance of birth control. Contraception was highlighted as the most important method of family planning. Both mechanical and chemical devices became widely available, birth control clinics were established and small, trained teams visited government offices, schools, factories and the countryside to give practical advice. The ban on abortion was relaxed, but people were not encouraged to regard it as a contraceptive method. Sterilisation was considered only in exceptional cases and then only with the unqualified agreement of both husband and wife. Later marriage was also encouraged. The Marriage Law set the lowest age for marriage as eighteen for girls and twenty for boys, but this was largely seen as a compromise with folk custom and young people were generally encouraged to marry in their mid-twenties so that they themselves had the fullest opportunity to exercise their talents and acquire skills which would put them in a better position to have a family. The use of birth control was left to the discretion of the family, and once a woman decided to have children, every facility was to be made available including fertility counselling and a wide range of child-care facilities.

In the early years of the 1950s a network of child-care facilities either in enterprises or in neighbourhoods and villages were established. These included 'nursing rooms' for the youngest babies where the mothers could feed and care for their babies at intervals during the working day from the end of their maternity leave, nurseries for children from eighteen months and kinder-gartens for ages $3\frac{1}{2}$ to 7 years. They were run by neighbourhood organisations, factories, schools, shops or co-operatives on a daily or weekly basis or on a seasonal basis in the countryside. By 1952 the number of nurseries in factories, mines, commercial enter-prises, government organisations and schools had expanded to twenty-two times their original number in 1949.[66] Trained child-care nurses and teachers were required to meet the expansion of facilities and in the major cities the Women's Federation initiated a series of short-term classes to train members in collective child care. In the rural areas the establishment of child-care facilities were less widely distributed and were at first small scale and of an experimental nature. In many areas the district and village administrations had co-operated with the Women's

Federation to organise mutual-aid groups to take care of the children at busy seasons in the agricultural cycle. In the year of 1952 seasonal nurseries were said to have increased tenfold. Many co-operatives did not permit women to take up outside employment unless there was adequate provision for child care and guidelines for the establishment of successful village creches were published. The Women's Federation of one county suggested that before organising creches it was necessary, 'first and foremost to look into the needs and possibilities'. For instance it should be known beforehand how many women are unable to take part in public activities and production because they have to look after their own babies and how many old women are available to supervise the creche. After preliminary investigations the women should meet to talk the matter over, and air their problems and worries, and arrange for the division of labour and the payment of staff so that all parties concerned can benefit. It also suggested that after creches were formed, meetings at regular intervals should be held to discuss problems or worries that either mothers or those that care for their children might have. It concluded that 'only when all these tasks are carried out can the creches be run well, expanded and improved step by step'.[67]

One village reported the history of their nursery so that others might avoid some of the difficulties which they, the Women's Federation and village welfare committee, had encountered. The main problem had been finding suitable people to care for the children. Strong and energetic women had preferred to do farm work which they thought had more status. Older women were found to lack the strength and energy necessary to keep up with a roomful of lively youngsters. When women whose own small children were of nursery age were put in charge, other mothers claimed that they picked up their own children more than others. The nursery limped along for some time as staff came and went for no one wanted to bear for long the emotional wear and tear of bored, unruly children and sensitive mothers. It was not until young unmarried women were sent on short training courses and put in charge of small child-care centres where they were assisted by older women, that educational and recreational activities for pre-school children were well planned and organised.[68] As Kang Keqing, head of the Child Welfare Department of the Women's Federation said, 'it was the large-scale training of personnel for child welfare' and 'the establishment of creches, public nurseries and village nurseries in various parts of the country' that enabled women 'to participate more fully in the productive and political life of the country'.[69]

A great handicap to women's entrance into social production was their illiteracy and lack of technical skills. Literacy classes were very often the first step into public life and women were encouraged to take the opportunities presented by the evening, winter and spare-time classes. According to figures published in 1951, of the 56 million peasants of both sexes attending winter and spare-time schools about half were women, and in 1952 more than 3 million men and women working in offices and factories were attending workers' spare-time schools.[70] Many found great difficulty in mastering the complicated characters of the Chinese written language, others, like Ye Heng Zhan, learned to write short letters after only a three-month study course.[71] The government was also well aware that if women were to play a full part in a society in which technological innovations, mechanisation and industrialisation were to feature greatly in its development, every effort must be made to acquaint them with new technological developments. If they did not, they would be increasingly relegated to the more menial occupations in a new division of labour between skilled and unskilled work. Women must acquire skills. As the head of a co-operative said to the women of his work team, 'there are still some jobs that are too heavy for women. But when we get tractors and machinery in the future—there'll be nothing the women won't be able to do.'[72] Women everywhere were encouraged to apply for short-term training programmes in any one of a number of skills, short-term courses in middle schools for workers and peasants, and courses in technical colleges and universities. Like Li Jinzhi many found the courses taxing and it was only perseverance that saw them through to the finish. Li Jinzhi was one of three peasant girls enrolled in a training class in the nationally famous Anshan Iron and Steel Works. She was to be trained to operate the control board at the new seamless tubing mill there. She recalled the initial difficulties she faced in mastering the necessary technical skills. At the first lecture she was nervous but keen. The tutor slowly drew a sort of picture on the blackboard—the side elevation of a re-heating furnace. 'Side elevation? What on earth's that?' she wondered. But she noticed everyone else taking notes like mad and started to follow suit. Then she couldn't remember the Chinese character for 'elevation' and had to put a cross instead. The tutor was going on '. . . and the furnace is lined with fire-proof brick'. 'Fire-proof brick? Oh dear,' thought Li, 'where do they get all these queer terms? Never heard of them.' She began to get flustered and panicky. Casting a glance about her, she saw all the other trainees busily taking notes, their pens scratching on the paper. In the end, she closed her notebook and sat there, pursing her lips with mortification. She couldn't take in a thing. She made her way home tired after the intensive effort to understand and depressed at her own poor showing. The other girls too feared the classes were too much for them, but, determined not to prove the conservative foremen right in their prejudiced appraisal of women's abilities, they didn't give up and at the end of the course they were to be found among the operators of the control panel of the new seamless tubing mill at the Anshan Iron and Steel Works.[73]

One group with particular problems were the former prostitutes for which the main cities and ports of China had been notorious. The brothels were closed down shortly after the new government took office. In Peking alone, 237 were closed and overnight 1,290 prostitutes mostly between the ages of 18 and 25 lost their jobs.[74] They were taken to the Women's Institutes for Education and Production to train in some new skill. At first the girls, influenced by past experience at the hands of the Guomindang government and anti-Communist rumours, viewed any attempt to help them with great suspicion. They feared that they would all be sent to distant regions to reclaim land or be distributed to 'grimy-faced workers' who were too poor to get wives by any other means. It was some time, and only after they had been encouraged to arrange for their children or mothers to live with them at the Institute if they so desired, and they had experienced kindness and help over a period of time, before they began to co-operate in their rehabilitation. All but 79 of the 1,000-odd prostitutes were in need of treatment for venereal diseases and the girls were encouraged to talk of their bitter experiences in the past. It was hoped that by talking about things they would be released from their past guilt and bitterness. They began to understand that they were more the victims of a particular social and economic system rather than individually responsible for their former occupation. They saw that they were no longer prisoners of their past. Literacy classes and vocational courses were also organised and soon most of the former prostitutes took up occupations with a new sense of worth and confidence in themselves.

Women were not only encouraged by the government and the women's movement to redefine their public role through involvement in social production and their improved economic bargaining position. The Women's Federation was convinced from past experience that women would remain isolated and outside the mainstream of events so long as they were under-represented in the membership and leadership of political institutions and popular occupational or community associations. In their support, they cited cases when men had failed to notify women of meetings that they should have attended or had defined women's needs to suit themselves. In one village, where a woman was responsible for woman work and was the elected head of the co-operative and its representative on county committees, one of the men leaders tried to persuade her to give up one or other job. 'I can manage both jobs,' she assured him and cited the policy of the Party in her defence. 'One of the reasons why the Party wants women as well as men in leading posts is that we understand women's special problems and men don't.' He retorted that she was always trying to get something special for the women and contrasted their present lives with the old days 'when they used to work right up till the day their children were born and start again directly afterwards'. She replied that that was before liberation and anyway 'what of yourself then, you were a hawker trying to make a living selling brooms. Now you are a deputy-head of a co-operative. I haven't heard you suggest that you should go back to the old days.' With the strength of her new position behind her she rallied the support of the villagers and, with the man leader roundly criticised for his attitude, she was able to continue to support both interests.[75]

In the early 1950s women were represented in top government posts and elected to the government councils and people's representative conferences. Women constituted 20 per cent of the total number of public functionaries working in the Central People's Government.[76] Women members elected to provincial and municipal people's government councils numbered 287, or 4.7 per cent of the total in 1952.[77] In some places the percentage was higher. In five cities of north China, 8 per cent of the municipal council members were women.[78] The sixteen district government councils of the city of Peking had 35 women members or 16 per cent of the total.[79] In rural areas too, women participated in the administration. In 43 villages on the outskirts of Peking, 13 per cent of the village council members were women.[80] In Wu village, 7 out of 15 members of the village council, including the vice-chairman, were women,[81] and in one model village in Hebei province, the village head, deputy head and supervisors of public security and education were all women.[82] In 1950 the percentage of women participating in people's representative conferences averaged around 10 per cent of all levels. In 1951 this number had increased to approximately 15 per cent and in some cities and counties it reached 30 per cent.[83] It was the nationwide election of 1953 to elect people's congresses at all administrative levels—district, county, municipal, provincial and national—which convinced many women of their new importance in society. As one representative of the Women's Federation said at the time, 'it was not until she saw her name on the electoral roll that she realised that not only had she a new public place in society, but also a responsibility to help in the building of a new society'.[84] Of the total number of registered women voters 84 per cent exercised their new right.[85] Women not only voted, but were elected as deputies to the people's congresses at all levels. At the lowest levels 17 per cent were women, in 14 provinces an average of 16 per cent of the deputies were women and 20 per cent were women in the 5 municipalities of Peking, Tientsin, Shanghai, Jinan and Qingdao.[86] In the National People's Congress, women constituted 12 per cent of the deputies.[87] They included leaders of women's organisations, authors, artists, teachers and scientists, and others were peasants and factory workers.

These figures had nowhere reached the ideal of equality of representation, but for each woman elected it was the end of a long personal struggle to overcome age-old prejudices. Each had a history of personal struggle to recount. They had had to counter severe social constraints that had in the past produced sayings such as 'a mare can't go to the front, and a woman can't take up a post'; and the fact that in the past women themselves wouldn't have even dreamed of taking part in government. In Shahe village where a young peasant woman was proposed as a candidate for election, some of the men of the village voiced their opposition. 'We are electing a deputy. How can a woman do that job?' This provoked a sharp response from the women who disclaimed these backward ideas and with their support she was elected to the local people's congress.[88] In other areas, especially the older liberated areas, the records of older individual women made them more obvious choices. Li Fanglan had been active in her village for several years and she was unanimously elected as a deputy. She felt great excitement, 'she an ordinary peasant woman elected as a deputy to the *xiang* people's congress!' She described it as an unprecedented honour, but also a daunting responsibility. How could she cope with this new type of work?[89] Many of the new deputies felt their lack of education and public experience. Zhao Songjia, in the city of Shenyang, and Liang Guoying of Huailai county shared the fears and doubts of Li Fanglan. Zhao Songjia, despite her work in the community didn't know where to start when many new problems crowded in on her.[90] Liang Guoying, the daughter of a peasant, had only attended primary school for two years. Later she worked in women's welfare and in 1952 became head of Huailai County in Hebei Province. As the first woman to do so, the people doubted her ability and with her lack of experience, she initially also had no confidence in herself. But undaunted, she carefully studied all the relevant documents, discussed her work with others and went to the villages to check on the results of her work.[91] Like Zhao Songjia she kept in constant touch with her constituents in order to know their needs and listen to their proposals and opinions. Slowly they both began to master the intricacies of their work.

Women were also encouraged to take part in rural and urban class associations. It was proposed that in these joint associations they would both raise their class consciousness and bring their collective strength to bear and further safeguard their rights and contribute to the building of the new society. Local women's federations encouraged peasant women to take a full part in the poor and lower-middle Peasant Associations, mutual aid teams and later co-operatives. The exclusive Women's Associations supported the activities of women within the joint peasants' associations. In 18 agricultural producers' co-operatives in Shanxi province, 95 of the co-op directors and assistant directors were women. In the 812 co-operatives established in Xingdai county there was a total of 2,817 leading women workers including 472 co-op leaders, 917 management committee members and 1,482 brigade leaders.[92]

In the towns, women workers in factories were encouraged to take part in trade union organisations. As early as 1920 women leaders had found that only by involving themselves at the point of production in the daily struggle of the women workers could they hope to negotiate some improvement in their working conditions and raise women's self-awareness of their role in society. In 1928 a resolution on the women's movement passed at the Sixth Communist Party Congress had stated that woman work among industrial workers fell naturally within the work of the trade unions.[93] The responsibilities of the trade union movement to women factory workers were again reiterated in 1950 when *Gongren Ribao* (*Workers' Daily*) emphasised that 'work among industrial working women was an indispensable and important part of trade union activity'.[94] According to the women's representative in the Municipal Trade Union Headquarters in Shanghai in 1973, the category 'industrial working women' included women working in four different types of work—heavy and light industry, communications, construction and finance, and trade. At each administrative level of the trade union movement, special women's departments were set up to care for women's special needs in these types of work. Within each factory or enterprise there was, depending on its size, usually a full-time or part-time women's representative or committee for woman work at each level of production. For instance, at the large Peking Number 2 cotton mill there was a trade union committee for work among women at three levels, one small full-time committee had overall responsibility for the women workers of the whole factory, and the others were established within each workshop and each work group. By 1952 it was estimated that over 70 per cent of industrial women workers were members of the trade union movement.[95] It was understood that if the trade unions were to pay special attention to the technical and social needs of women workers, the women themselves would have to fully participate and represent their numbers in leadership positions. It was with this in mind that the Women's Federation established itself as a kind of external watchdog to prevent the traditionally male-dominated trade unions from ignoring the interests of its women members and neglecting woman work. In 1953 the Second All-China Women's Congress discussed the division of labour between the Women's Federation and the trade unions and established channels to facilitate co-operation between the two. The secretary of the Women's Federation outlined the duties of the Women's Federation. These were to assist, advise and supervise the unions in their task of improving the position of women workers and solve their special difficulties. Branches of the Women's Federation were therefore asked to 'concern themselves with the establishment, improvement and progress of women workers' departments of unions and study the work of women workers in conjunction with these departments, as well as assisting the unions by carrying on woman work which was not within the province of the unions and solving the special problems of women workers'. City branches of the Federation were exhorted to recognise this inter-relationship between the work of the trade union women's departments and the branches of the Federation, and to this end the National Women's Federation was to set up committees to encourage regular liaison and the exchange of information and opinions between the two.[96]

The trade union movement was also concerned with the political and technical education of women workers, the establishment of welfare facilities and the improvement of their working conditions. It immediately arranged for literacy and technical classes to train women to take administrative and management responsibilities and to encourage them to initiate new methods of production. It held meetings to discuss the new Marriage and Labour Laws which safeguarded the domestic and occupational rights of women, and cared for the personal welfare of its members. Every workshop in a factory had a trade union committee which met and discussed any problems of the workers. The women often met separately to discuss any special problems which they might have. Typical of the problems were those brought to one of the trade union women's groups in Number 1 cotton mill in Shanghai.[97] Sun Xiaomei was caught between the old and new customs. She had married a young man of her own choice, but of whom her mother disapproved. Her mother had never reconciled herself to this state of affairs and carried on a regular feud with her son-in-law. Eventually her marriage broke up despite the fact that she was expecting her first baby. With the support of the women's trade union representative, they began to sort out their domestic and housing problems. Sun Xiaomei's temper improved, she was no longer regarded as a trouble-maker, she became more popular with her workmates and she began to take an active part in discussion meetings held in the workshop. Another woman, Xu Zaizhen was said to take full advantage of her years and was feared for her tongue and manner. In her trade union group, relations became strained until the subject was brought out into the open. Xu Zaizhen had learned from long experience to stand up for herself against the foremen and her fellow workers in the previous decades. 'In the old days', she said, 'if I didn't get the upper hand of others, they'd bully me.' The members of the group began to understand the cause of her domineering manner and she herself came to see it was unnecessary in the new conditions of work. Their separate collectives within local trade unions acted to safeguard their rights in the factory and keep their interests in the forefront of the national trade union movement.

Urban housewives who did not immediately enter social production were encouraged to step outside the domestic sphere and participate in the newly established neighbourhood organisations. The street committees were local voluntary community self-help or self-government organisations centred around residential location. They generally included 200–300 households or the lanes between two main roads. From the very beginning the Women's Federation worked alongside these community organisations which were responsible for local welfare, public safety, sanitation, hygiene and educational work within each local area. Within each local area meetings were held among small groups of residents and they elected representatives to meet regularly with other groups to discuss mutual problems and local programmes of work. The proportion of women elected to street committees increased from 22 per cent in 1950 to 48 per cent in 1953.[98] Classes in literacy and hygiene were organised by the Women's Federation through the street committees, and newspaper and magazine reading groups kept the women in touch with outside events. The president of the local Women's Federation, who was also a member of a street committee in Shanghai, told Dymph Cusack how for women in her district the world had previously stopped at their front doors and one of the main aims of both organisations had therefore been to teach women to live as a part of a community rather than exclusively for any single household. A leader in the same street committee described the changes in her neighbourhood as a 'little revolution in itself'. Since 'through it we have learned to play our part in society. In the past we lived in the small family circle concerned only with our personal affairs and our children. We took it for granted, for we had always been taught that we were inferior and could play no part in life outside the home. But now all that is changed.'[99] In some areas though change did not come so easily. In one neighbourhood in Shenyang many of the women thought that they could not take much of a part in social life because they were too much occupied with household work. They did not even participate in the meetings of residents in their own neighbourhood. The local women's representative fought vigorously against such old ideas. 'In the old days, people declared, "women can't deal with big affairs",' she said to them, 'but we can see today that in our new society women can do any kind of work—they drive trains, run tractors and take part in state affairs. We housewives musn't lag behind others. We must step out and learn to serve our country.'[100]

Housewives were also encouraged to take an active part in local political activities as part of the 'Five Good Movement' launched in the middle 1950s. It was primarily a movement to encourage housewives to plan their domestic budgets, establish hygienic standards in the home, help their husbands and children, study and co-operate with each other on a neighbourhood basis. It was recognised that in this transitional period there were not yet sufficient opportunities to allow every woman to enter paid employment. Until an urban and rural economy required an expanded work force, many women would have to remain in the traditional category of 'housewife'. In an interview given by a leader of the Women's Federation, she said that the 'Five Good Movement' campaign was designed to enable each housewife to 'link up closely the household work with the work of constructing a socialist society'.[101] Women were to be encouraged to manage their household efficiently, but she emphasised that the campaign in no way aimed to confine women to their houses as had sometimes been surmised by interpreters abroad. The principle of mutual self-help took the practical form of various welfare services including literary and vocational classes, house-repair teams, street cleaning, meals-on-wheels for the house-bound and short-period creches to enable women to take part in all of these. In caring for others and working together, housewives were beginning to co-operate and look beyond their homes to community and national affairs.

The women's movement had been criticised by the government in its implementation of the Marriage Law, now it was the turn of the women's movement to criticise the government. In its encouragement of women into political activities the women's movement became very dissatisfied at the level of government co-operation. The government, the Party and the trade unions and other popular organisations all came under fire at various times from the Women's Federation for neglecting women's interests. The most conspicuous occasion was the Eighth Party Congress held in 1956 where Deng Yingzhao and Cai Zhang, officers of the Women's Federation, criticised continuing discrimination against women and the disregard of the functions of the Women's Federation by the Party and other organisations.[102] They criticised those leaders of rural and urban enterprises who continued to look down upon women, discriminate against them and 'employ their labour power improperly'. In their report they cited cases where enterprises had flatly refused to employ women or had laid down conditions which restricted their chances of being employed. Others had overlooked women's physiological characteristics and their household duties or had imposed work quotas which proved too much of a physical strain for women. Until there were sufficient social services to lighten the burden of housework, they thought enterprises should see to it that women had as much time as possible to attend to their household affairs. Instead of helping women to solve practical domestic problems many had left them to be solved by the women themselves. Above all the Party, the Young Communist League, the trade unions and urban and rural enterprises were criticised for neglecting to give sufficient consideration to the needs of the increasing number of working women within their organisations, to discussing their special problems and to consulting with the Women's Federation at various levels. Women were under-represented in the local and national leadership of these organisations. The leaders of the Women's Federation gave examples where cadres thought that 'even three women are not equal to one man' or where they were afraid that women cadres, if promoted to a higher position, would not prove equal to the tasks assigned to them, would not work for sustained periods of time and would be a 'burden' to the organisations they worked in. These fears accounted for the fact that men cadres were more likely to be promoted than women, even where it was a choice between men and women of equal competence. Deng Yingzhao pointed out that so long as conditions such as these existed, women were in need of their own separate organisation which would collectively 'give expression to their aspirations, protect their rights and interests as well as those of their children, and supervise the implementation of the policy and decrees regarding the equality of men and women'.

The criticisms of each movement by the other confirmed their common assumption that there was a direct correlation between participation in production and female status. If only the opportunities and facilities to enable women to enter social production were available, then women would acquire access to and control over the products of their labour and the strategic resources of society. Women who had entered social production attributed their new satisfaction with and importance in society to their entry into this new life. A widow described the changes in her life in one rural village.[103] She and her child had received a portion of land during land reform. Now she worked in the fields and at home. Her son was studying in the primary school and she was the new chairperson of the Women's Federation of the village. She summed up her life history and that of the other women in her village with the following words: 'Almost every woman in our village has a past history of bitterness, that is why we are happy.' In a village on the outskirts of Peking, a young 26-year-old woman who was now vice-director of the newly established co-operative spoke of her past. She had previously been illiterate and had had her marriage arranged on her behalf. She also pointed to the contrasting life-history of her friend, who had studied up to lower middle school, had become a young kindergarten teacher and had now chosen her own husband. The fact that there was only seven years difference in their ages pointed to the degree of social change since 1949.[104] Shen Jilan, a village woman, emphasised that 'we become really equal when we start to work outside the home, when we win our right to the jobs that men do and get equal pay for equal work'.[105] Like other women it seemed to her, from her own experience and the struggles they had shared, that above all entry into social production was the key to equality. Deng Yingzhao, a leader of the women's movement, wrote in 1956 that although there had been profound and unprecedented changes in the lives of women this did not mean that 'in our present-day society the question of the emancipation of women has been completely solved. A great deal remains to be done before the emancipation of women can be complete.'[106] It was the limited material conditions, preventing an increased entry into social production with its correlating individual economic independence and collective access to local and national decision-making bodies, which were interpreted as the primary obstacles inhibiting the emancipation of women.

9 A New Stage: New Problems

> The people's commune movement created the most favourable conditions for the complete emancipation of women. This has brought the women's movement in China to a new historic stage.
> (Li Dezhuan, 8 March 1959.)[1]

The plans to rapidly expand the economy and establish new social institutions, especially the rural people's communes, which were initiated in 1957–8 as part of the Great Leap Forward, were welcomed by the women's movement as signalling a new age for women. The president of the Women's Federation expressed the new mood of optimism and excitement when she said that the women's movement had 'leapt forward into a new historic stage', a stage of the 'thorough emancipation of women' and the realisation of genuine equality with men.[2] It was the organisation of social production and collective living on a grand scale, and their implications for the lives of women, that were said to have created the 'unprecedented conditions favourable to the emancipation of women' and given the women's movement an 'extraordinary momentum' during these years of the Great Leap Forward.

It was commonly appreciated that the first few years of the People's Republic had provided the legal basis for the equality of women in all areas of social, economic and political life. The redistribution of land and the partial collectivisation of industrial and commercial enterprises had reduced the private ownership of the means of production, but many felt that the material conditions for women's emancipation were still limited. Cai Zhang, the president of the Women's Federation, summed up the situation that existed just prior to the Great Leap Forward when she stated that so long as the small peasant economy remained so did the patriarchal system.[3] The establishment of the agricultural co-operatives had marked the first step in transforming the productive relations of a small producer economy and women had often contributed their labour to the co-operative, but its establishment had not gone far enough in providing women with new opportunities to enter social production. The employment of women in the co-operatives had remained limited in scope and

scale. Rural co-operatives, for example, engaged only in agriculture and some small side-line occupations, had not facilitated
their wide-scale entry into the work force. Moreover, where they
did work the wages of each member of the household were tallied
and paid to its head. Women were therefore still economically
dependent and this was at a time when it was work, with its
potential independent source of economic support in the form of
individual wages, which had become the symbol of the new
emancipation. In an open letter addressed to all women, the
Women's Federation reminded them of the significance of
employment. It revealed that for the women's movement active
participation in social labour was 'the fundamental condition for
the complete emancipation of women', and one through which
women would 'raise their economic status still further and so
achieve all-round development in politics, ideology, culture,
science and technology'.[4] The Great Leap Forward constituted a
movement to expand the economy and increase rural and
industrial production on a scale previously unknown in China. It
brought with it a new opportunity to put into nationwide practice
the premises of Marx, Engels and Lenin that the introduction of
women into social production was a precondition of their
liberation.

The rural people's communes were a new form of economic,
social and political organisation which was first established in
1958. They varied in size from 10 to 20 thousand households and
usually several co-operatives had merged to form one commune.
They differed from agricultural producers' co-operatives in that
they were a further step towards the development of common
ownership and not solely devoted to agricultural production.
Members were only paid according to the amount of their labour
and no longer was the amount of land or tools which they had
originally contributed taken into consideration. These passed into
public ownership. The communes diversified their economy to
include forestry, animal husbandry, fisheries and other side-
occupations, and they also engaged in industrial, trade and
banking enterprises. The establishment of the latter aimed at
reducing the differential distribution of resources between town
and country, and between industry and agriculture. Apart from
economic activities the people's communes were responsible for
cultural, educational and military institutions. The national
newspaper, *Renmin Ribao*, summed up their activities in 1958. In
all, 'the people's communes combine industry (workers),

agriculture (peasants), exchange (traders), culture and education (students), and military affairs (militia) into one and take charge of political, economic, cultural and military affairs at the same time.'[5] The women's movement welcomed the new opportunities it had made available for women, and directed its main efforts from 1958 to 1960 to further encouraging women to step outside the confines of the small circle of the family and take up new jobs and learn new skills.

In most communes women began to enter into agricultural production. In classes and through practice, women learned the techniques of ploughing, raking, seed mixing, manure application and the techniques of harvesting. Women also took part in the large numbers of industrial, water conservancy and construction projects. In Henan province, women did roughly one third of the conservancy work in the province, digging and building 880,000 reservoirs, ponds and canals.[6] Women's dams, women's dikes, March 8 reservoirs, March 8 forests, and so on, appeared in all provinces. The establishment of the people's communes speeded up semi-mechanisation, and the mechanisation and electrification of agriculture gradually lessened the labour-consuming manual work and made it more convenient for women to take part in various kinds of productive labour. Women themselves were encouraged to master and improve various kinds of farm tools. In Lushan Xien, Henan province, over 150 kinds of traditional farm implements were improved and some by women, including a wooden-track earth mover and a waterwheel.[7] In another area in the same province the women were said to have collectively created a new hand-cranking mill which was eleven times faster than the ordinary stone ones in milling wheat.[8] Women took part in experimentation with new methods of agriculture and in many areas experimental plots were attended by women. One village woman, Zhang Jiuxiang, who developed new strains of cotton, was acclaimed as one of the first peasants to turn scientist.[9] The people's communes operated iron-smelting plants, farm-tool factories, lathe factories, fertiliser works and agricultural-product processing factories. Rural women began to participate in the commune-operated industry and learned new industrial techniques. Some women took part in the nationwide movement to smelt iron in the locally built 'backyard' furnaces. In many communes several special 'women's blast furnaces' were built. In the Leap Forward Commune, Taihe County, Anhui, women set up a 'March 8 ball-bearing works' of which 64 per cent of the labour force were women.[10] In another, the women fitted hundreds of carts with the ball-bearings they had made themselves.[11] In a commune in Hangzhou, twelve women set up a cement plant after sending a representative to a nearby cement works to learn the appropriate techniques. Within a few weeks their plant was employing 103 workers and producing 60 tons of cement daily.[12] Example upon example could be cited to illustrate the diversity and scale upon which women took advantage of the new opportunities. It was estimated that the organisation of communes probably added close on a hundred million women to China's available labour force.[13] Women were said to have moved from a subsidiary role where they were merely considered to be 'all right and helpful' to one where they were 'essential, necessary and important'.[14]

Although women were encouraged to enter production alongside their menfolk and undertake a wide variety of jobs, they were also reminded that equality was not to be confused with sameness. Women were equal, but physiologically different, and because of their special functions they were entitled to certain privileges. An editorial in the women's magazine, *Zhongguo Funu*, was typical of a number of articles warning women not to strain their physical strength.[15] They warned women not to 'indulge in physical contests and think that women must carry what men can carry and do what men can do'. They cited examples where women, eager to prove their work capacity, had challenged the men of the commune in exercises often beyond their individual capacity. Some women thought that the protection of women's labour, far from being necessary or desirable, reflected their weakness or the delicacy of women and they were often shy and embarrassed about telling other people when they were menstruating or became pregnant. That is, 'they take a lead in production but dare not in protection'. The Women's Federation called on its members to remedy this state of affairs. They were reminded of the special arrangements to be made in the allocation of work during menstruation, pregnancy, birth and breast feeding. During these four events it was stipulated that their labour should be adjusted in the following ways: women should be assigned 'to a place nearby but not far away, to the dry field but not the paddy field, and to lighter work, but not heavy work.' They recommended that women production team leaders particularly concern themselves with the welfare of the women members. They were to acquaint themselves with the general situation of the whole team and confer with the male team leaders in the allocation of labour. They drew the attention to the fact that although new standards in labour protection had been achieved in some areas they were still far from adequate in other communes where women had recently been recruited into the work force in large numbers.

In urban areas women were also encouraged to enter social production in large numbers. Many factories were built and expanded but by far the largest number of women began to work in neighbourhood production units known as street or neighbourhood factories. These small-scale undertakings were collectively owned, based on low capital investment, labour intensive, often utilised recycled waste materials as their raw materials and many undertook simple manufacturing work for larger factories. In Peking, for example, 200,000 women including 190,000 former housewives entered social production in 1958–9. Of these women, one-quarter were apprentices, workers in factories and the service industries, capital construction and commercial departments, and three-quarters joined the community-organised projects.[16] More than 2,400 neighbourhood production units had been established, including special handicraft-works such as embroidery, lacquer-coating, tailoring, shoemaking, book-binding, paper boxes, toys, spinning of yarns or wool, glassware and small chemical works. Many of these products were made of materials discarded by factories or of obsolete articles. For instance odd scraps of leather were used to make leather belts, the residue of limestone was used to make calcium carbonate, and leftovers of various materials were used to make studs, buckles, shoe-laces, springs and keys. Most were established by the housewives themselves, who, inspired by the efforts of other sections of the population during the Great Leap Forward, were determined not to be left behind in their contribution to the building of a new society. They nearly all started from very humble beginnings—no ready factory accommodation and no equipment or funds to work with bar their own contributions. Many had never seen the inside of a factory before and felt they had few technical skills to offer. One way they gradually gained the necessary technical knowledge was to send one of their number to the large modern factories for short spells of study and practical training. An alternative was to invite a technician from a nearby factory to come and teach them skills.

The neighbourhood factories not only took part in textile, food and other light industries, but also in heavy industry. In Shijiazhuang, an industrial and railway centre in Hebei province, more than 22,000 housewives began making industrial products in small workshops they had built themselves. In Right East Street, for example, most of the younger married and unmarried women were already at work in industrial or other jobs, but not so the middle-aged housewives. One group included about thirty wives of workers at a local pump plant who, though eager to have their own workshop, were sensitive about the fact that none of them had had much education and nearly all were tied down by children. They began by making suggestions along the lines of 'sewing, knitting or making boxes' or what seemed to them to be traditionally 'women's work'. Fan Xiuyong disagreed. 'My husband says that the plant has so many orders for pumps from the farms that they can't make them fast enough. Let's set up a foundry for casting pump parts.' The other women at first greeted the idea with some scepticism. Without technical knowledge, experience in production and no capital, premises, equipment or materials, how could they even think of embarking on this project? They were assured that they would be given every assistance and, as the women said, 'If we can't build socialism as well as men, how can we say we're equal?' One team of women made arrangements with the pump plant, which gave firm orders for the component parts. With borrowed bamboo poles and straw mats, others constructed a shelter in an empty area near their houses. The pump plant and other nearby factories agreed to supply the equipment and the initial materials. The pump plant assigned two of its skilled workers to teach the women the art of casting. Within a few weeks their workshop was in full production.[17] Many such enterprises expanded fast. Zhou Junjiao and three housewives in Wuhan began a small production team to install and repair electric lamps and water pipes. Trained by workers in nearby factories, they had begun in a borrowed backroom with a few tools. One-and-a-half years later the factory consisted of six workshops employing 130 ex-housewives and turning out good quality electrical appliances.[18] According to a report by the chairman of the local Women's Federation, housewives living in Changchun city set up 135 workshops producing electrical dynamos, cloth, ironware, linen, saw blades, chemicals and other items.[19] Forty women in Jinjiao, Liaoning province, built a small workshop and produced good quality active carbon. Eighteen housewives in the coal centre of Fushun set up an improvised oil refinery which produced heavy diesel oil, fuel oil, lubricating oils, sulphate of ammonia and other chemicals.[20] Every city, every town, every urban neighbourhood could boast its range of street industries.

The government also introduced policies to socialise or collectivise housework during the Great Leap Forward. The previous collectivisation of production on a small scale had been able neither sufficiently to expand the employment opportunities for women nor to solve the conflict of interests or contradiction between collective social production and individual private consumption, or for individual women that between their work and private or individual household chores. The co-operatives, especially those in the rural areas, had been unable to provide facilities on a large scale and household work had remained the primary responsibility of the wife and the mother. Too often women in employment had found themselves with not one job, but two—in the home and at work. Working women in the urban areas often rose earlier and went to bed later in order to fit their household chores of cooking, shopping, cleaning and sewing into a busy day. In rural areas housework was especially time consuming and onerous. Water had to be fetched and carried, often from the outskirts of the village, grain had to be ground at a stone mill turned by a donkey or the housewife herself; fuel had to be gathered, clothes and shoes sewn by hand and vegetables pickled, sliced and dried for the long winter months. All this on top of daily cooking and washing.

Li Yangjing, a 29-year-old housewife in Liuling village, worked in the house and in the fields during the busy seasons. She described a typical day when she also worked in the fields. She got up before 5 o'clock in the morning to get breakfast ready, clear away and tidy her cave house, dress the children, feed the pig and see to the hen and six chicks. She worked in the fields from 7 a.m. until mid-day when she came home and cooked a meal. In the evening she returned to her home about 7 or 8 o'clock in the evening. 'The first thing,' she said, 'is to feed the family; then I feed the pig, the hen and six chicks, then I see to the children and when they're asleep, I do my sewing and make clothes and attend to such things, until about 10 o'clock, when I am tired and fall asleep.' She described the additional household tasks particular to each season. During the tenth portion of the Moon Year she 'puts down' cabbage, turnips and radishes by preparing and layering them with salt and pressing them in stoneware jars. In the spring she prepared and dried mustard-root and beans, and stored maize and potatoes, and during the first and second portions of the Moon Year she had to devote all her spare time to making clothes and shoes for the family. 'That is a lot of work, because the children are growing and wear things so.' She either made a new, or remade a quilted coat, an unquilted coat, a pair of quilted trousers and a pair of unquilted trousers for everyone in the family each year. It was the quilted clothes which were the most time-consuming. Each old garment had to be unpicked and the old wadding cleaned, washed and carded before mixing it with any new wadding to form the lining for the new season's clothes. She made a whole new quilted coat for each member of the family every other year and in between she unpicked, washed and mended the old one. The most laborious task was the making of shoes—two pairs per person each year and each pair took ten days to make. 'First,' she said, 'I collect all the old worn-out cloth that can't even be used as lining any more. I wash it carefully, then I paste the pieces together each on top of the other, between layers of new cloth. When this has dried, I cut it out into soles. I make thicker soles for my husband and thinner soles for the children. Then I sew them with jute thread. This is the most laborious. You have to stitch very close and pull hard. The wear of the shoes depends in the first place on how the soles are sewn together. It is the jute you wear, not the cloth. I make the paste myself; I take roughly equal quantities of wheat and bean flour, mix it with water and boil it. I also make the jute thread myself. I cut the jute, remove the leaves etc., then I put it in the stream. I dam this up with stones on the bundles of jute to keep them in place, and there they have to stay for a week, rotting. After that I take the jute out, peel it and there the fibres are. I wind those into thread by rolling them on my thigh.'[21] Under conditions like these most women found it impossible to take part in regular production or social and political activities or take full advantage of the new opportunities for cultural and technical education.

It was explicitly recognised that while restrictions of this kind were imposed upon women they could never be completely equal to men. A spokesman for the government pointed out at a conference for women in 1958 that the main task was to remove the contradictions between social production and household labour.[22] The solution was said to lie 'not in the negation of household work' nor in the mechanisation of household chores. Mao told the French writer André Malraux that 'to liberate women is not to manufacture washing machines'.[23] China had neither the resources nor the inclination to go in for a range of household gadgetry. Rather, the constraints hindering the redefinition of women's traditional role were to be overcome by socialising household chores and turning scattered and individual home chores into collective paid social work. In this the Chinese felt they were very much following the precepts of Marx and Lenin. The following words of Lenin were widely quoted in the newspapers and internal documents of the Women's Federation: 'When women are busy at household chores they suffer inevitably from certain limitations' which could only be overcome with the 'transformation of the sundry household chores into the great socialist economy'. Only then will any 'true liberation of women be possible, or true communism'.[24] The Women's Federation exhorted its members to realise these ideals in practice. Its Executive Committee advocated the development of a network of community dining rooms, nursing rooms, day nurseries, kindergartens, neighbourhood service centres and maternity hospitals to 'make all-round arrangements for the people's livelihood'. Those which already existed were to improve the quality of their services and expand their scope. They recommended that there should be no hard and fast rules governing the particular form of their development, rather 'we should develop collective welfare and social service undertakings in diverse forms and at different scales and standards so as to meet as far as possible the needs of different persons, different seasons and different production pursuits.'[25] Under the auspices of the new social organisations, the people's communes in rural areas and the urban neighbourhoods, domestic labour was to be gradually socialised.

During the Great Leap Forward many forms of household labour, such as preparing meals, processing food or grain, sewing clothes and caring for children gradually became collective enterprises in many areas. By 1959 it was estimated that in rural areas there were 4,980,000 nurseries and kindergartens, more than 3,600,000 public dining rooms and numerous flour mills and sewing centres.[26] In the rural outskirts of Peking 92.4 per cent of peasant households were said to use the community dining rooms.[27] Much importance was attached to the establishment and smooth running of the community dining rooms which would free women from the responsibility of providing daily meals and preserving food for long-term use. Commune and brigade secretaries were encouraged to personally participate in the kitchens and management to ensure their smooth running. Working in the public dining rooms was a new type of community service, but old ideas and attitudes often died hard. In many areas there was initially some feeling that serving in a community dining room was 'waiting on others' and a more menial occupation. In one village in Zhejiang, Zhang Amei, the director of the stock-breeding yard in the commune, volunteered for the job of cooking, saying 'I'm a Party member and head of the co-operative. It's my duty to take the lead.' To set an example her daughter-in-law and her second daughter went into the nursery.[28] Two foreigners, resident in another village, thought the new services looked as though they were the key to the freeing of women from housework and to their taking part in productive employment and public life. They described the establishment of the community dining rooms in Yangyi commune in September 1958, and by the summer of 1960 a total of 315 community dining rooms had been established with each work team having at least one. They ranged in quality of service from one to three stars! In Ten Mile Inn village, for example, not one of the team members had to walk more than a few doors to get to the dining room, the cooking was good, the menu varied and the accounts were detailed, business-like and public. The public dining room quickly became a kind of community centre with a reading room, recreational facilities and a bath-house.[29] The canteens tended to be popular at least for a short time if they were reasonably run and physical conditions were not unfavourable. In other areas experiments in establishing community dining rooms were less successful.

Sewing centres and kindergartens also aimed at lightening women's household tasks. Perhaps sewing centres were the easiest of all services to set up. Although the villagers in many communes had started to buy ready-made undergarments most of the outer garments, shoes, and cotton-padded mattresses and quilts were still made at home. In many communes sewing machines, still beyond private means, were collectively bought for the sewing centres. By the summer of 1960, for instance, the Ten Mile Inn Sewing Centre had a total of six machines which made clothes for roughly 65 per cent of the villagers.[30] A Resolution on People's Communes published in December 1958 recommended that 'nurseries and kindergartens should be run well, so that every child in them had better living conditions and education than at home and so that the parents want to put them there and the children want to stay there.'[31] Parents should be given the choice to decide whether their children should board or not and may change their minds at any time and take them home. In order to run nurseries and kindergartens well, the communes should have the facilities to train a large number of qualified child-care workers and teachers. In the middle 1950s many rural areas were still without child- and baby-minding facilities. Ten Mile Inn village fell into this category. In 1959 a kindergarten was established for the children of the village. It was staffed by two elderly women and to entice the villagers to send their children a special canteen was established to give them nutritious meals. At first it was not a success. The work of the kindergarten had been limited to keeping the children fed well, and out of mischief and danger. Many of the children, bored, ran away beyond the reach of the bound-footed attendants and many parents took their children home again. The brigade leadership acted and sent representatives to observe the more successful kindergartens in neighbouring areas. The nearby brigade in Bailin had long experience in this field. Small and temporary nurseries and kindergartens had been expanded, improved and made permanent during the Great Leap Forward. Now in this one brigade alone there were 27 nurseries and kindergartens taking in 93 per cent of the village children of pre-school age. All the children wore gay pinafores and the toddlers 'never went around in wet pants'. The kindergarten children had learnt thirty written characters and the new romanised alphabet. They could sing songs from local operas, recite ballads to their own castanet accompaniment and dance. Their visit to Bailin convinced the Ten Mile Inn brigade leaders that what was needed was a competent kindergarten teacher and one of the young girls subsequently attended a course run by the Women's Federation. Soon she and two young assistants attended to the health, hygiene and diet of the children and taught them songs, dances and handicrafts and general educational skills. The kindergarten soon became a recognised part of the life of this brigade.[32]

In the cities many new collective welfare and service facilities were established and old ones were extended. These included nurseries, creches and other child-care services, public dining rooms, and neighbourhood service centres or shops which undertook a wide range of former domestic chores. They were organised by the urban neighbourhoods a few of which had formed themselves into urban communes, especially in the provinces of Henan, Hebei and Heilongjiang. Like the rural communes the principle behind the urban communes was to create a single integrated unit of production, living and administration. Urban communes were easier to establish in areas where there was a central production focus and many centred on factories, mines, schools and offices. In other areas, attempts were made to give a residential unit some common production focus by setting up a number of small handicraft shops. But even at the height of the Great Leap Forward, the term 'urban people's commune' was not widely used and by 1960 the term was loosely used to describe urban neighbourhoods with small-scale street production and collected welfare and living facilities. Initial statistics showed that the communes and neighbourhood organisations in the large and medium-sized cities had already established some 50,000 community dining rooms catering for more than 5.2 million people. The number of street nurseries and kindergartens had reached more than 42,000 with more than 1.2 million children in their charge. This figure did not include canteens and nurseries set up by factories, government offices and schools. Neighbourhood service centres run by the urban people's communes and neighbourhood organisations numbered more than 66,000 with over 440,000 people working in them.[33] All these services took a variety of forms in accordance with the specific conditions and needs of the people in each locality. For instance nurseries instituted different systems—half-day, whole-day, twenty-four hour, and weekly care. Their time schedules fitted in with local production schedules and they were located as closely as possible to the work place of the majority of the mothers. Street nurseries and community dining halls ranged from those established on a grand scale to the more simple nursery classes and dining rooms serving a few dozen families. When the 250 residents of Xinjiehou street in Peking started their own dining rooms, they were able to complete five kitchens, a dozen stoves and whitewash ten rooms, and operated a dining hall to serve the residents of eleven neighbouring streets. Some 800 people took their meals there. A meals-on-wheels service was instituted for those unable to get to the dining rooms in person.[34] Other urban community dining rooms were far less ambitious.

In the capital city of Peking, there were by 1959 more than 1,250 street kindergartens and nurseries which accommodated approximately 62,000 children or triple the figures of 1957. There were 670 community dining rooms where more than 46,000 dined, 1,200 service centres and more than 230 units to mend, sew, patch and wash clothes for the residents.[35] These services were further expanded and a year later it was estimated that there were some 12,000 community dining rooms, more than 1,200 service repair shops, 3,700 service centres and more than 18,000 nurseries and kindergartens taking more than 610,000 children.[36] Neighbourhood service centres had been widely established throughout the city. Their range of services was varied and diversified including all-hour shopping services, street services and individual household services. The Baochi street neighbourhood service centre provided such services for more than 1,300 families housed in seven blocks of the neighbourhood.[37] They formed their own carpentry, tilemaking, electric fixtures, wall-papering, washing, mending and sewing work teams. Many working wives, on leaving for work in the mornings left their keys at the service centre. In their absence the staff of the centres would have water carried to their rooms, start a fire going in the stove and have their washing and other housework completed. In another area in Peking, the neighbourhood service centre in Er Long Street in the West City district of Peking was set up by the street committee with the help of the district Women's Federation and the local government in 1958. It maintained a twenty-four-hour service handling about 300 people a day from the area's 1,000 families. Its original aim had been to aid working housewives but it had gradually expanded its facilities to serve the entire neighbourhood, the workers in local factories and passers-by. Most of its sixty different types of work were done without charge, but to pay salaries and small maintenance expenses, the service centre received a monthly subsidy from the organisations for which it acted as an agent. These included the bank, the cinema and the post office for which it handled sales and subscriptions to newspapers and periodicals. It also acted as a distributor for the local Xinhua Bookstore. The service centre made part of its income from books which its staff sold at schools, offices and factories during lunch hours. From its office it also sold paper, pencils, common medicines and other necessities for unexpected needs after the retail stores were closed. There was also a small charge for mending, sewing and laundry services. A correspondent to a Chinese magazine describes a typical day's work and 'the atmosphere' of the Er Long Service Centre as:

> homelike. Both big and small affairs are handled quickly and
> efficiently by its staff of eight housewives and two elderly men.
> A middle-aged woman drops in to rest her feet and have a cup of
> hot water between shopping errands. An old woman asks for
> help in writing a letter to her daughter in another province. A
> housewife brings a bundle of socks and children's clothes for
> washing and mending. A newly married couple ask for help in

cleaning and moving into their new apartment. A boy wants a ticket for the evening show at the local cinema. A man wants to call a taxi to take his pregnant wife to the hospital.

The service centre would also make a client's deposits and withdrawals or pay the rent. The correspondent goes on to say that even more important than the staff's many helpful services however, was 'the feeling throughout the neighbourhood that it is a friend to depend upon whenever there is a need'.[38]

These services were not limited to the capital city. Chungking, the largest city in southwest China, was said to have established 27,000 neighbourhood dining rooms, thousands of service centres and other facilities. Special committees, composed of people's deputies, representatives of the Women's Federation and other public bodies, the state shops, the banks, factories, offices and schools had been responsible for the establishment of these community facilities. The neighbourhood service centres were run by the residents themselves on a mutual aid basis. They sold consumer goods, books and newspapers, received savings deposits for the bank, repaired furniture and household utensils, washed and mended clothing, did housework and performed a hundred and one other services. Women returned home from work to find hot meals locally available and their homes neatly cleaned. There were nurseries where mothers might leave their babies for a few hours to go shopping, see a film or go to spare-time school. In Chungking's Shangxinjie district which pioneered this work in the city, state shops and service centres were sufficient to ensure roughly every seventy households with a retail sales centre.[39] In far away Harbin, a northern industrial city, more than 4,000 neighbourhood service centres staffed by 16,000 people were established to take over virtually all the household chores of women in employment. There it was said that the rise in the numbers of women entering the work force and the pressing need for socialising housework had given impetus to the growth of service centres which were described as a form of mutual aid among neighbours. When a working housewife went to work in the morning she could entrust all her domestic jobs for the day to the service centre by leaving a note in the box on the door. Such services might include shopping, booking train tickets, mailing letters, drawing savings from the bank, mending furniture and utensils, sending clothes to the laundry and cleaning and decorating homes.[40] The Dongfeng urban people's commune in Changchun city organised around the Number 1 motor-car plant set up twenty-two service centres and 304 service points to serve 20,000 residents. The commune provided the street dwellers with 7 dining rooms, 27 food-processing centres, in addition to special units to serve the motor-car plant workers and the surrounding agricultural areas.[41] These examples are typical of the extensive network that had been developed by 1960. Not all community projects lived up to the expectations of the women, but as one of the leaders of the women's movement said in 1960 it was the establishment of new institutions which had turned housework from a scattered occupation into a public service that 'was a great revolution in the lives of the people'. It was the first steps in the organisation of production *and* livelihood that had brought into being a 'new way of life'.[42]

During the Great Leap Forward the transformation and expansion of production not only facilitated the wide entry of women into social production and the public sphere, but the transformation in the mode of production also had broad repercussions for the position of women in the domestic sphere. The organisation of collective production and the socialisation of domestic work potentially reduced the economic basis of patriarchal relations within the household. As the Resolution on Questions Concerning People's Communes stated, 'we stand for the abolition of the irrational patriarchal system inherited from the past and for the development of family life in which there is democracy and unity'.[43] Many articles elaborated the theoretical basis for the policies aimed at its abolition. The system of patriarchy was said to have assumed different forms in different historical periods. But whatever the difference in form, the relations within the domestic group had the following characteristics in common: the relations between men and women and between the old and the young were not equal. These relations were determined by the mode of production, the sexual division of labour and the principle of subordination.[44] In 1949 it was the feudal system of patriarchy which prevailed over most of the country and many articles in the media at the beginning of the Great Leap Forward linked the continuing existence of a small-producer economy with the patriarchal system. In the feudal mode of production the household had been both a unit of production and of consumption. The household was a productive unit combining agriculture with side-line activities and handicrafts. This was said to be true for all classes, peasant and landlord, toilers and leisured, and exploiters and exploited, for so far as private ownership and the organisation of production were concerned each were small-scale units of production. The households of the landlord class met the needs of its members through the possession of land and the exploitation of the surplus, or even a part of the necessary, labour of peasants while the peasant family was a small-scale unit of production based on plots of land and tools of production and individual labour. It was pointed out in a number of articles that it was one of the conditions of the small-producer economy that the household, as the unit of production, must necessarily have its own system of authority and subordination or patriarchy. Lenin's words, 'Paternalism is a product of a small-producer economy,' were often quoted in this conjunction,[45] and Mao Zedong following on from Lenin had described China as 'a country of small-scale production and one dominated by the patriarchal system'.[46]

Primarily the authority and control of the patriarch was thought to have been incorporated into the traditional ruling ideology to maintain the domestic group as a unit of production, extract its surplus and to submerge variations in the division of labour within the mode of production. As one article has said, 'it is precisely because the landlord class and the feudal states want to ensure, through the patriarchal system, that their economic and political demands are met by the domestic group, that they especially strengthened his authority over the family and gave him undisputable control over the members of the family.' According to an old maxim, 'as the Emperor should have a father's love for his family, so a father should have the sovereign's power over the family.' His lawful authority gave him control such that only he could dispose of properties, distribute labour power within the household and supervise the recruitment of labour through marriage. His control and authority were incorporated into the ruling ideology to the extent that it had the effect of submerging the class differences in the sexual division of labour within the household. In their analysis of the feudal mode of production the principle of subordination of women was grounded in the division of labour. Man's labour power was identified as the principle means of subsistence while the activities of women were confined to the transformation of raw materials for consumption. Although the basis of the power of the patriarch was often weaker in peasant households, where women frequently participated in the principle means of subsistence as well as the transformation activities, and their labour power was necessary for the maintenance of the unit of production, the authority of the patriarch remained intact. To abolish the patriarchal system necessitated the entry of women into social production and transformations in the mode of production itself. The articles in the Chinese media constantly quoted Engels:

> Participation in social labour by all women is a prerequisite to their emancipation. To attain that aim, it will be necessary to eliminate the family as an economic unit of the society. . . . Once men voluntarily form themselves into society and transform private domestic affairs into public enterprises, the socialisation of youth education, the establishment of genuine free relationships between family members are at hand.[47]

The development of new economic relations had begun with the introduction of policies to establish the collective ownership of the means of production in the early 1950s. The establishment of the co-operative system had turned the former individual mode of production, in which the household was the dominant unit, into a form of collective production. Henceforth the household was basically no longer the primary unit of production, but it still remained the major unit of consumption. The establishment of the communes was seen to further reduce the function of the household as a socio-economic unit. The involvement of women in social production and the gradual socialisation of household work undermined the traditional division of labour, and as wages were paid directly to the earners, irrespective of sex, every working member of the family, man or woman, was able to maintain independence and acquire equal ranking in the distribution of social resources. Because the new community services such as the dining rooms and child-care centres and the system of distribution were managed by the communes, a large part of the consumption of the people did not take place within the household as before. It was concluded that in these new circumstances the household was neither the economic unit of production nor entirely one of consumption, and in consequence the power once vested in the patriarch to manage and supervise production and dispose of domestic property had lost its 'sense and utility'.[48] Although this transformation in the mode of production was designed to reduce the role of the household as a unit of production and consumption the organisation of collective production and consumption were not designed to eliminate the household or the family.

The *Kirin Ribao* clearly stated that 'the family system will not be destroyed and the family members will regularly live and get together even when we have reached the Communist stage.'[49] The *Hebei Ribao* also reiterated that the establishment of the communes and collective living facilities will not and cannot lead to the destruction or elimination of the family. It distinguished between the system of patriarchy and the family as a form of joint life of two sexes united in marriage.

> The existence of this form of joint life is dictated not only by the perpetuation of the race. Even in the Communist society we cannot conceive any objective basis and necessity for the elimination of the family. In contrast a breakdown in the system of patriarchy would signify a 'real and complete emancipation of women and children'.[50]

It was anticipated that a reduction in the functions of the household would allow for the entry of women into social production and at the same time break down the hierarchical relations within the household which were traditionally based on the exclusive power of the household to organise production, consumption and primarily control the processes of socialisation. The power of the patriarch was to be replaced by a more 'democratic, harmonious and united' family. As Cai Zhang said, 'the family we want is one of democracy and unity, of equality between men and women, of respect for the old and love for the young.'[51] In a socialist society it was said that it need no longer be a cage imprisoning men, women and children. Family relations between husbands and wives and parents and children could be based on genuine affection and not on the economic considerations and social standing of its members. The legal rights and economic independence of women meant that they could take an equal part in decision-making. In the ideal family, the only difference between men and women was seen to be a physiological one and just as they had similar authority, rights and responsibilities in society so did they in the family. Parents were still to be responsible for bringing up their children, although they now shared their socialisation and education with child-care and other educational institutions. Children were still to be subject to the discipline of their parents, but their relationship was not to be one of blind obedience and still less of a subordination of personality. Children, like women, were 'independent persons', instead of a form of private property, and the former were still less to be regarded as a form of social insurance for the well-being of their parents. It was hoped that the family life based on the ideals of 'democratic consultation' would be full of vitality and contribute to the well-being of the 'big family'—the commune.

The practical application of the policies introduced to implement these ideals had far reaching consequences, and potentially affected every village, every neighbourhood and every family. It was a change not easily acceptable to each family or every member of the family. For some, their response was governed by the amount of authority they were likely to lose, and for others it was a genuine fear for the future of the family life as they had known it. In 1959 *Kirin Ribao* noted that among some sections of the people, there was a growing fear that the rise of the people's communes spelt doom for the family institution.[52] They surmised that the establishment of collective living facilities meant the end of 'natural and kindred relationships' between persons. In many areas where these doubts and fears were evident, communes held discussion meetings where individual members could voice their fears and opinions. The members of a brigade in Beiyuan people's commune in Shandong province recorded their debate on the nature of the 'small' family. In 1959 its members generally took their meals in the public dining rooms, and a nursery, kindergarten, a sewing team, a laundry team and home for the aged had been established. These innovations had caused some people to express concern over the question of whether there would still be 'small families' in the future and if so what role would they play in their lives. The first speaker asked if 'after the establishment of our people's commune where we have been served free meals, and since the people's commune is described as our big family, are there still small families?' Others were not sure of the relationship between life in the 'small families' and life in the 'big families' or the commune. Some welcomed the new facilities for public consumption in that they broke down the divisions between the richer and poorer households. Other women felt that even with the new policies their households continued to have a common budget and they still had no share in its disposal. Many worried about the fate of the old and the very young now that women were undertaking paid employment outside the household. They warned the women that 'they should not regard themselves as having no more to do with the old and the young' now that they were economically independent. On a national level the Women's Federation stressed the interdependence of the policies of the Great Leap Forward and the goals of the women's movement. It emphasised that it 'had come to realise that when our collective life is improved, the family is more democratic and united, greater equality between men and women is achieved, and the feudal patriarchal system is thoroughly ended'. After the whole family is engaged in productive labour and living 'all its members young and old, will be together with affection and joy and family life becomes happier and happier'.[53]

Indeed the combination of the above factors, the consequences of their increased involvement in social production, the introduction and extension of collective facilities to socialise domestic labour, the ensuing changes in family relations and more particularly in the individual and collective position of women, convinced the women's movement that it had indeed entered a new stage.

At the close of the Great Leap Forward it was estimated by the Women's Federation that 'the broad masses of women throughout the country had generally taken part in industrial and agricultural production and other construction projects, and the overwhelming majority of the labour-capable women had already become social labourers.'[54] A National Conference on Women and Work estimated that in rural areas 90 per cent of the feminine population had participated in production[55] and in 26 cities, including Peking, Canton, Harbin, Kirin and Taiyuan, preliminary statistics indicated that 80 per cent of residents had participated in production in each of these cities.[56] Individual women recorded great changes in their personal lives. Zhu Jin, tied to her home and her children, had often felt left out of things and was only vaguely aware of the changes taking place in the city where she lived. When she was out at meetings or at study sessions her mind had wandered—'Are the children alright? What will she cook for dinner?' Yet when she returned home she would catch herself feeling lonely. She would stand still and wonder to herself: 'Is this all there is to a woman's life? You grow up, get married, have children, cook and then you grow old and just die. Other people seemed to have time for all sorts of jobs. Will my life ever be different?' At the time of the Great Leap Forward, a neighbourhood factory was established near her home. Her children went to a new local nursery while she trained for a job. She began to earn her own wages, met other women and had an outside interest which she now shared with her husband and others living and working in the same community.[57]

Wang Wenlan was a 38-year-old mother with five children who lived in a small village. By reputation she had been a nagging housewife and a bedraggled and nervous mother. Once the commune was formed and nurseries and kindergartens and public dining rooms established her youngest children were taken care of and the family often ate in the communal facilities. Wang Wenlan went to work with her husband in the fields, she began to go out in the evenings and learned to read and write 700 Chinese characters at night school. She described how she became cheerful, busy and confident and was aware how much she owed to the commune. 'The commune,' she said, 'has given me a bigger world, now I am beginning to know lots of things besides babies, nappies and pots and pans.'[58] Mei Zheng wrote a letter to one of the newspapers in 1958 expressing her satisfaction in the new developments in her life. She described how previously marriage had symbolised security and she had given birth to children, brought them up, prepared meals, washed clothing and preoccupied herself with sewing and mending. She said that 'ten years had passed like a fleeting moment. But I suffered really badly through those years.' It was several years before she thought about getting a job, partly because of her domestic commitments and partly because of her lack of inclination. It was not until the Great Leap Forward and the new opportunities for work and household help that she went to work during the day leaving her children in the care of nurseries and kindergartens. She and her family ate in the dining room for meals, washed in the bath-house and put out the laundry if they did not have time to do the washing themselves. They lived and worked together in the 'big family' during the day and spent the evenings in the 'small family', resting and chatting with each other. She felt their lives to be greatly enriched from the combination of the two 'families', for they had also become interested members of the immediate community and the commune.[59]

The acquisition of new roles and the accommodation of old roles were presented in the media as marking a dramatic breakthrough in each individual life and in the history of the women's movement. In the period of a few short years it seemed as if they had satisfied the preconditions of their liberation and were on the brink of 'a thousand years of happiness'. Many songs expressed their joy and satisfaction at the new developments:

> In the past, women kept houses and were tied down by domestic affairs.
> They spent their days beside the pots and millstones and had to carry their babies on their back.
> When they went to the fields to work, their hearts remained at home.
> But now domestic labour has been socialised.

Everyone praises people's communes.
There are community mess halls to cook and serve food.
There are nurseries to look after their babies—
When they go home after working, they have plenty of time for
learning culture.[60]

Another similar song was written and sung by the members of
another commune:

Everyone sings in praise of the people's commune,
The young women say it is like a flower;
Our children go to the nurseries and kindergartens,
And the dining-rooms prepare the food for us,
We go to work with a light heart,
We learn to read and write after work;
We women are fully emancipated,
We sing in praise of the commune.[61]

In the excitement and exhilaration of the initial months of the Great
Leap Forward, when it seemed that the new policies had eliminated
or at least reduced many of the glaring inequalities of the past, it was
a temptation to fête the new age as if all the goals of the women's
movement had been achieved. Many women were working, they
were earning their own living and some were no longer afraid to
speak out in defence of their interests at village meetings. There
was a growing feeling in some local areas that now women were
involved in social production on a large scale there was no further
need for their own organisation. In Yangyi Commune for instance,
the work of many of the local women's organisations in brigades and
villages was found to suffer from a lack of vitality and purpose.[62]
The women's organisation in Liuling village was abolished in 1961
'because it was no longer needed'.[63]

Perhaps it was the almost exclusive emphasis on production that
had caused emancipation to be defined in terms of employment, and
within these confines had caused the achievement of emancipation
to be prematurely acclaimed. The Women's Federation itself had
stressed the necessity to involve women in social production and this
single precondition had taken priority in all its work. At the
beginning of the Great Leap Forward it had made a statement to the
effect that the present task of the women's movement was to
mobilise all women with labour power to take part in social labour
and constantly elevate their role in industrial and agricultural
production and construction.[64] They also maintained that through

social production women could go on to improve their status in the family and in public, economic, political and social life, but it was the more tangible goal, *paid work* which had become the symbol of emancipation. A song sung by women in Jiangxi province was perhaps symbolic. It began with the lines 'The power of women is inestimable, it fills half the world of *production*' (my emphasis).[65] Their role in holding up half the world, the sky or heaven was narrowly defined. But out of the experience of the Great Leap Forward, the women's movement came to recognise that the apparent satisfaction or partial satisfaction of the precondition of their liberation, their entry into social production, was not enough. Although female productive labour was a necessary condition for the redefinition of the role and status of women, it was not a sufficient condition. Other factors interfered with and discouraged their emancipation. The period of the Great Leap Forward had highlighted other conditions or problems, the solutions of which were essential to the achievement of liberation. In the concluding months of the Great Leap Forward the leaders of the women's movement were more cautious in their estimation of its achievements. They stated that 'though in the work of women, very rich experiences had been gained these provided still more favourable conditions for *further* development of work among women.'[66]

In the domestic sphere the household was no longer the same small-scale unit of production as before. An individual was no longer solely reliant on the household for economic support or social services. Women had access to the processes of social production and their own means of economic support. Thus to a large extent women were no longer reliant on their relations with their sons, gossip or threatened suicide in bargaining to improve their position in the household. No longer were daughters considered to be economic burdens and no longer were they subject to the same flagrant forms of discrimination that had been grounded in the traditional sexual division of labour. Marriage reforms had introduced the rights of individual choice, by free will and divorce, which considerably strengthened the position of the younger women in the household. But incomplete transformations in the mode of production and the continuing though reduced role of the household as a unit of production and consumption continued to work against the reduction of patriarchal relations within the household and sexual division of labour within the public sphere.

A problem common to both rural and urban areas concerns the role of the household in society and especially the accommodation of domestic labour. The separation of the public and domestic spheres underlay the traditional division of labour and their merger was crucial to its alteration. Articles in the media had made it clear that what is to be avoided is the entry of women into the public sphere with the result that they merely acquire dual roles with ensuing conflict and role strain. During the Great Leap Forward the government had attempted to resolve the problem by socialising as many domestic roles as possible by taking them out of the household and establishing the relevant community services. The collectivisation of household chores within the rural commune or the urban neighbourhood was designed to either substitute or at least supplement individual household tasks. Although an impressive array of these services was established in 1958–9 it was a very uneven implementation with a lesser number of services available to rural households and not all the various services were established with equal success. For example the establishment of child care and community dining rooms in rural areas proved to be very expensive as formerly unpaid domestic labour became paid labour in the public sector. Popular opinion often worked against their successful establishment, as did certain pragmatic factors. In Yangyi commune it was reported that people were unaccustomed to eating in community dining rooms and at a fixed time and place and any defects in management and cooking aroused complaints such as 'The food's no good', 'Always the same old stuff', and 'You can't eat what you want when you want to'. These were especially to be heard among the better-off members of the community who were accustomed to superior fare. There were also complaints of some waste or extravagance especially since the dining rooms were seen to involve considerable expenses which did not arise in individual household cooking.

To make a success of cooking for so many people a staff of some numbers was necessary. The work was skilled and the hours long. The cooks had to begin their day at three in the morning to light the fires and steam the maize cakes on a large scale for breakfast, others attended to the kitchen garden, food preparation and other odd jobs and the accounting and management were time-consuming jobs. Formerly, when cooking was done at home, people had hardly given these jobs a thought; they were just the unpaid work of the housewife! For instance household fuel had consisted of brushwood found by the children who scoured the hillsides after school. The big canteen stoves, however, needed coal and this had to be bought and transported by carts and animals belonging to the work team. The cost of the wages and fuel, which nobody in the village had had to face before, had now to be borne by the work team and took a sizeable slice out of the funds prior to their distribution to work-team members. In many families the new wages of the women less than compensated for these other costs. Moreover in the Yangyi area, as in the whole of north China, household cooking was done on a little stove in the front of the *kang* and the flue from this stove, passing under the brick bed had heated it and the whole house. Even if cooking was done in the community dining room, in winter these stoves still had to be lit for space-heating and brushwood collected as before.[67] In many areas such problems combined to force the closure of the community dining rooms although many became seasonal in operation, that is they continued to provide meals at the busy periods in the agricultural cycle. Others were closed altogether.

Community dining rooms were easier to establish and more popular among urban dwellers. They were often attached to places of employment and open to all members of the family. Long after the Great Leap Forward most workers continued to eat their main meal in factory or work canteens which were also open to their families and they often took home ready-prepared food for the evening meal. Many families ate in the canteens on work days and cooked their own food on their days off. This pattern of living in urban areas continues to the present day. Overall, though, the collectivisation of domestic activities was often not accorded equal parity with questions of production. In rural areas in production brigades the household remained the main institutional provider of these services and everywhere the women remained the ones who provided these services within the household.

In the rural areas the situation was complicated by the existence of certain private properties and opportunities for earning income outside the collective sector. Their existence strengthened the household as a unit of production though it was still greatly reduced in scope compared to the pre-collectivisation period. Although the private sector of the economy was based on a maximum of 5 per cent of the total lands owned by the production brigade, private means constituted a larger proportion of the household income and were an important cash component. The existence of these privately worked plots and privately owned housing meant that labour continued to be also organised by and within the household and this provided an opportunity for the head of the household to maintain his traditional authority and control. The total surplus of the household very much depended on the ratio of wage-earners to wage-dependants and this could work in favour of the early reproduction of labour power and the interests of the elder generation in controlling the recruitment and exchange of labour power in marriage. The traditional form of patrilocal marriage also encouraged a preference for sons, for only they were permanent members of the household, and only they could recruit additional labour power into the household on marriage.

In the public sphere women had certainly entered into new economic and political roles which were hitherto male preserves. The value attached to their labour power had increased and women had been encouraged to attend classes aimed at increasing their levels of education and technical skills in order to reduce the division of labour within the work force. Many facilities had also been provided to accommodate the biological roles of women. But by the end of the Great Leap Forward a new division of labour grounded in the traditional subordination of women characterised the public sphere. Not a division between the public and domestic spheres, but within the public sphere itself. Women in the non-professional sectors of the economy still tended to be found predominantly among the less skilled and lower paid. Although entry into social production and the individual receipt of wages redefined the economic position of women, the actual amount they earned each week often fell below that of the men. This was so despite the stipulations of national policy that women should receive the same remuneration as the men alongside whom they worked. 'Equal pay for equal work' was a common slogan of the times. 'Equal pay for equal work' was taken to mean that all labourers, whether they were men or women, were entitled to the same rating and the same remuneration when they had completed the same job of the same quality. This maxim was applied in the professions and the state factories where women were present in large numbers and tended to perform the same kind of work as the men, but it proved more difficult to implement in the rural communes and urban neighbourhoods. It was widely thought that women did not deserve equal pay because they did not do the same work as men. In the rural communes, where the great majority of the people lived and worked, wages were based on the number of work points accorded per day which were based on the type and amount of work performed. Where new projects of capital construction required labour power, the agricultural tasks were left to the women. In Weixing people's commune in Jianxi province for example, more than four fifths of the male labour force were transferred to smelting iron and irrigation works, leaving the work of autumn harvesting and winter sewing to the women. But generally the main, heavy and skilled agricultural work which was traditionally performed by men, scored higher work points than the lighter, less skilled subsidiary tasks or women's jobs. For instance the number of work points accorded to collecting grass was much less than those accorded to ploughing. Even where women did perform the same tasks, lower ceilings limiting their work points and prevented them from earning the same number as men. For instance in a brigade in Jiu Bao commune where two women and one man worker carried manure from the cowshed, the man worker was awarded ten points while the women members only received eight points although the quantities were the same.[68] Some women did learn new skills and undertook capital construction projects and main agricultural tasks, but in many areas a new division of labour had arisen.

In the street industries women often confined themselves to jobs that were traditionally thought of as women's work such as sewing, embroidery, light assembly work and other repetitive jobs. In the case of Right East Street in Peking the women there had first suggested projects along the lines of 'sewing, knitting or making boxes or what seemed to them to be traditionally women's work', until they had lighted on the idea of casting pump parts.[69] Some types of street industries did lie outside of what was traditionally labelled as 'women's work' and became very successful, often expanding into state-run industrial enterprises, but the work of the majority remained unskilled, repetitive or utilised women's traditional handicraft skills. Their subsidiary nature was perhaps reflected in the level of their wages which were usually half those paid to workers in state factories. To the women themselves, however, these were often more than compensated for by the convenience of their locality and hours, the fact that they collectively owned their factory, and controlled their work environment and their wages resulted from the sharing of profits; as the profits increased so did their wages. For many housewives it was the collective experience and satisfaction of working outside the home and knowing they were contributing to the future of their society and country that was enough. But there was no doubt that though these women had moved from the domestic to the public sphere, their activities within the public sphere reflected the traditional division of labour.

Despite policies to the contrary, the division of labour was sanctioned by the legacy of the traditional value placed on women's

labour power, their physiology and their household responsibilities. These factors supported the views that women had never
earned the same wages as men, they had seldom been the main
bread-winner before and moreover they were hardly capable of
earning the same as men. In one brigade the men defended their
higher wages, even where women performed the same tasks as
competently, on the grounds that women could only 'take small
steps'. That is they lacked the 'staying power and could neither
carry heavy loads nor cover long distances'. Therefore they said,
women should have to fulfil three conditions before they qualify
for the same number of work points. They must be able to plough the
field, turn the earth and transplant rice plants, carry regularly a
load of over 100 catties and show the same attendance rate as that
of men members.[70] Although policies of labour protection were
meant to help accommodate and compensate women's biological
functions, many brigades still used these measures to plead the
delicacy of women and give them jobs befitting the 'weaker sex'.
These brigades took the assignment of lighter tasks at certain times
of the month and life-cycle to mean lighter and subsidiary tasks at
all times. It was the women who were given time off to attend to
unpaid domestic chores. In many communes the basic working
days for women members were fixed according to the extent of
their household burden and the number of their children. By this
means women's traditional household responsibilities were taken
care of, but these measures also served to reinforce the idea that
housework was the sole responsibility of women and their time off
for unpaid domestic labour had repercussions for their level of
earnings. There was no doubt that many women had moved into
social production, but the new division of labour reflected
traditional attitudes towards women and women's work.

One measure of female status in China is taken to be the number
of women cadres or women who hold positions of responsibility in
the Party, government organs and production units. In the Great
Leap Forward women were soon to unite and take part in economic
activities but not in politics. The expansion in the numbers of
women entering social production was not reflected in the numbers
of women admitted to Party membership or selected for positions
of decision-making in high-level or government organs. To take the
membership of the Communist Party and the Youth League as
examples, women made up only 10 per cent of the Party
membership in the 1950s[71] and 30 per cent of the Young
Communist League membership,[72] and of the basic-level people's

deputies elected in all parts of the country the proportion of women rose from 17.3 per cent in 1953 to 20 per cent in 1958.[73] These percentages were far below the proportion of women entering social production and the government and the women's movement set out to discover the foundations of this discrepancy. They found that the traditional ruling ideology which had taught that women should have no public influence or knowledge of affairs outside the home remained to influence the attitudes of both men and women. Women's domestic roles also prevented them from fully participating in political processes, many of which at the local levels were spare-time and unpaid. This was particularly so in rural areas where the distribution of women's labour power in favour of the domestic and private sector had direct repercussions on their opportunities to participate in the decision-making processes of the collective production unit. Too often the women cadres were exclusively relegated to woman work, creche and nursery attendance and all-women production teams. Moreover, the custom of patrilocal marriage by which women were both temporary or 'outsider' members of the production unit worked to their disadvantage in the holding of or training for responsible political posts.[74] In the past there had been a high correlation between adopted child-brides or brides remaining within the village and women cadres. There were obvious advantages in being able to remain in one's home community after marriage, but it was still unusual for women to do so.

By the 1960s it was becoming evident that certain obstacles were inhibiting the further redefinition of the role and status of women. These various obstacles can be categorised into three main problem areas—the existence of certain ideological constraints, the structural implications of the incomplete transformations in the mode of production and the ambiguities surrounding the general role of woman work or female solidarity groups in the transition to socialism. Recent campaigns of the 1960s and 1970s have attempted to identify and rectify each of these in turn.

The Cultural Revolution: Socialism versus Feminism 10

> We must have a clear historical materialist viewpoint and make a
> clear class analysis of the ideological viewpoints of the women of
> different periods and different class positions, and not raise
> questions of conception of life and viewpoints of love, which
> have a strict class nature, as abstract, general questions of the
> 'female and the male'.
>
> (Wan Mujun, 28 October 1964.)[1]

During the first decade the women's movement and the
government had co-operated to incorporate women into social
production and thus apparently satisfy both the demands of
economic development and the necessary condition prescribed for
the liberation or emancipation of women. But once the goals of the
two movements moved beyond this initial premise and into the
sphere of ideology in the 1960s, some differences emerged in the
approach of the women's and the wider revolutionary movement
towards woman work. It seems that in the first instance they
commonly agreed that the experience of the 1950s had shown that
changes in the economic base, or transformations in the mode of
production, did not necessarily mean the creation of new norms
determining social behaviour. Indeed it was the wide-scale entry of
women into social production or into the labour force after the
Great Leap Forward, and the initial establishment of new social
institutions designed to remove certain of the structural constraints
inhibiting the redefinition of their roles which were said to be
responsible for highlighting the fundamental problem that
confronted women—the removal of a whole history of cultural
oppression or institutionalised and internalised subordination. It
was not only the attitudes of male supremacy inherited by men
which seemed to perpetuate the traditional structures, but women
too colluded in their persistence by internalising and perpetuating
attitudes of inferiority, self-abasement and dependence.

At the end of the first decade an editorial in *Renmin Ribao*
concluded that 'only by enabling women to obtain their ideological
emancipation will it be possible for them to develop their infinite
source of power.'[2] The Peking Women's Federation also made it
clear, as the following statement illustrates, that it was the

289

ideological aspects of women's emancipation which now demanded attention.

> Now that the broad masses of the women have taken part in productive labour, can one say that there is no more work to be carried out among women? No; on the contrary, the contents of woman work are now richer than before, and we are now required to carry out this work more penetratingly, carefully and solidly. For instance, though the broad masses of women have taken part in production, they still have many special problems in production, living and thought. The thought that women are inferior and dependent is present to a greater or lesser degree among the women themselves, and, in society, the vestiges of the feudal thought that women are contemptible cannot be thoroughly eliminated within a short time. . . . For this reason, it is not true to say that 'there is not more work to be carried out among women'; on the contrary, the work in this respect must be reinforced.[3]

Despite this common goal, the early 1960s saw the development of two separate movements, one to raise the consciousness of women as members of their sex suffering a particular form of cultural suppression and the other to raise the class consciousness of men and women.

In order to redefine the role of women, women's movement embarked on a 'conscious learning process' in the 1960s to raise the consciousness of women to an awareness of the ways in which the traditional ideology continued to circumscribe their lives. 'Without self-awareness,' they said, 'women will be unwilling to fly though the sky is high.'[4] The consciousness-raising movement was organised on the twin premises that the continuing social secondariness of women had ideological foundations and that 'first we [women] must begin with ourselves.'[5] On the basis of the first premise, many articles were published which defined the individual and collective problems of women in ideological terms. For instance, the problem of combining the demands of home, children and careers, or of equal payment and rewards could be overcome by simply identifying and then eliminating the continuing influence of old beliefs and attitudes. The Women's Federation conducted a survey and concluded that the greatest obstacle preventing the immediate implementation of the policy of 'equal pay for equal work' was the persistence of traditional thought patterns and prejudices. The traditional evaluation of the sexes, the long-time subsidiary nature of their labour power and their physiological restrictions were all used as excuses to pay women less than men. This was so even in areas where women had not only learned to do the same work as men but had equalled them in performance. Instead of women being compensated for their biological role and remaining household responsibilities, they had continued to be the subjects of discrimination. The Women's Federation pointed out in a number of editorials and articles in their magazine and other periodicals that once the people had the correct way of thinking then the principle of 'equal pay for equal work' would be easily implemented.[6]

The degree to which individual women could successfully combine public and domestic roles was also primarily determined by the level of a woman's consciousness of the problems involved. This was the conclusion of a special commentary in *Zhongguo Funu* which asked if the relationship between work, children and household chores should be treated as an ideological or practical problem?[7] The article recognised that the expansion of a woman's public role had often led to conflicting demands, caused considerable tension whose resolution was no easy matter. It pointed out that women's reproductive functions and the traditional definition of women's roles meant that they would continue for some time to face a number of difficulties if they wanted to work yet also bear children and share in their upbringing. It would create serious problems if these difficulties and tensions were to be neglected or swept under the carpet. 'In the course of their advance', the article emphasised, 'women will always encounter difficulties and often old problems will be solved only to be followed by new ones.' The kind of ideological consciousness necessary was defined as that incorporating a preparation for and will to overcome these difficulties, together with a belief that after marriage and the birth of children they would be able to continue in employment and contribute to and enjoy both. The article concluded that without this belief in 'objective social conditions' women would individualise the difficulties, and the resulting tensions would lead to conflict and the neglect of one or other role. In support of this argument two cases in which women overcame ideological constraints to successfully combine their two roles were quoted in the article.

Fu Sui had worked in a university but until recently she said she had devoted so much time to her home and children that she had lagged behind in study and work. She had excused herself with the thought that 'women are after all women' and have special domestic responsibilities hence 'a chicken feather never could fly to the sky'. She had begun to worry as she fell further and further behind in her work and in the end she had no alternative but to make use of the community facilities available to share child care. She herself found that she was able to keep apace with her work without worry and as to the children she found they grew to be stronger and more independent now that she was not tempted to spoil them. She concluded from her own experience that her way of thinking in the past had been detrimental to her own way of life and that of the rest of the family. In the other case quoted a leader of a local women's organisation had written that before her marriage she had worked actively, but as soon as she got married she had become very preoccupied with the very comfortable and pleasant life of her 'little family'. She and her husband had a good income and they had a lovable child. She had indulged in 'this little sweet home' and although she had someone to help her look after the child she did not have confidence in her and spoiled the child in every possible way. She spent a lot of time thinking about her and her husband's clothes. In sum, although she was working in the office physically she was 'engaged at home mentally'. She refused to meet any of the abnormal demands of her job such as visiting rural areas or undertaking woman work in the evenings. Her work suffered and she was far from happy. Only after criticism from her colleagues and husband did she decide that her priorities had not only undermined her own capacity for her work in the women's movement, but had also been against the interests of her husband and child. She determined to change her life-pattern. The article pointed out that in both cases the correspondents were the same people in the same situation and with the same problems. Owing to the raising of their consciousness coupled with the 'correct thinking' they were able to combine work, children and household chores to their own satisfaction. On this basis the women's movement encouraged individual women to self-consciously take up the task of raising the consciousness of women to a new stage of self-awareness.

In the early 1960s the women's movement set out to remove ideological constraints by making the raising of consciousness and confidence of women their prior area of work. One article in the national women's magazine outlined what this process of consciousness-raising was to entail.[8] In reply to the question, 'In what respects should we women be self-conscious?' it recommended that to bring the unconscious to the conscious women should be encouraged to study their own individual life-histories and the collective history of women, analyse the foundations of past subordination and compare it to their present and potential positions in society. Such a self-examination, it suggested, would reveal the thought patterns which governed the daily practice of their lives and the continuing, and often quite unconscious, influence of beliefs such as 'the husband is responsible for supporting a family, while the wife is responsible for household chores' or 'a man is superior to a woman' which underlay the sexual division of labour and the evaluation of the sexes into superior and inferior categories. As a first step women were encouraged to 'begin with themselves' and articulate their individual experience and learn from each other in an 'exchange of experiences' in their local groups.

The basis for the separation of women into their own solidarity and study groups was reiterated. This was a necessary step because in the years immediately following the Great Leap Forward the sometimes limited working definition of emancipation or liberation to refer to entry into social production had caused local women leaders to feel that the goals of the women's movement had been achieved and local female solidarity groups had sometimes all but disappeared. Women's groups of class associations such as the trade and peasant unions were reactivated and the separation of women into their own exclusive study groups was defended on the grounds that though men and women workers could be said to view many questions in the same light, there were also questions specific to women. For example, issues concerning the role of the Communist Party and the working class in the revolution, the question of who is working for whom, the relationship between individuals and the state and between production and livelihood were all said to be common to both sexes. But certain beliefs and thought patterns were said to be still peculiar to women because of the influence of the traditional ruling ideology, different physio-logical conditions and different social obligations in the past.[9]

The women's movement also criticised the tendency to look down on woman work and regard it as a subsidiary and less urgent task which remained outside the mainstream of economic and political activities. They criticised those who would rather not be bothered with what they saw as the 'complications of the personal lives of women' and were impatient with the apparently petty details of this work and the 'backward' ideological levels of so many women. Some women Party members of cadres were accused of thinking that working with non-Party women or housewives was beneath them and that contact with them would affect their own political position and their level of thought.[10] A document published by the Women's Federation in Peking criticised these tendencies and set about to re-educate women leaders by re-establishing the importance of woman work as a necessary part of socialist construction and one that demanded as much attention as any other form of political activity.

> It must be realised first of all that every kind of work is part of the revolutionary work, and that the work among women is an indispensable part of the work of socialist revolution and socialist construction . . . and is something which women cadres should do wholeheartedly and energetically. . . . It is certainly not something of no importance or something which it is entirely up to oneself to do or not to do. The view that the work among women is tedious and troublesome, does not involve any policy and does not have any political significance, is wrong. The work with women, like any other kind of revolutionary and construction work, cannot be smooth sailing all the way. Difficulties cannot be avoided in it.[11]

To publicise the new attitudes towards woman work role models portraying women cadres who had broadened the definition of emancipation beyond entry into social production and given due importance to the individual experience of women, were introduced into *Zhongguo Funu*. The case of Chen Yunjing was cited as an example of a woman leader who had initially disparaged woman work. She was a graduate of a senior middle school and on graduating from a three-month engineering course she had been asked to go to a commune and lead a women's construction group there. She didn't mind the thought of working in an all-woman team, but she was determined to steer clear of any other relations with them and especially those that would involve her in woman work. In the past she said she had been reluctant to categorise herself as a woman. 'I was even reluctant to hear the two words 'funu' [woman]. While in school, I would get angry with those who referred to me as a woman. I believed that a woman was one who had married and had children. . . . How could I be called a woman?' Initially she had felt ill at ease with the other women for was she not above concerning herself with the details of their personal lives? Her own attitudes and the evident sensitivity of her fellow workmates to these views increasingly isolated her from the rest of the group until the resulting estrangement began to affect her own work progress and the construction work of the rest of the group. It was not until the commune leaders of the women's movement began to talk with her and correlate her own reluctance to identify with the other women with her own levels of consciousness, that she began to take a course of study and slowly and painfully began to establish close relations with the other women. Long talks over shared domestic activities revealed that although the group as a whole were active in production, their thoughts had not kept pace. They began to learn from each other's personal experience and attitudes and she began to take an interest and initiative in the affairs of the local women's representative conference. As her identification with their concerns and activities increased she reported that she actually began to enjoy this aspect of her work and realise the 'importance of woman work and of its rich content'.[12]

A special commentary on woman work in *Zhongguo Funu* pointed out that consciousness-raising involved consistent efforts to establish sisterly relations and go beyond abstract generalities and categoric statements to analyse the practical problems and specific conditions of individual women.[13] The Women's Federation sponsored a number of courses to train women representatives and women production team leaders in the new type of woman work. In one course women leaders pointed out that the delicate and intimate nature of consciousness-raising demanded more than ever before the ability and will of the women who were of a comparatively higher level of consciousness, and who were likely to be leaders and group representatives, to establish sisterly relations with those whose ideological consciousness still remained in a 'middle-of-the-road' or even in a 'backward state'.[14] As one article said, ideological emancipation or raising the consciousness of women should be based on the solution of practical problems met in their individual experience and not on abstract slogans.[15] The Women's Federation thought that these methods of work were applied in the Peking Municipal Bus Company and it became a nationwide model for woman work.

The women's movement thought that the experience of the First Maintenance Centre of the Peking Bus Company deserved wider study because the committee for woman work had regarded ideological education as the most important aspect of their work and they had linked it to the solution of women workers' practical problems in day-to-day life.[16]

The work force of the First Maintenance Centre of the Peking Municipal Bus Company had expanded dramatically as a result of the rapid growth of public transport services during the Great Leap Forward. More than 90 per cent of the workers were women, and for the majority of the maintenance workers and bus conductors this was their first job. They had either stepped straight from the confines of the home or had very recently left school, hence they were often unskilled in their work and many experienced difficulty in adjusting to their new work role. It had not been easy for those responsible for woman work to establish a practical work style for the work force was exceptionally dispersed and mobile. The Maintenance Centre extended to a number of depots scattered along nine different routes in the suburbs of Peking. The women worked in shifts and apart from a few residential hostels for the younger girls, they were drawn from many dispersed residential areas in Peking. There was one full-time cadre, several part-time workers' committee members and women workers' team leaders in all workshops and all bus fleets who were responsible for woman work. With such a large, dispersed and mobile work force they could not possibly have handled all the woman work themselves, therefore they had concentrated on establishing close relationships with the other women workers with a view to raising their consciousness and eventually actively involving them in the solution of their own practical difficulties. For all those interested they had held report meetings and forums to discuss topics such as the meaning of work, practical difficulties encountered in combining work and living, and current events and policies. Young and old women were encouraged to exchange their experiences and learn from each other. There were demonstrations in the skills of their jobs and they discussed the ways and means of improving their job situation and policies of labour protection in the workshop. They met in each other's homes and in this way they got to know the women workers and their family backgrounds. They found that if they knew approximately how many people there were in their households, how many children, where their husbands worked, how the family budget was arranged, and how the husband and wife or wife and mother-in-law got on, then when problems arose it wasn't difficult to find the cause and work out a solution particularly suited to the individual circumstances.

The most common types of problems arose from a non-committal attitude to work, low job performance, the weight of household chores, failure to budget and from poor family relations. Li Weixin was one who was disappointed with her job, it seemed to have 'no prospects' and as a result she was sometimes late for work or did not show up at all. Lo Yiwei often made mistakes and after losing several dollars each month she became despondent and lost confidence in her abilities to do the job well. One young girl, Li, who had recently begun her first job, was inexperienced in monthly budgeting. With her new salary she could not deny herself the pleasure of buying things. First a pair of sandals, then a silk shirt and a pair of woollen trousers and so it went on. She ate several popsicles and drank several bottles of soda each day. After she had spent every cent she had, she would borrow from her fellow workers. This affected her relations with them and she spent much of each month half-heartedly working and anxiously awaiting the next pay day. Another woman worker had difficulty in finding a nursery place for her child, one was unable to pay the school fees for all her children at once and quite a few of the women workers found it difficult to make and mend clothes for their children at the change of seasons. Some women workers were newly married and were inexperienced in cooking and other kinds of household chores. For other workers the problem was tension in the home. Of 480 families of workers there was said to be some tension between mother and daughter-in-law in 26 and between wives and husbands in another 34. For each one of these problems, individual women were assisted by their workmates, their groups or committee members on an individual 'one to one' or collective basis. The women's committee found that those who were helped and impressed by the care shown for their day-to-day life, were in their turn ready and eager to help others and in this way woman work was constantly being expanded. The results had shown that it would never have done to 'simply and harshly criticise' the women workers as 'backward' ideologically. Many had real problems which required a solution and unless they had received practical help, and at the same time come to a position of new self-awareness, they would never have overcome these difficulties and those they were bound to meet in the future. It was pointed out in a special commentary that consistent efforts had been made to establish sisterly relations and go beyond generalities and categoric statements so as to analyse specific conditions and treat individual cases according to their particular circumstances. Because they had involved the women workers themselves in carefully and regularly analysing their own ideological problems through the establishment of report meetings, forums and small groups, they were able to discover and achieve results by promptly solving real problems.

To supplement the work of local groups, the women's magazine established a national forum in which it invited readers to write in and relate their own life experience on two separate but linked questions: the more general question asking 'What do women live for?' which arose from another, more particular, question 'What should be the criteria in selecting a husband?' Although these two questions were treated under separate headings the issues raised by them were closely linked. One was an abstract discussion of the meaning of individual 'happiness' and its sources, while the other took a more practical turn and debated the actual choices open to women on marriage. The main question for both comprised 'What concept of happiness should one cultivate?' Women were invited to contribute their opinions. There were many different views expressed in letters published in *Zhongguo Funu* in 1963–4. Some women thought that their biological functions determined their primary social roles and were therefore the main foundations of their 'personal happiness'. Xiu Feng of Shanghai wrote that women primarily 'lived for the purpose of bearing and bringing up children'. 'Women's peculiar physiological structure', she said, 'determines their role of taking up the natural and sacred duty towards society, that is bringing up the next generation.' She went on to say that this is woman's inescapable function and once achieved they can say without feeling conscience-stricken that they have fulfilled their 'social obligation'. Their role was to bring up the next generation and support their husbands so that they can perform their jobs well and gain promotion.[17] Children and the cultivation of 'warm and enjoyable small families' were full-time jobs for women, and the sense of well-being and the loving relationships generated were the main sources from which they were to derive their happiness. Many wrote that they had entered marriage with these aims in mind.

Others felt that the quality of their personal and family happiness was very much dependent on the material standard of living which their husband was able to provide. They had either looked for or had chosen husbands who had high positions, good salaries and marketable skills. Ai Zhuan was friendly with one boy whom she felt was compatible in every way, but he held a low rank and earned a small salary. This provided a gnawing source of dissatisfaction which had begun to outweigh all other considerations. She felt she had to consider 'the economic possibilities' of her would-be husband as she had always hoped for a comfortable married life. 'For in my mind's eye', she wrote, 'I always felt that happiness consisted of a good economic condition and a comfortable and happy.'[18] In another letter, a reader expressed graded and high-salaried cadre in Shanghai whom she later decided to marry. 'I thought that after we married, our life would be very comfortable and happy.'[18] In another letter, Ai Zhuan expressed similar views. She thought that if a woman can find a husband of a comparatively high position and live well materially 'it will be a very fortunate thing' for 'living well materially is happiness'.[19] Kang Hua of Peking wrote a letter in support of Ai Zhuan:

> I think Comrade Ai Zhuan's views on the happiness of living well materially is in a way quite correct. Material conditions, whether good or bad, not only have a direct bearing on a man's life, but also will directly affect his work and study. . . . In choosing a husband, it is therefore my opinion that consideration should also be given to the other party's pay and income, apart from his political attitudes, age and cultural level.[20]

A husband's salary was not just important for the provision of security and home comforts, but was a source of status and prestige in which they could share. Another source of prestige for a woman was her husband's progressive political attitudes and high level of ideological consciousness. This was the main criterion for Yu Jin when she chose her husband. He was a member of the Communist Party, deputy chief of his work section and rated as an activist in study. He was involved in many social activities and loved singing and painting. She would have liked him to be less single-minded about his work, dote on her more and spend money on his lover in the same way as other men did, but she finally decided that 'it would be nice to have a husband like him'. 'Although I did not change my view of him, I still felt that a young Party member and section chief like him would make a good husband in whom I could take pride in the presence of other people. Thus I married him.'[21]

Others sought a companion in the pursuit of the pleasures of life. Cai Yin from Heilongjiang was in no doubt about the ideal type of husband she wanted to marry.

> I think a woman will find her life the happiest, the most joyous
> and the most amusing if she can find a husband who works in
> the city, if she lives in a modern industrial city, does a little light
> social work and leads a rich diversified urban life with her
> husband.[22]

Many were put off by a young man's serious attitude to work and
leisure. They preferred to have a good time in the evenings strolling
in the park, going to the cinema and dining in restaurants. Jin Gu
wrote that she had 'always believed that those who, when choosing
a husband, attach importance to performance in work and study
and neglect the pleasures of life—which is the most important
aspect—are the greatest fools in the world'. Kong Guihua soon
grew tired of her friend, a college student, who was reluctant to go
to the cinema or the park of an evening. He preferred to read or get
an early night. 'When I asked him to take me out and have some
fun, he would tell me what he read from the book. I soon realised
that he was like a "bookworm". His life was too dull and he had
no tender feelings for me.' Her attentions were soon diverted by a
young man from the city. He continually expressed his tender
feelings for her and sought to please her by taking her expensive
presents. 'Things like these', she said, 'impressed me greatly and,
therefore very soon we developed fond feelings for one another.'
She said she found it very difficult to decide between them.[23]

Views like the above were countered point for point by other
signed letters and articles. Li Yu or Hubei thought that women
who only think of their husbands and children, their warm feelings
for one another and the comforts of their family life were pursuing
'personal happiness' to the exclusion of all else. They put the
interests of the small family above everything else and fail to see
that the purpose of the revolution was to enable all labouring
people in society to lead a happy life. Moreover, after they
themselves have achieved a happy family life, they do not bother to
think how this small family has come about or bother to work out
the dependence of individual happiness on collective happiness.[24]
Others were horrified by the manner in which their sisters could
ignore the present opportunities, economic, political and social
which were open to all women. It seemed as if they wished
themselves back into a position of dependence on their husbands
and families. Hu Bairen responded to Ai Zhuan's views that a
woman should find a husband of a comparatively high position to
live well materially. She asked how was it that in the present

society, Ai Zhuan still wanted to stay under her husband's wing? She thought that women like Ai Zhuan had been strongly influenced by feudal and bourgeois ideas. They do not respect their abilities or regard themselves as equals in work and society. 'Instead', she says,

> they regard themselves men's auxiliary belongings. They avidly aspire after security, leisurely living and the comforts of life, shunning arduous labour and think of relying on their husbands and expecting them to provide things they want without having to work for them. This is a reflection of the bourgeois idea of having fun in the mind of women. It is also a reflection of the idea prevailing in the feudal society, which asserts that when a man is successful and becomes prosperous, his wife takes for granted that she shares his good fortune. Instead of recognising the fallacy of this idea, Comrade Ai Zhuan has gone so far as to regard the chance of leading the life of a parasite as her concept of 'happiness', a concept 'way behind the thought of our times'.[25]

Others suggested that if women are prepared to contribute their share of skills and work to the family budget then a husband's salary and position need not be the most important criteria in choosing a husband. In a letter Meng Yun tells how she met a young man who was working and studying, and despite the fears of her family that she would suffer financially if she continued the relationship, she knew that she was still young and if she learned well and mastered skills his financial position would not matter. They married and although their joint income was still not high they managed to save a little, and, more importantly, this had not in any way hindered the good relationship they had built up together.[26] Huang Xiaozhong pointed to the differences in the salary and position between herself and her husband, she was a doctor and he a low-grade government worker but this gap had not affected their feelings for one another and the type of relationship which they had developed. As far as she was concerned this was far more important than the opinions of others towards their overall financial position and status in society.[27]

The letters which emphasised the importance of love and the pleasures of life evoked a large number of critical responses. Many accused the original correspondents of placing 'love' on a pedestal and presuming that the greatest source of happiness was to be found in one's 'love-life'. They criticised those who demanded that their boyfriends or husbands give all their hearts and attention to them and those who accused their boyfriends or husbands of being inconsiderate and cold if they worked, studied or talked of such 'serious' things in their leisure hours. Hai Zhao disagreed with Jin Gu's condescending view and low evaluation of those who devote time to work and study. Her husband worked hard, studied seriously and lived simply. 'I have never held that his studying and loving his work and studies means that he does not know how to live. Nor have I ever got angry with him because he did not have time to have fun with me. I feel that work and study themselves are a kind of pleasure.'[28] Dong Hui also recommended that husbands and wives share each other's interests in work and pleasure. She emphasised that everyone enjoys talking, a good meal, a rest and leisure activities such as watching a stage or film show, reading or strolling in the park after work. But this is only one part of life, and a small one at that. She argued that work, study, family and community life and cultural recreation were more important and it was selfish to live for pleasure and love alone.[29]

The letters to *Zhongguo Funu* on what type of happiness a woman should cultivate make no mention of her sexuality. As Simone de Beauvoir and others who have visited China in the past 25 years have reported this seems not to have been an issue for the women's movement in China. Simone de Beauvoir has noted that, for most Chinese women, the bed so long signified a form of slavery so odious that for them to have the right to choose their own marriage partners was seen to be a great advance in itself. Once she attended an opera in which the young heroine was desperately struggling to free herself from the Emperor's lewd embrace. Her companion explained to her that the Revolution had given women 'the right to say no to that sort of thing'.[30] There are several references to the importance of enjoying sex within marriage in articles written on birth-control.[31] But what seems to have been a far greater problem has been the establishment of a whole new category of social relations between young men and women which are neither of avoidance or of marriage. Letters and articles in *Zhongguo Funu* and *Zhongguo Qingnian* frequently refer to the difficulties young people have in meeting and talking together especially in the rural areas.[32] The very establishment of courting patterns has been one of the problems in establishing marriage based on free choice of partners even in the 1970s.

This national forum was designed to allow women to exchange their individual experiences and to use these pages as part of their

own consciousness-raising process *as women*, and it was anticipated
that their publication would mark the first stage in the development
of a coherent analysis of the present position of women in society.

At the same time as the women's movement was raising the
consciousness of women as women, the government had begun a
nationwide attempt to raise the class consciousness of both men and
women. The movement for political study had been first taken up by
the People's Liberation Army in the early 1960s as an example to the
rest of the population. Like other popular organisations, the
women's movement too was encouraged to take up political study to
raise the class consciousness of women. Women's political study
groups were formed and the role models selected for emulation were
seen to devote a large part of their time to political study which aided
them in distinguishing between the proletarian and bourgeois lines
of social development. *Zhongguo Funu* published an article on the
purpose and importance of political study for women in 1964. It
recommended that readers follow the example of Wang Huizheng,
an intellectual, and Shi Bing, an actress, who had both utilised their
studies to overcome the individualist pursuit of fame and change
their attitudes to one of service to the people. The article concluded
that the main purpose of study was to raise the class consciousness of
women and to distinguish between proletarian and bourgeois
attitudes and beliefs.

It can be seen that Wang Huizheng and Shi Bing have a purpose
in their study of Chairman Mao's works, and made demands on
themselves. That is why they do not evade their own ideological
problems, on the contrary they regard Chairman Mao's works as
a weapon with which to fight against their non-proletarian
ideas. Thus, through studies, they have continued to raise their
class consciousness, and their thoughts and feelings have
changed.[33]

The habit of serious political study was not an easy one to acquire
and many women, individually and collectively, found they needed a
lot of support and encouragement to develop the habit of study. Liu
Fengshe was a female worker in her early thirties in a metal
workshop who was married and had two children. She described the
struggle she had in trying to study:

I was quite enthusiastic about the study of Marxism-Leninism at
the outset, but I lost heart with the study of Marx and Lenin as I
was unable to understand some of the long names. I thought that

perhaps only university graduates could study such works whereas I only had a primary school education. But then I thought that what was adding to my difficulties was that I have these kids at home. My eldest son is in a nursery. They are quite naughty; their clothes soon tear. They like to imitate the People's Liberation Army and fight with each other! They make a mess at home. So faced with such a situation I did not know whether to laugh or cry. Furthermore I suffer from arthritis. Therefore I thought that since I failed to stop the civil war in my family why should I study the civil war in France. I became quite discouraged. But this time my leading colleagues came to my help and encouraged me to persevere. They told me that I should think of the past. In pre-liberation days women had no political status, were not even allowed to speak in the presence of men let alone join political groups.

She went on to say how the position of women had improved and how she knows it is important to study. She began again with the study of 'The Foolish Old Man who Removed the Mountains' an ancient Chinese fable which told of an old man who lived in northern China and was known as the Foolish Old Man of North Mountain. His house faced south and beyond his doorway stood the two great peaks, Taihang and Wangwu, obstructing the way. With great determination and hoe in hand he led his sons in digging up these mountains. He replied to derisive comments: 'When I die, my sons will carry on; when they die, there will be my grandsons and then their sons and grandsons and so on to infinity. High as they are, the mountains cannot grow any higher and with every bit we dig they will be that much lower. Why can't we clear them away?' Undaunted, he went on digging. Mao Zedong likened the two big mountains to those of imperialism and feudalism, which lay like a dead weight on the Chinese people. Liu Fengshe read 'The Foolish Old Man Who Removed the Mountains', and began to think that

Since he could remove mountains why could I not overcome such minor difficulties. With the help of my comrades and inspired by the spirit of the foolish old man I joined a study group. In the study sessions I carefully listened. If I was unable to understand something I asked the other comrades to help me. At home I studied on my own initiative, and even wrote some articles on my study experiences. When I was trying to understand the special terms in these works my boys came to me one after another telling me stories about each other so I threw away my books and felt I would never be able to study in such an atmosphere. When my anger cooled down I recalled the spirit of the foolish old man and also the heroic deeds of the fighters in the French Civil War, for example a woman who, carrying a baby in her arms, went on with her stubborn struggle against the enemy. I tried by every means to squeeze out some time. For example, I thought about what I read while doing my washing and mending, and after the kids were in bed. I wrote a few lines and studied six works by Marx and Lenin, for example, the 'Critique of the Gotha Programme'. In the past I thought a woman worker was a good one if she fulfilled her eight hours and then went home to her family. Now I think differently, and am involved in factory activities.[34]

Separate study groups were established to encourage women to study, but even some of these ran into difficulties. For instance in one street in Peking a newspaper-reading group made up of housewives, mostly 'middle-aged and grey-haired grandmothers' who did not know enough characters to read the newspapers themselves, had the support and help of the local neighbourhood women's committee, backed by the Municipal Women's Federation. Five readers were found who had more than four years of schooling, and to help them read they often gathered together to prepare material for study prior to meetings. The local Women's Federation often recommended suitable materials and gave guidance for its use to the readers. But as time went on some participants dropped out and some even chatted with each other while the reading was going on. When the local women's committee looked into the matter, they discovered that the chosen meeting place and time were not suitable for some members and that the materials chosen for reading were often too long and abstract. The women felt that the materials which were the most useful and relevant to the details of their own lives were the real-life experiences of other women.[35]

Although the 1960s had seen the development of two movements to raise the consciousness of women both as members of their sex and as members of different classes, and there were moments of co-operation, the two movements tended to remain quite separate and eventually they were to fall out over the apparent failure of the women's movement to translate the individual experiences of women into a coherent analysis of their oppression which required the recognition of the class identity and class consciousness of women. In turn it was these same issues, the relevance of class struggle to their further emancipation and the applicability of the political and economic goals of the government to the feminist goals of the women's movement, which divided the women's movement itself. The controversy surrounding the question of whether women should primarily identify with their sex or with their class associates became explicit with the publication of an article in *Hongqi* in 1964 entitled 'How the problem of women should be viewed'.[36]

The article itself analysed the present state of the women's movement and revealed that there was an acute internal struggle between the primarily feminist and primarily socialist viewpoints. It was written as a critique of those who tended to look at the question of women as if it were merely a question of physiology and to distinguish a single female or woman's as opposed to a male or man's conception of life. The author thought that where physiology was emphasised, the question of women was usually 'covered with a veil of sentiment' with continual reference made to the so-called 'blessings of women', the 'joy of womanhood' and their 'natural duties' or 'natural functions' in society. If women were allowed to speak with authority on any subject it was usually those traditionally associated with their reproductive and domestic roles such as romantic love, marriage, housework, child-bearing and child-rearing. But even discussions on these subjects, the article pointed out, eventually reverted to, and got bogged down in, circular arguments involving difficult and abstract theories of human nature based on 'natural functions' and confused biological and social needs. Such consequences were seen to be inevitable when the differences between the sexes were taken as the primary division in society.

The author of the article rejected the primacy of the social division between the sexes in favour of that between classes. Women just could not be said to have a single special or separate world viewpoint distinct from that of men, but were themselves divided by class. Did not women of different times and different classes display widely disparate social attitudes? 'In different societies', says Wan Mujun, 'the women of different classes, because they are in different class positions, have completely different purposes and ideals of life and viewpoints of marriage and love.' The author concluded that to look at questions like these from a single women's viewpoint and distinguish their 'special conception of life' was to recognise the existence of 'abstract above-class' women, and 'abstract above-class' women like 'abstract above-class' men did not exist in the world. The article argued on behalf of the critics that the only way to understand and handle the women's question was to apply a class analysis and the only way to change the position of women was to arouse the awareness in women of their interests as members of a class as well as a sex. The article urged women to apply a class analysis to their own and wider problems and take part in the class struggle between the bourgeois and the proletariat.

The controversy within the women's movement between these two points of view was to centre primarily around the control of the form and content of the women's magazine *Zhongguo Funu*. With a nationwide circulation its contents were thought to be symbolic of the interests and priorities of the women's movement. The conflict for control of the magazine resulted in the removal of the editor, Dong Bian, from her duties as editor in 1966. At this time forums were held in many provinces to analyse the contents of the magazine in order to understand why it had been necessary to remove Dong Bian from her office. From an examination of some of these criticisms which were published in *Zhongguo Funu* in July and August 1966 it is clear that it was the two correspondences 'What do women live for?' and 'On what criteria should one choose a husband?' which were singled out for criticism. The chief arguments cited in the correspondence columns indicate that they were thought to be symbolic of the amount of space and attention directed towards the narrow definition of women's biological and domestic roles. It turned their attention away from political and revolutionary issues and encouraged them to personalise and individualise their problems. It seemed to some that in devoting their energies to the ideological emancipation of the individual and consciousness-raising these had become ends in themselves and the women's movement had arrived at an impasse. It had become extraordinarily introverted by separating itself off to an intolerable degree from the wider political and social questions of the day. There was a growing feeling that the women's movement could not work itself out of this stalemate without referring to the political and economic system. Ideology just did not exist in a vacuum and beliefs did not spring fully fledged from within the individual consciousness but were determined by economic and political systems.

This criticism was not new. In 1963 some correspondents had noted this aspect of the debates. For example one woman had written:

It suddenly dawned upon me, that this was not merely a question of whether it was good to choose this or that man, not merely a question of how to solve the 'realistic problem'. Rather it reflected a struggle between two conceptions of life. I began to realise that the problem of livelihood is not a long way from the class stand and that livelihood is permeated with class struggle.[37]

In July and August 1966 Dong Bian was again criticised for dividing the 'personal' from the 'political'.

Displaying the signboard of solving so-called personal problems of women, the magazine publicised revisionism and tried to make the women's class viewpoint blurred and lead women to show no concern over major state affairs, but merely to show concern over the life of their individual families and go after so-called happiness of husbands and children.[38]

This view was said to be especially evident in her attitudes towards the movement to encourage political study and the raising of class consciousness. Some critics said that they had analysed the contents of sixty issues of *Zhongguo Funu* from 1961 to 1965 and found that only 33 or 2.3 per cent of its articles referred to the form that political study should take and its application to practical problems.[39] *Zhongguo Funu* reported that Dong Bian had thought that articles such as these were not written from the feminist perspective and anyway they 'had nothing to do with women'. Rather it was reported that she had preferred to develop an authoritative feminine viewpoint on all issues to do with women which precluded the application of a class analysis. She was even reported to have said that the idea of protracted class struggle or continuous revolution was like 'frying rice that had gotten cold'.[40] What especially seems to have incensed some readers was Dong Bian's attempt to negate the whole history of struggle by the women's movement to redefine the role and status of women. As one correspondent said, this was an 'extremely serious slander and disparagement of us revolutionary women which tried to make us forget the revolution, do away with the revolution and return once more to the kitchen'.[41] Readers who had suffered greatly in the old society, or lost all but their lives in the civil war, were especially incensed.

Zhang Yubing, chairman of the Women's Congress of a brigade in Hebei province, wrote that she was 'nearly bursting with anger'. She had fought against the Japanese, was assaulted herself and lost all her family, many killed in front of her own eyes. Did Dong Bian and others who agreed with her point of view think that then 'a woman had lived for money, betrayal of fellow-villagers or self-betrayal?' 'No . . . I would go on struggling against the enemy'. Just as it was then so it is now absurd to think that 'a good material life means happiness' or 'a nice little family constitutes happiness'. She went on to say, 'It was only with the liberation of their country that most women had the opportunity to even think of or enjoy a secure livelihood and family life, and present happiness was due to the form of the new society not to the individual situations within it.'[42]

Another reader concluded that the offending articles were a

> vain attempt to make our revolutionary women cadres and
> masses of the revolutionary women indifferent to major affairs
> of the country and of the world, and make them go only after
> the 'happiness of the small family' and fall into the quagmire of
> bourgeois love for good food, good wine and good times, so as
> to achieve your [Dong Bian's] objective of a 'peaceful evolution
> and capitalist comeback'. Dong Bian, you are just dreaming. We
> revolutionary women . . . will never fall into your trap.[43]

At the same time as the new staff of *Zhongguo Funu* published the letters criticising Dong Bian and her colleagues, it also published letters recommending the form which the magazine should now take. For example women workers from government offices, factories, mines and schools in one district in Shanxi province met to discuss and compose such a letter. They wanted the magazine to become more relevant to the lives of the majority of the women—the peasants, and the workers. They wanted it to publish the biographies of ordinary women and they hoped that it would not neglect the individual and personal problems of women but put them into their political context.[44] The Women's Federation said it promised to take these and other similar suggestions seriously and to signal a new beginning they requested Mao Zedong to inscribe in his own calligraphy a new title page for the magazine. The staff of the magazine wrote that they were using this occasion to pledge themselves to 'pursuing proletarian politics and helping revolutionise the ideology of women workers and commune members, People's Liberation Army women, revolutionary girl students, revolutionary women cadres, and revolutionary women intellectuals.' This new start would inspire them to carry out the two-line struggle and pay attention to state affairs and 'carry the Great Proletarian Revolution through to the end'.[45] But despite these pledges to begin anew and the telegrams and letters of congratulations which flooded into the editorial offices, it almost immediately ceased publication. Whether the differences between the opposing points of view within the staff of the women's magazine ran too deep for there to be any agreement on form and content, or whether it is more likely that the women's movement was subjected to pressure from the outside, is difficult to tell. In the women's movement at large it seems as if continuing dissension and conflict had almost brought it to a standstill as a national functioning organisation and by early 1967 the Party seems to have recommended the suspension of the Women's Federation. Other popular organisations including the Youth League and the trade union movement were also disbanded.

The suspension of the Women's Federation was not meant to signal the end of woman work. For during the Cultural Revolution, although there was no separate organisation of women, the very definitions of class terms were elaborated to include attitudes to and by women. The primarily feminist viewpoint was accorded to the bourgeois class and hence to be struggled against and in this manner the struggle for women's liberation was integrated into the current class struggle. Women were therefore to be encouraged to raise their class consciousness and to take part in politics.

A group in Hunan province reported that while it was accepted that women would partake in productive labour, the idea that 'politics is certainly not for them' prevailed. The influence of the traditional practice of belittling the public activities of women and the idea that 'men do not rule inside and women not rule outside' remained.[46] Another group in Guangxi reported that many women there were in the state of 'carrying the hoe outdoors, handling the pot indoors, and taking a back seat in a meeting or in study'.[47] Women leaders were more often than not leaders of women's groups or sections rather than of the joint organisations including both sexes. As part of the Cultural Revolution to heighten class consciousness and involve as many as possible in political affairs, the government encouraged women to participate and lead in political and state affairs and recommended that all bodies and associations take steps to include women in their affairs. As a first step women were encouraged to take up the habit of political study on the grounds that women should become aware that ideas such as 'if men earned more, women wouldn't have to work' and 'somebody has to look after the practical affairs of the home and why not the women, for men have enough responsibility outside the home' were associated with particular classes whose viewpoints continued to influence government policy and permeate Chinese society despite the history of the revolution.

Nearly all the films, operas and ballets produced during this period had a clear message for women. They reminded women that lots of them had led bitter lives when political power had been the monopoly of the warlords, the landlords and factory employers. Two of the most famous ballets originating in this period, 'The Red Detachment of Women' and 'The White-Haired Girl', both remind women of their grim past. In one a slave girl in the house of a warlord ran away, was beaten and sold. In the other, based on the play of the same name, the landlord had appropriated the only daughter of his tenant. But despite the disadvantages of their background they had played an essential part in the struggle to overthrow those power holders. Many of the films and operas first produced during the Cultural Revolution were set in the 1920s, 1930s and 1940s and the leadership roles were often played by women who as the local leaders helped and counselled the villagers, men and women, to victory in their struggle against local landlords, warlords or the occupation forces of the Japanese. Operas and films set in contemporary China, too, very often portrayed women leaders of the enterprises or brigades. For instance the operas 'The Song of the Dragon River' and 'On the Docks' both portray women leaders who were politically astute and capable. Films such as these were designed to challenge old attitudes of patronage and popularise the importance of women in political affairs.

Women were exhorted to learn from Wei Fengying, a worker engineer of the Northeast Machinery Plant who was a well-known model woman worker and a member of the technical innovation brigade of her factory.[48] She had 'tirelessly persevered' in remoulding her ideology and adopted a 'proletarian world outlook' which she applied to her work, class struggle and to her home life. She identified three areas which had persistently worried women. 'The three problems which women comrades frequently meet up with in the course of their advance along the revolutionary road are love, marriage and children.' Wei Fengying has often described how she experienced difficulties at each of these stages as first she courted, then married and later had two children. During her courtship she and her future husband always put their work and studies first, frequently forgetting to turn up for dates. Because of the common understanding and priorities which they had worked out for themselves, these occasions caused no dissension between them. After they were married she found herself faced with buying food, cooking, sewing and other chores. 'I realised what running a home meant and how much bigger the responsibilities of a wife were than those of the husband.' As a result they drew up a four-point plan to study, share the housework, budget and plan their family. She reports that they kept to this charter.

> With a common understanding and these specific four points, household chores have become a minor matter. When crucial problems appear in production I think up ways to make technical innovations and make models. Sometimes in the course of making these we forget to put soda into the dough, forget to put salt in our cooking and even forget our meals entirely. But we are happy, family life has not hampered us.

After the birth of her first child and when her maternity leave was about up, she did not want to continue to breastfeed her child when she went back to work. 'If I breastfed the baby it would mean a couple of hours off each day, and over a year it would mean three months off work.' She arranged for one of the grandmothers to share the upbringing of the two children and bought them books to read to enable her to continue her studies in the evenings. Where the interests of the collective or class struggle came into conflict with her personal interests she said she was determined 'to serve the people wholeheartedly'.

During the Cultural Revolution the lack of women in leadership positions was viewed as a serious shortcoming in Chinese society and one which demanded immediate attention. The old ideas that 'women are backward and women are useless' and were less qualified and less capable than men, was directly countered by another: 'Times have changed, men and women are equal. What men can do, women can do too.'[49] Many articles argued the case for involving women in class struggle now despite their lack of experience. In Liuling village women began to participate in class struggle during the Cultural Revolution. When the Swedish writer Jan Myrdal returned to Liuling village in Shaanxi province in 1969, seven years after his previous visit, he found that one of the greatest changes in the village was the attendance of the women at the meetings.[50] But they had not achieved this right without a struggle. Before the Cultural Revolution there had been a few female activists, but during the Cultural Revolution the women had insisted on condemning the idea that women are only capable of housework. One woman there described the sequence of events to Jan Myrdal. 'Since we women are half of heaven we want to take part in all political activities and in all decisions too!' The brigade discussed this a great deal. If the women were to have the same right as men to participate in meetings surely then men were under an obligation to share the housework. At first some of the men had got up and said that the women simply couldn't make decisions. To look after children, that was woman's work, look how the children cried for the mummies at nights! They used the rights of the children as a form of blackmail. It just wouldn't be good for the children's sake for women to attend meetings while the men sat at home. The women became impatient with the excuses. 'We women put the question to the brigade: are we, or are we not, to participate in political work?' Many discussions followed. Finally the brigade adopted the principle that women should have the same right as men to go to meetings. Not merely the same formal right, either, but the same right in practice. On evenings when the women went to meetings, it was right that the men should stay at home and look after the children. 'In this way it wouldn't only be men who spoke at meetings and decided things.' The women began to speak about state affairs. Wang Gulan, elected to the leadership of the brigade, told how she had previously never spoken at meetings.

> I was selfish, I had my household and children to look after. I thought of my own private interests and was not an active member of the board. No one criticised me during the Cultural Revolution. But from studying Chairman Mao I soon realised what a mistake I'd been making, to sit silent at the meetings of the management board, thinking of my own household instead of the affairs of the community or the state. Before the Cultural Revolution women were too tied to their home. Then we discussed the importance of interesting ourselves in state affairs, just as much as the men do. During these discussions I became more politically aware. Now we women are studying Chairman Mao. We read newspapers and discuss things. Formerly it was only the men who discussed things when resting from their work in the fields. Now women, too, talk things over. . . . The young women say we women must be capable of making up our minds

L*

and arriving at decisions. . . . Now I take part in all discussions of the brigade management committee. If someone makes a suggestion, I state my opinion, like the others do, whether it's right or wrong. . . .

In a commune in south Henan there had been a number of women cadres appointed before the Cultural Revolution which had become rather unpopular. Some had buried themselves in office work and took no heed of politics or were sleeping partners on committees. Now classes were set up and they were encouraged to change their work style.[51] In Dazhai Production Brigade the Party intervened in support of Ku Ailin. One night in winter 1967 she returned home from a meeting in the commune to find that her baby had cried all evening, her husband was in a dither and her mother-in-law less than pleased. She was met by the fuming husband and a row ensued. When the women of the Party branch heard this they immediately sent one of their husbands to talk with Ku Ailin's husband. 'If we men are away at work, the women hold the fort and never complain when we come home late', he said. 'So why can't we look after the children for a change when they go to meetings? Women are the "other half" of the brigade, you know—just imagine half the brigade chained to the home—how can production and revolution go ahead then?' In the meantime women cadres had chatted with the mother-in-law, 'In the old society we women were less than human beings. We had no say in anything. Now that Chairman Mao and the Communist Party have liberated us, we should support women running public affairs.' So peace was restored to Ku Ailin's family and special classes were held for women cadres with help given to solving the problems regarding children and housework.[52]

There is plenty of evidence to suggest that women played a significant part in the events of the Cultural Revolution on a national and local level. It was a continuation in the work of the Communist Party to bring about changes in the belief system or the superstructure, to break down the divisions between public and domestic spheres and to effect a political solution for all the problems of women. The very definition of class terms was elaborated to include attitudes to and by women. But there was also some evidence that in incorporating women's interests in broader class definitions and the wider political aims of class struggle, the special interests and history of women were neglected.

During the Cultural Revolution there was little attention given in the media to the position of women in society after the suspension of the women's movement and its magazine. Articles published in the newspapers after the Cultural Revolution suggest that many individuals, associations and enterprises had come to feel that so long as general revolutionary aims were fulfilled there was no need to pay particular attention to the position of women. During the Cultural Revolution revolutionary committees were established as new organs of leadership to replace the single line of management that had been established in the 1950s. As leadership collectives the new forms included representatives from all the constituent groups in, for example, the factory or commune. Normally they were based on a three-in-one combination consisting of party members, technicians, and representatives from the constituent workshops, agricultural production or other units. However, they ignored the special problems of women. When the revolutionary committee assumed overall responsibility for the affairs of Lochang Xian, for example, they thought that women cadres with special responsibilities for woman work were unnecessary. As a result the women there found that their special interests were ignored because the revolutionary committee had more work than it could possibly manage and there was no one person who was specifically charged to remind them of their responsibility.[53] Again in Henan province it was reported that revolutionary committees there followed one of two tendencies. Either they thought that anything they could do would have little bearing on the general position of women or they tended to assume that their work would automatically include the interests of women. They tended to generalise that 'since work in every field included women, there was no need to grasp woman work as a separate task'.[54] In 1968 an article had generally warned revolutionary committees against the new tendency that had arisen of 'showing concern' for women without involving the women themselves.[55]

During the Cultural Revolution the 'real' concerns of women were defined as politics and production. The heroines of the new films were only seen in their leadership roles with no hint of the many and competing demands which these women might have experienced in practice. In describing their own priorities, role models such as Wei Fengying never questioned the assumption that politics and production took first place at all times. In describing her 'personal' as opposed to 'political' interests she often referred to her child-bearing, child-rearing and domestic roles. She personalised the difficulties in these areas and rarely assessed their importance to society.[56] The slogan, 'anything men can do, women can do' had its own pitfalls. The author's interviews with national and local leaders in the women's movement in the summer of 1973 substantiate the impression that many women, because of their experience in the Cultural Revolution, came to recognise that although work in every field did include women, it was not enough to include women in every field and neglect their special difficulties inherited from the past or their reproductive roles. Both the articles published after the Cultural Revolution and the author's own impressions and interviews suggest that for the first time in the history of the women's movement and the revolution, a period of heightened class struggle had not been accompanied by heightened activity within the women's movement. It was the experience of the Cultural Revolution which re-established the value of the women's organisations among women and led to the rebuilding of the women's movement in the late 1960s and 1970s.

A Political Solution: Socialism and Feminism

We cannot discuss women's liberation, women's independence and women's freedom in isolation. I'm not for what is called women's rights in and for itself, as opposed to men's rights. We cannot make the men our target of struggle. Oppression of women is class oppression. When we talk about this we must remember that the liberation movement of women cannot be separated from the liberation of the proletariat. It is a component part of the proletarian revolution.

(Wang Zi, 1973)[1]

The day when the women all over the country rise up, that will be the day of victory for the Chinese Revolution.

(Mao Zedong)[2]

If we ask whether the women's liberation movement in China has come to an end, the answer is definitely no . . . the women's liberation movement will be ended when and only when . . . the process of the social transformation of society as a whole is completed. . . .

(Song Qingling, 11 February 1972)[3]

What we want is equality and we will struggle until we get it.

(Young Chinese girl, 1973)[4]

In the late 1960s the women's movement was re-established as a separate social movement distinguished by the sex of its members. A number of internal documents were circulated calling for a new attitude towards women and their movement in preparation for the rebuilding of the women's movement on a new basis. For instance in 1971 one commune in Guangdong province described in *Hongqi* how it had recently put woman work on its agenda and appointed one of its vice-chairmen to take overall charge of it.[5] In turning its attention to handling and solving the problems of the women in the commune it said it was following recent instructions that special meetings be held in each enterprise and area to discuss the role of woman work in society. An instruction from Mao Zedong was quoted as saying 'it is still necessary to struggle against the concept of despising the women's movement because the people holding this concept fail to see its importance in redefining the role of

women and the importance of their participation in the revolution.'
In a brigade in Guangxi province leaders reported that they had
taken the new instructions very seriously and studied the
recommendations that Mao Zedong had made with regard to
woman work.[6] They reported his three points for communities to
keep in mind when rebuilding the women's movement. The first
was that the problem of women must be analysed from a class point
of view and was not an area exempt from class struggle. The
bourgeois point of view had penetrated the women's movement as
much as any other organisation, association or enterprise and it
was therefore as imperative for the future of the women's
movement, as it was for the whole of society, for women to be
involved in class struggle. Second, the revolution could not continue
without the support of half of the population therefore woman
work was a serious matter and, third, the women's movement was
to make political study its priority.

In the same article the leaders of the brigade described how they
had endeavoured to put these recommendations into practice. First,
they had held a number of meetings of the Party branch and of the
members of the brigade to ascertain the present state of woman
work. They then found that in the past few years during the
Cultural Revolution those in leadership positions had been too
preoccupied with the general class struggle to pay attention to
woman work. They revealed that they had thought that since they
were busy with work of central importance they 'must not allow the
women to drag their legs' and that 'woman work really had no
bearing on the general situation within the brigade'. After studying
the recommendations of Mao Zedong they realised that the
question of whether they thought highly of, or understood well,
woman work or slighted and neglected woman work by regarding
women simply as units of labour power was really not a subsidiary
question, but one that was directly related to their class viewpoint
and levels of class consciousness. They held a meeting to criticise
their tendency to slight woman work, and to rebuild the original
women's organisations on a new basis they formed a women's
committee in the brigade. This committee was to set up women's
leading groups in various production teams to investigate and
report on the requirements of women prior to the re-establishment
of a new branch of the Women's Federation there. Women's study
groups were established and the men were to be encouraged to
mind the children and share the housework so their wives could
attend the meetings.

In these same discussions the women said that they realised too that many of them had tended to drag their feet in political activities as a result of not recognising their importance. They had been more interested in their jobs and work inside the household in order to maintain their 'small families' than in serving the community and their country. One of the study groups drew up a programme which was labelled 'the destruction of the five old ideas and the establishment of five new ideas'. These included the destruction of the

theory that women are useless and the establishment of the
ability of women of strong will in holding up 'half of heaven';
the destruction of the narrow feudal definition of women as a
'worthy wife and good mother' and the establishment of a new
broader economic, social and political definition of woman as
proletarian revolutionaries; the destruction of dependence and
the establishment of ambition and resolution to liberate
themselves; the destruction of old customs, habits and beliefs
and the establishment of new habits and beliefs worthy of the
proletariat; the destruction of a narrow individual or
family-centred view of the world and the establishment of an
interest in national politics and world events.

On these platforms the women said they aimed to build anew the women's movement in their brigade.

These debates and discussions were published as an example to other brigades who were re-establishing local Women's Federations or committees for woman work. How far they were followed it is impossible to know, but certainly by the time of my visit to China in summer 1973, woman work and the separate organisations of women had been re-established at local levels with the avowed aims of both developing women's class interests and their interests as women.[7] At each social institution in the urban and rural areas visited by the author, there was a branch of the Women's Federation or a women's representative committee. In each place the dual demands based on class and sex membership were combined with top priority given to the encouragement of political study and political participation. Women leaders without fail isolated this aspect of their work as constituting the major change since the Cultural Revolution. Only after this aspect of their work had been discussed did they go on to detail the other main categories of their work. In a production brigade near Jinan city in Shandong province, the representatives of the four constituent work teams and three others elected by the women of the brigade, met for a half-day every ten days for discussion of woman work and to hear the reports of those of their number who had represented the brigade at higher administrative levels. Each month all the women of the brigade devoted two full days to political study and two to three evenings a month to the study of current affairs and to look at their own lives. Sometimes the meetings were given over to 'criticism and self-criticism'. At the most recent of evening meetings one woman had explained the reasons for her reluctance to attend public meetings. In addition, on one half-day a month all the women of the brigade met to discuss and voice their opinions of the affairs of the brigade. At the previous meeting they had discussed the problem of housework and in small groups studied and assessed the lives of those who seemed to have solved this problem.

In another commune on the outskirts of Shenyang in northeast China, the Women's Federation had been reorganised, although it had not been formally disbanded during the Cultural Revolution. The women there had participated in a number of discussions similar to those reported in *Hongqi* for the brigade in Guangxi province. The eleven part-time representatives of the brigades that met at commune level gathered together to plan meetings, undertake their own study and exchange the experiences of their brigades. Within each of the brigades the women met three times a month for political study and three times a month to assess their own problems, criticise the past and correct shortcomings. In one brigade within the past month they had had one special meeting to discuss ways of improving their productivity and another joint meeting with men to discuss the distribution of housework. In a commune near Peking, the Women's Federation had been disbanded, but at the request of the women it had resumed activities in 1969. Now the women held their own separate meetings to discuss both ideological and practical problems twice a month. They had studied three works of Mao Zedong: 'Serve the People', 'The Foolish Old Man' and 'On Contradictions' and studied articles from the newspapers. At a recent meeting they had put forward suggestions on ways to improve their work style for the next year and also mediated in a quarrel between two women, one of whom always took the easy work in the field to the chagrin of the other. They felt their interests were better served by their own organisation. Among the problems they felt they faced was that the enthusiasm and the participation of the younger members was not shared by married women once they had their homes to look after. The older members still tended to disapprove of free social activities and the mingling of the sexes. At another meeting they had invited the men in order to remind them of the role of women in history and the importance of sharing housework. Men were occasionally criticised at their meetings, but they said it was more common for them to take their complaints to joint class organisations for discussion.

A similar re-establishment had taken place in the factories and the urban neighbourhoods. At Peking Number 2 Cotton Mill, for example, a woman-work committee now met at each of three levels, in work groups, in each workshop and for the mill as a whole. It had two main tasks, one was to politicise the women workers and the other was to cater for their special interests. Their aim was to raise the workers' political consciousness and remove the influences of the traditional ruling ideology as well as arrange for their welfare and ensure that women's interests were represented on all the leading bodies of the factory. For a certain time women would form their own separate study groups to discuss these two areas of work. Among the subjects they had discussed at their meetings was the role of love and marriage in their lives and the problems in combining the demands of their families, housework and work. Many of the women felt that they had not seen enough of their children of pre-school age and at a recent meeting they had requested that the factory nursery hours be made more flexible in order that they might keep their children at home when they were not at work. As a result the nursery now operated a shift system. Women leaders here said that plans for woman work were still being worked out and were very much in a state of experimentation in this and in most other factories. They said they were very much feeling their way in the search for new forms of organisation and priorities.

By the summer of 1973, elections of representatives to higher administrative levels of the women's movement had taken place. At one brigade visited by the author, fifteen local communes had elected representatives to the county Women's Federation. At the first county meeting they had summed up the recent history of the women's movement in the Cultural Revolution, the shortcomings of the old organisation of women, and the need to give priority to political, ideological and theoretical study to prepare women for further participation in political and vocational activities. During the latter half of 1973 most provinces and municipalities held congresses of elected women representatives. In the Tientsin municipality local Women's Federations had elected representatives to attend a conference there in June 1973. It was the first congress of women to be held at this level since the Cultural Revolution and its agenda set the pattern for those to follow.

The Congress summed up the contribution of women to the Cultural Revolution. The recent history of the women's movement was discussed in terms of the struggle between two attitudes towards the problem of women and criticism of the bourgeois line and the working out of its new relationship with the Communist Party.[8] The Congress emphasised the importance of political study and political activities in solving the problems of women. Speakers at the Congress stressed that the present position of women in China was very much due to the establishment of the proletarian dictatorship whose future would be greatly threatened unless women took part in the class struggle and in the work of their separate organisation. Women who had been active in class struggle during the Cultural Revolution reported on their experience and much of the Congress was given over to formulating resolutions which were to become the basis of future programmes for woman work. Women were encouraged to take up political study and participate in class struggle and production. The number of women leaders was to be increased and the Women's Federation to be represented on all leading bodies in the Municipality. The ideological beliefs that men were superior to women were to be fought at all times. Women were to be given all the information and facilities for birth-control, childbirth and child-rearing. Care should be taken to ensure that every facility should be made available to enable women to combine work, a family and household responsibilities. Finally it was hoped that women would benefit from an 'exchange of experiences' with women of other countries. One young delegate who had represented her commune at this Congress told the author that she had welcomed the re-establishment of the Women's Federation as she had felt that the revolutionary committees had previously not given enough attention to women. There had been a shortage of articles on women and guidance on how to undertake woman work. Women leaders in Tientsin interviewed by the author were adamant that the women's movement was set on a new course of development and by the end of 1973 most provinces and municipalities had followed the example of Tientsin and held representative conferences in preparation for the Fourth National Congress of Women. Despite several references in the press referring to its preparation it has not yet been held. This may reflect the preoccupation with other political events in China rather than continuing divisions within the women's movement itself, although why it was not held during the recent anti-Confucian and anti-Lin Biao campaign when there was much attention given to the ideological emancipation of women is a perplexing question.

At the outset of the recent anti-Confucian and anti-Lin Biao campaign it was forecast that this movement would 'surely create still more favourable conditions for the emancipation of women'.[9] To create conditions advantageous to women, the campaign set out to identify the remaining obstacles inhibiting the redefinition of the role and status of women. On the eve of the campaign a national newspaper noted that so far in China it had been impossible to completely eliminate the remnants of the Confucian ideology advocating male supremacy and the division of labour into the domestic and public spheres and that the persistence of old habits and customs underlying the discrimination against women was a reflection of the influence of the old ruling ideology.[10] Again it stressed that if women were determined to identify and criticise the influence of the ruling ideology they would be able to 'emancipate their minds, do away with all fetishes and superstitions and press ahead despite the difficulties'.[11] The identification of the ideological constraints is not a new element introduced in the recent movement, indeed the problem has been stated many times. What is significant about the campaign is that it is the most concentrated and analytical attempt to date to integrate the redefinition of the female role into a nationwide effort to change the self-image and expectations of men and women and combine a consciousness of both women's and class interests. Through a nationwide study programme the campaign has aimed to identify and trace the origins and development of the ideology responsible for the oppression of women, and identify, criticise and discredit the remaining influence of the traditional ruling ideology.

For the first time women have been widely encouraged to rediscover and study their own history with a view to understanding the role of the Confucian ideology, its origins, development and limitations in determining the expectations and self-images of women. Numerous study groups have been formed in factories, government institutions, schools, neighbourhoods and some have aimed to combine peasant, worker and student women in the one group. Some have reported on their studies in the media. The historical studies mainly aimed to draw attention to the 'social origins and class foundations' of the code of ethics which so discriminated against women. It was stressed that male supremacy was neither an immutable social principle ordained by Heaven nor one dating back to time immemorial, but was a principle developed by Confucius in a specific historical period at the time of the transition from the slave to the feudal society. One women's theory group pointed out in *Guangming Ribao* at the beginning of the campaign that Confucius lived in a period which witnessed the gradual decline of the system of slavery and the ascendancy of the newly emerging feudal forces, and to bolster the authority of the declining slave owners he established the authority of the husband and the suppression of women as one of the foundations of their rule.[12] If the relationship between man and woman was likened to that of master and slave, then not only would the ruling classes operate the exchange of women in their favour, but in turn the subjugation of women would to some extent compensate for the class position of the slave himself.[13] In this belief Confucius is said to have established the maxims that 'women like slaves were hard to manage', 'the subordination of women to men was one of the supreme principles of government' and that 'the relations between husband and wife, like those between King and minister and between father and son were all, as those between master and servant, universal under Heaven'. It was on these foundations that ethical codes of conduct for women were elaborated in the Sung dynasty. The groups have contrasted the division of labour during the Tang and Sung dynasties and concluded there to be a direct correlation 'between the exaltation of Confucius and the degree of subjugation of women'.[14]

It was in criticising Confucius that the women's groups said they began to realise that the traditional division of labour and the evaluation of the sexes into inferior and superior categories rested on social rather than biological foundations. As one women's group concluded from its studies, 'the cruel oppression of women was not due to the biological distinction between men and women, but was rooted in the social system directed by a small handful of the exploiting classes'.[15] Male supremacy was found to be a common feature of societies under the rule of exploiting classes be it slave-owners, the feudal lords or, nearer their own time, the capitalists. In the recent campaign Lin Biao was also singled out for criticism as one representative of a long line of statesmen who utilised the idea of male supremacy to bolster an outmoded social system. Lin Biao is reported to have continuously slandered women, using such phrases as 'women are backward in thought and ideas', 'a woman cannot be expected to have a bright future', 'a woman's future is determined by her husband' and 'women think only about how to get oil, salt, vinegar, soy sauce and firewood'.[16] His recommendation to restore the feudal code of ethics was seen as an attempt to turn the wheel of history back and once more segregate women into a separate and inferior social category,[17] but above all he was accused of believing that these concepts 'still possessed a logic of their own'.[18] Women authors of an article on the Confucian persecution of women in history pointed out that identifying the source of women's oppression was of immense significance in diminishing the remaining influence of Confucius on the position of women.[19] Some groups came to the conclusion that only the demise of the Confucian ideology itself ensured its disappearance as a resource available for manipulation by those in positions of political power. They believed that in this respect it was only the identification and widespread knowledge of the social origins of the idea of male supremacy which allowed for the very possibility of change.

In rediscovering and studying their own history one study-theory group reported that the present criticisms were part of a long tradition of resistance by women to the ruling ideology. The study-theory group of the Message Station of a women's unit of the People's Liberation Army, and another made up of women from a railway loading machinery plant, peasant women and students from the Department of History at Peking Teachers' University, suggested that where there was a history of oppression, there was also a history of resistance. Far from being passive recipients of ideological forces women had participated in and even led some of the movements of resistance against the Confucian ruling ideology.[20] Many more groups wrote articles reporting on the role of individual women and the women's movement in the history of the revolution in the twentieth century. In documenting their history, one of the study groups was very impressed by the fact that despite the centuries of oppression, these women, their forebears, had thrown overboard the Confucian fallacy that women should stay at home and work and not concern themselves with political affairs.

During the recent campaign, study groups drew attention to the ways in which the traditional rules of propriety defined and affected women's individual and personal life histories. First they studied these traditional rules of propriety. The Weaving Workshop of the Shanghai No. 30 Cotton Textile Mill singled out for study the Women's Classics (*Nü er Jing*) as one of a number of written codes which had popularised the rules of propriety. To demonstrate its influence in practice, the older women were asked to relate their life histories in order that the group might identify and analyse the precise influence of the Confucian code of ethics on their lives. The group concluded that the Confucian ideology as popularised by the Women's Classics and reflected within the experience of working women was 'like a spiritual yoke weighing a thousand catties'.[21] The Dazhai iron women's team held similar study groups. They reported that through the study of women's histories 'they were reminded that the masses of working women were the most oppressed and humiliated victims of the old ethical code and their life experiences served as a warning against the restoration of the Confucian rites and rules of propriety'.[22]

The women's groups used this experience in analysis in order to identify the remaining influence of the old ideology on their lives today. In these same study groups women identified the discrimination and prejudices which they currently experienced and which shaped their own expectations of themselves. Few women today had the ethical codes quoted to them in their classical forms, but many groups pointed to the numerous folk sayings and proverbs which continued to operate within their everyday experience to disparage women and belittle their social contribution.[23] Under their influence young women were said to still feel themselves to be less than equal with men. To give women more confidence the media has described how many women have already broken ancient prohibitions and taboos and entered into new spheres of work which were traditionally male preserves.[24] An analysis of the recent history of individual women and the women's movement was said to illustrate that change was possible and prove that women have and should 'smash the traditional myths by their own action'.[25]

Throughout the campaign the government seems to have been particularly anxious that women should understand the role of ideology in society, not just to enable them to counter consciously the influence of the old ideology, but to also ensure they were not left out of the movement through lack of interest or knowledge. Never again it is said should men be in a position to monopolise and manipulate ideological resources to the disadvantage of women. A number of articles stress that during the historical period of socialism class struggle is acute and complicated in the sphere of ideology and therefore it is said to be imperative that women build up their number of theorists and strengthen the ideological understanding of all women.[26] 'To strike iron, we must first have a strong body.' Many groups were formed to raise their members' understanding of Marxist theory by studying the works of Marx, Engels, Lenin, Stalin and Mao Zedong. As the girls of the Dazhai theory group embarked on a study programme they said they were 'determined to read and study seriously the ideological weapon of Marxism'.[27] Many provincial revolutionary committees held numbers of workshops to cultivate a 'backbone of women Marxist theorists' to contribute to the movement to criticise Lin Biao and Confucius.

The particular and practical aims outlined in the campaign confirm that several problem areas continue to concern the government and the women's movement. These include the insufficient representation of women in political and leadership positions, the problem of equal pay for women in rural areas, the persistence of traditional customs in courtship and marriage and the division of labour within the household. The campaign has identified the particular ideological constraints which continue to hinder the resolution of each of these problems.

The government has once more referred to the disproportionately low percentage of women cadres despite the increases in their numbers since the Cultural Revolution. Of the 6 million new members admitted to the Party between 1966 and 1973, 27 per cent were said to be women.[28] In the provincial congresses of the newly reconstituted Young Communist League in 1973 an average of 40 to 45 per cent of the delegates were women.[29] In Peking, by 1972 women were said to comprise 16 to 20 per cent of all Party and revolutionary committee cadres at the district, *xian* and bureau levels[30] and in Shanghai women cadres accounted for 17 per cent and 22 per cent respectively of the city's Party and revolutionary committees.[31] In Honan province women accounted for 30 per cent of cadres of the agricultural production brigades.[32] But despite the improvements relative to the 1950s these figures were reported to be far from satisfactory. Just prior to the anti-Confucian campaign a national newspaper stated that 'although many new women cadres have emerged since the Cultural Revolution their number was still far from reaching the needs of the developing situation in China today'.[33] A number of articles point out that although the new opportunities in Chinese society make it possible for women to handle the affairs of the state, the training, selecting and promoting of female cadres remains an ideological problem. One article identified the nature of the problem when it said that some of the men comrades 'cannot correctly deal with women'. They always believe that women possess 'Low cultural standards and ability', that they have 'family complications' and that it is 'difficult to promote women cadres'.[34] It concluded that this kind of thinking had greatly lowered women's social status in the local and national community and the campaign set out to refute these assumptions. Similarly it was found in a number of study groups on rural communes that the traditional evaluation of the sexes, the long-time subsidiary nature of their labour power and their physiological restrictions had all been used as excuses to undervalue the labour power of women and award them fewer workpoints. This was said to be so even in areas where women had not only learned to do the same work as men, but had equalled them in performance.[35]

The domestic sphere, long identified as 'one of the most sensitive and difficult areas in which to introduce social change'[36] has also received considerable attention in the anti-Lin Biao and anti-Confucian campaign. The concept of 'superiority of men and inferiority of women' was said to be nowhere more evident than in the continued preference for sons over daughters. The sayings, 'just as men are superior to women so it was better to have sons over daughters', 'more sons more well-being', 'without sons there is no happiness' and 'a family with daughters is a dead-end family', were said to reflect this preference which was also thought to particularly inhibit the practice of birth control in many families.[37] On the eve of the campaign, one of the women leaders pointed out that the continuing division of labour in the public sphere was still rationalised on the grounds of 'the family complications of women'. On the eve of the campaign she wrote in *Hongqi* that in the domestic sphere it was above all the question of housework which had yet to be solved, chiefly she thought, 'because of the influence of the idea of male supremacy and limited material conditions'.[38] The division of labour within the household and its repercussions for the position of women were discussed during the campaign. It was pointed out that just as women were to be fully integrated into the public sphere so men must undertake their share in the domestic sphere.

With regard to the question of family complications of women, we must also conduct concrete analysis. For several thousand years the basic guiding thought of the feudal landlord and bourgeois classes was to take women as slaves and appendages, to put them in the kitchen, to tie them up with heavy household chores; and to deprive them of the right to participate in social production and political activities. One of the important tasks of the proletariat is to liberate women from this slavery. After liberation, the establishment of the socialist system and the participation in productive labour by the masses of women have brought fundamental changes in this situation. However due to the influence of the idea of the exploiting classes of looking down upon women and the restrictions of the material conditions, the question of household chores has not been completely solved. To solve this question, it is most essential to criticise the feudal thinking of looking down upon women . . . and to solve contradictions between revolutionary work and family work. It is necessary to promote the practice that men and women must share household chores. At the same time, it is necessary to pay attention to the specific characteristics of women and help them solve specific problems. Late marriage and planned parenthood should be promoted. It is essential to do a good job in running social public welfare facilities, such as health, insurance for women and children, and nurseries. So long as we adopt the correct attitude and a number of practical measures, it is not difficult to solve the specific difficulties of women.[39]

For each of these problem areas men's and women's groups were reported in the media as coming to a new awareness of an old problem through the recognition of the ideological constraints originating in the Confucian principle of male supremacy. The campaign has concentrated on the ideological constraints inhibiting the redefinition of the role and status of women. But it can be argued that some structural constraints discouraging the further redefinition of the role of women still exist in Chinese society, for incomplete transformations in the mode of production encourage the persistence of certain ideological constraints particularly in the rural areas. For instance the presence of the private sector of the economy based on private plots in rural areas the effect of encouraging a sexual division of labour between that of the collective and political and that of the private and domestic spheres and detract from women's value in the collective and political sphere. The persistence of the patriarchal rule of residence after marriage and the role of the household in the economy encourages marriage to be thought of as an exchange of female labour and reproductive capacities and thereby bolsters male supremacy. If structural changes in these spheres were implemented no longer would women tend to be either 'temporary' or 'outsider' members of the production brigade and be at a disadvantage when it came to training for or holding political positions. It seems as if certain measures to overcome these structural obstacles may have been introduced in various areas, but they are as yet in their early and experimental stages. The 'Learn from Dazhai' campaign is very much concerned with the mode of production in rural areas. Dazhai is a model production brigade which has abolished the private sector of the economy based on private plots and implemented new criteria for the distribution of work points and wages. There has been some attempt to establish matrilocal marriage as a normal rather than inferior form of marriage to raise the status of daughters in rural areas.[40] Drawing attention to the structural obstacles is not meant to negate the ideological constraints, indeed where transformations in the mode of production are more complete, as in the urban areas, ideological constraints continue to persist. But further redefinition of the role and status of women requires a dual strategy, at the economic and ideological levels and not in one rather than the other.

Perhaps the most important principle to come out of the experience of the Cultural Revolution was the re-establishment of the interdependence of both movements. Since the Cultural Revolution the leaders of the women's movement have again and again emphasised in western-language periodicals the necessity of socialism to the achievements of the goals of the women's movement.[41] But they have also pointed out that their experience in the Cultural Revolution has taught them that socialism is not a sufficient condition automatically bringing about a redefinition of the role and status of women in its wake. Women leaders say that they have learned this second valuable lesson from their own experiences. Women will only improve their own position if they fight for it themselves. As one woman leader said on Women's Day in 1974, 'the establishment of a socialist society does not automatically wipe out centuries of feudal male chauvinism all at once.' She stressed that to further the goals of the women's movement in the future, 'the women themselves still need to work for the further establishment of socialist principles and above all the women themselves need to struggle to overcome all kinds of obstacles'.[42] It seems as if the function of the women's movement is once again perceived to be twofold: to raise the consciousness of women both as members of a class and as women. The uneasy alliance between the two movements in the past and the competing claims on the identity of women have once again been theoretically resolved by giving priority to the class struggle on the grounds that without the establishment of a new political and economic system there can be no substance to women's liberation. The recent campaign to criticise Confucius and Lin Biao went some way to combine both women's special and class interests in the one nationwide study movement, but how these dual demands and competing claims that have characterised the history of the women's movement can again be juxtaposed in practice remains to be seen. In the past their own struggle has benefited enormously from the support of the wider revolutionary movement but at the same time it has also brought the women's movement into conflict with the wider revolutionary movement.

Whatever the twists and turns in the history of the women's movement the image and expectations of women have altered beyond all recognition. Women in China today are deeply committed to their present opportunities, the scope of which was unimaginable in the past. Gone are the days when women likened their secluded and confined existence to that of a 'frog in a well'. Both structural and ideological constraints have been reduced to encourage women to redefine their own roles in society. For women of an older age who have lived in the old and the new societies, the changes experienced in their own lives are little short of miraculous. As one woman said, the women of her country have 'undergone vast changes comparable to the reversing of heaven and earth, politically, economically, culturally, socially and in respect of family life'.[43] Yet in present-day China it is also recognised that women have not yet reached their full potential. The campaigns of 1973–4 reflect the very real problems which continue to face women in China today: equal pay for equal work, full representation in leadership groups, and the breaking down of traditional role differentiation in the domestic and public spheres. These campaigns like others in the past have arisen out of a continual and constant public recognition of the problems.

The women's movement in China has been and is a continuing movement. It is rare for even the most profound and far-reaching of revolutions to effect immediate and abrupt social and economic changes and in China each wave of revolution has given fresh impetus to the introduction of 'new' and the rejection of 'old' social norms and economic relations. For some time old and new social norms and economic relations interact to produce a state of transition. In one of the most recent village studies published in 1973, Jack Chen, who had lived in the village of Upper Felicity for a year, observed that despite far-reaching changes there, many traditional attitudes still persisted. Most of the old ideas and superstitious practices in Upper Felicity were gradually disappearing, but in others connected with betrothal and marriage customs the change in character had been more subtle. They could be said to be at a 'half-way stage' that reflected the present stage of wider social relations and outlook in the village. Jack Chen concluded that 'old feudal forms and content of life are being shed, the bourgeois ideas and forms that creep in are being rejected, but the socialist order has not yet fully taken over'.[44] The transitional state of Upper Felicity mirrors that apparent at a national level. Reflecting on the general state of Chinese society, Mao Zedong said in March 1974 that 'invariably remnants of old ideas reflecting the old system remain in people's minds for a long time and do not easily give way'.[45]

A history of the many many struggles of the women's movement in China has revealed to women the magnitude of the problem, both the depth and tenacity of the economic and ideological foundations of women's oppression in society, and the sensitivity that surrounds such a struggle. As a woman correspondent said in 1973, 'the thorough-going liberation of women is not something ready-made'.[46] In China there was no prepared definition or blueprint. Rather it had to be consciously shaped and worked out in a continuous process requiring constant assessment, analysis and experimentation. It is this aspect of the process of social change that has deserved such close attention and documentation. The women's movement of China has assessed, analysed and experimented and it has been no mere strike of fate that has allowed child labourers, illiterate peasant women and child-brides to redefine their role and status in society. As many women have testified, each step has been the result of their own struggle. Zui Yulan, summing up a lifetime in the women's movement, wrote in 1974 that 'actual life and struggle have taught us that real equality between men and women doesn't come of itself, and it can't be given by anybody.' She thought that in China it would only be won 'if the women themselves fight for it with a constantly heightened socialist consciousness'.[47]

M

Notes

Chapter 1 Introduction: The Women's Movement in China

1 F. Farjenel, *Through the Chinese Revolution*, London, 1915, p. 59.
2 I. Dean, 'The Women's Movement in China', *Chinese Recorder*, vol. LVIII, no. 10, 1927, p. 652.
3 J. Belden, *China Shakes the World*, London, 1951, pp. 316–17.
4 Committee for Concerned Asian Studies, *China: Inside the People's Republic*, New York, 1972, p. 266.
5 A. H. Smith, *Village Life in China*, London, 1900, p. 262.
6 Sarah Pike Conger, *Letters from China*, Chicago, 1909, p. 2.
7 The only books solely devoted to women in China in the English language available at the time this book was begun were: F. Ayscough, *Chinese Women Yesterday and Today*, London, 1938; D. Cusack, *Chinese Women Speak*, London, 1959; and H. Snow, *Women in Modern China*, The Hague, 1967. Each of these, and especially the latter, are invaluable sources of information and for records of interviews with women, but few have attempted to trace the development of the organised and collective effort of all Chinese women to expand their public role and attain equality in economic, political and social life from the turn of the century to the present day. There have been some specialist studies on particular periods and I am particularly indebted to Roxanne Witke's work on the May Fourth period and Delia Davin's work on the Liberated Areas.
8 There have been several studies published since this manuscript was drafted. These include:
S. Andors, 'Social Revolution and Women's Emancipation: China During the Great Leap Forward', *Bulletin of Concerned Asian Scholars*, Jan.–March 1975.
D. Davin, *Woman-Work: Women and the Party in Revolutionary China*, Oxford, 1976.
N. Diamond, 'Collectivisation, Kinship, and the Status of Women in Rural China', *Bulletin of Concerned Asian Scholars*, Jan.–March 1975.
M. Wolf and R. Witke, *Women in Chinese Society*, Stanford, 1975.
M. Young, *Women in China: Studies in Social Change and Feminism*, Michigan Reports in Chinese Studies No. 15, University of Michigan, 1973.
E. Croll, *The Women's Movement in China: A Selection of Readings 1949–73*, ACEI, London, 1974.
9 *Funu Yundong* (*Collection of Articles on Women*), Shanghai, 1925.
Liu (Wang Li-ming), *Zhongguo Funu Yundong* (*The Feminist Movement in China*), Shanghai, 1934.
Mei Sheng, *Zhongguo Funu Wenti Taolunji* (*Collection of Articles on the Women's Question in China*), vols 4, 6, Shanghai, 1934.

Chen Dongyuan, *Zhongguo Funu Shenghuoshi* (*History of the Life of Women in China*), Shanghai, 1937.

Guo Zhenyi, *Zhongguo Funu Wenti* (*Problems of Chinese Women*), Shanghai, 1938.

Liu Hengjing, *Funu Wenti Wenji* (*Articles on the Problems of Women in China*), Nanking, 1947.

Wen Yiduo, *Funu Jiefang Wenti* (*On the Emancipation of Women*), Shanghai, 1948.

Zhongguo Jiefangqu Funu Yundong Wenxian (*Documents of the Women's Movement in the Liberated Areas*), Shanghai, 1949.

10 Interview with Chin Chih-fang (Jin Zhifang), *PR*, 4 May 1973.

Chapter 2 'A Frog in a Well': Mechanisms of Subordination

1 *PC*, 16 August 1955.

2 Cheng Yu-kao, trans., *Manual of Chinese Quotations*, Hong Kong, 1903, p. 173.

3 M. E. Burton, *The Education of Women in China*, New York, 1911, p. 19.

4 *Book of Changes*, XXXVII, trans. by J. Legge and quoted in I. B. Lewis, *The Education of Girls in China*, New York, 1919, p. 8.

5 *Book of Rites*, IX:24 quoted in *Xin Qingnian*, vol. 2, no. 4, Dec. 1916.

6 Mencius, Book III, chap. 2, quoted in Lewis, *op. cit.*, p. 9.

7 *Nü Jie*, chap. III. translated by I. T. Headland, see Lewis, *op. cit.*, p. 8.

8 *Nü er Jing*, Sections IV & V, see I. T. Headland, *Home Life in China*, London, 1914, pp. 69–80.

9 See F. Ayscough, *Chinese Women Yesterday and Today*, London, 1938, p. 267.

10 Lewis, *op. cit.*, p. 15.

11 *Book of Rites*, I:24, quoted in *Xin Qingnian*, vol. II, no. 4, Dec. 1916.

12 *Book of Poetry*, III, Ode X, trans. J. Legge in *The Chinese Classics*, London, 1871, vol. 4, p. 561.

13 *Shui-hu chuan*, trans. as *The Water Margin*, quoted in C. T. Hsia, *The Classic Chinese Novel*, Columbia, 1968, pp. 105–6.

14 D. C. Graham, *Folk Religion in S.W. China*, Washington, 1961, p. 32.

15 *Book of Rites*, X:51, quoted in *Xin Qingnian*, vol. II, no. 4, Dec. 1916.

16 A. Waley, Translations from the Chinese, New York, 1941, p. 72.

17 From 'Chin Ping Mei', trans. as *The Golden Vase Plum*, c. 1650, quoted in S. Rowbotham, *Women, Resistance and Revolution*, London, 1972, p. 171.

18 Ayscough, *op. cit.*, p. 187.

19 Pa Chin (Ba Jin), *The Family*, trans. S. Shapiro, FLP, 1958 (first published in 1931).

20 J. Myrdal, *Report from a Chinese Village*, London, 1963, pp. 65, 285.

21 A. H. Smith, *Village Life in China*, London, 1900, p. 262.

22 *Ibid.*

23 Myrdal, *op. cit.*, p. 48.

24 I. Pruitt, *A Daughter of Han: An Autobiography of a Working Woman*, Stanford, 1967, p. 29.

25 I. Crooks and D. Crooks, *The First Years of Yangyi Commune*, London, 1966, p. 211.

26 Pruitt, *op. cit.*, p. 22.

27 S. Couling, *Encyclopaedia Sinica*, London, 1917, p. 186.

28 H. S. Levy, *Chinese Footbinding: The History of a Chinese Erotic Custom*, New York, 1966, pp. 26–7.

29 Pruitt, *op. cit.*, p. 22.

30 Lin Yu-tang, *My Country and My People*, London, 1936, p. 159.

31 H. S. Levy, *op. cit.*, p. 41.

32 *Nü er Jing*, Section VII, trans. Headland, *op. cit.*, p. 77.

33 H. S. Levy, *op. cit.*, p. 41.

34 *Ibid.*, p. 30.

35 Fei Hsiao-tung, *Earthbound China*, London, 1949, p. 112.

36 J. L. Buck, *Land Utilisation in China*, Chicago, 1937, p. 303.

37 Pruitt, *op. cit.*, p. 55.

38 Waley, *op. cit.*, p. 72.

39 *Book of Odes*, quoted in *NCH*, 10 Feb. 1931.

40 A. H. Smith, *Proverbs and Common Sayings from the Chinese*, Shanghai, 1902, p. 302.

41 Smith, *Village Life*, p. 326.

42 C. H. Plopper, *Chinese Religion Seen Through the Proverb*, Shanghai, 1926, p. 99.

43 Smith, *Proverbs*, p. 302.

44 Smith, *Village Life*, p. 307.

45 Myrdal, *op. cit.*, p. 59.

46 H. Kulp, *Country Life in South China*, vol. 1, New York, 1925, p. 164.

47 *Nü er Jing*, Section LL, in Headland, *op. cit.*, p. 71.

48 Professor S. L. Kiang, quoted in Lewis, *op. cit.*, p. 14.

49 'Primer for Girls', in Headland, *op. cit.*, p. 23.

50 Wang Tsang-pao, *La Femme dans la société chinoise*, Paris, 1933, p. 16.

51 Chen Dongyuan, *Zhongguo Funu Shenghuoshi* (*History of the Life of Chinese Women*), Shanghai, 1937, p. 188.

52 *Book of Rites*, X:3, quoted in *Xin Qingnian*, vol. II, no. 4, Dec. 1916.

53 *Nü er Jing*, Section VIII, in Headland, *op. cit.*, p. 78.

54 'The Twenty-Four Patterns of Filial Piety', quoted in *ibid.*, pp. 33–4.

55 Smith, *Proverbs*, p. 67.

56 Zhao Shuli, 'Meng Xiangyin Stands Up' in W. F. Jenner, *Modern Chinese Stories*, Oxford, 1970, pp. 121–38.

57 See Vermier Chiu, 'Marriage Laws of the Ching Dynasty . . .', *Contemporary China*, vol. II, Hong Kong, 1958.

58 C. K. Yang, *The Chinese Family in the Communist Revolution*, Boston, 1959, p. 48.

59 Lu Hsun (Lu Xun), *Selected Stories*, Peking, 1972, pp. 125–44.

60 M. J. Levy, *The Family Revolution in Modern China*, New York, 1968, p. 94.

61 M. Wolf, *Women and the Family in Rural Taiwan*, Stanford, 1972, p. 37.
62 S. D. Gamble, *Ting Hsien: A North China Rural Community*, Stanford, 1954, p. 38.
63 'Chin Ping Mei' (*The Golden Vase Plum*) quoted in O. Lang, *Chinese Family and Society*, Yale, 1946, p. 50.
64 Cao Zhan, *Hung-lou Meng*, trans. by Wang Chi-chen, as *The Dream of the Red Chamber*, London, 1959.
65 Lin Yu-tang, *op. cit.,* p. 157.
66 E. A. Ross, *The Changing Chinese*, London, 1911, p. 201.
67 Smith, *Proverbs*, p. 292.
68 J. McGowan, *Sidelights on Chinese Life*, London, 1917, p. 32.
69 Wolf, *op. cit.,* p. 40.
70 C. K. Yang, *A Chinese Village*, New York, 1946, p. 90.
71 Smith, *Village*, p. 277.
72 Levy, M. J., *op. cit.*, p. 117.
73 Wei Tao-ming, *My Revolutionary Years*, New York, 1943, pp. 1–5.
74 M. B. Treadley, *Men and Women of Chung Ho-cheng*, Taipei, 1971, p. 202. Based on Tsu Yu-chi and others' field study of the 1940s.
75 Kulp, *op. cit.*, pp. 278–81.
76 P. Leboucq, quoted in F. Blackburn, 'The Role and Organisation of Secret Societies', M. Phil. thesis, London, 1968, p. 198.
77 *Ibid.*, p. 199.
78 *Ibid.*
79 V. Purcell, *The Boxer Uprising*, Cambridge, 1963, pp. 235–8.
80 A. H. Smith, *Chinese Characteristics*, London, 1892, p. 221.
81 McGowan, *op. cit.,* p. 32.
82 Waley, *op. cit.*, p. 72.
83 Hu Shih, 'A Chinese Declaration of the Rights of Women', *Chinese Social and Political Science Review*, vol. VIII, no. 2, 1924, pp. 100–9.
84 *Ibid.*
85 H. S. Levy, 'Yellow Turban Religion and Rebellion at the End of the Han', *Journal of America Oriental Society*, 76, 1956.
86 V. Shih, *The Taiping Ideology*, Washington, 1957, p. 69.
87 Lin-le, *Ti-ping Tien-Kwoh: The History of the Ti-ping Revolution,* vol. I, London, 1866, pp. 234–5.
88 Shih, *op. cit.*, p. 61.
89 R. Alley (trans.), *Poems of Revolt*, Peking, 1962, p. 13.
90 Shih, *op. cit.*, p. 65.
91 Alley, *op. cit.*, p. 30.
92 Shih, *op. cit.*, pp. 69, 71.
93 *Ibid.*
94 *Ibid.*, p. 73.
95 *Ibid.*, p. 72.
96 Lewis, *op. cit.*, pp. 18–19.
97 Burton, *op. cit.*, pp. 45–6.
98 Lewis, *op. cit.*, p. 24.
99 *Ibid.*
100 Burton, *op. cit.*, p. 34.

101 M. E. Burton, *Notable Women of Modern China,* New York, 1912, pp. 20, 163.

102 M. G. Guinness, *The Story of China*, London, 1894, p. 298.

103 See: Ross, *op. cit.*, p. 204; Smith, *Village Life*, p. 287; Lang, *op. cit.*, pp. 108, 201; Yang, *The Family*, pp. 197–8.

104 Smith, *Village Life*, pp. 287–8. For a fuller account, published since this book was written see M. Topley, 'Marriage Resistance in Kwangtung', in M. Wolf and R. Witke, *Women in Chinese Society*, Stanford, 1975.

Chapter 3 New Expectations: Patriotism and the Vote

1 Wei Chin-chih, 'An Early Woman Revolutionary', *CR*, June 1962.

2 Zhang Zhidong, 'Exhortation to Study', 1898, trans. by Teng Ssu-yu and J. K. Fairbank, *China's Response to the West, A Documentary Survey 1839–1923*, New York, 1967, p. 169. H. S. Levy, *Chinese Footbinding: The History of a Chinese Erotic Custom*, New York, 1966, p. 72.

3 Zhang Zhidong, 'Education Makes European Countries Strong' (a diary entry of 11 Feb. 1891), in Teng and Fairbank, *op. cit.*, p. 145.

4 *NCH*, 11 Dec. 1903.

5 Quoted in H. Levy, *op. cit.*, p. 72.

6 Quoted *ibid.*, p. 81.

7 *Ibid.*, pp. 82–3.

8 A. Smedley, *The Great Road: Life and Times of Chu Teh,* New York, 1956, p. 51.

9 *NCH*, 23 Dec. 1904.

10 H. Levy, *op. cit.*, p. 86.

11 *Ibid.*, pp. 84–5.

12 *NCH*, Aug. 10, 1906.

12 *NCH*, 10 Aug. 1906.

13 H. Levy, *op. cit.*, p. 20.

15 S. Couling, 'Antifootbinding', *Encyclopaedia Sinica*, London, 1917, *NCH*, 4 Jan. 1913.

16 'The New Republic', 18 Dec. 1915, trans. in J. Bashford, *China: An Interpretation*, London, 1916, p. 139.

17 H. Levy, *op. cit.*, p. 74.

18 See S. D. Gamble, 'The Disappearance of Footbinding in Tinghsien', *American Journal of Sociology*, Sept. 1943, pp. 181–3.

19 H. Levy, *op. cit.*, pp. 91–2.

20 M. E. Burton, *The Education of Women in China*, New York, 1911, pp. 100–1.

21 *Ibid.*, p. 102.

22 M. E. Cameron, *The Reform Movement in China 1898–1912*, Stanford, 1931, p. 83.

23 Quoted in Burton, *op. cit.*, p. 122.

24 'The Feminist Movement in China', *Review of Reviews*, New York, Jan. 1909, p. 101.

25 Burton, *op. cit.*, pp. 122–3.

26 *NCH*, 18 July 1908.

27 Burton, *op. cit.*, p. 126.
28 *Ibid.*, p. 127.
29 *Ibid.*
30 *Ibid.*
31 *Ibid.*, p. 128.
32 *Ibid.*, p. 127.
33 *Ibid.*, p. 129.
34 *Ibid.*, p. 150.
35 Reported in Headland, *op. cit.*, p. 223.
36 Burton, *op. cit.*, p. 161.
37 '*Women's Missionary Friend*', Oct. 1906.
38 Burton, *op. cit.*, pp. 153–4.
39 *Ibid.*, p. 122.
40 E. A. Ross, *The Changing Chinese*, London, 1911, p. 206.
41 Burton, *op. cit.*, p. 139.
42 Zhou Rong, *The Revolutionary Army 1903*, trans. by J. Lust, The Hague, 1968, pp. 123, 126.
43 M. Rankin, *Early Chinese Revolutionaries: Radical Intellectuals in Shanghai and Chekiang, 1902–11*, Boston, 1971, p. 66.
44 Wei Chin-chih, *op. cit.*, pp. 31–3.
45 Wei Tao-ming, *My Revolutionary Years*, New York, 1943, p. 31.
46 I. Dean, 'The Women's Movement in China', *Chinese Recorder*, vol. LVIII, no. 10, 1927, p. 653.
47 Rankin, *op. cit.*, p. 71; R. S. Britton, *The Chinese Radical Press, 1800–1912*, Shanghai, 1933, p. 116.
48 *Nuzi Shijie* (*Women's World*), no. 1, 1903.
49 Burton, *op. cit.*, p. 174.
50 Sarah Pike Conger, *Letters from China*, Chicago, 1909, p. 373.
51 Fan Wen-lan, 'Chiu Chin—A Woman Revolutionary', *ZF*, Oct.–Dec. 1956.
52 *Beijing Niubao* quoted in 'The Feminist Movement in China', *op. cit.*
53 *Ibid.*
54 Burton, *op. cit.*, p. 177.
55 *Ibid.*, p. 176.
56 F. Ayscough, *Chinese Women Yesterday and Today*, London, 1938, p. 150.
57 C. F. Remer, *A Study of Chinese Boycotts*, Taipei, 1966, p. 41.
58 Burton, *op. cit.*, p. 177.
59 *The Association Monthly*, April 1911, quoted in Burton, *op. cit.*, pp. 178–9.
60 M. Wright, *China in Revolution: The First Phase 1900–1913*, Yale, 1968, p. 33.
61 *Ibid.*, p. 34.
62 G. L. Harding, *Present-Day China*, London, 1916, pp. 48–53.
63 Wei Tao-ming, *op. cit.*, pp. 40–52.
64 Harding, *op. cit.*, pp. 40–5.
65 'The Suffragettes of China', *Literary Digest*, vol. 44, 3 Feb. 1912, p. 239.
66 *Ibid.*, pp. 241–2.
67 *Ibid.*, p. 239.

68 Wei Tao-ming, *op. cit.*, pp. 55–62.
69 M. E. Baldwin, *Revolution and other Tales*, London, 1913, pp. 16–19.
70 LCC, 'The Women's Movement in China During the Last Thirty Years', *Chinese Recorder*, Oct. 1941, p. 562.
71 M. T. Z. Tyau, *China Awakened*, New York, 1922, p. 57.
72 E. J. Dingle, *China's Revolution, 1911–12*, London, 1912, p. 53.
73 F. Farjenel, *Through the Chinese Revolution,* London, 1915, p. 59.
74 Baldwin, *op. cit.*, p. 19.
75 Nai-cheng Shen Nelson, 'The Changing Chinese Social Mind', *Chinese Social and Political Review*, vol. 8, 1924, p. 155.
76 Wei Chin-chih, *op. cit.*, p. 31.
77 Ayscough, *op. cit.*, p. 143.
78 *Ibid.*, p. 162.
79 Wei Chin-chih, *op. cit.*, pp. 32–3.
80 *Ibid.*, p. 32.
81 Harding, *op. cit.*, p. 56.
82 *Ibid.*
83 *NCH*, 30 March 1912.
84 *Ibid.*, 21 Dec. 1912.
85 Farjenel, *op. cit.*, pp. 60–1; *NCH*, 23 March 1912.
86 *NCH*, 27 Sept. 1913.
87 J. Myrdal, *Report from a Chinese Village*, London, 1963, p. 357.
88 Account based on A. Zell, 'Early Beginnings of the Development of Working Class Institutions in China', MA thesis, University of London, 1969.
89 *NCH*, 8 Feb. 1913.
90 Harding, *op. cit.*, p. 53.
91 Wei Tao-ming, *op. cit.*, p. 29.
92 Burton, *op. cit.*, pp. 183–4.
93 *Ibid.*, p. 187.
94 Burton, *op. cit.*, p. 199.
95 Zhang Zhidong, in Teng and Fairbank, *op. cit.*, p. 165.
96 Ross, *op. cit.*, pp. 202–3.
97 *The World's Students' Journal*, 1907, trans. M. Bromhall, *Present Day Conditions in China*, London, 1908, pp. 30–1.
98 *NCH*, 9 Aug. 1907.
99 'The Feminist Movement in China', *op. cit.*
100 *Ibid.*
101 *NCH*, 15 June 1912.
102 *NCH*, 10 Aug. 1912.
103 Chow Tse-tung, *The May Fourth Movement*, Stanford, 1960, p. 43.
104 *NCH*, 6 Dec. 1913.
105 Wright, *op. cit.*, p. 34.
106 Harding, *op. cit.*, p. 61.
107 *NCH*, 11 July 1908.

Chapter 4 A Personal Solution: Feminism

1 G. T. Seton, *Chinese Lanterns*, New York, 1924, p. 232.

2 Quoted in A. M. Anderson, *Humanity and Labour*, London, 1928, p. 1.

3 As estimated by Hu Shi, see Chow Tse-tung, *May Fourth Movement*, Stanford, 1960, p. 178.

4 P. Hutchinson, *China's Real Revolution*, New York, 1924, p. 54.

5 *Ibid.*, p. 55.

6 *China Weekly Review*, 4 Feb. 1922.

7 Quoted in J. T. Chen, *The May Fourth Movement in Shanghai*, London, 1971, p. 40.

8 Chen Duxiu, 'The Way of Confucius and Modern Life', *Xin Qingnian*, Dec. 1916.

9 Chen Duxiu, 'Call to Youth', 1915, trans. by Teng Ssu-yu and J. K. Fairbank, *China's Response to the West, A Documentary Survey 1839–1923*, New York, 1967, p. 240.

10 Manifesto, *Xin Qingnian*, 1 Dec. 1919.

11 Seton, *op. cit.*, p. 237.

12 M. T. Z. Tyau, *China Awakened*, New York, 1922, pp. 59–60.

13 Chow Tse-tung, *Research Guide to the May Fourth Movement*, Harvard, 1964, p. 64.

14 *NCH*, 30 April 1921.

15 H. C. E. Liu, 'The Chinese Women's Movement and Magazines', *Chinese Recorder*, Feb. 1934, p. 85.

16 *NCH*, 30 April 1921.

17 Trans. Seton, *op. cit.*, pp. 232–4.

18 M. E. Burton, *Women Workers of the Orient*, London, 1920, p. 135.

19 Nym Wales, *The Chinese Communists: Autobiographical and Biographical Sketches*, Connecticut, 1972, p. 265.

20 Speech to club quoted in Hutchinson, *op. cit.*, p. 105.

21 H. Snow, *Women in Modern China,* The Hague, 1967, p. 236.

22 Seton, *op. cit.*, pp. 235–6.

23 Hutchinson, *op. cit.*, p. 72.

24 *Ibid.*, pp. 73–4.

25 *Ibid.*, pp. 103–4.

26 R. Witke, 'Mao Tse-tung [Mao Zedong], Women and Suicide in the May Fourth Era', *C.Q.*, July–Sept. 1967, p. 143.

27 Wales, *op. cit.*, p. 265.

28 Pa Chin, *The Family*, trans. S. Shapiro, FLP, Peking, 1957, p. 43.

29 Wales, *op. cit.*, p. 265.

30 Witke, *op. cit.*, pp. 131–2.

31 Snow, *op. cit.*, p. 235.

32 A. Smedley, *The Great Road: Li Fe and Times of Chu Teh*, New York, 1956, p. 123.

33 Witke, *op. cit.*, p. 134.

34 Tyau, *op. cit.*, p. 63.

35 Seton, *op. cit.*, pp. 209–10.

36 Anderson, *op. cit.*, p. 226.

37 *Ta Kung Pao*, 8 June 1919, quoted Witke, *op. cit.*, p. 133.

38 *Ibid.*

39 *Ibid.*

40 LCC, 'The Women's Movement in China During the Last Thirty

Years', *Chinese Recorder,* vol. LXXII, no. 10, Oct. 1941, p. 567;
NCH, 9 May 1925.

41 Hsieh Ping-ying (Xie Bingying), *Autobiography of a Chinese Girl,*
London, 1943, p. 67.

42 Burton, *op. cit.*, p. 164.

43 Tyau, *op. cit.*, pp. 63–5.

44 *NCH*, 7 June 1919.

45 Chen Dongyuan, *Zhongguo Funu Shenghuoshi* (*History of the Life
of Women in China*), Shanghai, 1937, pp. 127–9; Witke, *op. cit.*,
p. 133.

46 *China Weekly Review*, 18 June 1921.

47 *NCH*, 2 April 1921.

48 Hutchinson, *op. cit.*, p. 102.

49 Seton, *op. cit.*, p. 125.

50 Hutchinson, *op. cit.*, p. 102; *NCH*, 14 Oct. 1922.

51 *NCH*, 4 April 1925.

52 LCC, *op. cit.*, p. 567.

53 *NCH*, 13 Oct. 1923.

54 *Ibid.*, 4 April 1925.

55 Based on Tyau, *op. cit.*, pp. 60–2; *NCH*, 20 Mar. 1920.

56 Seton, *op. cit.*, p. 207.

57 Nym Wales, *The Chinese Labour Movement*, New York, 1945, p. 16.

58 'Women's Work in Kwangtung Provinces', *Chinese Economic
Journal*, vol. 1, 1927, p. 570.

59 Quoted in Hutchinson, *op. cit.*, p. 125.

60 Seton, *op. cit.*, pp. 176–7.

61 *Ibid.*, p. 312.

62 Chen Ta, 'Working Women in China', *Monthly Labour Review*,
vol. 15, 1922.

63 Based on *NCH, passim*, 1920–5; Seton, *op. cit.*, p. 303; Chen Ta,
ibid., p. 144.

64 *NCH*, 19 Aug. 1922.

65 Snow, *op. cit.*, p. 204.

66 Witke, *op. cit.*, p. 142.

67 *Ibid.*, p. 147.

68 Hsieh Ping-ying (Xie Bingying), *op. cit.*, pp. 140–2.

69 Witke, *op. cit.*, p. 147.

70 *Ibid.*, p. 145.

71 Interview with Deng Yingzhao in Snow, *op. cit.*, p. 255.

72 Hsieh Ping-ying (Xie Bingying), *op. cit.*, pp. 111–13.

73 *NCH*, 9 May 1925.

74 Anderson, *op. cit.*, p. 222.

75 Wales, *The Chinese Communists*, p. 256.

76 *Ibid.*, p. 231.

77 Hutchinson, *op. cit.*, p. 128.

78 Seton, *op. cit.*, p. 275.

79 Anderson, *op. cit.*, p. 222.

80 *NCH*, 29 Dec. 1923.

81 *Ibid.*

82 *Ibid.*, 9 May 1925.

83 Snow, *op. cit.*, p. 235.
84 Interview with Deng Yingzhao in *ibid.*, p. 256.
85 *NCH*, 14 Oct. 1922.
86 Wales, *op. cit.*, pp. 256–7.
87 *NCH*, 28 Oct. 1922.
88 Hsieh Ping-ying (Xie Bingying), *op. cit.*, p. 67.
89 *NCH*, 5 Dec. 1925.
90 *Ibid.*, 12 Dec. 1925.

Chapter 5 An Uneasy Alliance: Feminism and Socialism

1 Hsieh Ping-ying (Xie Bingying), *Autobiography of a Chinese Girl,*
   London, 1943, p. 110.
2 Xinchao, 11, 2 Dec. 1919, quoted in R. Witke, 'Transformation of
   Attitudes of Women during the May Fourth Era of Modern China',
   Ph.D. thesis, University of California, 1970, pp. 257–8.
3 Jianshi (Construction), II, 2 March 1920 in *ibid.*, p. 271.
4 A lecture to the Guangdong Women's Alliance reprinted in *Funu
   wenti taolunji (Collected Discussions of the Woman Problem)*,
   Shanghai, 1934, p. 271.
5 K. Marx, *The Holy Family*, Moscow, 1945 (trans. 1956), p. 259.
6 Alexandra Kollontai, *Women Workers Struggle for their Rights*,
   trans. Celia Britton, London, 1971.
7 V. I. Lenin, *Women and Society*, New York, 1938, pp. 11–13 (Speech
   at the First All-Russian Congress of Women Workers, 19 Nov. 1918).
8 'The Task of the Working Women's Movement in the Soviet
   Republic', 23 Sept. 1919, in *ibid.*, pp. 15–20.
9 *Op. cit.* C. Brandt *et al.*, *A Documentary History of Chinese
   Communism*, London, 1952, p. 63.
10 Brandt, *op. cit.*, p. 64.
11 Lieshi Xiang Jingyu (*Life of the Revolutionary Martyr, Xiang
    Jingyu*), Peking, 1958; Witke, *op. cit.*, p. 283; Wang Yizhi, 'A Great
    Woman Revolutionary', *CR*, March 1965; H. Snow, *Women in
    Modern China*, The Hague, 1967, p. 247.
12 Wang Yizhi, *op. cit.*, pp. 25–6.
13 *Ibid.*
14 *Ibid.*
15 Witke, *op. cit.*, p. 263.
16 Snow, *op. cit.*, p. 247.
17 H. Isaacs, *The Tragedy of the Chinese Revolution*, Stanford, 1962,
    pp. 62–3.
18 *Ibid.*
19 I. Dean, 'The Women's Movement in China', *Chinese Recorder*,
    vol. LVIII, no. 10, 1927, p. 654.
20 LCC, 'The Woman's Movement in China During the Last Thirty
    Years', *Chinese Recorder*, Oct. 1941, p. 569.
21 *Ibid.*
22 Quoted in Dean, *op. cit.*, p. 655.
23 Quoted in R. L. Lo, *China's Revolution from the Inside*, New York,
    1930, p. 264.

24 Dean, *op. cit.*, p. 635.
25 C. K. Yang, *The Chinese Family in the Communist Revolution*, Boston, 1959, p. 120.
26 Dean, *op. cit.*, p. 658.
27 *China Weekly Review*, 12 April 1926 and 26 April 1924.
28 A. L. Strong, 'New Women of Old Canton', *Asia*, June 1926.
29 Dean, *op. cit.*, p. 655.
30 *Ibid.*
31 *Ibid.*, p. 656.
32 Nym Wales, *Red Dust*, Stanford, 1952, pp. 201–2.
33 Yang, *op. cit.*, p. 120.
34 A. L. Strong, *China's Millions*, London, 1936, p. 113.
35 Based on description of Hunan women's movement in *CR*, March 1975.
36 Lo, *op. cit.*, pp. 265–6.
37 *Ibid.*, p. 263.
38 Strong, *China's Millions*, pp. 112, 114.
39 Statement Issued by Committee of Advancement for Women's Rights in Henan, trans. Lo, *op. cit.*, pp. 257–9.
40 Trans. in *ibid.*, pp. 270–4.
41 *NCH*, 14 May 1927.
42 Published in complete form in Hsieh Ping-ying (Xie Bingying), *op. cit.*
43 *Ibid.*, p. 92.
44 *Ibid.*, p. 107.
45 *Ibid.*, p. 100.
46 *Ibid.*, p. 110.
47 *Ibid.*
48 Strong, *China's Millions*, p. 114.
49 Lo, *op. cit.*, pp. 270–2.
50 Strong, *China's Millions*, p. 115.
51 *Ibid.*, p. 117.
52 *Ibid.*
53 *Ibid.*, p. 123.
54 Snow, *op. cit.*, p. 107.
55 *NCH*, 19 March 1927.
56 Strong, *China's Millions*, p. 115.
57 Lo, *op. cit.*, pp. 262–3.
58 H. O. Chapman, *The Chinese Revolution, 1926–7*, London, 1928, p. 86.
59 *Ibid.*
60 Trans. in Dean, *op. cit.*, p. 654.
61 Strong, *China's Millions*, pp. 125, 131.
62 Wales, *Red Dust*, pp. 201–2.
63 Strong, *China's Millions*, p. 121.
64 *Ibid.*, p. 120.
65 Lo, *op. cit.*, p. 274.
66 *Ibid.*, p. 273.
67 Strong, *China's Millions*, p. 126.
68 *Ibid.*, pp. 104–10.

69 Nym Wales, *The Chinese Communists: Autobiographical and Biographical Sketches*, Connecticut, 1972, pp. 243–4.
70 Interview with textile workers, in Strong, *op. cit.*, pp. 107, 111.
71 Dean, *op. cit.*, p. 656.
72 Strong, *China's Millions*, pp. 105–6.
73 Wales, *The Chinese Communists*, p. 238.
74 Interview, in Strong, *China's Millions*, p. 108.
75 *Chinese Toiling Women*, Modern Books, London, 1932, pp. 24–5.
76 *NCH*, 14 March 1927.
77 Strong, *China's Millions*, pp. 199–200.
78 Wales, *Red Dust*, pp. 201–2.
79 Strong, *China's Millions*, pp. 121–2.
80 See Lo, *op. cit.*, pp. 274–5.
81 Interview with Dean of Women's Training School, in Strong, *op. cit.*, p. 119.
82 Strong, *China's Millions*, pp. 137–45.
83 *Ibid.*, p. 144.
84 Wales, *The Chinese Communists,* pp. 234–42.
85 E.g. *NCH*, 19 Feb. 1927; 14 March 1927.
86 Chapman, *op. cit.*, pp. 86–8; *NCH*, 14 May 1927.
87 Strong, *China's Millions*, p. 27.
88 *Ibid.*
89 Han Suyin, *Birdless Summer*, London, 1968, p. 133.
90 Dean, *op. cit.*, p. 659; Strong, *China's Millions*, pp. 112, 121.
91 Hsieh Ping-ying (Xie Bingying), *op. cit.*, pp. 130–1.
92 *Ta Kung Pao*, 1927, quoted in Isaacs, *op. cit.*, p. 290.
93 Strong, *China's Millions*, p. 190.
94 *Ibid.*, pp. 145–6.
95 *China Weekly Review*, 20 August 1927.
96 Snow, *op. cit.*, p. 241.
97 R. Alley (trans.), *Poems of Revolt*, Peking, 1962, p. 43.

Chapter 6 'The Feminine Mystique': Guomindang China

1 Tseng Pao-swen, 'The Chinese Women Past and Present' in Sophia H. Chen, *Symposium on Chinese Culture*, Shanghai, 1931, p. 344.
2 E. M. Pye, 'The Women's Movement in China', *Asiatic Review*, vol. 25, 1929, pp. 204–19.
3 Strong, *China's Millions*, London, 1936, p. 17.
4 *Ibid.*
5 Pye, *op. cit.*, p. 214.
6 *Ibid.*, pp. 214–17.
7 *Ibid.*
8 *Ibid.*, p. 217.
9 Wei Tao-ming, *My Revolutionary Years*, New York, 1943, pp. 168–70.
10 Quoted in Jen Tai, 'The Status of Women in China', Information Bulletin, Council of International Affairs, Nanking, 1936, p. 184.
11 *Ibid.*, p. 175.

12 Quoted in F. Ayscough, *Chinese Women Yesterday and Today*, London, 1938, p. 99.

13 Tseng Pao-swen, *op. cit.*, p. 339.

14 O. M. Green, *China's Struggle with the Dictators*, London, 1941, pp. 107–8.

15 E.g. *NCH*, 17 Aug. 1929.

16 Tang Leang-Li, *The New Social Order in China*, London, 1936.

17 Tseng Pao-swen, *op. cit.*, pp. 343–4.

18 Soong Mei-ling (Song Meiling), *We Chinese Women*, New York, 1943, p. 111.

19 Mme Chiang Kai-shek, *China Shall Rise Again*, London, 1941, p. 52.

20 Hu Shih, 'A Chinese Declaration of Rights', *NCH*, 10 Feb. 1931.

21 Tang Leang-li, *op. cit.*, pp. 219–28.

22 Lin Yu-tang, *My Country and My People*, London, 1936, pp. 131–63.

23 Tang Leang-li, *op. cit.*, p. 219.

24 LCC, 'The Women's Movement in China During the Last Thirty Years', *Chinese Recorder*, Oct. 1941, p. 570.

25 Ayscough, *op. cit.*, p. 100.

26 Yi Fang-wu, 'Women in the War', *Chinese Recorder*, June 1940, p. 372.

27 Tsu Yu-chi in M. B. Treadley, *Men and Women in Chung Ho-cheng*, Taipei, 1971, pp. 196–7.

28 Tseng Pao-swen, *op. cit.*, p. 339.

29 Lin Yu-tang, *op. cit.*, p. 146.

30 *Ibid.*, p. 148.

31 *Ibid.*, p. 140.

32 H. C. Mei, 'The Role Women's Clubs Play in the Social Reconstruction of China', *Chinese Recorder*, vol. LXVII, no. 12, Dec. 1936, pp. 751–5.

33 Soong Chingling (Song Qingling), 'The Chinese Women's Fight for Freedom', *Asia*, July 1942, p. 165.

34 Soong Mei-ling (Song Meiling), *op. cit.*, p. 111.

35 Mei, *op. cit.*, p. 751.

36 *NCH*, 1 April 1930.

37 LCC, *op. cit.*, p. 570.

38 *NCH*, 20 May 1930.

39 *Ibid.*, 7 July 1928.

40 *Ibid.*, 21 July 1928.

41 *Ibid.*

42 *Ibid.*, 18 Feb. 1928.

43 *The Chinese Year Book,* 1937, pp. 1048, 1073.

44 Li Dezhuan, 'Guomindang tongzhizhu minzhu funu yundong baogao' (Report of the Democratic Women's Movement in Guomindang Controlled Areas at First Women's Congress), Peking, 1949.

45 Soong Chingling (Song Qingling), 'The Chinese Women's Fight for Freedom', p. 164.

46 Li Dezhuan, *op. cit.*

47 H. Snow, *The Chinese Labour Movement*, New York, 1945, p. 17.

48 Li Dezhuan, *op. cit.*

49 *From Struggle to Victory*, ACDWF, Peking, 1949.

50 Quoted in E. R. Wolf, *Peasant Wars of the Twentieth Century*, New York, 1969, p. 134.
51 J. Myrdal, *Report from a Chinese Village*, p. 268.
52 See Pa Chin, *The Family*, trans. S. Shapiro, FLP, Peking, 1958.
53 See *Selected Works of Lu Hsun*, FLP, Peking, 1960.
54 Han Suyin, *Birdless Summer*, London, 1968, pp. 132–56.
55 *Ibid.*, p. 167.
56 Special Women's Work Supplement, *China Weekly Review*, 25 Dec. 1937.
57 E. Hahn, *The Soong Sisters*, London, 1942, p. xvii.
58 H. Snow, *Women in Modern China*, The Hague, 1967, pp. 164–5.
59 Hahn, *op. cit.*, pp. 212–13.
60 Soong Chingling (Song Qingling), in *People's Tribune*, Hankou, 14 July 1927, quoted in Hahn, *op. cit.*, p. 111.
61 Belden, *op. cit.*, pp. 311–12.
62 Lu Hsun (Lu Xun), 'On the Emancipation of Women', 21 Oct. 1933, see *Selected Works of Lu Hsun,* vol. III, Peking, 1959.
63 O. Lang, *Chinese Family and Society*, New York, 1946, p. 123.
64 S. D. Gamble, *Ting Hsien: A North China Rural Community*, New York, 1954, p. 379; Fei Hsiao-tung, *Peasant Life in China*, London, 1939, p. 40.
65 Lang, *op. cit.*, p. 194.
66 Fei Hsiao-tung, *op. cit.*, p. 81; *Earthbound China*, London, 1949, pp. 111–12.
67 M. Yang, *A Chinese Village*, New York, 1945, pp. 52, 55.
68 C. K. Yang, *A Chinese Village in Early Communist Transition*, Mass. 1959, pp. 89–90.
69 J. L. Buck, *Land Utilisation in China*, Chicago, 1937, pp. 373ff.
70 Tsu Yu-chi in Treadley, *op. cit.*, pp. 196–7.
71 Lang, *op. cit.*, p. 123.
72 *Ibid.*, pp. 203–12.
73 Tien Ju-kang, 'Female Workers in a Cotton Mill in Shih Kuo-leng', *China Enters the Machine Age*, Harvard, 1944, pp. 178–98.
74 *NCH*, 14 March 1934.
75 Soong Chingling (Song Qingling), 'The Chinese Women's Fight for Freedom', pp. 155–6.
76 Soong Mei-ling (Song Meiling), *op. cit.*, p. 54.
77 Mme Chiang Kai-shek, *op. cit.*, p. 68.
78 Soong Chingling (Song Qingling), 'The Chinese Women's Fight for Freedom', p. 159.
79 *Ibid.*
80 *Ibid.*; Hsu Meng-hsiung, 'Women of Free China', *Asia*, March 1941.
81 Ayscough, *op. cit.*, p. xiv.
82 Mme Chiang Kai-shek, *op. cit.*, p. 67.
83 *Ibid.*
84 *Ibid.*, p. 223.
85 D. T. Wang, 'Mobilising the Chinese Women', *Chinese Recorder*, Jan. 1939, p. 18.
86 Wang Hsiao-yin, quoted in Ayscough, *op. cit.*, p. 111.
87 Wei Tao-ming, *op. cit.*, p. 214.

88 *Ibid.*, pp. 215–16.
89 Mme Chiang Kai-shek, *op. cit.*, p. 223.
90 Snow, *Women in Modern China*, pp. 167–9.
91 Mme Chiang Kai-shek, *op. cit.*, p. 223.
92 Mei, *op. cit.*, p. 754.
93 Nym Wales, *The Chinese Communists: Autobiographical and Biographical Sketches*, Connecticut, 1972, pp. 259–60.
94 Nym Wales, *Notes on the Chinese Student Movement 1935–6*, Hoover Inst., 1959, p. 181.
95 Soong Chingling (Song Qingling), 'The Chinese Women's Fight for Freedom', pp. 155–6.
96 *From Struggle to Victory*, p. 50.
97 Han Suyin, *op. cit.*, p. 132.
98 Mme Chiang Kai-shek, *op. cit.*, p. 227.
99 Hahn, *op. cit.*, p. 242.
100 Interview, in Snow, *op. cit.*, pp. 251–2.
101 Soong Chingling (Song Qingling), 'The Chinese Women's Fight for Freedom', p. 165; Hahn, *op. cit.*, pp. 244–5.
102 Soong Chingling (Song Qingling), *ibid.*
103 *NCH*, 4 Sept. 1940.
104 Li Dezhuan, *op. cit.*
105 *Ibid.*
106 Hahn, *op. cit.*, p. 239.
107 E.g. LCC, *op. cit.*, pp. 573–5.

Chapter 7 'Woman Work': Communist China

1 Resolution passed on the Women's Movement, *Documents of the Sixth Communist Party Congress*, Moscow, 1928.
2 *Ibid.*
3 'Resolution on Present Political Tasks Adopted by the CCP Politburo, 11 June 1930', trans. in C. Brandt, *A Documentary History of Chinese Communism*, London, 1952, p. 159.
4 Nym Wales, *The Chinese Communists: Autobiographical and Biographical Sketches*, Connecticut, 1972, p. 243.
5 Mao Tse-tung (Mao Zedong), 'Report on an Investigation of the Peasant Movement in Hunan, March 1927', see *Selected Works*, Peking, vol. 1, pp. 44–6.
6 *Ibid.*
7 Wales, *op. cit.*, pp. 212–15.
8 A. Smedley, *China's Red Army Marches*, London, 1936, pp. 54–5.
9 A. Smedley, *The Great Road: Life and times of Chu Teh*, New York, 1956, p. 271.
10 'Resolution on Present Political Tasks Adopted by the CCP Politburo, 11 June 1930', in Brandt, *op. cit.*, p. 198.
11 *Ibid.*
12 M. J. Meijer, *Marriage Law and Policy in the Chinese People's Republic*, Hong Kong, 1971, pp. 38–9.
13 *Chinese Toiling Women*, Modern Books, London, 1932, p. 27.

14 See Mao's Report to Second Congress of Chinese Soviets, quoted in A. Strong, *China Fights for Freedom*, London, 1939, p. 63.
15 D. Davin, 'Women in the Liberated Areas', in M. Young (ed.), *Women in China*, Michigan Papers in Chinese Studies, no. 15, 1973, p. 75.
16 Smedley, *China's Red Army Marches*, p. 295.
17 Report by Mao Tse-tung (Mao Zedong), 23 Jan. 1934, see *Selected Works*, vol. 1, p. 142.
18 Wales, *op. cit.*, p. 244.
19 Strong, *op. cit.*, p. 63.
20 Nym Wales, *Red Dust*, Stanford, 1952, p. 216.
21 R. Alley (trans.), *Poems of Revolt*, Peking, 1962, p. 114.
22 Wang Ming and Kam Sing, *Revolutionary China Today*, London, 1934, p. 48.
23 The Marriage Regulations of 1931, see Meijer, Appendix 1.
24 *Chinese Toiling Women*, p. 28.
25 *Ibid.*
26 *Ibid.*, p. 29.
27 *Ibid.*
28 Meijer, *op. cit.*, p. 39.
29 *Ibid.*, pp. 41–2.
30 *Ibid.*, p. 39.
31 *Ibid.*, p. 41.
32 D. Cusack, *Chinese Women Speak*, London, 1959, p. 189.
33 Smedley, *The Great Road*, p. 271.
34 Meijer, *op. cit.*, p. 39.
35 *Ibid.*, p. 43.
36 *Chinese Toiling Women*, op. cit., p. 27.
37 *ZF*, 1 Feb. 1962.
38 Wales, *Red Dust*, p. 217.
39 Wales, *The Chinese Communists*, p. 245.
40 Cusack, *op. cit.*, p. 190.
41 *ZF*, 1 May 1965.
42 *Ibid.*
43 Wales, *Red Dust*, p. 217.
44 Wales, *The Chinese Communists*, p. 247.
45 D. Wilson, *The Long March, 1935*, London, 1971, p. 69.
46 I. Epstein, *The People's War*, London, 1939, p. 249.
47 A. Smedley, *Battle Hymn of China*, London, 1944, p. 190.
48 Hsu Kwang (Xu Guang), 'Women's Liberation through Struggle', *CR*, March 1973.
49 I. Crooks and D. Crooks, *The First Years of Yangyi Commune*, London, 1966, pp. 16–17.
50 J. Myrdal, *Report from a Chinese Village*, London, 1963, p. 48.
51 J. Belden, *China Shakes the World*, London, 1951, p. 82.
52 Tsai Chang (Cai Chang), 'Welcome the new Policy in Woman Work, March 1943', *Documents of the Women's Movement*, ACDWF, Peking, 1949.
53 Cusack, *op. cit.*, p. 198.

54 M. Selden, *The Yenan Way in Revolutionary China*, Harvard, 1971, p. 116.
55 Epstein, *op. cit.*, p. 249.
56 Cusack, *op. cit.*, pp. 197–8.
57 W. Hinton, *Fanshen*, New York', 1966, p. 157.
58 'Present Policy of Woman Work', 26 Feb. 1943, in *Documents, op. cit.*
59 E. Snow, *Red Star over China*, London, 1937, p. 226.
60 I. Crooks and D. Crooks, *Revolution in a Chinese Village*, London, 1959, p. 45.
61 Selden, *op. cit.*, p. 258.
62 *From Struggle to Victory*, pp. 14–15.
63 Teng Ying chao (Deng Yingzhao), *PC*, 16 March 1950.
64 Crooks and Crooks, *Chinese Village*, p. 45.
65 Chang Kiang, 'Reunion', *Women in China Today*, ACDWF, Peking, 1951, no. 8, p. 13.
66 Belden, *op. cit.*, pp. 315–16.
67 Yang Yu, 'The Story of Tung Yu-lan', *PC*, 16 Dec. 1954.
68 Tsai Chang (Cai Chang), *op. cit.*
69 *From Struggle to Victory*, p. 15.
70 See interview with Li Kuei-ying, Myrdal, *op. cit.*, p. 281.
71 Chang Chung-chih, 'Liu Hu-lan', *PC*, 1 July 1952; Ruben Sanchez, 'Communist Heroine, Liu Hulan', *CR*, March 1972.
72 Liu Su-ying, 'Autobiography', *Women in China Today*, ACDWF, Peking, no. 7, p. 4.
73 Smedley, *Battle Hymn*, pp. 190–4.
74 Selden, *op. cit.*, p. 165.
75 Resolution of the Party 1939, trans. Brandt, *op. cit.*, p. 326.
76 Crooks and Crooks, *Chinese Village*, p. 45.
77 Xu Guang, 'Women's Liberation is a Component Part of the Proletarian Revolutionary', *PR*, 8 March 1974.
78 Selden, *op. cit.*, p. 111.
79 *Ibid*.
80 Belden, *op. cit.*, p. 122.
81 Wales, *The Chinese Communists*, p. 258.
82 Belden, *op. cit.*, p. 211.
83 Crooks and Crooks, *Yangyi Commune*, p. 268.
84 H. Snow, *Women in Modern China*, The Hague, 1967, p. 225.
85 Yang Yu, *op. cit.*, p. 30.
86 Hinton, *op. cit.*, p. 157.
87 Crooks and Crooks, *Chinese Village*, p. 107.
88 *Ibid.*, p. 108.
89 Belden, *op. cit.*, p. 316; *Women in New China*, FLP, Peking, 1950, p. 36.
90 Hinton, *op. cit.*, p. 465.
91 W. Jenner (ed.), *Modern Chinese Stories*, Oxford University Press, 1970, p. 129.
92 Crooks and Crooks, *Chinese Village*, pp. 100–4.
93 M. Goldman, *Literary Dissent in Communist China*, Mass., 1967, pp. 23, 27, 43.

94 Hsu Kuang (Xu Guang), *op. cit.*, p. 9.
95 Gunther Stein, *The Challenge of Red China*, London, 1945, p. 206.
96 Hsu Kuang (Xu Guang), *op. cit.*, p. 9.
97 *Ibid.*
98 Hinton, *op. cit.*, p. 397.
99 Yang Yu, *op. cit.*, p. 29.
100 'Woman Work in the Rural Districts of the Liberated Areas', 20 Dec. 1948, *Documents, op. cit.*
101 Hinton, *op. cit.*, p. 158.
102 Belden, *op. cit.*, pp. 289–310.
103 Hinton, *op. cit.*, p. 159.
104 *Ibid.*, p. 160.
105 Belden, *op. cit.*, pp. 316–17.
106 Crooks and Crooks, *Chinese Village*, p. 44.
107 Belden, *op. cit.*, p. 307.
108 Davin, *op. cit.*, pp. 80–1.
109 Belden, *op. cit.*, p. 316.
110 *Women in New China*, p. 36.
111 Selden, *op. cit.*, p. 142.
112 Snow, *op. cit.*, p. 225.
113 *Ibid.*
114 *Ibid.*
115 *From Struggle to Victory*, ACDWF, Peking, 1949, pp. 14–15.
116 Teng Ying chao (Deng Yingzhao), 'Present Policy and Tasks of the Women's Movement', 1949, *Documents, op. cit.*
117 Hsu Kuang (Xu Guang), *op. cit.*, p. 11.
118 'Present Woman Work in Rural Districts of the Liberated Areas', *Documents, op. cit.*

Chapter 8 A New Society: New Standards

1 Teng Ying chao (Deng Yingzhao), Speech, 14 May 1950, in *RMRB*, 26 May 1950.
2 Mao Tse-tung (Mao Zedong), Speech, 1 Oct. 1949.
3 See Common Programme of the People's Republic of China adopted 29 Sept. 1949 in *PC*, 16 March 1950.
4 Shen Chilan (Shen Jilan), 'How We Became Equal', *CR*, March 1955.
5 *RMRB*, 26 May 1950.
6 'Resolutions on the Present Tasks of the Women's Movement of China, Passed by the First All-China Women's Congress', 1 April 1949, *Documents of the Women's Movement*, ACDWF, Peking, 1949.
7 Mao Tse-tung (Mao Zedong), 'On the Correct Handling of Contradictions among the People', 27 Feb. 1957, see *Selected Readings*, FLP, Peking, 1967, pp. 350–85.
8 Chang Yun, *Xiandai funu (Modern Women)*, Sept. 1950, quoted in C. K. Yang, *The Chinese Family in the Communist Revolution*, Boston, 1959, p. 283.
9 J. Myrdal, *Report from a Chinese Village*, London, 1963, pp. 285–6.

10 'Woman Work in the Rural Districts of the Liberated Areas', 20 Dec. 1948, *Documents, op. cit.*

11 C. K. Yang, *A Chinese Village in Early Communist Transition*, Mass., 1959, p. 178.

12 'Women's Federation Report on Woman Work in the Agricultural *China's Countryside*, Peking, 1957, p. 283.

13 Chang Su, 'Women of Chaoshou Ward', *PC*, 1 March 1955.

14 *PC*, 1 March 1955.

15 'Women's Federation Report in Hsingtai County', *op. cit.*, pp. 283–4.

16 Tie Lien-li, *Diary of a Visit to China*, printed for private circulation, 1958, pp. 25, 30.

17 'The Second All-China Women's Congress Report', *PC*, 16 May 1953.

18 'China's New Womanhood', *CR*, March 1956.

19 *Marriage Law of the People's Republic*, FLP, Peking, 1950.

20 Shih Liang (Shiliang), 'Attend Seriously to the Thorough Implementation of the Marriage Law', *RMRB*, 13 Oct. 1951.

21 *Ibid.*

22 R. Lapwood and N. Lapwood, *Through the Chinese Revolution*, London, 1954, p. 88.

23 D. Cusack, *Chinese Women Speak*, London, 1959, p. 211.

24 C. Yang, *The Chinese Family*, pp. 203–4.

25 Yang Yu, 'The Women of Wu Village', *Women in China Today*, ACDWF, No. 1952, vol. III.

26 *Zhongguo gudai shenhua gushi*, Shanghai, 1957. (I am indebted to Paul Clifford for drawing my attention to, and translating these.

27 *Ibid.*

28 *Ibid.*

29 Ling Mei-li, 'The Growth of a New Outlook on Marriage', *PC*, 1 June 1951.

30 *Ibid.*

31 Yang Yu, 'Freed from Unhappiness', *PC*, 1 March 1951.

32 *Ibid.*

33 Cusack, *op. cit.*, p. 54.

34 Yang Yu, *op. cit.*, p. 12.

35 Teng Ying chao (Deng Yingzhao), 'Breaking the Yoke of the Feudal Marriage System', *PC*, 1 March 1953.

36 *Ibid.*

37 Shih Liang (Shiliang), *op. cit.*

38 Teng Ying chao (Deng Yingzhao), *op. cit.*

39 Shih Liang (Shiliang), *op. cit.*

40 *RMRB*, 29 Sept. 1951.

41 *RMRB*, 4 July 1952.

42 Fang-yen, 'Making the Marriage Law Work', *CR*, Sept.–Oct. 1953.

43 Yang Yu, 'Three Conditions', *PC*, 1 March 1953.

44 'Directive of the Government Administrative Council Concerning the Thorough Implementation of the Marriage Law, 1 Feb. 1953', *NCNA*, 1 Feb. 1953.

45 'General Report of the Central Committee of the CCP on the

Movement for the Implementation of the Marriage Law, 19 Feb. 1953', *NCNA*, 19 Feb. 1953.

46 See *The Upsurge of Socialism in the Countryside*, FLP, Peking, 1960, p. 286.

47 V. I. Lenin, 'The Tasks of the Working Women's Movement in the Soviet Republic', 23 Sept. 1919, in *Women and Society*, New York, 1938, pp. 15–20.

48 Mao Tse-tung (Mao Zedong), Inscription for the Magazine, *Women of New China*, 20 July 1949.

49 Teng Ying chao (Deng Yingzhao), 'The Women's Movement in China', *PC*, 1 March 1952.

50 Shen Chi-lan (Shen Jilan), *op. cit.*, p. 3.

51 Yang Yu, *op. cit.*, pp. 2, 6–7.

52 'Report of Women's Federation of Hsingtai County', pp. 274–84.

53 Shen Chi-lan (Shen Jilan), *op. cit.*, p. 3.

54 *Ibid.*, p. 4.

55 Chou Min-yi, 'Shen Chi-lan, Woman of New China', *PC*, 16 Aug. 1953.

56 Nan Ting, 'Tien Kuei-ying (Dian Guiying) Earns a Licence', *PC*, 1 April 1950.

57 Pu Chun-sheng, *Women in China Today*, Part 6, pp. 1–12.

58 Cusack, *op. cit.*, pp. 63–9.

59 *Ta Kung Pao*, 15 Aug. 1958.

60 Kao Shan, 'A Village Maternity Centre', *PC*, 16 July 1953.

61 Han Suyin, *Birdless Summer*, London, 1968, pp. 155–65.

62 *RMRB*, 25 April 1952.

63 Chou Ngo-fan, 'Birth Control in China', *PC*, 1 June 1957.

64 *Ibid.*

65 *Ibid.*

66 'Mother and Child Care', *PC*, 1 June 1953.

67 'Report of Women's Federation of Hsingtai County', p. 280.

68 Sun Tan-wei, 'A Village Nursery, How it Grew', *CR*, Aug. 1956.

69 Kang Ke-ching (Kang Keqing), 'Child Care in New China', *PC*, 1 June 1950.

70 Teng Ying chao (Deng Yingzhao), 'China's Women Advance', *PC*, 1 Dec. 1972.

71 *Ibid.*

72 Shen Chi-lan (Shen Jilan), *op. cit.*, p. 5.

73 Wen Chun-chuan and Shan Fu, 'The Girl at the Control Board', *PC*, 1 May 1955.

74 Liang Yin-mei, 'Peking Prostitutes Reform Themselves', *PC*, 16 Feb. 1950; Hsiao-Kun, 'The Return to Daylight', *PC*, 1 April 1950.

75 Chin Yueh-ying, 'Country Midwife', *CR*, May 1959.

76 Teng Ying chao (Deng Yingzhao), 'China's Women Advance', *RMRB*, 26 May 1950.

77 Teng Ying chao (Deng Yingzhao), 'The Woman's Movement in New China', *PC*, 1 March 1952.

78 *Ibid.*

79 *Ibid.*

80 *Ibid.*

81 Yang Yu, *op. cit.*, p. 4.
82 Teng Ying chao (Deng Yingzhao), *op. cit.*
83 *Ibid.*
84 Cusack, *op. cit.*, p. 121.
85 Tso Sung-fen, 'New China's Woman in State Affairs', *PC*, 1 March 1955.
86 *Ibid.*
87 *Ibid.*
88 San Chan-ko, 'Election in Shaho Village', *PC*, 16 Dec. 1953.
89 San Chan-ko, 'Li Fanglan—People's Deputy', *PC*, 1 Jan. 1954.
90 *PC*, 16 March 1954.
91 Tso Sung-fen, *op. cit.*, pp. 17–18.
92 'Report of Women's Federation of Hsingtai County', p. 280.
93 'Resolution on the Women's Movement', *Documents of the Sixth Communist Party Congress*, Moscow, 1928.
94 *NCNA*, 14 Sept. 1950.
95 'Facts on China', *PC*, 16 April 1951.
96 Report of Women's Federation, *Survey of World Broadcasts*, no. 217, 11 Jan. 1953, p. 24.
97 'Trade Union Report', *PC*, 1 Jan. 1957.
98 Teng Ying chao (Deng Yingzhao), *PC*, 1 Dec. 1952.
99 Cusack, *op. cit.*, pp. 116–21.
100 *PC*, 16 March 1954.
101 Interview with ACDWF official, *RMRB*, 13 June 1957.
102 Speeches by Teng Ying chao (Deng Yingzhao) and Tsai Chang (Cai Zhang), *Report of the Eighth Party Congress*, FLP, Peking, 1956.
103 Yang Yu, *op. cit.*, pp. 14–15.
104 Cusack, *op. cit.*, pp. 51–2.
105 Shen Chi-lan (Shen Jilan), *op. cit.*, p. 1.
106 Teng Ying chao (Deng Yingzhao), *Speech at Eighth Party Congress*, p. 227.

Chapter 9 A New Stage: New Problems

1 Li Teh-chuan, 'On Women's Emancipation in China', *NCNA*, Peking, 8 March 1959.
2 *RMRB*, 7 Oct. 1959.
3 'Report of the Second Executive Committee of 3rd NWF Committee', *NCNA*, Peking, 24 Feb. 1960.
4 Open letter sent by National Women's Conference to all Women, *NCNA*, Peking, 16 Dec. 1958.
5 *RMRB*, 4 Sept. 1958.
6 'Chinese Women's Achievements in 1958', *NCNA*, Peking, 4 Jan. 1959.
7 *RMRB*, 2 June 1958.
8 *NCNA*, Chengchow, 7 May 1958.
9 *RMRB*, 2 June 1958; *PR*, 12 July 1960.
10 Wang Yin, 'Women's New Life in Rural Communes, *China News Service*, Peking, 24 Feb. 1959.

11 'Women's Contribution to Agricultural Upsurge', *NCNA*, Peking, 10 Dec. 1958.
12 Wang Yin, *op. cit.*
13 Editorial, *RMRB*, 8 March 1960.
14 Cao Guanchan, 'Further Liberate Women's Labour Capacity', *RMRB*, 2 June 1958.
15 *ZF*, 1 Aug. 1961.
16 Chang Xiaomei, 'The Broad Masses of the Housewives take up Social Labour', *RMRB*, 5 May 1959.
17 Fang Wei, 'Housewives Build Up their Own Factories', *CR*, Feb. 1959.
18 *NCNA*, Wuhan, 27 April 1960.
19 'Greater Role of Women in Industry', *NCNA*, Peking, 13 Dec. 1958.
20 *Ibid*.
21 Interview with Li Yang-ching, J. Myrdal, *Report from a Chinese Village*, London, 1963, pp. 295–306.
22 'Peng Teh-huai greets Women's Conference', *NCNA*, Peking, 3 Dec. 1958.
23 Interview with Mao Tse-tung (Mao Zedong), in A. Malraux, *Anti-Memoirs*, New York, 1970, pp. 463–5.
24 See *PR*, 15 July 1958.
25 Tsai Chang (Cai Zhang), Report of Second Executive Committee Meeting of Third NWF Committee', *NCNA*, Peking, 24 Feb. 1960.
26 *RMRB*, 8 March 1959.
27 Teng Ying chao (Deng Yingzhao), 'Towards the Emancipation of Women', *PR*, 15 March 1960.
28 'Report of the National Conference of Women', *PR*, 9 Dec. 1958.
29 I. Crooks and D. Crooks, *The First Years of Yangyi Commune*, London, 1966, pp. 68–71; 151–8.
30 *Ibid.*, pp. 158–9.
31 'Resolution on Some Questions Concerning the People's Communes', Dec. 1958, trans. in *Contemporary China*, 1958–9, pp. 213–34.
32 Crooks and Crooks, *op. cit.*, pp. 159–61.
33 Li Chieh-po, 'Urban People's Communes', *PR*, 19 April 1960.
34 *Beijing Ribao* (*Peking Daily*), 19 March 1960.
35 *RMRB*, 5 May 1959.
36 Teng Ying chao (Deng Yingzhao), *op. cit.*, 1960.
37 *Beijing Ribao* (*Peking Daily*), 19 March 1960.
38 'The Service House', *CR*, Dec. 1959.
39 'Working Women Freed of Household Work in Southwest China', *NCNA*, Chungking, 13 March 1960.
40 'Harbin Working Women Freed of Household Burdens', *NCNA*, Harbin, 16 March 1960.
41 'Tungfeng People's Commune', *NCNA*, Changchun, 24 April 1960.
42 Tsai Chang (Cai Zhang), *RMRB*, 7 Oct. 1959.
43 Resolutions on Questions Concerning People's Communes, 1958.
44 See Fan Ruoyu, *Hongqi* (*Red Flag*), no. 5, May 1960.
45 V. I. Lenin, 'On the Historical Experiences of the Dictatorship of the Proletariat', *Collected Works*, New York, 1942.

46 Mao Tse-tung (Mao Zedong), 'The Role of the Chinese Communist Party in the National War', Oct. 1938, see *Selected Readings*, FLP, Peking, 1967.

47 F. Engels, *Origins of the Family, Private Property and the State*, New York, 1942.

48 Fan Ruoyu, *op. cit.*, 1960.

49 *Kirin Ribao (Kirin Daily)*, 10 Jan. 1959.

50 *Hebei Ribao (Hebei Daily)*, Tientsin, 8 April 1959.

51 'Tsai Chang's (Cai Zhang) Report to Women's Conference', *NCNA*, Peking, 4 Dec. 1958.

52 *Kirin Ribao (Kirin Daily)*, 10 Jan. 1959.

53 *RMRB*, 17 Jan. 1959.

54 *RMRB*, 20 Aug. 1959.

55 *Ibid.*, 7 Oct. 1959.

56 *NCNA*, 31 July 1958.

57 Interview with author, private mss.

58 Kung Ying-chao, 'Commune Opens New World for Women', *NCNA*, Peking, 18 Dec. 1958.

59 Meizheng, Letter to *Renmin Ribao*, 13 July 1958.

60 'Historic Change of Several Million Rural Women', *NCNA*, Peking, 22 Sept. 1959.

61 *Women in the People's Commune*, *NWF*, Peking, 1960.

62 Crooks and Crooks, *op. cit.*, p. 251.

63 J. Myrdal, *Report from a Chinese Village,* London, 1963, p. 289.

64 See 'Report Secretariat of the Women's Federation', *Renmin Ribao*, 2 June 1958; 'Open Letter to all Women', *NCNA*, Peking, 16 Dec. 1958; 'Report on National Conference on Woman Work', *NCNA*, Peking, 31 July 1958.

65 'Report of the Second Plenary Meeting of the Third Executive Committee of the National Federation of Women held in Peking', *NCNA*, 24 Feb. 1960.

66 'Report by Women's Conference on Experiences of the Great Leap Forward in Guangdong', *Nanfang Ribao (Nanfang Daily)*, 27 March 1962.

67 Crooks and Crooks, *op. cit.*, pp. 68–71; 151–8.

68 Report Women's Fed. from Jiuji Xian, *ZF*, Nov. 1961.

69 Fang Wei, *op. cit.*

70 Report from Jiuji Xian, 1961.

71 J. Lewis, *Leadership in Communist China*, New York, 1963, p. 109.

72 *RMRB*, 3 May 1959.

73 *NCNA*, 22 Sept. 1959.

74 For an elaboration of this point published since this chapter was drafted see N. Diamond, 'Collectivisation, Kinship, and the Status of Women in Rural China', *Bulletin of the Concerned Asian Scholars*, Jan.–March 1975.

Chapter 10 The Cultural Revolution: Socialism versus Feminism

1 Wan Mujan, 'How Should the Problem of Women be Viewed', *Hongqi (Red Flag)*, 28 Oct. 1964.

2 *RMRB*, 2 June 1958.
3 'Reference Materials for Training Basic-level Women Cadres', *ZF*, Feb. 1962.
4 Liao Suhua, 'What is Revolutionary Women's True Happiness?', *ZF*, 1 Oct. 1963.
5 Liao Suhua, 'In What Respects Should We Be Self Conscious?', *ZF*, Oct. 1963.
6 'Same Pay for Same Work to Men and Women in the Qingxi Production Brigade', by the Work Section of the Jiuji Xian Women's Federation, *ZF*, Nov. 1961.
7 'Special Commentary', *ZF*, Nov. 1963.
8 Liao Suhua, *ZF*, Oct. 1963.
9 Chu Guohua, 'Strengthen Political and Ideological Work Among Women Workers', *Gongren Ribao* (*Workers' Daily*), 8 July 1959.
10 Editorial, *RMRB*, 8 March 1962.
11 'Reference Materials for Training Basic-level Women Cadres', *op. cit.*
12 Chen Yunjing, 'Why I Love Woman Work', *ZF*, Aug. 1964.
13 *Ibid*.
14 'Reference Materials for Training Basic-level Women Cadres', *op. cit.*
15 Editorial, *RMRB*, 8 March 1962.
16 Reported in *ZF*, Sept. 1961.
17 Xiu Feng, Letters, *ZF*, Sept. 1963.
18 Ai Zhuan, Letter, *ZF*, Aug. 1964.
19 Commentary, *ZF*, 1 Sept. 1963.
20 Kang Hua, Letter, *ibid*.
21 Yu Jin, Letter, *ibid*.
22 Cai Yin, Letter, *ibid*.
23 Kong Guihua, Letter, *ZF*, May 1964.
24 Li Yu, Letter, *ZF*, Sept. 1963.
25 Hu Bairen, Letter, *ibid*.
26 Meng Yun, Letter, *ZF*, May 1964.
27 Huang Xiaozhong, Letter, *ZF*, Aug. 1964.
28 Hai Zhao, Letter, *ZF*, July 1964.
29 Dong Hui, Letter, *ZF*, May 1964.
30 Simone de Beauvoir, *The Long March*, London, 1958, pp. 153–4.
31 E.g. Letter to Lin Shan, *ZQ*, 28 July 1963.
32 E.g. Letter from Jian Feng, *ZQ*, 27 Oct. 1964.
33 Editorial, *ZF*, 1 July 1964.
34 Quoted in R. Buxton and P. Langton, 'Women in Socialist Equality', *China Now*, Jan. 1973.
35 *Women of China*, no. 3, March 1965.
36 Wan Mujan, *Hongqi*, 28 Oct. 1964.
37 Wang Ajiu, *Zhongguo Funu*, Sept. 1963.
38 'Letter from Women's Federation Meng xian, Shaanxi', *Zhongguo Funu*, 10 July 1966.
39 *Zhongguo Funu*, 10 July 1966.
40 Report of staff of *Zhongguo Funu*, 10 July 1966.
41 Tang Guiying, 'Women's Militia', *Zhongguo Funu*, 10 Aug. 1966.

42 Zhang Yubing, Chairman of Women's Congress, *Zhongguo Funu*, 10 Aug. 1966.
43 Chan Koubao, *Zhongguo Funu*, 10 Aug. 1966.
44 'Letter from Women's Federation, Meng xian Shaanxi', *op. cit.*
45 *Zhongguo Funu* (editorial), 10 Sept. 1966.
46 'Report of the Writing Group, CCP Hunan Provincial Revolutionary Committee', *Hongqi (Red Flag)*, no. 10, 1 Sept. 1971.
47 'Investigation and Report on the Tungchin Brigade, Kwangsi', *Hongqi (Red Flag)*, no. 2, 1 Feb. 1971.
48 Wei Fengying, *RMRB*, Nov. 1966; *PR*, 2 Dec. 1966.
49 'Report of the Writing Group, CCP Hunan Provincial Revolutionary Committee', *op. cit.*
50 J. Myrdal and G. Kessle, *China: The Revolution Continued*, London, 1973, pp. 111–18.
51 'Cadres in Henan', *RMRB*, 15 Nov. 1969.
52 'Training Women Cadres in Dazhai', *PR*, 30 March 1973.
53 'Report of the Revolutionary Committee, Lochang Xian, Guangdong Province', *Hongqi (Red Flag)*, no. 2, 1 Feb. 1971.
54 'Report of the Writing Group, CCP Hunan Provincial Revolutionary Committee', *op. cit.*
55 'Role of Women on Revolutionary Committees', *Wenhuibao* (Shanghai newspaper), 14 June 1968.
56 Wei Fengying, *RMRB*, Nov. 1966; *PR*, 2 Dec. 1966.

Chapter 11 A Political Solution: Socialism and Feminism

1 Wang Tse (Wang Zi), *PR*, 9 March 1973.
2 Quoted *ZF*, 10 Sept. 1966; *PR*, 5 April 1974.
3 Soong Ching-ling (Song Qingling), 'Women's Liberation in China', *PR*, 11 Feb. 1972.
4 Quoted in E. McFarquar, 'What Mao can do for Women', *Nova*, Nov. 1973.
5 'Report of the Revolutionary Committee, Lochang Xian, Guangdong Province', *Hongqi*, 1 Feb. 1971.
6 'Investigation Report on the Tungchin Brigade, Guangxi, *Hongqi*, 1 Feb. 1971.
7 Account based on interviews with women's representatives in summer 1973 at communes, trade unions, factories, urban neighbourhoods and other institutions in the vicinity of Peking, Shenyang, Nanjing, Tientsin, Qingdao, Jinan and Shanghai.
8 Account based on author's interviews and *Xinhua News*, 5 July 1973.
9 'Let all Women Rise Up', editorial, *Renmin Ribao*, 8 March 1974.
10 *Ibid.*
11 Yang Bolan and Chan Beizhen, 'Smash the Mental Shackles that Bind and Enslave Women', *Renmin Ribao*, 2 Feb. 1974.
12 Red Detachment of Women Squad, 'Women Can Prop Up "Half of Heaven"', *Guangming Ribao*, 14 Jan. 1974.
13 Ching Fu-wen, 'The Ways of Confucius and Mencius are Ropes that Bind and Enslave Women', *Renmin Ribao*, 27 Jan. 1974.

14 Sun Loying and Lu Lifen, 'On Confucian Persecution of Women in History', *Xuexi yu Pipan*, 10 Jan. 1975.

15 Red Detachment of Women Squad, *Guangming Ribao*, 14 Jan. 1974.

16 Iron Girls' Team of Dazhai Brigade, 'We Revolutionary Women Bitterly Hate the Doctrines of Confucius and Mencius', *Hongqi*, 3 March 1974; Women Oil Extracting Team of Daqing Oilfield, 'Smashing the Iron Chains of 1,000 Years' Standing', *Guangming Ribao*, 6 March 1974; Ching Fuwen, *Renmin Ribao*, 27 Jan. 1974.

   Whether Lin Biao (Lin Piao) has said all these is yet to be verified, but what is important for the position of women in this campaign is that these are the types of views which were to be criticised.

17 Yang Bolan and Chan Beizhen, *op. cit.*

18 Red Detachment of Women Squad, *op. cit.*

19 Sun Loying and Lu Lifen, *op. cit.*

20 *Ibid.*; Theory Group of a People's Liberation Army Unit, 'Women are a Great Force in the Revolution', *Renmin Ribao*, 8 March 1975.

   They singled out a number of peasant uprisings for study: in 17 AD occurred the first identifiable peasant uprising to have been launched and led by a woman; in a peasant rebellion during the Tang dynasty, a woman, Chen Shizhen, had led a peasant force 10,000 strong and had become the first woman empress; and the Taiping Rebellion of the mid-nineteenth century had produced the most ambitious programme to redefine the role of women.

21 No. 30 Cotton Mill Shanghai, 'Reveal the Reactionary Features of Women's Classics', *Xuexi yu Pipan*, 20 Sept. 1974.

22 Iron Girls' Team of Dazhai Brigade, *Hongqi*, 3 March 1974.

23 The most common saying cited disparages the leadership of women. For example when a woman assumed a leading role men were found to use sayings which meant that it was like a donkey taking the place of a horse which can only lead to trouble.

24 Of particular note is the number of articles referring to women who have overcome taboos to enter occupations to do with agriculture and fishing.

25 Women Oil Extracting Team of Daqing Oilfield, *op. cit.* A few study groups were reported to be so challenged that they immediately set out to prove their own abilities and the fallacy of ancient sayings. For examples see CCP Committee of the Shanghai Iron and Steel Plant, No. 5, 'Our Primary Task is to go on Carrying out well the Movement to Criticise Lin Biao and Confucius', *Guangming Ribao*, 18 Feb. 1975; *NCNA*, 7 April 1975.

26 Party Committee of Second Wuzhou Municipal Light and Chemical Industries Bureau, 'Pay Attention to Developing Female Membership of the Party', *Hongqi*, 1 July 1974.

27 *Ibid.*, 3 March 1974.

28 'Let All Women Rise Up', *RMRB*, 8 March 1974.

29 J. Maloney, 'Women Cadres and Junior-Level Leadership in China', *Current Scene*, vol. XIII, nos 3–4, 1976.

30 *NCNA*, 11 March 1972.

31 *RMRB*, 16 March 1973.

32 *RMRB*, 6 March 1973.
33 'Working Women are a Great Revolutionary Force', *ibid*., 8 March 1973.
34 Xia Ping, 'Make Energetic Efforts to Train Women Cadres', *Hongqi*, 1 Dec. 1973.
35 Theory-Study Group of Dian Chun Commune *et al*., 'The Anti-Lin Biao and Confucian Campaign', *RMRB*, Nov. 1974; *CR*, March 1975.
36 *RMRB*, 13 Dec. 1963.
37 *Ibid*., Nov. 1974; *Guangming Ribao*, 18 Feb. 1975.
38 *Hongqi*, 1 Dec. 1973.
39 *Ibid*., 1 July 1974.
40 *Anhui Radio*, 6 Feb. 1975; *Peking Radio*, 6 Feb. 1975.
41 Wang Tse (Wang Zi), *PR*, 8 March 1973; Hsu Kuang (Xu Guang), *PR*, 8 March 1974.
42 Tsui Yu-lan (Zui Yulan), *CR*, March 1974.
43 *ZF*, 10 Aug. 1966.
44 J. Chen, *A Year in Upper Felicity*, London, 1973, p. 60.
45 Quoted in Liu Chao, 'Safeguarding Women's Interests', *PR*, March 1974.
46 Woman Correspondent, *PR*, 9 March 1973.
47 Tsui Yu-lan (Zui Yulan), *CR*, March 1974.